LITERARY WOMEN

LITERARY WOMEN

❂ Ellen Moers

New York
OXFORD UNIVERSITY PRESS

Copyright © 1963, 1972, 1973, 1974, 1975, 1976, 1977 by Ellen Moers
First published in 1976 by Doubleday & Company, Inc., Garden City, New York
First issued in paperback in 1977 by Anchor Press/Doubleday
This paperback edition published in 1985 by
Oxford University Press, Inc., 200 Madison Avenue, New York, NY 10016

Reprinted by arrangement with Doubleday & Company, Inc.

Some of the material in this book has appeared in the following publications: *The New York Review of Books, The American Scholar, Saturday Review, The Columbia Forum*. Other material originally appeared in *Harper's Magazine* as "The Angry Young Women," and in *Commentary* as "Money, the Job, and Little Women," copyright © 1972 by American Jewish Committee.

LIBRARY OF CONGRESS CATALOGING IN PUBLICATION DATA

Moers, Ellen.
  Literary women.
  Reprint. Originally published: Garden City, N.Y.:
Doubleday, 1976.
  1. Women authors.   I. Title.
[PN471.M63   1985]   809'.89287   84-25437
ISBN 0-19-503582-8 (pbk.)

Printing (last digit): 9 8 7 6 5 4 3 2 1

Printed in the United States of America

Grateful acknowledgment is made for permission to include the following:

Lines from "Hawk Is a Woman" by Hildegarde Flanner, from *If There Is Time* by Hildegarde Flanner, copyright 1942 by New Directions. Reprinted by permission of the author.

Lines from "Prologue/The Evidence" from *Half-Lives* by Erica Jong. Copyright © 1971, 1972, 1973 by Erica Mann Jong. Reprinted by permission of Holt, Rinehart and Winston, Publishers.

Lines from "Fatal Interview" by Edna St. Vincent Millay, Harper & Row, Publishers, Inc. Copyright 1931, 1958 by Edna St. Vincent Millay and Norma Millay Ellis.

Four lines from "The Exorcists," from *To Bedlam and Part Way Back*. Copyright © 1960 by Anne Sexton. Reprinted by permission of the publisher, Houghton Mifflin Company.

Lines from "The Insatiable Baby" by Cynthia MacDonald, George Braziller, Inc. From *Amputations* by Cynthia MacDonald. Reprinted with the permission of the publisher. Copyright © 1972 by Cynthia MacDonald.

"Epigram" by Anna Akhmatova, copyright © 1973 by Stanley Kunitz and Max Hayward. Originally appeared in *Poetry*. From *Poems of Akhmatova*. Selected, Translated and Introduced by Stanley Kunitz with Max Hayward. By permission of Little, Brown and Co. in association with The Atlantic Monthly Press.

Material from "Dedicatory" by Willa Cather, reprinted from *April Twilights* (*1903*) by Willa Cather, edited with an introduction by Bernice Slote, copyright © 1962, 1968 by the University of Nebraska Press.

This one is for Mary—and in memory of Celia

Preface

The subject of this book is the major women writers, writers we read and shall always read whether interested or not in the fact that they happened to be women. But the fact of their sex is, frankly, fascinating—one of those facts which raise questions, open perspectives, illuminate and explain. The open question with which I began was: what did it matter that so many of the great writers of modern times have been women? what did it matter to literature? For this was something new, something distinctive of modernity itself, that the written word in its most memorable form, starting in the eighteenth century, became increasingly and steadily the work of women.

This book deals with women's literature, not Women in general, but for those who undertake to theorize about the female sex, literature is a unique resource. It is the only intellectual field to which, for hundreds of years, women have made an indispensable contribution. One cannot talk rationally of the English novel, or of French Romanticism, or of the American short story and modern poetry without discussing women writers.

The historical boundaries of the book have been set not arbitrarily but by the subject itself: from the eighteenth century to the present (with a principal exception made for the first American poet, Anne Bradstreet, who wrote in the seventeenth century). For all practical purposes, literary professionalism for women began with the rise of the Richardsonian novel, that historic event which must once again be summoned to account for change, here a change for writing women: their chance to achieve, to influence, and to be decently paid.

Most of the writers discussed are English, American, and French; by general consent they are the women writers who can truly be called major literary figures of the latter eighteenth and the whole of the nineteenth century. Scandinavian and Russian women writers of the early twentieth century, especially the poets, would also demand attention from critics who can read them in their own language as, regrettably, I cannot. As to contemporary women writers, many are mentioned and more were in my mind as I wrote, but here my choice of texts was inevitably somewhat haphazard. Limitations of time, space, and knowledge have kept me from discussing many of the innumerable gifted women who write in German, Spanish, Italian, Russian, Japanese, and other languages—not to mention many other Canadian, African, Australian, English, and American women who write in my own.

The literary women themselves, not any doctrine of mine, have done the organizing of the book—*their* concerns, *their* language. I have worked not to narrow the focus but to widen the range of literary materials upon which psychologists and philosophers always draw to support their theories about women. There is no discussion here of Dr. Helene Deutsch's use of George Sand's *Petite Fadette* to shore up psychoanalytic doctrines on proper womanhood; but there is a good deal about George Sand's development as a writer and thinker on social and religious issues, about the place of *La Petite Fadette* among the hundred or so works Sand wrote, about their influence on her century. As I understand it, my principal obligation is to record without simplification what it has meant to be at once a woman and a writer.

Some sense of the range, the development, the variety of women's literature will be provided, I hope, by this book—especially the variety. Literary women have worked in every available form and style, have exhibited every mood and character, have been radical and conservative, narrow and wide-ranging, tragic and comic in their writings. There is no point saying what women cannot do in literature, for history shows they have done it all.

From the start my approach has been essentially a practical one. If there seemed something new worth saying about a major writer as a woman writer, that is what I say here: Jane Austen's precise concern with money, Mary Shelley's creation of a birth myth, Emily Dickinson's use of the metaphors of girlhood, George Sand's obsession with the illiterate, Harriet Beecher Stowe's access as a woman to the matter of slavery, Willa Cather's access as a woman to the drama of landscape, Emily Brontë's access as a woman to the savagery of childhood, the ending of mothers in Virginia Woolf and modern fiction after her, George Eliot's place in a tradition of women's literature originated by Mme de Staël, which made a myth of glory, of the public appurtenances of fame, for the woman of genius. . . .

All this was new, and has seemed worth saying; none of it had occurred to me before I read these writers with a heightened and concentrated sense of their being women writers. Because they are major literary figures, we have examined and reexamined them as Americans, or Evangelical Protestants, or Romantics, or Celts, or socialists; we have grouped them with writers of the American renaissance or the French enlightenment; we have located them on the frontier or in Bloomsbury; we have approached them as victims of madness or consumption, as students of Shakespeare, or Freud, or Rousseau, as naturalists or surrealists. But by some accidental or willed critical narrowness, we have routinely denied ourselves additional critical access to these writers through the fact of their sex—a fact surely as important as their social class or era or nationality, a fact of which women writers have been and still are conscious. How, as human beings, could they not be?

Being women, women writers have women's bodies, which affect their senses and their imagery. They are raised as girls, and thus have a special perception of the cultural imprinting of childhood. They are assigned roles in the family and in courtship, they are given or denied access to education and employment, they are regulated by laws of property and political representation which, absolutely in the past, partially today, differentiate women from men. If they denied their bodies, denied whatever was special about being a woman in their time and class and place, they would be only narrowly human and could hardly be much good as writers. The great writers have always chosen brilliantly, individually, imaginatively among the varying feminine facets of the human condition; and transformed this material, along with all the other materials a writer uses, into literature. Thus the task at hand is not to assemble documents (such as letters and diaries) for an account of the surfaces of women's lives, but to track the deep creative strategies of the literary mind at work upon the fact of female.

It was not my intention to attempt a history of women's literature, but I have organized one chapter chronologically (Chapter 2: The Epic Age) as a sample of the way such a history might read. The scholarly apparatus at the back of the book has been designed to provide a resource for historians in the form of a checklist of literary women. As the Guide to the Notes explains in detail, the notes are arranged not seriatim but dictionary fashion, that is, alphabetically under the name of each writer discussed, plus a few extra dozen who appear only in the notes. The correct literary names of women writers, their nationalities and dates are given, and, where space permits, a chronology of their literary production.

At one time I held the narrow view that separating major writers from the general course of literary history on the basis of sex was futile, but several things have changed my mind. As an approach to literature in general, and to much besides literature, it has turned out to be surprisingly productive. Every subject I have had to consider—Romanticism, opera, pronouns, landscape, work, childhood, mysticism, the Gothic, courtship, metaphors, travel, revolution, monsters, pedagogy—has broadened and changed in the light of some knowledge of the women's issues and women's traditions that have been shaping forces in all modern literature. Everything special to a woman's life, its most trivial aspects as well as its grandest, has been claimed for literature by writers who share the quality Thackeray saw in Charlotte Brontë: "the passionate honour of the woman."

The suspicion has grown upon me that we already practice a segregation of major women writers unknowingly, therefore insidiously, because many of them have written novels, a genre with which literary historians and anthologists are still ill at ease. Neither Jane Austen nor Harriet Beecher Stowe is mentioned (no less included) in the standard anthologies which today are the staple introductions to English and American literature for students. Thus, where young readers are concerned, English Romanticism is deprived of its greatest non-poet; and all the clichés about the American renaissance and about the antisocial American romance tradition go on being repeated without testing against the major female exception to the rule.

But the main thing to change my mind about a history of literary women has been history itself, the dramatically unfolding, living literary history of the period of my work on this book. Its lesson has been that one must know the history of women to understand the history of literature.

. . .

The generosity of the National Endowment for the Humanities, which gave me a Senior Fellowship and a Research Grant for this book, cut me loose from teaching in 1972, 1973, and 1974. The new wave of feminism, called women's liberation, pulled me out of the stacks and made the writing of this book much more of an open-air activity than a bookish person like myself could otherwise have expected. My table of contents evokes for me the widespread places where most of these chapters were first born as public lectures—lectures some of which I was asked to give as contributions to that burning topic of the day, women.

I talked to the New England College English Association, during their annual meeting at Smith College, about biography and women's literature; to the New York Browning Society about Mrs. Browning; to the English Institute about Anne Bradstreet; at the University of Wisconsin about Emily Dickinson; at Hofstra University about Harriet Beecher Stowe; to the Victorian Studies Department at Indiana University about the Epic Age; at the University of Warwick (where Germaine Greer was a superbly scholarly heckler) about Female Gothic; to the American Society for

Eighteenth Century Studies, during their annual meeting at the University of Pennsylvania, about Traveling Heroinism; at St. John's University and again at Brooklyn College about Loving Heroinism; at Harvard University about Educating Heroinism; at the University of Rochester about the landscape metaphor in a lecture celebrating the Willa Cather centennial, an occasion which also drew me to the University of Nebraska, and to Red Cloud. My thanks go not only to my many gracious hosts, but to members of the audience, some of whose names I never learned, who informed, corrected, and inspired me, who made the writing of this book a dialogue.

My thanks go also to the many editors who opened pages of their publications to drafts of most of these chapters, and again to the many readers who wrote me and thus contributed to their final revision. Some were writers who shared their manuscripts and projects with me, among these, Tillie Olsen, Ruth Ann Lief, and Judith Johnson Sherwin, who have become friends.

Part of the Tradition chapter ran in the *Columbia Forum;* Realism in *Commentary;* Female Gothic in the *New York Review of Books,* where some of the material on Richardson and Stowe also first appeared; Performing Heroinism in *Harvard English Studies,* except for the Italy material, which appeared in the *American Scholar;* some of the Cather/Colette material ran in *World.* All these articles appeared in the 1970s, but the first writing I did for this book, scraps of which reappear in the Epic Age chapter, goes back to 1963: an article called "Angry Young Women," about the Victorian writers, which *Harper's Magazine* commissioned for a special issue on Women published at the end of that year. When I take out that article now, I marvel at the change caused by a few years of women's history, for in 1963 I was mainly irritated with the quiescent spirit of current women writers, and mainly concerned to show the creative power of women's anger in a past age.

In 1963 Betty Friedan published *The Feminine Mystique,* which turned out to be the start of the political organization of feminists in America. In 1963 Sylvia Plath killed herself and was born again to a dominant role in the world of letters; her autobiographical novel *The Bell Jar,* appeared in 1963, *Ariel,* her last great book of poems in 1965, and her work has been constantly published, debated, followed ever since. No writer has meant more to the current feminist movement, though Plath was hardly a "movement" person, and she died at age thirty before it began. She provides a first practical lesson in the complexities of chronology that face the historian of women's literature, which sometimes runs before, sometimes after, sometimes in tandem with the history of feminism, but is not the same thing.

Just as we are now trying to make sense of women's literature in the great feminist decade of the 1790s, when Mary Wollstonecraft blazed and died, and when, also, Mme de Staël came to England and Jane Austen came of age, so the historians of the future will try to order women's literature of the 1960s and 1970s. They will have to consider Sylvia Plath as a woman writer and as a poet; but what will they make of her contemporary compatriot, the playwright Lorraine Hansberry? Born two years before Plath, and dead two years after her in her early thirties, Hansberry was not a suicide but a victim of cancer; she eloquently affirmed life, as Plath brilliantly wooed death. Historians of the future will undoubtedly be satisfied with the title of Lorraine Hansberry's posthumous volume, *To Be Young, Gifted and Black;* and they will talk of her admiration for Thomas Wolfe; but of Sylvia Plath they will have to say "young, gifted, and a woman." And when they try to place Plath in the history of women's literature, perhaps they will look back to the turn-of-the-century Russian religious poet Zinaida Hippius, some of whose poems—if translations are any guide to them—are astonishingly like Plath's in imagery and tone.

Future historians will automatically place in the context of women's liberation the young women who first began to publish their poems and polemics, their ribald and outrageous fictions in this feminist era. They will use the same context to explain much of the change that came over the work of the poet Adrienne Rich, whose first volume, published in the Yale Series of Younger Poets in 1951, won praise from W. H. Auden for "good manners": hers were poems, Auden wrote, which do not "bellow at the reader." In 1974 Rich won the National Book Award for *Diving into the Wreck,* the central section of which is all a bellow, called "The Phenomenology of Anger"; and she accepted the award, jointly with two other women poets, "in the name of all the women whose voices have gone and still go unheard in the patriarchal world. . . ."

The women's movement has brought back dead writers, created new writers, changed established writers, and summoned old writers to literature again. Much of the excitement in the literary scene of the past decade has come from the vitality of women in their sixties and seventies and perhaps older who have been republished and have begun to write again. Christina Stead, Jean Rhys, Tillie Olsen belonged to the 1920s and 1930s, but they also belong to our time. And there has been in the past decade a golden harvest of memoirs by distinguished women whose lives have transformed and been transformed by the whole erratic course of our century—memoirs by Margaret Mead, Lillian Hellman, Hannah Tillich, Anne Morrow Lindbergh, Svetlana Alliluyeva, Pamela Hansford Johnson, Simone de Beauvoir. Thus the voices of the old and the young have come together in testimony to the human quality of a woman's life.

The book that follows is not precisely history, nor is it theory; it is plainly a celebration of the great women who have spoken for us all, whatever our sex. Elizabeth Barrett Browning's injunction has stayed in my mind:

> Deal with us nobly, women though we be,
> And honor us with truth if not with praise.

Poets will never understand how much work goes into truth. Hard as I have tried, however, to avoid error, I have made no effort at all to avoid praise.

Publisher's Note

For the first paperback edition of this book, published in 1977, the author wrote that no substantive changes had been made, "except that a few more writers were mentioned, especially in the notes, in response to requests by readers of the hardcover edition." For this edition, the publisher has included these writers in an addendum (p. 321) to the original notes section. This edition reproduces the original hardcover edition published in 1976, with a few minor corrections of typographical errors and other infelicities prepared by the author for the 1977 edition; the preface, however, includes the author's revisions for the 1977 edition.

Contents

List of Illustrations

LITERARY WOMEN

PART I

⊞ HISTORY AND TRADITION

THE LITERARY LIFE:
SOME REPRESENTATIVE WOMEN

> The poet is representative. She stands among partial women
> for the complete woman. . . . The young woman reveres
> women of genius, because, to speak truly, they are more her-
> self than she is. . . . For all women live by truth and stand in
> need of expression.
>
> —Emerson

A woman's life is hard in its own way, as women have always known and
men have rarely understood. Literary women speak for themselves on this
matter, as on every other, with finality. The horrors of the housewife's lot
have never been more powerfully evoked than in this letter of 1850, by
Harriet Beecher Stowe, about her plumber:

> So this same sink lingered in a precarious state for some weeks, and
> when I had *nothing else to do,* I used to call and do what I could in
> the way of enlisting the good man's sympathies in its behalf.
>
> How many times I have been in and seated myself in one of the
> old rocking-chairs, and talked first of the news of the day, the railroad,
> the last proceedings in Congress, the probabilities about the millen-
> nium, and thus brought the conversation by little and little round to
> my sink! . . . because, till the sink was done, the pump could not be
> put up, and we couldn't have any rain-water. Sometimes my courage
> would quite fail me to introduce the subject, and I would talk of
> everything else, turn and get out of the shop, and then turn back as if
> a thought had just struck my mind, and say:—
>
> "Oh, Mr. Titcomb! about that sink?"
>
> "Yes, ma'am, I was thinking about going down street this afternoon
> to look out stuff for it."

"Yes, sir, if you would be good enough to get it done as soon as possible; we are in great need of it."

"I think there's no hurry. I believe we are going to have a dry time now, so that you could not catch any water, and you won't need a pump at present."

These negotiations extended from the first of June to the first of July, and at last my sink was completed. . . . Also during this time good Mrs. Mitchell and myself made two sofas, or lounges, a barrel chair, divers bedspreads, pillow cases, pillows, bolsters, mattresses; we painted rooms; we revarnished furniture; we—what *didn't* we do?

Then on came Mr. Stowe; and then came the eighth of July and my little Charley. I was really glad for an excuse to lie in bed, for I was full tired, I can assure you. Well, I was what folks call very comfortable for two weeks, when my nurse had to leave me. . . .

During this time I have employed my leisure hours in making up my engagements with newspaper editors. I have written more than anybody, or I myself, would have thought. I have taught an hour a day in our school, and I have read two hours every evening to the children. The children study English history in school, and I am reading Scott's historic novels in their order . . . ; yet I am constantly pursued and haunted by the idea that I don't do anything. Since I began this note I have been called off at least a dozen times; once for the fish-man, to buy a codfish; once to see a man who had brought me some barrels of apples; once to see a book-man; then to Mrs. Upham, to see about a drawing I promised to make for her; then to nurse the baby; then into the kitchen to make a chowder for dinner; and now I am at it again, for nothing but deadly determination enables me ever to write; it is rowing against wind and tide. . . .

To tell the truth, dear, I am getting tired; my neck and back ache, and I must come to a close.

It is a letter to leave one between laughter and tears, probably just the effect Mrs. Stowe intended, for she was already an accomplished writer of sketches and other journalism, the income from which was required by her large family. "Now, Hattie," her sister-in-law wrote, "if I could use a pen as you can, I would write something that would make this whole nation feel what an accursed thing slavery is"; but there was, after all, little Charley, just born, the last of her seven children. "As long as the baby sleeps with me nights I can't do much at anything, but I will do it at last. I will write that thing if I live." The first installment of *Uncle Tom's Cabin, or Life Among the Lowly* did in fact appear a little less than a year after Mr. Titcomb took care of Mrs. Stowe's sink.

. . .

But there were some lucky ones, lucky by birth, circumstance, physique, temperament especially: that miracle of temperament which creates its own luck. Two nineteenth-century women stand out in this respect, George Sand and Elizabeh Barrett Browning; what positively miraculous beings they were. A magnetism emanates from their life stories, some compelling power which drew the world to them—and all the goods and blessings of the kind that facilitate and ornament the woman's life in letters. It was not that their lives were without the difficulties that plague other women—hardly; but they made those difficulties into resources with a wave of the magic wand of their—what shall we call it: charm? power? egotism? energy? confidence? pride? genius? or just plain luck? Whatever it was, Elizabeth Barrett always knew it was hers, as we can see from the "Glimpses into My Own Life and Literary Character" that she set down in 1820.

Perhaps these pages may never meet a human eye—and therefore no EXCESSIVE vanity can dictate them tho a feeling akin to it SELF LOVE may have prompted my not unwilling pen.

. . . I was always of a determined and if thwarted violent disposition. My actions and temper were infinitely more inflexible at three years old than now at fourteen. At that early age I can perfectly remember reigning in the Nursery and being renowned amongst the servants for self love and excessive passion. . . . At four and a half my great delight was poring over fairy phenomenons and the actions of necromancers. . . . At five I supposed myself a heroine. . . .

I perfectly remember the delight I felt when I attained my sixth birthday. I enjoyed my triumph to a great degree over the inhabitants of the Nursery, there being no UPSTART to dispute my authority. . . .

At four I first mounted Pegasus but at six I thought myself privileged to show off feats of horsemanship. In my sixth year for some lines on virtue which I had penned with great care I received from Papa a ten shilling note enclosed in a letter which was addrest to the *Poet Laureat of Hope End;* I mention this because I received much more pleasure from the word *Poet* than from the ten shilling note. I did not understand the meaning of the word laureat but it being explained to me by my dearest Mama, the idea first presented itself to me of celebrating our birthdays by my verse. *"Poet Laureat of Hope End"* was too great a title to lose—

. . . At SEVEN I began to think of *"forming my taste."* . . . I read the History of England and Rome—at 8 I perused the History of Greece. . . .

At nine I felt much pleasure from the effusions of my imagination in the adorned drapery of versification. . . . The subject of my studies was Pope's "Illiad" some passages from Shakespeare & novels which I enjoyed to their full extent.

. . . At ten my poetry was entirely formed by the style of written authors and I read that I might write. . . . At eleven I wished to be considered an authoress. Novels were thrown aside. Poetry and Essays were my studies & I felt the most ardent desire to understand the learned languages—To comprehend even the Greek alphabet was delight inexpressible. Under the tuition of Mr. McSwiney I attained that which I so fervently desired. For 8 months during this year I never remember having diverted my attention to any other object than the ambition of gaining fame . . . and never had a better opinion of my own talents—In short I was in infinite danger of being as vain as I was inexperienced! During this dangerous period I was from home & the fever of a heated imagination was perhaps increased by the intoxicating gaieties of a watering place Ramsgate where we then were and where I commenced my poem "The Battle of Marathon" now in print!!

. . . At twelve I enjoyed a literary life in all its pleasures. Metaphysics were my highest delight. . . . At this age I was in great danger of becoming the founder of a religion of my own. . . . This year I read Milton for the first time *thro* together with Shakespeare & Pope's Homer. . . . I had now attained my thirteenth birthday! . . . I perused all modern authors. . . . I read Homer in the original with delight inexpressible, together with Virgil. . . .

I am now fourteen and since those days of my tenderest infancy my character has not changed—

. . . My admiration of literature, especially of poetical literature, can never be subdued nor can it be extinguished but with life. . . .

My views of every subject are naturally cheerful and light as the first young visions of aerial hope but there have been moments, nay hours when contemplation has been arrayed in sorrows dusky robe. . . . And yet I have not felt miserable even then. . . .

My mind is naturally independant and spurns that subserviency of opinion which is generally considered necessary to feminine softness. But this is a subject on which I must always feel strongly for I feel within me an almost proud consciousness of independance which prompts me to defend my opinions & to yield them only to conviction!!!!!!!

. . . Better oh how much better to be the ridicule of mankind, the scoff of society, than lose that self respect which tho' this heart were bursting would elevate me above misery—above wretchedness & above abasement!!! These principles are irrevocable! It is not—I feel it is not vanity that dictates them! it is not—I know it is not an encroachment on masculine prerogative but it is a proud sentiment which will never allow me to be humbled in my own eyes!!!

And so it went; no one and nothing could resist her. She wanted Greek —there was that tutor; before she was done she read "nearly every word extant in Greek," published her translation of Aeschylus, wrote as a specialist on Byzantine Greek literature, and also learned Latin, Hebrew, French, German, Italian, and Portuguese without ever going to school. She wanted a learned friend with whom to discuss as an equal the technicalities of Greek prosody and such matters; he was provided—it had to be a he—in a shape which permitted long hours of intimate converse without scandal: a blind scholar. She wanted to do nothing but read and write; it has been estimated that her curiously convenient regime as an invalid gave her more time, daily, for those occupations than any other modern young person has ever enjoyed.

Only a woman, perhaps, can fully appreciate the luxurious scholarly idleness of Elizabeth Barrett's life when a young woman, and the female head of a large household (after her mother's death). Her younger sisters and brothers, who all adored her, tiptoed by her door; while full of affection, so devoid of responsibility was she, that she confessed to confusion about their ages. And so protected was she from even the awareness of domestic responsibilities that her own room was cleaned only once a year—a ritual occasion, managed by others so that she need not observe servant industry. Whenever her large family moved house, she herself was transported separately, a precious burden, to the new residence made ready by others for her convenience. Elizabeth Barrett was not to be disturbed.

She wanted fame: published in her teens and twenties, her poetry was hailed round the world, and she was nominated for the laureateship. She wanted a share in the normal masculine literary life, and without unseemly effort on her part, almost without leaving home, she saw that life come to her: epistolary friendships with writers, assignments from the quarterlies, collaborations on a modernization of Chaucer and on a critical assessment of contemporary writers; even appointment as literary executor of an important man she had never met.

She wanted love as well: what poet does not? Her father did not remarry when her mother died, which is extraordinary, for he was only forty-three, and handsome, vigorous, and rich. All his amatory energies (which had produced twelve children) were turned to the worship of his brilliant and pretty eldest daughter, who was merely twenty-one years younger than he. Mr. Barrett comes down to us in legend as a patriarchal tyrant of black religiosity; but what woman can help relishing his style? Those nightly prayers in Elizabeth's room, only the two of them; she stretched on her couch like an invalid queen, and he on his knees before her. . . .

She wanted more love; and it came, it came—

> O liberal
> And princely giver, who has brought the gold
> And purple of thine heart, unstained, untold,
> And laid them on the outside of the wall . . .

Robert Browning came for Elizabeth Barrett just the way a lover should come for every literary woman, out of the blue, fascinated, en-

chanted, magnetized by her writing—the two-volume 1844 collection of
her poetry. "I love your verses with all my heart, dear Miss Barrett," this
unknown lover wrote; and this first letter of his, shot through with critical
raptures and sexual metaphors, climaxed with ". . . my feeling rises altogether. I do, as I say, love these books with all my heart—and I love you
too. . . ."

The rest of their courtship produced some of the finest love poems and
love letters in the language. "My letters!" she wrote—

> My letters! all dead paper, mute and white!
> And yet they seem alive and quivering
> Against my tremulous hands which loose the string
> And let them drop down on my knee tonight.
> This said,—he wished to have me in his sight
> Once, as a friend: this fixed a day in spring
> To come and touch my hand . . . a simple thing,
> Yet I wept for it!—this, . . . the paper's light . . .
> Said, *Dear, I love thee;* and I sank and quailed
> As if God's future thundered on my past.
> This said, *I am thine*—and so its ink has paled
> With lying at my heart that beat too fast.
> And this . . . O Love, thy words have ill availed
> If, what this said, I dared repeat at last!

. . .

Alfred de Musset, young, handsome, and a poet, read George Sand's
novel *Indiana,* met her, reread it, wrote her a letter containing much critical admiration and the poem called "After Reading *Indiana*":

> Sand, quand tu l'écrivais, où donc l'avais-tu vue,
> Cette scène terrible où Noun, à demi nue,
> Sur le lit d'Indiana s'enivre avec Raimond?
> Qui donc te la dictait, cette page brulante
> Où l'amour cherche en vain d'une main palpitante
> Le fantôme adoré de son illusion?
> . . . .
> As-tu rêvé cela, George, ou l'as-tu connu?

She answered, in part:

> . . . If I write literary criticism in response to your verses, which are
> so beautiful in thought and feeling, it is because I am very much at a
> loss as to how to answer the questions of the poet who addresses them
> to me . . . for I cannot forget that the poet is twenty years old, that
> he has the good fortune still to doubt, still to inquire, and it would be
> a bad grace on my part to reveal to him the mournful secrets of my
> own experience. . . .
> When I had the honor of meeting you, I did not dare invite you

to come and see me. I still fear that the somberness of my domestic
interior may alarm and bore you. However, if on some day of weariness and disgust with the active life, you were tempted to enter the
cell of a recluse, you would be received with gratitude and cordiality.

He came.

To Musset, to everyone, she was George Sand—usually Madame
George Sand. No one could tell the story of the birth of that pen name better than Sand does herself, in Part IV of the *Histoire de ma vie,* where she
interweaves it with the story of her adoption of male dress when she
began her literary life in Paris.

> . . . I yearned to deprovincialize myself and became informed about
> the ideas and the arts of my time . . . ; I was particularly thirsty for
> the theater.
>
> I was well aware that it was impossible for a poor woman to in-
> dulge herself in these delights . . . I took this problem to my mother.
> . . . She replied: ". . . When I was young and your father was short of
> money, he had the idea of dressing me as a boy. . . . That meant a
> saving of half our household budget." . . .
>
> So I had made for myself a *redingote-guérite* [the long, shapeless
> man's outer coat of the 1830s] in heavy gray cloth, pants and vest to
> match. With a gray hat and a large woolen cravat, I was a perfect
> first-year student. I can't express the pleasure my boots gave me: I
> would gladly have slept with them, as my brother did in his young
> age, when he got his first pair. With those little iron-shod heels, I was
> solid on the pavement. I flew from one end of Paris to the other. It
> seemed to me that I could go round the world. And then, my clothes
> feared nothing. I ran out in every kind of weather, I came home at
> every sort of hour, I sat in the pit at the theater. No one paid attention
> to me, and no one guessed at my disguise. . . .
>
> Myself, I had the Ideal lodged in a corner of my brain . . . I
> carried it about in the street, my feet on the icy pavement, my
> shoulders covered with snow, my hands in my pockets, my stomach a
> bit hollow every now and then, but my head all the more filled with
> dreams, melodies, colors, shapes, gleams and phantoms. I was no
> longer a *lady,* but I wasn't a *gentleman* either. . . . No one knew me,
> no one looked at me, no one found fault with me; I was an atom lost
> in that immense crowd. No one said to me, as they did in La Châtre:
> "There's Madame Aurore going by; she's got the same hat and dress
> on"; nor, as they did in Nohant: "Take a look at our ladyship riding
> on her big horse; she's got to be crazy to sit a horse that way." In
> Paris, nobody thought anything of me. . . . I could make up a whole
> novel as I walked from one side of town to another without running
> into someone who would say: "What the devil are you thinking about?"

The year was 1831. She was starting out in the world of letters just as
all young Frenchmen from the provinces did in those romantic days. That
she was a woman writer rather than a man writer is not the most remark-

able fact about Sand's literary debut. Something else about it, something so remarkable as to be almost unbelievable, turned out to be the characteristic note of Sand's whole literary career; and that is, its speed.

Before she came to Paris to earn her way as a writer, she had done a little scribbling, but had hardly shown any particular interest in or talent for a writing career. Once in Paris, she made contact with leading editors and writers, joined the staff of *Le Figaro,* and contributed regularly to the *Revue de Paris.* To learn her craft, she wrote alone or in collaboration numerous articles, tales, and novels; some of this apprentice work was never published, some appeared anonymously, some under various pen names. *Rose et Blanche,* a five-volume collaborative novel signed "J. Sand," marked the end of her apprenticeship. Next came *Indiana,* entirely her own work, the novel Musset read as did many others. ("Very brilliant and powerful," said Elizabeth Barrett of *Indiana,* "and eloquent beyond praising.") It established the fame of "George Sand," the pen name she used for the first time for *Indiana.*

The whole business took some fifteen months, only about half of which she was able to spend in Paris or devote to the literary life. She was twenty-six years, six months, and five days old when she came to Paris, and when she was done with her debut—with the contacts and the journalism, the hack fiction and sketches, the thousands of pages and dozens of volumes, and the writing of *Indiana* as well—she was twenty-seven years and nine months old. It took her friend Balzac, that dynamo of literary energy, about ten years to complete a similar apprenticeship in journalism and hack fiction.

There is certainly nothing remarkable about Jules Sandeau, her lover and collaborator during this period. He was a timid, aspiring, unpublished poet of nineteen, from her part of France, when she fell in love with him in 1830. She swept him off with her to Paris the next year, there to mother him, support him, introduce him around, and manage his literary debut while she attended to her own. From Sandeau she took nothing but the first syllable of the pen name she required—for what other name was she to use? Her maiden name was Amantine-Aurore-Lucile Dupin, of which Aurore was the operative first name (fortunately for literature: from "Aurora" Mrs. Browning derived a heavenly host of images for *Aurora Leigh*). Had she used her maiden name, it would have been an offense to her mother, Mme Dupin; and her married name, an outrage to her mother-in-law, the Baronne Dudevant.

Her marriage at eighteen to young Casimir Dudevant, which began as a love match, had in any case long since deteriorated into a marriage of form, with infidelities on both sides; but the form was extremely important. She was the mother of two children and the *châtelaine* of Nohant, her country estate by birth, her husband's property by marriage. They made an unusual separation agreement in 1830 under the terms of which her literary career unfolded. Dudevant made her a very modest allowance (out of her own money) on which to live part of every year in Paris. The rest of the time she would spend at Nohant, still officially a wife, still tied to her beloved countryside, still passionately a mother. But she would have to earn enough by writing to support a Paris establishment including one or both of her children, as their schooling dictated. This she did, with a drive, a speed, a versatility, and a force that can hardly be equaled in literary history. And in addition she supplied herself with an abundance of the goods of this earth which she so relished—lots of sex, lots of travel, lots of friends, lots of wholesome country life, lots of music.

The picture of George Sand that stays most in my mind (because she described it often and brilliantly) is that of her typical country evening at Nohant. At the center sits Madame Sand, with the needlework she loved in her hands, surrounded by a houseful of friends, children, lovers, guests, neighbors. Nohant was a messy household, full of laughter and games and theatricals and family arguments and good intellectual talk and tobacco smoke and music—just like yours and mine. With Sand, in fact, begins a literary life-style distinctly modern in its middle-class informality, and child-centered domesticity, and dominating presence: the efficient, versatile, overworked, modern mother. But there is one old-fashioned detail—live music on the piano, rather than recordings. Sand herself did not play but loved to listen, and what with the frequent visits of her friend Liszt, and the long residence of her lover Chopin, she managed to provide herself with the very best in piano-playing.

How did she do it? It is not the management of Sand's sex life that is baffling (except for one detail: what contraceptive device she relied on) but the management of her working life; for throughout all her years of passions, pleasures, politics, and domestic responsibilities, she went on producing at the rate of at least two long novels a year, and hundreds upon hundreds of pages of other kinds of writing. This is really the interesting question about George Sand, and it has always fascinated literary professionals. "It's taken me a long time to scribble some forty volumes," Colette once wrote.

> So many hours stolen from travelling, idleness, reading, even from healthy feminine stylishness! How the devil did George Sand manage? That sturdy woman of letters found it possible to finish one novel and start another in the same hour. And she did not thereby lose either a lover or a puff of the narghile, not to mention a *Story of my Life* in twenty volumes, and I am overcome by astonishment.*

* Translation by David Le Vay from *L'Étoile Vesper*. Unless otherwise indicated, as in this case, all translations are by E.M.

And Henry James, a prolific romancer himself, took a highly professional interest in the mystery of Sand's productivity. "During the five-and-forty years of her literary career," he wrote in one of his eight essays on George Sand,

> she had something to say about most things in the universe; but the thing about which she had least to say was the writer's, the inventor's, the romancer's art. She possessed it by the gift of God, but she seems never to have felt the temptation to examine the pulse of the machine.

James combed the prefaces Sand wrote for the popular edition of her novels (irresistible documents, the writer at her professional best) for clues to Sand's technique for managing time, and came up with what is probably the essence of her secret and of her luck. On the one hand, James saw, George Sand had "an extraordinary physical robustness"; and on the other, "it was her constant practice to write at night, beginning after the rest of the world had gone to sleep." That was it: she was a night worker. This inalterable physiological bias to the night hours probably accounted for more in George Sand's development as a writer than the fact of her sex.

As women writers especially know, there is no better way to stretch the day than by working late at night when human claims upon one's time are still. It was all very well for Sylvia Plath to get up to write her astonishing last poems "at about four in the morning—that still blue, almost eternal hour before the baby's cry, before the glassy music of the milkman, settling his bottles." Poets can manage with an hour or two of writing time, before the baby cries, because they carry their work in their head the rest of the day; but the novelists like James and Colette and Sand need more time for turning out copy, and night is the longest time when a woman's two hands are free to hold pen and paper.

The picture of George Sand that most people remember best is the one that became celebrated after the Musset/Sand love affair ended in great bitterness on his side. Late at night, when he awoke after an exhausting *nuit d'amour,* Alfred de Musset would see George Sand—heartless bitch! —sitting up in her wrapper in their bedroom, scratching, scratching away at the pages with her pen by candlelight.

THE EPIC AGE: PART OF
THE HISTORY OF LITERARY WOMEN

I heard an Angel speak last night,
  And he said *"Write!*
Write a Nation's curse for me,
And send it over the Western Sea."

. . . "Not so," I answered once again.
  "To curse, choose men.
For I, a woman, have only known
How the Heart melts, and the tears run down."

"Therefore," the voice said, *"Shalt thou write*
  My curse to-night.
Some women weep and curse, I say
(And no one marvels), night and day.

"And thou shalt take their part to-night,
  Weep and write.
A curse from the depths of womanhood
Is very salt, and bitter, and good."

Elizabeth Barrett Browning:
"A Curse for a Nation" (1856)

You may not know what I mean by the Angel in the House.
. . . She was intensely sympathetic. She was immensely
charming. She was utterly unselfish. She excelled in the difficult arts of family life. She sacrificed herself daily . . . she
never had a mind or a wish of her own. . . . And when I
came to write I encountered her with the very first words. . . .
She slipped behind me and whispered: "My dear, you are a
young woman. . . . Be sympathetic; be tender; flatter; de-
ceive; use all the arts and wiles of our sex. Never let anybody
guess that you have a mind of your own. . . ."

Virginia Woolf:
"Professions for Women" (1931)

Virginia Woolf was the most brilliant of all critics of women's literature, and the most sensitive to its womanly quality of rage. But she was also, besides a critic, an original creative artist in her own right, and therefore invariably at odds with her predecessors. Her aesthetic ideals and moral principles were those of twentieth-century Bloomsbury, not of the Victorian age. The literary Angel who lived in her house was clearly not the same Angel who ordered Mrs. Browning on the eve of the Civil War to curse the hypocrisy of the American nation, which, while standing up for Freedom, was all the while trampling down

> On writhing bond-slaves,—for this crime
> This is the curse. Write.

Virginia Woolf wanted an end to women's cursing. In *A Room of One's Own,* her most important work on the subject, she drew a close causal bond between the literature that denounces, protests, and agitates and the anger of women writers who do not have a room of their own. "Her books will be deformed and twisted. She will write in a rage where she should write calmly. . . . She is at war with her lot." And looking back on what she called "the epic age of women's writing," when women's rage had lashed out at injustice and oppression of every kind, Woolf asked the women writers of her own time "to use writing as an art, not as a method of self-expression. . . . It is fatal," she went on, "for a woman to lay the least stress on any grievance; to plead even with justice any cause; in any way to speak consciously as a woman. . . . Anything written with that conscious bias is doomed to death . . . it cannot grow in the minds of others."

Writers of the epic age, however, thought differently of literature: they cared less for the growing than for the changing of minds, and less for art than action. No period of women's literature more requires the writing of its history on the grounds that it did in fact, as much as any literature can, change the world. *Uncle Tom's Cabin* is the case in point. It was regarded around the world as "the most successful book printed by man or woman" (as Mrs. Browning put it) because of what it did to advance the abolition of slavery in America. Even today there is hardly an historian so skeptical about public opinion, so scornful toward the force of the printed word, who does not assign Harriet Beecher Stowe some causative role in the onset of the Civil War. Receiving Mrs. Stowe at the White House, President Lincoln is said to have exclaimed, "Is this the little woman who made this great war?" The famous story may be inexact or even apocryphal; but there is no lack of documentation for the furor the novel caused when it was published in 1852; for its enormous sales in England and America; for its universal translations and readership; for its stimulus to Fugitive Slave Law opposition in the North; for its citation by all writers as the model for activist literature; and for its preciousness to women writers as the proof of what women without votes, or property, or platform, or even a room of their own could do with the pen. English reviewers called *Uncle Tom's Cabin* the "Iliad of the Blacks," thus providing one of many justifications for the rather grand title Virginia Woolf bestowed on the "epic age."

Woolf's own choice of novel to summarize all that she felt was both "epic" and wrong in women's literature was *Jane Eyre,* which is a romance, a melodrama, or, in its greatest pages, a fantasy of female childhood, but nothing, at first glance, like the panoramic pamphleteering of *Uncle Tom's Cabin.* Yet *Jane Eyre* was read as a dangerous and angry book in its own time, a woman's book in the radical sense of the term; "we do not hesitate to say," said the *Quarterly Review* in 1848, "that the tone of mind and thought which has overthrown authority and violated every code human and divine abroad, and fostered Chartism and rebellion at home, is the same which has also written *Jane Eyre.*"

Chartists in England, millhands in Yorkshire, revolutionaries on the Continent, patriots in Italy, Catholics and Jews and atheists and foreigners —all victims of prejudice and oppression found champions among women writers, but no race of mankind was so widely and commonly assigned to angry women as the slave. To "conservative and sagacious people," as Mrs. Stowe wrote in her Introduction to *Uncle Tom's Cabin,* slavery was a subject "dangerous to investigate," and indeed it was a subject avoided by the major literary men of America in the 1850s; but she heard on all sides voices urging her, as a woman writer, to make slavery her subject; and most of the voices were female. There was the sister-in-law who urged her to write her book; there were women predecessors who had written slave novels (Harriet Martineau and Frances Trollope); there was Fredrika Bremer, the Swedish novelist, who predicted that a great fiction about the runaway slave would be written by "noble-minded American women, American mothers who have hearts and genius." Miss Bremer, in her play *The Bondmaid* (translated in 1844), was one of innumerable writers to draw obvious parallels between the condition of women in the early nineteenth century and that of the slave.

"As the friend of the negro assumes that one man cannot by right hold another in bondage, so should the friend of Woman," Margaret Fuller wrote, "assume that Man cannot by right lay even well-meant restrictions on Woman. If the negro be a soul, or the woman be a soul, to one Master only are they accountable." Margaret Fuller's *Woman in the Nineteenth Century* is a principal feminist text from the pre-Civil War period, when the emancipationists and the feminists were working in hopeful concert. The more somber post-Civil War mood, when political emancipation was extended to black males but not to women of any color, is reflected in

John Stuart Mill's *On the Subjection of Women* (1869). "No slave is a slave to the same lengths, and in so full a sense of the word," wrote Mill, "as a wife is. . . . 'Uncle Tom' under his first master had his own life in his 'cabin' . . . but it cannot be so with the wife." Thus even that "room of one's own" which Virginia Woolf would still be demanding for women in the twentieth century was in the nineteenth century perceived to parallel Uncle Tom's cabin.

Virginia Woolf's concern, however, was not with the feminist texts but with the great works of literature of the epic age. Because Charlotte Brontë was the greatest woman novelist of the post-Austen nineteenth century, her *Jane Eyre* is indeed the prime source, as Woolf discerned, for the language of rage and the metaphors of slavery as they permeated the literary imagination of Victorian women. Familiar *Jane Eyre,* the schoolgirl's classic, is where Virginia Woolf found the characteristic mood of the epic age: "an acidity which is the result of oppression, a buried suffering smouldering beneath her passion, a rancour which contracts those books, splendid as they are, with a spasm of pain." In the opening chapters of *Jane Eyre*— indeed on its very first page—there is writing with that special female ink trampled from the grapes of wrath: an extravagant biblical image Virginia Woolf would never have used, but written into "The Battle Hymn of the Republic" by a female contemporary of Charlotte Brontë.

The spray of hostile negatives—one to a sentence—in the first paragraphs of *Jane Eyre* is Brontë's way of establishing her self-conscious "I." Before she gives Jane Eyre a name, or a class, or an age, Brontë makes her speaker both a person and a female in the quickest shorthand available to women writers: she has her say no. Then comes the family-round-the-fireside scene from which Jane is excluded; then Jane's retreat to her books; then violence, in the person of John Reed, the boy of the family that wants none of Jane; then punishment, by solitary confinement. The whole of the three first chapters of *Jane Eyre,* including the crisis of pre-pubic sexuality that is their climax, is the female equivalent to chapters 2, 3, and 4 in *David Copperfield,* the classic Victorian dramatization of the Oedipal crisis in a boy's life, which Dickens wrote after he read *Jane Eyre.* But hatred, not guilt, dominates Jane Eyre's childhood crisis; and vengeance—or what Sylvia Plath called the "Electra complex"—is its cry. Jane Eyre uses language that would never occur to David Copperfield: "bullied," "bleared," "bilious," "disgusting," "ugly," "menaces," "insults," "inflictions." These are the words Jane spits at John Reed, the tyrant. " 'Wicked and cruel boy!' I said. 'You are like a murderer—you are like a slave-driver—you are like the Roman emperors!' " Though only a child, Jane has been reading, and has "drawn parallels in silence, which I never thought thus to have declared aloud."

No-saying, for a woman writer, is not quite the same unimportant thing it is for a man. "The first and most important qualification in a woman is good nature or sweetness of temper"—that is Rousseau, in his *Émile,* as quoted by Mary Wollstonecraft in her *Vindication of the Rights of Woman* half a century before *Jane Eyre.* Wollstonecraft, who was a novelist and critic as well as a feminist, went on to point the literary moral. In novels, she wrote, virtuous male characters were allowed to be of many temperaments, choleric or sanguine, gay or grave, overbearing or submissive—"but all women are to be levelled, by meekness and docility, into one character of yielding softness and gentle compliance." Not Jane Eyre, indeed; and not Catherine Earnshaw, whose childhood journal, at the start of *Wuthering Heights,* opens with the words "An awful Sunday!", moves on to rebellious threats, and climaxes with Cathy's hurling a dingy tract "by the scroop" and "vowing I hated a good book." And not Aurora Leigh, who, just like Jane Eyre, is told that females must "keep quiet by the fire/And never say 'no' when the world says 'ay.' "

On the first page of *Jane Eyre* the first issue raised is in fact the issue of style. The wrong style, in girlhood and in language, is the reason why Jane is kept by Mrs. Reed from joining the other children around her by the fire.

> Me, she had dispensed from joining the group; saying, "She regretted to be under the necessity of keeping me at a distance; but that until she heard from Bessie . . . that I was endeavouring in good earnest to acquire a more sociable and childlike disposition, a more attractive and sprightly manner—something lighter, franker, more natural, as it were—she really must exclude me from privileges intended only for contented, happy little children."

And, immediately after style, the next issue, raised by Jane herself, is justice—the one most calculated to make trouble in the nursery, or anywhere else.

> "What does Bessie say I have done?" I asked.
> "Jane, I don't like cavillers or questioners; besides, there is something truly forbidding in a child taking up her elders in that manner. Be seated somewhere; and until you can speak pleasantly, remain silent."

From justice in the personal context there is, for Jane Eyre, no distance at all to justice in a social context wide enough to frighten the *Quarterly Review.* "My blood was still warm," says Jane; "the mood of the revolted slave was still bracing me with its bitter vigour"; and, "like any other rebel slave, I felt resolved, in my desperation to go all lengths." These slavery metaphors in Brontë's language emphasize not the pathos of victimization but the dangerous recoil of revolt and revenge: "How all my brain was in tumult, and all my heart in insurrection!" These eloquent words begin a

passage which explains as fully as would volumes of feminist history why
chattel slavery was a woman's literary subject in the epic age:

> I was a discord in Gateshead Hall; I was like nobody there. . . . If
> they did not love me, in fact, as little did I love them. They were not
> bound to regard with affection a thing that could not sympathize with
> one amongst them; a heterogeneous thing, opposed to them in tempera-
> ment, in capacity, in propensities; a useless thing, incapable of serving
> their interest, or adding to their pleasure; a noxious thing, cherishing
> the germs of indignation at their treatment, of contempt of their
> judgment. . . .

Jane Eyre is here only a child—she is only ten; but childhood is where
the self is created, in the female as in the male sex; and where, incidentally, as these opening chapters indicate, the principal agent of repression
in a girl's life is not a father or any father-figure; but a boy who is an unnatural brother and, most important, a woman who is an unnatural
mother. In *Jane Eyre* and elsewhere, the testimony of literary women is
that the cultural command—"until you can speak pleasantly, remain
silent"—is imposed on girls primarily by women.

"You may try—but you can never imagine," a gifted woman says to a
man in one of George Eliot's novels, "what it is to have a man's force of
genius in you, and yet to suffer the slavery of being a girl." Literary women
of the epic age did not need to imagine; they knew. To the author of *Jane
Eyre* there was no mystery about Harriet Beecher Stowe's access as a
woman to the epic subject matter of *Uncle Tom's Cabin*. "I doubt not,"
Charlotte Brontë wrote when that work appeared, "Mrs. Stowe had felt the
iron of slavery enter into her heart, from childhood upwards. . . ."

. . .

When asked by her novelist friend and biographer Mrs. Gaskell for her
opinion on the "Condition of Women" question, Charlotte Brontë replied
that there were "evils—deep-rooted in the foundation of the social system,
which no efforts of ours can touch: of which we cannot complain; of
which it is advisable not too often to think." Out of the clear, un-
complicated light of day (where petitions are circulated and meetings organized); down below the surface of the mind, where Jane Eyres and Lucy
Snowes are born, seethed the feminine discontent that produced the literature of the epic age. To Virginia Woolf, it pulled the novelist's pen from
the straight; to us, it appears the source of the fire and passion that made
Jane Eyre more than a melodrama, and *Uncle Tom's Cabin* more than a
tract. But it did not produce feminist polemics.

There were many active Victorian feminists, of course; it was they
whose speeches and organizations and petitions yielded the slow but
steady achievements—in education, careers, property rights, divorce laws,

contraception—which made the nineteenth century the greatest period of female social progress in history. And feminist activists made part of the spectrum of opinion through which the great literary women of the age saw the world. For just as every woman writer knew conservative women, who urged her toward convention and silence, she also knew active feminists, who prodded her pen from the other, radical side of the Woman Question.

George Eliot knew Barbara Leigh-Smith (founder of the Association for Promoting the Employment of Women); Mrs. Gaskell knew Bessie Parkes; and Charlotte Brontë knew Mary Taylor (early settler and business-woman of New Zealand), who wrote home to Yorkshire denouncing the author of *Shirley* as "coward" and "traitor" for the hesitant ambivalence she sensed in Charlotte Brontë's attitude toward work for women. *Shirley* (1849), Charlotte Brontë's second published novel, contains more feminist writing than any of her other works, but it is more importantly concerned with industrial warfare between the millhands and the masters of York-shire, for Brontë was not a feminist so much as she was a writer of the epic age. Like the child Jane Eyre, her imagination was stimulated by drawing "parallels in silence" between her personal condition and that of other classes and races of mankind that suffered under oppression, and threat-ened to rebel.

This outreaching of the feminist impulse is the essence of the "epic age" phenomenon; this submersion of private, brooding, female resent-ment ("of which it is advisable not too often to think") in the Christian humanitarianism which, for women and men both, was the major current of Victorian thought. In this, the "epic age" is distinguished from the ages of women's literature which preceded it, and from the ages which followed it, including Virginia Woolf's—and our own.

Self-pity was not considered a virtue by the Victorians. To do for others, rather than to feel for oneself was what Harriet Martineau meant by "the most serious business of life" which she urged on her female con-temporaries in reaction to the passionate feminism of an earlier day. "Mary Wollstonecraft was, with all her powers," wrote Miss Martineau, "a poor victim of passion, with no control over her own peace, and no calm-ness or content except when the needs of her individual nature were satisfied." The judgment is harsh, but shrewd. Another way to put the matter would be to say that, while Wollstonecraft's writings had ushered in the Romantic age for English literary women, Harriet Martineau's began the Victorian reaction.

In 1832 Miss Martineau began to publish her *Illustrations* not of Women's Rights (though she was a suffragist) but *of Political Economy,* and so began the educating of the nation to the facts and theories of industry, labor, and trade. Her achievement was a remarkable one, and not only because she was "a little deaf woman at Norwich!" as Lord Brougham exclaimed; the knowledge she taught was essential to social change. That Harriet Martineau addressed herself to the Condition of England question rather than to the Condition of Women question may deprive her of a place in feminist history, but it certainly does not mark her as unambitious.

The medium through which Martineau taught economics was fiction; her *Illustrations* are lively novels in miniature, but complete in cast of characters, setting, dialogue, and plot as well as a concluding "Summary of Principles illustrated in this Volume." Narrative brought her the wide popular readership that other writers on economics had for decades been trying in vain to secure, and, because she wrote fiction, her influence was to be literary as well as political. The novel and the poem were women's only instruments of social action in the early nineteenth century: literature was their pulpit, tribune, academy, commission, and parliament all in one. "I want to be doing something with the pen," said Harriet Martineau, "since no other means of action in politics are in a woman's power." That flat statement, from 1832, announces the dawning of the epic age as surely as Virginia Woolf's peroration to *A Room of One's Own*—"Do not dream of influencing other people. . . ."—announces its close.

That the novel in particular was a national resource, and that women in particular wrote fiction with the ease and confidence of long tradition impressed foreign visitors to England in the nineteenth century. Karl Marx, for example, saluted "the present splendid brotherhood of fiction-writers in England, whose graphic and eloquent pages have issued to the world more political and social truths than have been uttered by all the professional politicians, publicists and moralists put together." To the credit of the epic age, half of the "brotherhood" Marx had in mind was female, for two women novelists, Charlotte Brontë and Mrs. Gaskell, shared his praise (in 1854) with two men, Dickens and Thackeray. And indeed, *Mary Barton: A Tale of Manchester Life,* the Gaskell novel Marx must have had mainly in mind, is a remarkable work not only for its subject matter, but for its smoothness of execution, its relaxed and confident intermixing of the traditional young-woman-in-search-of-a-husband story of female fiction with illustrations of the particularly brutal political economy of the Hungry Forties. *Mary Barton* was its author's first novel, but Mrs. Gaskell was a careful student of Jane Austen's realism, and a beneficiary of the enormous legacy of fiction that women had been writing since Richardson's day.

Another foreign visitor of radical views provides even more interesting testimony to the professional readiness of English literary women at the outset of the epic age, for she was a woman, herself a novelist, and a radical feminist named Flora Tristan. She came to England from Paris in the

1830s to study industrial slums and factories from London to Manchester, to investigate prostitution and parliament, upper-class corruption and working-class organization; she was a disciple of Robert Owen as well as of Mary Wollstonecraft. The Chartists, whose meetings Tristan attended, impressed her mightily, but the generality of English women revolted her, for she found no residue of Wollstonecraft's feminism in England.

Promenades dans Londres is the fascinating radical's-eye view of England that Tristan published in 1840. Its deceptively peaceable title, which means *Walks in London,* may account for the work's never having been translated, and for its being ignored by English (not French) historians of industrial strife. For historians of feminism, Tristan provides a bleak summary of the condition of early-Victorian womanhood. English girls in general she found coarse and corrupt because, she decided, they derived their entire moral education from that notoriously indecent work, the Bible. (Though part Peruvian in background, Tristan was very French.)

English wives in general she found stupid and idle, ignorant of housewifery—what a footnote to Dickens!—and ignored by their husbands except as "machines for making babies," babies they were incompetent to rear. But Anglophobe as she was, Flora Tristan had to admit that the *exceptional* women of England had not their like in France; and that they were the literary women. The list she discusses—Harriet Martineau, Lady Morgan, Rosina Bulwer, Lady Blessington, Mrs. Trollope, Mary Shelley, Mrs. Gore—shows she was well informed about the principal women writers of the 1830s, as well as a reader of Mary Wollstonecraft.

"What a revolting contrast exists in England," wrote Tristan, "between the slavery of women and the intellectual superiority of women writers." Their tradition of literary professionalism seemed to her very old (she dated its beginning to Lady Mary Wortley Montagu); and they published in greater numbers, and to greater effect than the *femmes-auteurs* of France, though French women were, in her opinion, generally more intelligent, more sophisticated, more used to equal converse with men and to political influence. To this apparent paradox, Flora Tristan found what appears to be the correct answer: the energies of exceptional English women were directed into literature because of their enforced social and political inactivity, because of their exclusion from what she called "le mouvement social." Flora Tristan's own life points up the trans-national paradox. Her one novel, with a hero named "Méphis le prolétaire," is poor literature; but her role as an activist among and on behalf of the proletariat has no parallel among English women of her day.

It was not only stifled feminism that inspired women's literature of social action—whether the feminism of the sickly, ugly daughter, or the poor spinster, or the servile governess, or the abandoned, brutalized wife, or the overworked mother, bitter at the death of a child. It was also women's craving for a share in "le mouvement social," the march on progress which absorbed an activist age. The literary energies of English women, wasting on the annuals and the tracts of the 1830s, were bubbling, perfecting, spoiling for themes of epic grandeur.

In their own terms, the call to new and dangerous and important subject matter was the call of duty, and no one put that call, as literary women heard it, better than Mrs. Gaskell. "When a man becomes an author," she wrote,

> it is probably merely a change of employment to him. He takes a portion of that time which has hitherto been devoted to some other study or pursuit; . . . and another merchant or lawyer, or doctor, steps into his vacant place, and probably does as well as he. But no other can take up the quiet, regular duties of the daughter, the wife, or the mother . . . ; a woman's principal work in life is hardly left to her own choice; nor can she drop the domestic charges devolving on her as an individual, for the exercise of the most splendid talents that were ever bestowed.

So far Mrs. Gaskell's statement is a commonplace of every age, whether wise or blind the reader will judge for herself; but the ringing challenge in her conclusion belongs only to the epic age. "And yet," Mrs. Gaskell continues,

> And yet she must not shrink from the extra responsibility implied by the very fact of her possessing such talents. She must not hide her gift in a napkin; it was meant for the use and service of others. In an humble and faithful spirit she must labour to do what is not impossible, or God would not have set her to do it.

Flora Tristan did not live to see the full historical unfolding of this spirit in the literature of the epic age. She died in 1844, a little over forty, while on a strenuous organizing tour among the French proletariat—a word which, incidentally, her writings did much to popularize. She is remembered today not primarily as a feminist but as founder of the *Union ouvrière,* as a bold and early spokesman for international working-class solidarity.

. . .

The factory setting, the new industrial cities of the north of England, the machines and manufacturing processes, the prices and wages, the tariffs and markets, the economic crises and layoffs, the capital investments and profits, the workers' associations, riots, and strikes—all the compelling, mysterious phenomena that underlay the Condition of England question were first opened up to literature by Harriet Martineau.

There is ample contemporary evidence that the simple, driving narratives which she devised as *Illustrations of Political Economy* were read for the story as much as for the principles of economic theory she taught; and that her capitalists and workers, new types to fiction, interested the public as characters in their own right. "Accurate and striking," said John Doherty, the trade unionist, of one of her tales, called *A Manchester Strike;* "very interesting and Robinson Crusoe-ish," said Miss Mitford, who was a great Whig, of another.

It was not, however, Miss Martineau, with her daunting rationality, who set the tone with which the Victorians would soon war on industrial misery. Carlyle and Dickens, of course, brought melodramatic fervor and wrenching pathos into Victorian prose; but neither of them, in their early works (*Sartor Resartus,* 1833–38, and *Oliver Twist,* 1837–39), explored the industrial setting. Instead it was the poets who first made pathos— effective pathos—out of the pale children, the maimed women, and the starving men of the mills and mines.

In the 1830s anonymous verses by Manchester workers, and by the Manchester radical Samuel Bamford, were written down, published in collections, set to music; and the poetesses of the annuals found their most effective material in *Tales of the Factories* (Caroline Bowles, 1833) and *A Voice from the Factories* (Caroline Norton, 1836). Mrs. Norton was a celebrity, the wit and beauty who is most remembered as the divorced feminist who fought for the legal right of mothers to custody of their children. Mrs. Norton hoped, however, to be remembered not for scandal, but for her *"real* occupations and aspirations," these best expressed in *The Child of the Islands* (1845), which returned to the subject of child labor. The two best-remembered poems written in the cause, which they advanced, of factory reform both appeared in 1843: Elizabeth Barrett's "The Cry of the Children" a few months before Thomas Hood's "The Song of the Shirt." But none of this factory verse can properly be stigmatized by the phrase "now forgotten," so dear to scholars, for a good share of it was absorbed into Mrs. Gaskell's *Mary Barton* (1848), the first great factory novel, where it is still read, and still makes a powerful effect. Mrs. Gaskell quotes radical verse, dialect verse, and women's verse in abundance; she has her characters copy out this verse in the novel, recite it, discuss it, and sing it, because she was centrally concerned with finding a new voice in which to "give some utterance," as she put it, to the agony of Manchester people.

Mary Barton is a remarkable work, but it was not the first in the field. The earliest factory novels were written by women—indeed, there appears to be a rule that wherever literary women achieve real distinction with an apparently new departure, there is a female literary model of less distinc-

tion in their past. Harriet Martineau paid full tribute in her autobiography
to the seeding inspiration of Mrs. Jane Marcet's *Conversations on Political
Economy,* which had popularized Ricardo's theories in the 1810s. Thus,
before *Mary Barton* there was *Michael Armstrong, the Factory Boy*
(1839–40), a crude but occasionally effective transposition of the *Oliver
Twist* formula to the industrial setting, by Frances Trollope (mother of
Anthony). Just back from America, where she had written one of the earliest fugitive slave novels, the energetic and passionate Mrs. Trollope
found a new cause in Lord Ashley's Ten-Hour Bill, a measure to limit
child labor in the factories. She announced to her publisher her intention
to write a factory novel, and, armed with Lord Ashley's introductions,
traveled by the new railway up to Manchester to see for herself.

Lord Ashley's name begins to appear everywhere in English literary
history as an imprimatur of earnest humanitarianism and effective social
action. Tory aristocrat that he was (later the seventh Earl of Shaftesbury),
he was the greatest political and professional philanthropist of the century,
first important for his leadership of the cause of factory reform in the
1830s and '40s, and later associated with the reform of slum housing,
public health, sanitation, education, and everything to do with the raising
of the children of the poor. (Dickens and Florence Nightingale, among
many others, paid tribute to his labors, from which their work benefited.)
We find Lord Ashley in Caroline Norton's *Voice from the Factories,*
which was dedicated to him, and in fact reads like a versification of one of
his parliamentary speeches. We find him roundly cheered in an important
scene of *Helen Fleetwood,* the influential early factory novel published in
the *Christian Lady's Magazine* in 1839–40, and in book form in 1841, by
a woman who signed herself "Charlotte Elizabeth."

Of all the minor women of the epic age, this lady, who is more conveniently known as Mrs. Tonna (after her second husband), is the one about
whom I most wish to satisfy my curiosity. The little I know of her seems
to set both the type and the extreme limits of the case of feminine outrage
diverted to non-feminist social causes. For example, after *Helen Fleetwood*
she wrote *The Wrongs of Woman* (1843–44), a title which is probably an
unintentional reminder of Mary Wollstonecraft's most feminist novel, *The
Wrongs of Woman, or Maria.* Mrs. Tonna's novel is not so much a feminist
work as a species of industrial fiction, for it narrates the miseries of
women workers in the factories.

Her maiden name was Charlotte Elizabeth Browne and she was, oddly
like Harriet Martineau in this single respect, a deaf woman from Norwich;
but where the Martineaus were Unitarians of the manufacturing class (and
Miss Martineau became an outspoken atheist), the Brownes were Establishment people (her father a rector) and Charlotte Elizabeth became

an Evangelical of what must be called maniacal fervor. An early, childless marriage to a Captain Phelan quickly turned to a disaster at which she merely hints in her *Personal Recollections*. In that surprisingly interesting volume she does explain, however, that she signed herself Charlotte Elizabeth to protect her anonymity, for "an attempt was suddenly made from another quarter to establish a claim to the profits of my pen," which in the 1820s and 1830s was busily producing religious tracts.

What does all this have to do with the factory novel? Not all the stages in her progression toward the new subject matter are clear, but it is not difficult to fill in the gaps: precocious girlhood; accidental deafness in adolescence; marriage; residence in Canada, then Ireland, where she became an Evangelical convert and developed a passion for the Irish people as fierce as her hatred for their religion; amateur teaching and converting of deaf children; tract writing "to instruct the poor in the blessed truths of the gospel"; England and Hannah More; first public activities—petitions, meetings, and so on—in the fruitless cause of opposition to Catholic Emancipation (1829).

Charlotte Elizabeth was a woman of passionate female hatreds, but she poured her passion not into feminism but into partisan devotion to Evangelical Protestantism, and partisan opposition to Roman Catholicism. To her there was no war so worth the fighting as that between "the arrogant assumptions of the Great Harlot" and "the sublime simplicity, purity, and modesty of the chaste Spouse of Christ." This kind of imagery was literally a godsend to nineteenth-century women of Mrs. Tonna's type.

In the 1830s she settled in London, edited magazines for Christian ladies and entered the highest Evangelical circles—of bishops, politicians, lords, and, who knows, perhaps even Lord Ashley.* Her new cause became London's wretched, growing Irish population; her new mission, a "campaign against starvation and Popery in St. Giles's," London's Irish quarter and one of its worst slums. "What visions of prodigies of wickedness, want and beggary, arose in my mind out of that place," Dickens told Forster. And there, at the outset of the Victorian age, Mrs. Tonna enters the world of *Oliver Twist*—and her *Recollections* break off.

* It would be odd if Lord Ashley had nothing to do with directing Mrs. Tonna's energies to the causes of factory and slum reform in the late 1830s. He was the leading Evangelical peer, and it was as chairman of a meeting of the Bible Society that he first appeared to Harriet Beecher Stowe, when she toured England in triumph after the publication of *Uncle Tom's Cabin*—which Lord Ashley was among the first to hail as a work of Evangelical humanitarianism. His own essentially religious dedication to social causes was hardly a family tradition, but the result of the influence upon him in his boyhood of an upper servant, Maria Millis, who "taught me many things, directing my thoughts to highest subjects," as he recalled in old age; "and I can even now call to mind many sentences of prayer she made me repeat at her knees. To her I trace, under God, my first impressions."

In *Helen Fleetwood,* Mrs. Tonna wrote in the language of the Evangelical tract on a subject to which it is thoroughly appropriate: child labor in the factories.

> Excluded from the free air, and almost from the pure light of day; shut up in an atmosphere polluted by clouds of fetid breath, and all the sickening exhalations of a crowded human mass . . . ; relaxed by an intensity of artificial heat which their constitutions were never framed to encounter in the temperate clime where God had placed them; doubly fevered, doubly debilitated, by excessive toil, not measured by human capacity to sustain it, but by the power of machinery . . . ; badly clothed, wretchedly fed, and exposed moreover to fasts of unnatural length . . . ; oh who could marvel though the little ones so fearfully forced into every way in which they should not go, became in riper years incarnate fiends!

Who read this sort of thing? Ladies who read publications like the *Christian Lady's Magazine,* where it appeared. Harriet Beecher Stowe, who was writing for similar Evangelical periodicals in America, not only read Mrs. Tonna, but in 1844 provided the introduction to the American edition of her *Works.* And there is a strong likelihood, as Aina Rubenius has argued, that Mrs. Gaskell read a great deal of Mrs. Tonna and was influenced throughout her own career as a novelist by her fiction.

There is an equally strong likelihood that Mrs. Gaskell did *not* read Disraeli, the single male exception (and with Disraeli's background, the one that proves the rule) to the predominating female presence in the early history of industrial literature.

Disraeli's *Sybil, or The Two Nations,* in any case, appeared in 1845, which seems too late to have affected Mrs. Gaskell's commitment to tell the Manchester story. And Disraeli's novel, however effective, is essentially a London politician's view of the industrial crisis in the midlands; while Mrs. Gaskell's approach to the same subject is that of Manchester resident and Christian womanhood.

. . .

I. M. Katarsky, in his introduction to the recent Moscow edition of *Mary Barton: A Tale of Manchester Life,* centers his claim for the novel on the figure of John Barton, the heroine's father. "For the first time in the history of English literature," he writes, "a novel appears whose author dares to make the hero of her work a 'rebel activist' [actually a "bundist"], a shaker of the social foundations, and she depicts him in a clear, strong, and humanly attractive way." The judgment is a little overdrawn but not eccentric, and it does point to the feature of the novel which was most original, which offended many readers, and which caused surprise that its author was a woman—and a minister's wife. Mrs. Gaskell portrayed with

all the sympathy at her command the awakening of radical views and revolutionary tendencies in the mind of a serious and thoughtful representative
of the industrial working class. "John Barton became a Chartist, a Communist," she writes in the novel, "all that is commonly called wild and
visionary. Ay! but being visionary is something. It shows a soul, a being
not altogether sensual; a creature who looks forward for others, if not for
himself." The figure of the social visionary looms large in Victorian
women's fiction—by Charlotte Brontë, Geraldine Jewsbury, George Eliot,
Mrs. Stowe, and Mrs. Browning, as well as Mrs. Gaskell.

John Barton works as a weaver in an industrial textile mill. He is
somewhat above the average in strength and sense, but not an intellectual;
above average too in steadiness and respectability, but no paragon, for he
can get drunk and even violent toward his womenfolk under the pressure
of unusual hardship. Routine hardship is a familiar thing to Barton (the
son of Manchester millhands), but so is a level of material prosperity well
above that attainable by agricultural workers, as Mrs. Gaskell points out.
What radicalizes the man is the fluctuations in trade against which workers
are powerless, but on which capitalists appear to him to thrive.

Economic crises struck cities like Manchester with increasing frequency
and severity between 1815 and 1839, the year John Barton's story opens;
that was also the dawning year of the "Hungry Forties" and of Chartism.
These crises were the striking flaw in England's prosperity to which Karl
Marx devoted his principal attention as economic analyst, and they, not
the general horrors of industrialism, are the particular issue of political
economy which Mrs. Gaskell's first novel "illustrates."

It was not that she loved the mills or Manchester; quite the contrary.
Indeed, so sensitive was Mrs. Gaskell to the horrors of the place that, in
the celebrated sixth chapter of *Mary Barton,* called "Poverty and Death"
—where a worker dies of fever in a sewer-like sub-basement before the
eyes of his starving family—she provides the only evocation of urban degradation to be compared for sheer power to scenes in Engels's *Condition
of the Working Class in England in 1844.*

But it is not the helpless, mindless surrender of the working class to
starvation, fever, and death that is the burden of Mrs. Gaskell's tale, any
more than it is of Engels's. Instead it is the workers' capacity to perceive
injustice, resent wrongs, speak hatred, and act in concert either to help
each other support misery—the role played by Barton in chapter 6—or to
rebel against the power of the bourgeoisie.

John Barton sees with clarity and bitterness that economic conditions
over which he has no control produce the personal tragedies that invade
his life, from the corruption of his sister-in-law, to the death of his wife,
to unemployment and poverty. A fall in markets causes the masters to
close their mills and lay off workers. Barton sees the masters profit by in-

surance, modernize their machinery, enjoy their leisure, increase their prosperity, and improve their style of life. "How comes it they're rich, and we're poor?" he asks. And his answer is the Manchester workingman's version of the labor theory of value:

> "I say, our labour's our capital, and we ought to draw interest on that. They get interest on their capital somehow a' this time, while ourn is lying idle, else how could they all live as they do? Besides, there's many on 'em has had nought to begin wi'; . . . and now they're worth their tens of thousands, a' getten out of our labour; but . . . whatten better are we? They'n screwed us down to th' lowest peg, in order to make their great big fortunes, and build their great big houses, and we, why we're just clemming, many and many of us. Can you say there's nought wrong in this?"

"Clemming" is the first word of Manchester dialect the reader learns from Mrs. Gaskell: it means "starving." But she heard more than dialect in working-class speech; she heard alert, well-informed, intelligent anger.

There is a good deal in *Mary Barton* about the intelligence of Manchester people—the acuteness of eye and the sharpness of tongue, even among the illiterate, which, she points out, markedly distinguish the industrial proletariat from the rural peasantry. And she goes out of her way to document the existence of "a class of men . . . whose existence will probably be doubted by many" that she finds not only in Manchester but "scattered all over the manufacturing districts of Lancashire": the intellectuals among the workers, weavers who read Newton's *Principia* at the loom, mechanics whose inventions advance industrial technology, botanists whose discoveries attract the attention of researchers in natural science throughout England. Do not discount the working men of Manchester, is what Mrs. Gaskell is saying; treat them "as brethren and friends," and speak to them "openly, clearly, as appealing to reasonable men." The moral impetus behind *Mary Barton,* as behind so much social fiction by women, is to reveal the essential humanity of a group, or class, or race by making its voice heard; and to suggest the hazards of society's failure to attend to that voice.

John Barton joins a trade union and becomes active at meetings; then he becomes a Chartist, is chosen a delegate, and goes to London to present the Chartist petition; finally out of class hatred, not a personal grudge, he assassinates a representative of the bourgeoisie. Two twists of plot advance Barton's progress from radical to dangerous revolutionary, and both illustrate the historical consequence of withholding attention from the voice of the working class. Mrs. Gaskell drew the first of these from history: Parliament's refusal to accept the Charter (which demanded merely a widening of political democracy) which tens of thousands of workers, tramping from every corner of the kingdom, carried to London in 1839. They were bent not on violent revolution, but on making their misery heard; and they were turned away unheard with disdain and ridicule. Mrs. Gaskell shows John Barton full of pride and hope on the eve of his departure for London, as his working-class friends crowd into his home to offer their views of what he should "speak on to the Parliament people." In the following chapter she shows him on his return from London, sullenly silent to his friends' questions about "what happened when you got to th' Parliament House."

> "If you please, neighbour, I'd rather say nought about that. It's not to be forgotten, or forgiven either, by me or many another; but I canna tell of our down-casting just as a piece of London news. As long as I live, our rejection of that day will abide in my heart; and as long as I live I shall curse them as so cruelly refused to hear us; but I'll not speak of it no more."

The second plot turn, by which Barton moves from cursing to killing, is a trivial event not drawn from history—a mere "by-play," Mrs. Gaskell says, of the kind "not recorded in the Manchester newspapers." A negotiation between masters and men is going badly, because neither side is talking seriously to the other. Instead of listening, one of the rich men present, the son of a principal Manchester manufacturer, scribbles a caricature of the workers in which he cleverly mocks their coarse and hungry look, their ragged clothes and spent bodies. This "admirable caricature" makes smiles pass across the faces of the masters when it is circulated among them; later, when passed among the union men, it sets off a demand for class murder. John is chosen to be assassin, and Harry Carson to be victim. He is the young man who drew the caricature, and thus provides a parallel, on a small and human scale, of the Londoners who ridiculed the Chartists, of the Parliament that "cruelly refused to hear." "The most deplorable and enduring evil that arose out of the period of commercial depression to which I refer," writes Mrs. Gaskell, "was this feeling of alienation between the different classes of society."

How seriously Mrs. Gaskell took the novelist's role of bridging the gap between masters and men she makes clear in her brief but important preface to *Mary Barton,* where she also outlines the steps in her own progress as a writer from distance and artificiality to immediacy and reality —to paying attention to the Manchester voice. The preface begins with a vague reference to an unspecified crisis in her personal life, in 1845, which made her "anxious to employ myself" in writing fiction. At that time she had in fact already begun a novel, but it was a rural tale set far in the past, the sort of fiction to be expected from an author with her "deep relish and fond admiration for the country." But the personal crisis which made her "anxious" also made her suddenly aware of the "romance" of the here and now: the industrial present, and the working people of Manchester all about her.

These last she refers to first as a presence neither seen nor heard but felt—a jostling crowd "who elbowed me daily in the busy streets." Then she notices their faces: "care-worn men, who looked as if doomed to struggle through their lives in strange alternations between work and want." Then she listens to their voices, giving "a little attention to the expression of feelings on the part of some of the work-people with whom I was acquainted." Because she pays attention and manifests sympathy, "the hearts of one or two of the more thoughtful" of the work-people were "laid open to me." She learns that their worst grievance is neither misery nor injustice, but the failure on the part of the prosperous to pay attention and manifest sympathy.

> The more I reflected . . . the more anxious I became to give some utterance to the agony which, from time to time, convulses this dumb people; the agony of suffering without the sympathy of the happy, . . . of believing . . . that the woes, which come with ever returning tide-like flood to overwhelm the workmen in our manufacturing towns, pass unregarded by all but the sufferers. . . .
>
> To myself the idea which I have formed of the state of feeling among too many of the factory people in Manchester . . . has received some confirmation from the events which have so recently occurred among a similar class on the Continent.
>
> October, 1848

The domestic event, incidentally, which turned Mrs. Gaskell's anxious attention to revolution was the death of her infant son. And John Barton's revenge leaves Carson the millowner a bitter but wiser man, bereft of his only son, the parent only of daughters—as was the case with Mrs. Gaskell.

* * *

During the early months of the February Revolution, the most important of those frightening Continental events of 1848 to which Mrs. Gaskell refers, George Sand played an active role in a revolutionary government—a "first," they say, for women's history. She threw no bombs and stormed no barricades and performed none of those symbolic gestures of violence which, in our stable times, pass for revolutionary action; instead she went to meetings, sat on committees, made speeches, nominated officials, debated doctrines, and, closely involved with both radical and socialist leaders, became enmeshed in party factionalism. In short, she engaged briefly in all the tedious if momentarily exciting work of a provisional government that must be carried on when the normal apparatus of the state has withered away. Principally, she wrote: journalism of all sorts, official propaganda for the Ministry of the Interior (a series of *Bulletins de la République* posted in the communes), and her *Letters to the People, to the Middle Class,* and *to the Rich.* Also published in 1848 were installments of *François le Champi* and *La Petite Fadette:* two of her *romans champêtres* (peasant tales, or rustic novels), those which, of all her works, have most securely held the status of "classics" in France.

In terms of worldwide effect, George Sand was the most important writer of the epic age. What actual role she played in French affairs, what particular slice of the ideological and utopian thought of early nineteenth-century France she made her own are subjects of some complexity on which much has been and more will be written; but that she expressed the general revolutionary aspirations of the age with a verve, a drama, and an eloquence heard around the world we know from contemporary evidence everywhere.

"She has passed *through* the crisis of the age," wrote Mazzini, the Italian patriot. "The evil she has depicted is not her evil, it is ours. . . . She has cried to us: *Behold your society.*" "George Sand is infinitely more than a novelist," wrote George Henry Lewes; "She is a Poet . . . uttering the collective voice of her epoch." Walt Whitman, whose carpenter-poet persona owed something to her work, said that George Sand was of the class of writers much needed "lest the world stagnate in wrongs"; and he succumbed to her power—"you have to lay down the book and give your emotions room." "George Sand is one of our saints," said Turgenev; and Dostoevsky assigned her "unquestionably the first place in the ranks" of the great European writers who suddenly burst on "the Russian idealists of the 1840s, . . . proclaiming that the regeneration of humanity had to be radical, complete. . . ." The "immense vibration of George Sand's voice upon the ear of Europe" was recorded by Matthew Arnold. And Karl Marx, no mean verbal agitator in his own right, quoted a sentence from George Sand to make the ringing, revolutionary conclusion to his 1847 polemic *The Poverty of Philosophy.* When Marx first arrived in Paris in 1843 he had been advised by his colleague Arnold Ruge to look up George Sand and Flora Tristan; for the French women, Ruge said, were on the whole more radical than the men.

A close interconnection between feminism and radicalism is no new idea to French historians of the nineteenth century. Proto-socialist ideologues in France at the beginning of the century placed a revision of marriage laws at the center of their utopias; and a female Messiah was envisaged by Saint-Simon and Enfantin as an essential partner in the revolutionary enterprise. Both Flora Tristan and George Sand were widely mentioned as candidates for this post—a suggestion which the former seems to have regarded seriously, the latter with characteristic humor. But George Sand comments herself on feminine access, via a sense of personal injustice, to the wider issue of social class injustice in modern society.

"George Sand never wrote just to write," as Taine put it, "but because she was animated by a faith." That is the impression all her work gives, just as much as the impression (about which she was quite candid) that she wrote for money. Sloppy in form, hasty in execution, slight in invention her works often were, but the convictions behind them ring true. In the dullest and stupidest of her fictions there will come a page of such brilliance, a paragraph or sentence of such irresistible and earnest eloquence that the reader who thought he was done with her forever goes on to the end—as Matthew Arnold did, for example, from the 1830s to the 1870s. And Ruskin, who placed her alongside Balzac among "good novelists of the second order," was something of a Sand addict: "George Sand . . . will not live," he said, "but she got [her] power from the sense of Justice. . . ."

The first impetus to write, in Sand's case, derived as all the world knows from her own marital situation. And the marriage question, from the unhappy wife's point of view, is the theme of *Indiana* (1832), which brought George Sand instant prominence as a novelist, and which in some ways—for its lush romanticism and lucid construction around a standard adultery motif—she never surpassed. But *Indiana* is also, in its simplicity, the least characteristic of Sand's works. With her second novel, *Valentine* (also 1832), she was already a messier, a more diffuse, and I think a more interesting novelist; there her social concerns fantasize her plot and complicate her characters.

Thus her heroine, Valentine, yearns not only for ideal love but for an ideal redistribution of property. Issues of women's education and men's careers permeate the "marriage question." Old people are set against young people not merely as agents of conformity, but as highly attractive spokesmen of class values and philosophical views; the first of Sand's marvelous old lady aristocrats appears in *Valentine*. Loyalties in the novel are even more regional than sexual: in *Valentine* Sand begins to do that remarkable landscape painting which so dazzled her English readers, who had not, before Sand, found Nature celebrated in the novel. And class barriers, aspirations, and curiosities, as well as marriage laws, complicate the course of true female love. There are almost as many types of heroine in George Sand's *oeuvre* as there are novels; but if one type can be considered most characteristic, it is the aristocratic woman like Valentine* who

---

* Others are Fiamma in *Simon*, Yseut in *Le Compagnon du tour de France*, Marcelle in *Le Meunier d'Angibault*, in a sense even Consuelo. The number of serious Victorians who admitted to being in love with these socially liberated ladies is astonishing, and suggests the value of Sand's fiction as an agent of sublimation. Ruskin, for example, said that he had fallen in love with four Sand heroines, one after the other, and was "quite vexed because I can't see them— seriously vexed I mean; made uncomfortable." The most important novelist to rework Sand's heroines was Dostoevsky. Henry James tried his hand at catching the charm of these social-justice-through-love heroines in his early neo-Sand tale, "Gabrielle de Bergerac" (1869), which is apprentice work, but more fun than *The Princess Casamassima* (1886).

loves a man of the people, and who attempts to work out through her female destiny—in its whole gamut, from virginity to maternity and old age—her own commitment to social justice.

But it was also George Sand who touched the extremes of feminine nihilism in *Lélia* (1833), that threnody of sexual despair and bitter skepticism which made the *maladie du siècle* a female as well as a male disease. *Lélia* was the only one of her works that Sand substantially revised, and through her long struggle to produce a second *Lélia* (1839) can be traced the development in her literary ethos from romantic egotism, to mystical humanitarianism, to radical activism. "I'm redoing *Lélia,* did I tell you?" she wrote midway in the process to her friend Marie d'Agoult (who wrote novels, history, and criticism of Emerson as "Daniel Stern"). "That book brought me to the depths of skepticism; now it is pulling me out. . . . Sickness created the book, the book made the sickness worse, and it's the same with the cure. To make this work of anger accommodate a work of gentle acceptance. . . ." And she went on to sketch the articles of her new doctrine according to which she was reworking *Lélia* as a social manifesto:

> To throw oneself on Nature's breast, taking her truly as *mother* and *sister;* stoically and religiously withdraw from one's life everything that is satisfied vanity; stubbornly resist the proud and the wicked; to become humble and small with the unfortunate, weep with the poor in their misery, and wish for no other consolation than the fall of the rich; to believe in no God other than Him who ordains justice and equality among men; to venerate the good, severely judge the strong, live on almost nothing, give almost everything away, in order to reestablish primitive equality and reinstitute the divine order—that is the religion I'll proclaim in my little corner, and that I hope to preach to my twelve apostles under the linden tree in my garden.
>
> As to love, that will be a book and a course to itself . . .

Had Sand been English instead of French, we would probably think of her as a Christian Socialist. Matters of religious faith were the first and always predominant issues in her intellectual development, as was the case with her Victorian readers, who would have been intrigued to learn of her lifelong attraction to Protestantism. Thackeray, however, was outraged by her *Spiridion* (1839), Sand's fantasy of mystical humanitarianism, because of her female pretension to pronounce on matters spiritual. In "Madame Sand and the New Apocalypse" Thackeray compared her to those tract-writing Englishwomen (among whom he might have meant Mrs. Tonna) "who step down to the people with stately step and voice of authority and deliver their twopenny tablets. . . ." The principal difference, Thackeray added ruefully, was Mme Sand's "wonderful power of language": "her brief rich melancholy sentences. . . . I can't explain to you the charm of them; they seem to me like the sound of country bells—provoking I don't know what vein of musing and meditation. . . ."

As a writer of the epic age, Sand comes closest to her Anglo-American women contemporaries with *Le Compagnon du tour de France* (1840), which reflects her friendship with Agricol Perdiguier, the worker-poet and radical leader who introduced her to the mysteries of *le compagnonnage,* to which the novel is devoted. This was the ancient system of worker's associations (somewhere between medieval guilds and modern street gangs) whereby young French workingmen trained in their skills and crafts by taking to the road and traveling far from their native villages in order to study, work, and especially fight with their fellows. Like Flora Tristan, Sand regarded *le compagnonnage* as a potential force for social change and deplored its component of divisive working-class violence. But she had no interest in or knowledge of the industrial proletariat; and she tended to see her carpenters and masons as folk-artists, rather than true workers. It was when she turned to the peasantry of Le Berry, with whom her ties were lifelong and quasi-familial, that accurate observation came together with social idealism in the fiction Sand devoted to *le peuple.*

Radicalism and regionalism are in any case inseparable in Sand's literary development. Her *romans champêtres* were written as part of a series she planned in the 1840s, in a fairly programmatic fashion, to present an epic of the working class: the carpenters, builders, shepherds, muleteers, lumbermen, millers, and farmers of *Le Compagnon du tour de France* (1840), *Le Meunier d'Angibault* (1845), *Le Péché de M. Antoine* (1845), *La Mare au diable* (1846), *François le Champi* (1847–48), *La Petite Fadette* (1848–49), and *Les Maîtres sonneurs* (1853). In the 1851 preface to the popular edition of the first of these, George Sand provided yet another context, another connotation for the word "epic" as applied to women's literature in the mid-nineteenth century.

Le Compagnon du tour de France brought her the accusation of flattering the people and idealizing the working class. Why not? she asks. Why isn't the writer permitted to idealize that class as he is all the others? Why not draw the worker's portrait in such a way that all intelligent and good workingmen will wish to resemble it? Why not show a woman in love with a man socially beneath her because of his mind and character? No one questions her attraction to such a man because of his good looks. . . . Sand recalls arguing with her friend Balzac about their different approach to literature. Your *Comédie Humaine,* she had told him, could just as well be called the Human Drama or Tragedy. Yes, he had answered, *"et vous, vous faites l'épopée humaine"*—you are writing the Human Epic. In this case, Sand said, the title would be too high-flown—*"mais je voudrais faire l'églogue humaine, le poëme, le roman humain."*

"But I would like to write the human eclogue, the human poem, the human novel. You want to, and know how to portray man just as he is, before your eyes—so be it! But I feel called upon to portray him as I wish him to become, as I think he should be." And as we weren't in competition, we might well agree on our mutual rights. . . .

The critical debate between realism and idealism, so important in nineteenth-century English literature, is I think meaningless without some knowledge of George Sand's prestige among English literary intellectuals (all of whom read her) as leading exponent of literary idealism. Mrs. Gaskell said much in favor of the workers because she was committed to sympathetic attention; a decade later, George Eliot created the Noble Workingman in the person of the carpenter hero of her first novel. The difference between John Barton and Adam Bede has many sources, but one is surely the relatively greater impact of George Sand on the later novelist.

The effectiveness of Sand's idealization of the French peasantry can be gauged by Matthew Arnold's reaction. He discounted Sand's "strong language about equality" ("The form of such outbursts . . . will always be distasteful to an Englishman"); but he was convinced by her peasants. "The French peasant is really, so far as I can see," Arnold wrote in 1876 (in his memorial tribute to George Sand) "the largest and strongest element of soundness which the body social of any European nation possesses."

Sand's method of idealization was essentially indirect: through the style she perfected in the 1840s for her peasant tales. The penetration of her language with the imagery, the rhythms, the old-fashioned locutions and syntax of *berrichon* speech gives the effect, at its best, not of the wearisome earnestness of dialect writing, but of a playful, sophisticated musicality, a balance of affectionate warmth, self-deprecating humor, and lyrical fantasy. The effect is to charm. Here the critic of women's literature must simply abandon principle and, faced with George Sand, call the style of *La Mare au diable* and *La Petite Fadette* plain seductive. These brief tales of love and labor in the fields, the woods, and the lanes, which center on childhood and sport with peasant superstitions and customs, remain the most delicious of all Sand's works to read in the original, because of style; for the same reason, they remain the most resistant to adequate translation.

While Mrs. Gaskell sought to voice the agony of the working class, Sand out of principle voiced the joy. Her vision was one of happiness for all, of life in its goodness, nature in its fecundity—for all men, of all classes. She protested (in the preface to *Le Compagnon du tour de France*) against the literature of bitterness and despair, which by presenting only the miseries of the poor simply aroused fear and disgust (and caused the wealthy to pay their governments for cannons and police . . .). The true mission of art, she said, was to bind men together with love, not to divide them with fear and hatred, for solidarity was the source of all human progress. Nevertheless, in their shared commitment to voicing the unheard, Sand and Gaskell appear to stand together as women writers. They shared that heightened feminine sense of the preciousness of language to those who are self-taught, who only yesterday, in the case of women and *le peuple* both, had no voice.

The theme of illiteracy is a major one in all George Sand's work, and it is plainly a woman's theme. Not only in her novels, where she attentively explores the thoughts and feelings of illiterate characters, but even in her autobiographical writings the subject of illiteracy is often in her mind. In her stunning peroration to the *Histoire de ma vie* she calls upon the workers and the peasants, those who have only recently learned to read and write, to record their own lives as she is doing, to enter history as until recently the nobility alone could pretend to do. For "oblivion is a stupid monster that has devoured too many generations. . . . Escape oblivion. . . . Write your own history, all of you who have understood your life and sounded your heart. To that end alone I am writing my own. . . ."

The link that binds *Adam Bede* to Sand's peasant fiction runs through Bartle Massey's night school where "three big men, with the marks of their hard labour about them" are "anxiously bending" over their worn readers. The link that binds Harriet Beecher Stowe's "Iliad of the blacks" to George Sand's "épopée humaine" is made by Sand herself on the first page of her review of *Uncle Tom's Cabin*. Writing in 1852, or only months after the novel was published in America, Sand was already struck by the immense French public that was reading Stowe's novel in translation; she was moved to regret that there were many condemned by illiteracy never to read *La Case de l'oncle Tom* at all. They too are slaves, Sand writes, slaves of ignorance.

Let the voice of women thank Madame Stowe, George Sand went on; let the voice of all the oppressed traverse the seas to express esteem and affection for this unknown woman writer far away. In the pride, the excitement, and the gratitude with which Sand greeted *Uncle Tom's Cabin* there is a characteristic expression of the "solidarity" among literary women which is a feature of the epic age. But her last word is pure George Sand. "All honor and respect to you, Madame Stowe," she concluded. "Some day or other your reward, which is already inscribed in the archives of heaven, will also be of this world."

. . .

Uncle Tom's Cabin achieved the greatest sales and the greatest social influence of any novel of the epic age; but it set a standard for women writers because it had the greatest subject: slavery. There is wistfulness as well as admiration in Charlotte Brontë's apology to her publisher for the modest purview of the novel on which she was working when *Uncle Tom's Cabin* appeared. *Villette,* she confessed, contained "no matter of public interest. . . . I voluntarily and sincerely veil my face before such a mighty subject as that handled in Mrs. Beecher Stowe's work. . . ."

It is today easier than it was in the 1850s to make high claims for *Uncle Tom's Cabin* as a work of literature, because we read Dickens better than his contemporaries did, because we can see in *Bleak House* as in Stowe's novel (they were published almost simultaneously) an organizing principle which makes sense out of a vast social panorama, and patterns underlying the apparent slapdash hazards of serial publication. The Mississippi River slashes through the center of *Uncle Tom's Cabin:* across its frozen northern tributary, the Ohio, Eliza crosses with her baby; its southern tributary, the Red River, borders the plantation where Simon Legree rules and Tom dies. Downriver is the descent to slavery, death, and hell; upriver, the flight to life and freedom, where George Harris sees the blue waters of Lake Erie rippling and sparkling in the fresh breeze off Canada's shore. Stowe uses the swelling waters of the Mississippi as vantage points—for *Uncle Tom's Cabin* is a novel of continental destiny as well as of slavery. Her gaze travels back to New England and forward to "all the broad land between the Mississippi and the Pacific" which may become "one great market for bodies and souls." In its dizzying geographical perspectives, *Uncle Tom's Cabin* is an epic work in another sense; alas for its misbegotten title, little of importance to the novel happens inside Uncle Tom's cabin.

But it must also be said that Mrs. Stowe's novel is proudly and openly a woman's work; George Sand was right to take particular delight in its rich variety of women characters and its children. For it was women, specifically the "mothers of America," on whom Mrs. Stowe squarely placed responsibility for the perpetuation or abolition of slavery. Surely no other woman writer has ever recorded the rattle and clutter of domestic life, the dressing, gardening, and cooking, the household budgets, the slovenliness or precision of housekeepers, the disciplining of children and managing of husbands, the granting or withholding of sexual favors with such evident confidence that upon these female matters rested the central moral issue before the nation: slavery.

For example, Mrs. Stowe's ideal of womanhood is presented by her Quaker mother Rachel Halliday, not only for her religion (earliest and firmest of all American faiths in opposition to slavery) but for her accordant domestic polity. Rachel's household offers ordered serenity, hospitable abundance, and an enviable technique—essential in a society without either hired or enslaved domestics—for eliciting, without scolding, the voluntary services of the young:

> busy girls and boys . . . who all moved obediently to Rachel's gentle "Thee had better," or more gentle "Hadn't thee better?" in the work of getting breakfast; for a breakfast in the luxurious valleys of Indiana is a thing complicated and multiform, and, like picking up the rose-leaves and trimming the bushes in Paradise, asking other hands than those of the original mother.

The girl-children of *Uncle Tom's Cabin* are more celebrated: treacly little Eva, white and golden-haired, bearer of the good news of the gospel of love, whom we excuse as a period piece because she serves to set off black Topsy, Mrs. Stowe's most brilliantly original creation. In the famous scene of Topsy's catechism ("I spect I grow'd. Don't think nobody never made me.") there is the Christian mother's passionate attack on an institution that gives children life without the knowledge that gives Life, of the God that made them; ideas for this scene seem to have come to Mrs. Stowe from the opening of the great Frederick Douglass memoir. But there is more to Topsy than tragedy; there is the comedy of the indomitable free spirit of the mischievous, deceitful, troublesome, eternal American child. For Topsy as "limb of Satan" Mrs. Stowe needed to draw only on childhood memories. As family letters show, little Harriet Beecher was the model for Topsy, as well as for little Eva.

· · ·

Mrs. Stowe seems to owe so much as a novelist to the early Dickens that it is interesting to note, without making too much of it, that she writes in her 1844 introduction to Mrs. Tonna that "this lady's delineations of factory life" were more useful models than "the fearfully graphic delineations of Dickens. . . . Our present question is not which evince the most talent, but which are the best adapted to practical purposes"—by which she meant the purposes of the "authoress." "The authoress is," as she wrote of Mrs. Tonna, "a woman of strong mind, powerful feeling, and of no inconsiderable share of tact in influencing the popular mind"; and the snapshot definition does nicely for Harriet Beecher Stowe as well.

That she stood squarely in the center of a line of ladies committed not to "mere secular literature" (as she said of Mrs. Tonna) but to "the simple effort to do good" was at the least a source of confidence, if not of the overweening and finally justified ambition to write that novel about slavery which no man would write. And Mrs. Stowe herself set similarly large ambitions for women writers after her. "As to the Jewish element in 'Deronda,' " wrote George Eliot in a famous letter about her last novel,

> . . . I therefore felt urged to treat Jews with such sympathy and
> understanding as my nature and knowledge could attain to. Moreover,
> not only towards the Jews, but towards all Oriental peoples with whom
> we English come in contact, a spirit of arrogance and contemptuous
> dictatorialness is observable which has become a national disgrace to
> us. There is nothing I should care more to do, if it were possible, than
> to rouse the imagination of men and women to a vision of human
> claims in those races of their fellow-men who most differ from them in
> customs and beliefs.

This remarkable statement is well-known because it has often been
reprinted as a prefatory statement to *Daniel Deronda,* the novel George
Eliot daringly devoted to Zionism at the end of her life. Less well-known is
the fact that she wrote it in a letter addressed to Harriet Beecher Stowe,
whom she honored as her predecessor in that great feminine enterprise of
rousing the imagination "to a vision of human claims" in races, sects, and
classes different from the established norm. The letter in fact echoes the
ideas, even some of the words of Stowe's preface to *Uncle Tom's Cabin.*
George Eliot was Mrs. Stowe's most important disciple among later
women writers of the epic age.

If there really was such an age in women's literature, it deserved an
epic in the classic sense of the term: a long narrative in verse of heroic
deeds. This idea clearly occurred to Elizabeth Barrett Browning:

> The critics say that epics have died out
> With Agamemnon and the goat-nursed gods;
> I'll not believe it . . . :
> . . . . every age,
> Heroic in proportions, double-faced,
> Looks backward and before, expects a morn
> And claims an epos.
> . . . . Ay, but every age
> Appears to souls who live in 't (ask Carlyle)
> Most unheroic. Ours, for instance, ours:
> The thinkers scout it, and the poets abound
> Who scorn to touch it with a finger-tip:
> A pewter age,—mixed metal, silver-washed;
> An age of scum, spooned off the richer past,
> An age of patches for old gaberdines,
> An age of mere transition. . . .
> . . . . But poets should
> Exert a double vision; should have eyes
> To see near things as comprehensively
> As if afar they took their point of sight,
> And distant things as intimately deep
> As if they touched them. Let us strive for this.

So she wrote *Aurora Leigh* (1856), from the fifth book of which this epic credo comes. The causes to which Mrs. Browning devoted some of her best and some of her worst poetry—in the 1840s, child labor, prostitution, and abolition; in the 1850s, Italian unification—prove her a writer of the epic age. When she met Harriet Beecher Stowe in Florence, and their correspondence began, they went naturally back and forth in their letters between such female subjects as abolitionist agitation in the Union and nationalist agitation in Italy. "Is it possible that you think a woman has no business with questions like the question of slavery?" wrote Mrs. Browning to a shocked reader of *Uncle Tom's Cabin.* "Then she had better use a pen no more. She had better subside into slavery and concubinage herself, I think, as in the times of old, shut herself up with the Penelopes in the 'women's apartment,' and take no rank among thinkers and speakers."

There are social causes a-plenty in *Aurora Leigh,* some of the best lines of which are devoted to factories and slums, but the poem is essentially an epic in another sense: it is the epic of the literary woman herself. The heroine's life, which she tells in her own voice—her rebellion against convention and family pressure, her independent career in London, her solitary journey to Italy, her rejection of marriage on the usual terms, and principally her determined, self-critical slugging away at the work a writer does—is the heroic matter of the poem.

A little, but not much self-portraiture entered into the creation of Mrs. Browning's heroine; that is why Aurora Leigh is a poet, not a novelist. But a principal pleasure the work offers today is its kaleidoscopic view of nineteenth-century fiction, mainly by women; Mrs. Browning had read it all. (On her tombstone, she once said, should be written: *"Ci-gît* the greatest novel reader in the world.") There are reminders of de Staël, Brontë, Sand, Gaskell, and many more. For example, the heroine's birth and childhood are returns to Mme de Staël's *Corinne.* The marriage proposal and the blinding of Romney Leigh in the poem are returns to *Jane Eyre,* though St. John Rivers, Charlotte Brontë's icy missionary, is more important than her Rochester in providing Mrs. Browning with ideas for the man a literary woman must not marry when he is in his arrogant prime, but may marry when he is suitably prepared to accept her guidance in the reformation of the world.

Why *Aurora Leigh* is not more read by feminists—for it is *the* feminist poem—puzzled writers like Alice Meynell and Virginia Woolf. The reason may be the title of the work. For if readers require an excuse for not plunging into a narrative poem in nine books and more than ten thousand lines of blank verse, they have the vaguely, oddly persistent impression that *Aurora Leigh* is a silly sentimental poem; and this may well be because of its confusion with "Annabel Lee," the very short, popular ballad by Edgar

Allan Poe. People must think they know something about Aurora Leigh because, according to Poe,

> . . . a maiden there lived whom you may know
> By the name of Annabel Lee;—
> And this maiden she lived with no other thought
> Than to love and be loved by me.

That is just the kind of sentimental heroine that male poets love to create, and to dispatch, a few quick stanzas later, to "her tomb by the side of the sea." But Aurora Leigh is everything that Annabel Lee is not, including tough-minded, independent, witty, and long-winded; and if there is a confusion between the two heroines, history has played an unfair joke on Mrs. Browning, because Poe was one of her best critics and most successful imitators (as "The Raven," in particular, reveals).

Aurora Leigh, however, may always be a heroine of limited appeal: the literary woman's heroine, as Mrs. Browning may always be the literary woman's writer. One cannot expect every woman to say with Virginia Woolf that "Elizabeth Barrett was inspired by a flash of true genius when she rushed into the drawing-room and said that here, where we live and work, is the true place for the poet." Nor can one expect every woman to relish Mrs. Browning's summons to the writers of the epic age:

> Never flinch,
> But still, unscrupulously epic, catch
> Upon the burning lava of a song
> The full-veined, heaving, double-breasted Age.

Such an unscrupulous mishmash of images; such brazen, female tastelessness—for those double breasts are flesh, not buttons—appealed mainly to eccentric lady writers, like Emily Dickinson. But that is another story.

⊞ 3

WOMEN'S LITERARY TRADITIONS AND THE INDIVIDUAL TALENT

> We dwell with satisfaction upon the poet's difference from her predecessors, especially her immediate predecessors: we endeavor to find something that can be isolated in order to be enjoyed. Whereas if we approach a poet without this prejudice we shall often find that not only the best, but the most individual parts of her work may be those in which the dead poets, her ancestors, assert their immortality most vigorously.
>
> —T. S. Eliot

I

To be a woman writer long meant, may still mean, belonging to a literary movement apart from but hardly subordinate to the mainstream: an undercurrent, rapid and powerful. The word "movement" gives an inaccurate idea of an association often remote and indirect. To use the word George Sand imposed, and speak of a "solidarity" of women, would also be misleading, for writing women have never felt much of a sentimental loyalty to their own kind—quite the contrary. The harshest criticism of trashy books by lady writers came from women writers themselves; sometimes, as in the case of Elizabeth Rigby's famous review of *Jane Eyre,* they denounced books that were not trashy at all. George Eliot's "Silly Novels by Lady Novelists" of 1856 is the classic of the genre, as well as one of the funniest pieces of serious criticism ever written; but long before, in 1789, there was Mary Wollstonecraft's swift dispatch of one of the worst specimens of female pap that she encountered as a reviewer with the line, "Pray Miss, write no more!"

Not loyalty but confidence was the resource that women writers drew from the possession of their own tradition. And it was a confidence that until very recently could come from no other source. Male writers have always been able to study their craft in university or coffeehouse, group themselves into movements or coteries, search out predecessors for guidance or patronage, collaborate or fight with their contemporaries. But women through most of the nineteenth century were barred from the universities, isolated in their own homes, chaperoned in travel, painfully restricted in friendship. The personal give-and-take of the literary life was closed to them. Without it, they studied with a special closeness the works written by their own sex, and developed a sense of easy, almost rude familiarity with the women who wrote them.

When fame at last propelled Charlotte Brontë to London and gave her the opportunity to meet her greatest male contemporaries, she exhibited an awkwardness and timidity in literary society that have become legendary—except in one encounter, that with Harriet Martineau, to whom she sent a brusquely confident note soliciting a meeting. "I could not help feeling a strong wish to see you," she wrote; ". . . It would grieve me to lose this chance of seeing one whose works have so often made her the subject of my thoughts." And George Eliot could write in her first letter to Harriet Beecher Stowe, though they had not and would not ever meet, that she knew her as a woman as well as a writer, for she had years before taken the liberty, rude but comprehensible, of reading Mrs. Stowe's intimate correspondence with another woman. Later Stowe and George Eliot would correspond about the source of Casaubon in *Middlemarch;* their letters provide a tragicomedy of mutual misunderstanding about each other's married life, but they also reveal that there is a human component to literature which a woman writer can more easily discuss with another woman writer, even across an ocean, than she can with the literary man next door.

Emily Dickinson's literary solitude was breached by the incorporeal presence of women writers she knew exclusively but intimately from reading their works and everything she could find about their lives. Jack Capps calls it an "intimate kinship," and the phrase is excellent, because it suggests a family relationship which can be either hostile or loving, competitive or supportive, but is always available. Through the closed doors and narrow windows that so often shut on the literary woman's life seeped a whole family of literary relationships for her to exploit: patterns to be followed, deficiencies to be made up, abuses to correct, achievements in works by other women to surpass. What was supplied for the nourishment of male literary production by simple acquaintance was replaced for women writers by the reading of each other's work, reading for intimate reverberation, for what Gertrude Stein called "a sounding board."

Take Jane Austen on the one hand, and her contemporaries Wordsworth, Coleridge, and Southey on the other. Wordsworth went to Bristol to meet Coleridge; both were Cambridge men, and they had university friends in common. At Bristol, Wordsworth found Coleridge rooming with an Oxford undergraduate named Southey: they were planning to emigrate to America. Instead, Wordsworth and Coleridge drew close together, settled near each other in the Lake District, and collaborated on a volume which made history, called *Lyrical Ballads*. Meanwhile Jane Austen, almost exactly the same age and from a similar social milieu (had she been a man, she would probably have gone to university), stayed home with her mother at Steventon, Bath, and Chawton. She visited a brother's family now and then, wrote letters to sister and nieces, and read Sarah Harriet Burney, Mrs. Jane West, Anna Maria Porter, Mrs. Anne Grant, Elisabeth Hamilton, Laetitia Matilda Hawkins, Helen Maria Williams, and the rest of the women writers of her day.

"I think I may boast myself to be, with all possible vanity," she once said, "the most unlearned and uninformed female who ever dared to be an authoress." Scholars have industriously scraped together evidence that softens if it does not essentially alter this self-portrait; for Austen of course knew something of the major English writers from Shakespeare to Johnson and read the best poetry of her day. But scholarship has averted its refined and weary eyes from the female fiction that Austen's letters inform us was her daily sustenance in the years that she became one of the greatest writers in the language. Who wants to associate the great Jane Austen, companion of Shakespeare, with someone named Mary Brunton? Who wants to read or indeed can find a copy of *Self-Control* (1810) by that lady, which Austen was nervous about reading while revising *Sense and Sensibility* for publication and starting *Mansfield Park,* nervous because she was "always half afraid of finding a clever novel *too clever—* and of finding my own story and my own people all forestalled." She did, however, read and reread the Brunton book, and said (jokingly), "I will redeem my credit . . . by writing a close imitation of 'Self-Control' . . . I will improve upon it."

It can be argued that Jane Austen achieved the classical perfection of her fiction because there was a mass of women's novels, excellent, fair, and wretched, for her to study and improve upon. Mary Brunton and the rest of the ladies were her own kind; she was at ease with them. They were her undergraduate fellows in the novel, her literary roommates and incorporeal collaborators, as someone like Walter Scott could never be. Austen's comment on Scott, when she learned he had turned to the then woman-dominated field of fiction, was wickedly female but also half-serious. "Walter Scott has no business to write novels, especially good ones. —It is not fair. —He has Fame and Profit enough as a Poet, and should not be taking the bread out of other people's mouths. —I do not like him, & do not mean to like Waverley if I can help it—but fear I must." The fact is that Austen studied Maria Edgeworth more attentively than Scott, and Fanny Burney more than Richardson; and she came closer to meeting Mme de Staël than she did to meeting any of the literary men of her age.

In the case of some women writers, Austen preeminent among them, women's literature has been their major tradition; in the case of others— and I think quality has nothing to do with the difference—it has mattered hardly at all: here Emily Brontë's name comes to mind. In the case of most women writers, women's traditions have been fringe benefits superadded upon the literary associations of period, nation, and class that they shared with their male contemporaries.

In spite of the advent of coeducation, which by rights should have ended this phenomenon, twentieth-century women appear to benefit still from their membership in the wide-spreading family of women writers. Willa Cather, exceptionally well trained to literature in the educational and journalistic institutions of a man's world, found her literary mentor in Sarah Orne Jewett; in that relationship sex easily canceled out the distance between Nebraska and Maine. Even wider incongruities appear in the productive pairings of Jean Rhys and Charlotte Brontë, Carson McCullers and Isak Dinesen, Nathalie Sarraute and Ivy Compton-Burnett. And the last provided, in her first novel, *Dolores,* the oddest exhibit that women's literature has to offer: a groping retrieval of what could be made modern in Austen and Gaskell, necessary to Compton-Burnett's development of her own apparently idiosyncratic fictional manner.

. . .

The case history of the birth of the novelist named George Eliot is particularly interesting, because there was a specialist in attendance, George Henry Lewes. Lewes believed in women's literature, and he had a method, thoroughly justified by results we know, for its perpetuation. "The appearance of Woman in the field of literature is a significant fact," he wrote. ". . . The advent of female literature promises woman's view of life, woman's experience: in other words, a new element." So Lewes wrote in 1852, before there was an author named George Eliot, and by that time he had already played an important role as critic, advisor, and friend, in encouraging the development of Charlotte Brontë, Geraldine Jewsbury, Harriet Martineau, Eliza Lynn Linton, and several other women writers. He was the principal interpreter of George Sand in England, and his knowledge of her work was astounding, especially to Mme Sand, for she did not take herself so seriously as Lewes did. "Distinguished" and "likable" were the words Sand applied to Lewes, "and more French than English in character. He knows my works by heart, and knows the *Lettres d'un voyageur* much better than I do."

The best way to discover what is both distinguished and likable in George Henry Lewes is to read the theater criticism he wrote in the midcentury over the pen name of "Vivian"; the next best way (as these columns are hard to find) is to approach him by reference to "Corno Di Bassetto," the persona George Bernard Shaw adopted for his own brilliant music criticism in 1888. "These articles of Lewes's are miles beyond the crudities of Di Bassetto," Shaw wrote,

> though the combination of a laborious criticism with a recklessly flippant manner is the same in both. Lewes, by the way, like Bassetto, was a musical critic. He was an adventurous person as critics go; for he not only wrote philosophical treatises and feuilletons, but went on the stage. . . . He also wrote plays of the kind which, as a critic, he particularly disliked. And he was given to singing—nothing will ever persuade me that a certain passage in The Impressions of Theophrastus Such about an amateur vocalist who would persist in wrecking himself on O Ruddier than the Cherry does not refer to Lewes. Finally he was rash enough to contract a morganatic union with the most famous woman writer of the day, a novelist, thereby allowing his miserable affections to triumph over his critical instincts . . . ; and so, having devoted some years to remonstrating with people who persisted in addressing the famous novelist by her maiden name instead of as "Mrs. Lewes," he perished after proving conclusively in his own person that "womanly self-sacrifice" is an essentially manly weakness.

Shaw's account of the Lewes/George Eliot relationship is so true to its spirit that one regrets having to point out where it is false to fact, but when this most important of all irregular unions began, the woman in the case was not a famous writer, was not even a novelist.

Before she met Lewes, before she took the pen name of George Eliot, the woman whose real name was Mary Ann (or Marian) Evans had lived over thirty years of a wider and more intellectual life than any Englishwoman before her, but, except for a schoolgirl exercise, she had never written a line of fiction, never seriously considered becoming a novelist. "September 1856 made a new era in my life," she recorded, "for it was then I began to write Fiction."

The "new era" actually dawned during the winter of 1854–55, when she read aloud to Lewes in Berlin—they had gone off together to Germany —a few pages she had written "describing a Staffordshire village and the life of the neighboring farmhouses." Staffordshire was her father's home county, where from the age of six Mary Ann Evans had been taken often to visit his relatives; her early perceptions of the differences between the Evanses of Staffordshire and her mother's people, the Pearsons of Warwickshire, would eventually inspire the chapters about "the life of the neighbouring farmhouses" that are the best things in her early novels. These reminiscent pages gave Lewes for the first time the idea that she might become a novelist, and with his encouragement she began to think of a subject, a title, for her first tale.

But there were two article assignments to be written first for the *Westminster Review,* and they required Marian Evans to ponder the highest and the lowest reaches of female ambition in the field of fiction. In "Silly Novels by Lady Novelists," which appeared in October 1856, she lambasted the kind of fiction that a highly intelligent woman would not become a novelist to write: novels pompous, pedantic, snobbish, sentimental, and pious. Her sharpest scorn was reserved for the Evangelical species, for her own religious experience as a young woman had taught her that Evangelicalism made its greatest appeal to people of simple and provincial situation, not to the improbably elegant societies that Evangelical lady novelists liked to invent. "Why can we not have," she asked, in a sudden lapse from mockery to seriousness, "pictures of religious life among the industrial classes in England, as interesting as Mrs. Stowe's pictures of religious life among the negroes?" In embryo, the subject of *Adam Bede* was here suggested: George Eliot's first novel would provide original and serious pictures of religious life among the working classes, not of industrial, but of rural England.

The model she had in mind was *Dred,* Harriet Beecher Stowe's second slavery novel, which Marian Evans reviewed in the *Belles Lettres* section of the same October 1856 issue of the *Westminster Review.* She found *Dred* a work of "uncontrollable power . . . inspired by a rare genius," not so much for its antislavery sentiments (even stronger than in *Uncle Tom's Cabin*) as for its religious matter:

> the exhibition of a people to whom what we may call Hebraic Christianity is still a reality, still an animating belief, and by whom the theocratic conceptions of the Old Testament are literally applied to their daily life.

She remarked upon the "wild enthusiasm" of Dred, the rebel slave leader, and such fine scenes in Mrs. Stowe's novel as the outdoor camp meeting of Presbyterians and Methodists. Religious revivalism in the woods of the Deep South would eventually be transformed into the village-green Methodism of Chapter 1 of *Adam Bede.* But something was to intervene to fuse George Eliot's childhood reminiscences (those pages on "the like of the neighbouring farmhouses") with her ambition to record the religious impulses of simple country people—and that was her reading of Jane Austen. Studying Austen's fiction was George Henry Lewes's program to turn Marian Evans into a great woman novelist—for "of all departments of literature," he believed, "Fiction is the one to which, by nature and experience, women are best adapted"; and of all novelists Jane Austen was "the greatest artist that has ever written, using the term to signify the most perfect mastery over the means to her end."

That Marian Evans was an accomplished writer of remarkable attainments Lewes knew well. When he met her in 1854 she was the anonymous

and unpaid but highly competent editor of the *Westminster Review,* and
with her excellent command of languages she had read widely (and reviewed and translated) the works of the best minds of her day, especially
the philosophers and the theologians, on the Continent as well as in England. Clearly she could instruct and improve the public, but could she
hold its attention with living characters, believable settings, interesting
events? Could she tell a story? "All the literary and philosophic culture
which an author can bring to bear upon his work will *tend* to give that
work a higher value," Lewes pointed out, "but it will not really make it
a better novel."

He made this comment in his article on Jane Austen in the July 1859
Blackwood's Magazine, an article devoted almost entirely to a celebration
of Austen's genius, but which also included a few paragraphs of compari-
son favorable and unfavorable to *Scenes of Clerical Life,* apprentice tales
by a new author Lewes referred to as "Mr. George Eliot." In all of English
fiction, Lewes said, Jane Austen was the master of the art of "dramatic
presentation," the only—but the essential—quality of the novelist that
George Eliot lacked. That was why, between February and September of
1857, Lewes had put George Eliot through a course of reading all of Jane
Austen's novels—reading them with him, slowly and aloud, one after the
other. As he said,

> . . . when it is considered what a severe test that is, how the reading
> aloud permits no skipping, no evasion of weariness, but brings both
> merits and defects into stronger relief by forcing the mind to dwell on
> them, there is surely something significant of genuine excellence
> when both reader and listener finish their fourth reading [of Austen's
> novels] with increase of admiration.

A few respectful mentions of Jane Austen can be found in George
Eliot's correspondence (after she met Lewes), but nothing like the pane-
gyrics she gave to Stowe, Scott, Rousseau, Brontë, and George Sand,
novelists of romantic fervor and depths of soul with whom she felt spiritual kinship. But Jane Austen? In temperament, social class, and literary
program—in everything but sex—she and George Eliot were a world and
several generations apart. Miss Austen (whose name George Eliot long
persisted in misspelling) was a product of the genteel classes, as Marian
Evans was not. As a writer, Austen was conservative, elegant, restrained,
unintellectual, impersonal—all that George Eliot the novelist was not and
did not want to be. I suspect her initial reaction to Jane Austen was much
like that of Charlotte Brontë when the same George Henry Lewes, a decade
earlier, as critic of and correspondent with the author of *Jane Eyre,* had
urged her too to read Jane Austen. "And what did I find?" Brontë wrote
Lewes. "A carefully fenced, highly cultivated garden, with neat borders
and delicate flowers; but . . . no open country, no fresh air. . . . I

should hardly like to live with her ladies and gentlemen, in their elegant but confined houses!"

Charlotte Brontë put her Austen reading to use, however, and so did George Eliot. Of all the Austen novels that George Eliot read in 1857, the one that made her a major novelist was, I am convinced, *Emma,* which she read aloud to Lewes out of doors one May afternoon when they were on holiday in Jersey, and finished the following evening. Published in 1816, the last year of Austen's life, *Emma* was the peak of Jane Austen's achievement and the most highly cultivated of her English gardens: "an idyllic world," in Lionel Trilling's phrase for the novel.

To read *Emma* and *Adam Bede* together is to sense a close, an almost uncanny association between the two novels; as if either could be pressed, a kind of thick transparency, upon the other, revealing below the traceries of dissimilar surfaces a single underlying structure. It is not "literary influence" of the standard sort, but the family relationship that women writers made work for themselves; here a relationship not of affection but of sibling rivalry. *Adam Bede* appears to be the novel that Austen rejected; it seems to hover below the surface of *Emma,* waiting to be born in the hands of another woman novelist, forty years later.

Thus, if Harriet Beecher Stowe offered a goal, Jane Austen indirectly provided a method of "dramatic presentation"; for what George Eliot seems to have done to become a novelist was turn her childhood memories into fiction by turning *Emma* inside out. She put at the center of her novel all that Jane Austen had relegated to the boundaries of her own, while moving all that was central to Austen to the outer fringes—to the place where the public sits, reading a novel. George Eliot broke through Austen's "highly cultivated garden" and found beyond its fences the open country that was her own proper material: "the life of the neighbouring farmhouses."

Emma is the story of the education, through love, of a snob, a spoiled young heiress who is the wealthiest of Austen's heroines and the most reprehensible. As the novel begins, Emma is shown wasting her time on matchmaking, an occupation which satisfies her lively imagination, encourages her idleness, and flatters her arrogant presumption to be the arbiter of her genteel and restricted world. Out on the farther edges of the novel, a subplot has to do with the nearly fatal effects of Emma's attempt to unmatch Harriet Smith and Robert Martin: the girl is a pretty nobody of uncertain parentage, taken up by Emma as plaything and protégée, and the man is a tenant farmer. The two lovers are united only at the end of the novel, in spite of Emma, through the agency of the all-wise Mr. Knightley of the vast and ancient estate of Donwell Abbey. He is the man Austen gives Emma to marry; he is also her final ideal of the English landlord, and stands at the center of Austen's idyllic vision of a fruitful land inhabited by a moral people.

The principal lesson Mr. Knightley teaches Emma is that she must not snub but respect and indeed sit down to table with the likes of estate managers and tenant farmers who are the landlord's most precious resource, for they are devoted to the proper management of the land. Emma, because she sees Robert Martin as a mere "clownish" rustic who moves clumsily, dresses unfashionably, and has not read the latest sentimental novel; because she hears in his talk not what he says but "the uncouthness of a voice, . . . wholly unmodulated," thwarts his love for Harriet Smith, forbids the girl any intimacy with his family, rations her visits to their home at Abbey-Mill Farm, and forces her to reject his honorable proposal of marriage—indeed dictates the letter of rejection herself. "The yeomanry," Emma says, "are precisely the order of people with whom I feel I can have nothing to do."

Nor does Jane Austen herself have much to do with this class in the novel. She never lets us penetrate the interior of Abbey-Mill Farm, never introduces us to the Martin family. Robert Martin himself is so shadowy a figure that few readers of *Emma* notice the character or remember his name. To such a reader as George Eliot, however, no character in *Emma* (no character in all Austen's fiction, where he has no parallel) can have been so fascinating to speculate upon, so stimulating to the imagination. For Robert Martin is in character, class, and social utility the very model of the man who dominated her childhood reminiscences: the real man who was Marian Evans's father.

Son of a carpenter and apprenticed to that trade, Robert Evans was a countryman of little schooling who spoke in the broad dialect of north Staffordshire (or, as Emma would put it, in an uncouth voice, wholly unmodulated). Because he grew remarkably wise in all to do with the land, its farms, its timber, its mines, he was raised to managership of a great estate. When his master inherited the even greater property of Arbury Hall (which stood, like Mr. Knightley's Donwell Abbey, on the site of an ancient monastery), he took Evans with him into Warwickshire to manage the estate and be tenant of South Farm, where Marian Evans was born. This was the man, shown as a young and handsome lover, whom George Eliot called Adam Bede and made the hero of her first novel—but not until she had read the praise that Austen's Mr. Knightley bestowed on Robert Martin. "I have a thorough regard for him and all his family," says that gentleman to Emma.

> ". . . I never hear better sense from any one than Robert Martin. He always speaks to the purpose; open, straight forward, and very well judging. . . . He is an excellent young man, both as son and brother."

And as surely as one can know anything about the mysteries of literary creation, there was Adam Bede born: the excellent son and brother, the dialect-speaking carpenter turned estate manager, the sensible and stalwart English yeoman hero of George Eliot's first novel.

It is as if George Eliot drew resolution from Jane Austen to write of the people she remembered best from childhood, and, in a new departure for English fiction, to make central to her novel agents and carpenters, dairymaids and farmers, "precisely the order of people," as Emma says, "with whom I feel I can have nothing to do." The people central to Jane Austen—landlords and vicars, dowagers and rakes—also appear in *Adam Bede,* but at its outer edges. Indeed, it is as if George Eliot addressed her new artistic program to Emma (and to that part of herself, which is in every woman, that was Emma-like) when she wrote, in the famous credo of realism in *Adam Bede,* "It is these people—among whom your life is passed—that it is needful you should tolerate, pity, and love . . . who can be chilled by your indifference or injured by your prejudice."

There is one page in *Emma* which, when I read it, makes me picture George Eliot bending over Austen's novel and planning her own. That is the page on which Emma makes her single near-approach to the Martin home at Abbey-Mill Farm, otherwise seen in the novel only as a distant, generalized vista "with all its appendages of prosperity and beauty, its rich pastures, spreading flocks, orchard in blossom, and light column of smoke ascending." Too prosperous to invite condescension or require charity, such farmhouses are not for Emma to visit. She drives only so far as the gate, where she drops Harriet and returns to retrieve her a quarter of an hour later: to the gate "at the end of the broad, neat gravel-walk, which led between espalier apple-trees to the front door."

If Jane Austen let the reader go up that gravel path, and threw open the farmhouse door, we would find within, I imagine, the wonderful interior of Hall Farm, where Adam Bede goes to court Hetty Sorrel. If we met Mrs. Martin, she might turn out to be a sharp-tongued farm matron like Hetty's Aunt Poyser. The Hetty Sorrel we do meet has the same delectable rosiness as Harriet Smith—the same dreams of fashion, the same capacity for letting her head be turned. George Eliot, too, pauses by the gate in her narration, but her intention is to invite, not to forbid the reader to enter:

> Yes, the house must be inhabited, and we will see by whom; for imagination is a licensed trespasser. . . . Put your face to one of the glass panes in the right-hand window: what do you see? A large open fireplace, with rusty dogs in it, and a bare-boarded floor

—and a spinning wheel, an eight-day clock, brass candlesticks, pewter dishes, and oak tables polished to such a smooth perfection that Hetty can use them as mirrors to reflect her beauty. The Hall Farm scenes, and their remarkable evocation of life on an English farm at the pitch of order and respectability, are today still the principal reason why we return to *Adam Bede.* And they seem to have been written not because of what Jane Austen wrote, but because of what she chose not to write. What George Eliot found in Jane Austen was a garden to break out of, a gate to push open, a doorway to enter.

． ． ．

George Eliot's first novel is not the only one to show the impress of women's literature in this rough, intimate way; *The Mill on the Floss,* her second, is an even more complex example. Mme de Staël's *Corinne,* the book which George Eliot places in its heroine's hands, deserves a chapter to itself in any study of the traditions of women's literature. And what George Sand meant to George Eliot as chronicler of English rural life is a large and fascinating subject that scholars are beginning to explore. It seems to me impossible for anyone who knows *The Mill on the Floss* to read the opening chapters of *La Petite Fadette* without seeing the relationship between Maggie Tulliver and her brother Tom take shape in the abnormally tense relationship between the siblings in *Fadette:* abnormal, because Sand's children are what the *berrichon* peasants called *des bessons*—identical twins, both males, one weak and querulously demanding, the other strong, stolid, and winning in temperament. That both George Sand and George Eliot enriched the novel by extending its terrain into the mind of the girl-child is beyond question; that the *bessons* of *La Petite Fadette* emboldened George Eliot to make as much of the sister-brother relationship as personal experience taught her that the novelist of girlhood should do seems more than probable.

From letters and other sources it is possible to establish the half-dozen or so Sand works that George Eliot definitely read (including *Fadette*) and to guess at the rest. From a dozen or so of his critical articles, we know that George Henry Lewes considered George Sand not only the greatest woman writer but the greatest writer of the age, an opinion seconded by George Eliot in her own criticism. We know George Eliot heard from all sides, especially from friends like Sara Hennell, Turgenev, and Frederic Myers, comparisons between her own work and George Sand's which were meant to flatter. But we do not have specific evidence of a debt owed by any one of George Eliot's novels to any one of Sand's. Instead we have a vague but nonetheless convincing statement of her gratitude, from the days when she was merely a reader of George Sand named Mary Ann Evans, not yet a novelist in her own right named George Eliot. "I don't care whether I agree with her about marriage or not," she wrote of Sand in 1849,

> —whether I think the design of her plot correct or that she had no precise design at all . . . —it is sufficient for me as a reason for bowing before her in eternal gratitude to that "great power of God" manifested in her—that I cannot read six pages of hers without feeling that it is given to her to delineate human passion and its results

— . . . some of the moral instincts and their tendencies—with such truthfulness such nicety of discrimination such tragic power and withal such loving gentle humour that one might live a century with nothing but one's own dull faculties and not know so much as those six pages will suggest.

All that is missing from this panegyric (otherwise something of a commonplace of the age) is the whoop of female exultation supplied by Elizabeth Barrett. In one of her sonnets to George Sand, Miss Barrett openly rejoiced that Sand was not only "True genius, but true woman!"

> . . . and while before
> The world thou burnest in a poet fire,
> We see thy woman heart beat evermore
> Through the large flame.

. . .

The most convenient and most delightful way to recover a sense of the way literary women read other woman writers is to go through Elizabeth Barrett's letters to Miss Mitford. They are wonderful letters and have been wonderfully edited by Betty Miller—so that, if one wants to know who was "poor Mrs. Sullivan" whose "tale of the wife with two husbands affected me very much"; or what were the dangerous attractions of Theodosia Garrow to a literary widower; or which Irish writer appeared in translation in Mme Amable Tastu's miscellany "which contains not a bit of naughtiness"—necessary information of the obscurest but hardly the dullest variety is at hand. (The first, Betty Miller tells us, was Arabella, daughter of Lady Dacre, who wrote *Tales of the Peerage and Peasantry;* the second was "a precocious musician and poetess"; the third was Mrs. S. C. Hall: "Dublin-born . . . she published more than fifty books, entertained spiritualists and street musicians, and helped to found both the Hospital for Consumptives at Brompton and the Home for Decayed Gentlewomen.") If one allows for the energetic nuttiness of the Victorians, which stamped the women as well as the men, the literary chitchat in these letters, full of enthusiasm and discrimination and gossip, is much the way literary women have always talked to each other about female colleagues.

Miss Barrett and Miss Mitford were both highly intelligent women of breeding and wit, both busy writers with much besides women on their minds. Mary Russell Mitford was much the older, a grand old lady of letters (exploited by her equally grand old father, a thorough reprobate she adored). She had won fame in the 1820s with her magazine sketches collected under the title *Our Village,* and she also did very well with the verse tragedies she wrote for the stage, and for which she was always requesting grand historical subjects from her young but learned friend,

Miss Barrett. Elizabeth Barrett's many interests are reflected in her equally numerous epistolary friendships. She was an indefatigable letter writer, and the letters she wrote to different correspondents on different themes have been published as separate series. Thus, if one wants the scholarly Miss Barrett, there are her letters, mostly on Greek poetry, to Hugh Boyd; for the amorous Miss Barrett, there are her letters to Robert Browning; and there are her family letters, her professional literary letters, her social thought letters. . . . But for her literary women letters, there are the letters to Miss Mitford.

Part of the fun of these letters is the drama that bubbles excitingly under their surface decorum. One act centers on Flush, the purebred spaniel Miss Mitford gave Miss Barrett; and one act on Robert Browning, whose victorious courtship burst upon Miss Mitford with all the astonishment of melodrama, for Miss Barrett had made no place for love in their literary-ladies correspondence. These two acts are celebrated: Virginia Woolf made a whole book out of Flush, and *The Barretts of Wimpole Street* made a perennial theater favorite and a permanent sentimental distortion out of the Browning courtship. But there is another act, centering on George Sand, which though less well-known would add at least comic interest to the Barrett-Mitford drama.

Miss Barrett tried to persuade Miss Mitford that they should send their latest books, tied together in a parcel for courage, to the great Mme Sand. They both enormously admired her, but, as respectable English literary spinsters, they were nervous about approaching her. For George Sand not only had lovers (which was known to happen, even in England, in the high social circles with which Sand, by family background, was associated); but she wore pants when it suited her convenience as a young woman, and she always smoked—depths of depravity which only twentieth-century women can appreciate at their true value. "Suppose you send her 'Belford Regis' or another work," Miss Barrett suggested to Miss Mitford,

> and let me slip mine into the shade of it? Suppose we join *so* in expressing, as two English female writers, our sense of the genius of that distinguished woman?—if it did not strike you as presumption in me to put my name to yours as a writer, saying '*we*.' We are equally bold at any rate. Mr Kenyon told me I was 'a daring person' for the introduction of those sonnets . . . [the two she wrote to George Sand, and published in her *Poems* of 1844]. Well!—are you inclined to do it? Will you? Write and tell me. I would give anything to have a letter from her, though it smelt of cigar. And it would, of course!

For once, Miss Barrett's wish was not immediately gratified; there was to be no tobacco-scented letter. But there were at last to be, though Robert Browning protested, two visits to Mme Sand.

Years later George Sand tried to recall their meeting for the benefit of Hippolyte Taine, the austere critic and literary historian, who sent her a copy of *Aurora Leigh* after Elizabeth Barrett Browning's death. Sand could remember only Mrs. Browning's long hair, and an air of illness and modesty and charm, which was a shame, for Taine wrote her that Aurora Leigh was a heroine related to Sand's Edmée (in *Mauprat*) and to Spiridion. "As for me," he wrote, "I love her too much, and just as Flaubert regrets never having seen Balzac, I have one desideratum in my life: never having listened to or looked at Elizabeth Browning for one hour."

As a poet, Elizabeth Barrett Browning was a post-Keatsian and can best be placed, as Jerome Buckley places her, among the early-Victorian "Spasmodics," with their virtues and their faults. Although she read with interest the women poets of the 1810s, 1820s, and 1830s (who were numerous), they seem to have contributed very little to her manner as a poet, which was in some ways so like Robert Browning's that one can only say how lovely it was that they married.

Among her contemporaries, the great women writers were (except for herself) novelists rather than poets; she shared important concerns with the Brontës, Mrs. Gaskell, and George Sand, and drew upon their fiction for plot ideas for her narrative poetry. But where poetic tradition is concerned, those professional matters on which poets are particularly dependent, there Elizabeth Barrett Browning was more a founder than a follower. All the way to Anna Akhmatova and beyond, the tradition of women's love poetry appears dominated by the creative presence of Mrs. Browning. The story of her role in the formation of the greatest woman poet of the nineteenth century provides a case history of particular fascination, for between Elizabeth Barrett Browning and Emily Dickinson there was no affinity whatever but their sex.

II

What is a Poet? To whom does she address herself? And what language is to be expected from her? —She is a woman speaking to women. . . .

—Wordsworth

"That Mrs. Browning fainted, we need not read *Aurora Leigh* to know . . ." Emily Dickinson wrote the Norcross sisters sometime in 1861; "and George Sand 'must make no noise in her grandmother's bedroom.' Poor children! Women, now, queens, now! And one in the Eden of God. I guess they both forget that now, so who knows but we, little stars from the same night, stop twinkling at last? Take heart, little sister, twilight is but

the short bridge, and the moon stands at the end. If we can only get to her!
Yet, if she sees us fainting, she will put out her yellow hands. When did
the war really begin?"

That is a fair sample of Emily Dickinson's epistolary style, with its
affected coyness (from a woman of thirty-one!) and its incoherence, as
well as the phrases that shoot like rockets through her prose as through
her poetry: *"Women, now, queens, now!"* The date of the letter is important, for 1861 was a watershed year for Emily Dickinson, the start of her
period of greatest creativity, when she began to pour out hundreds of
poems a year, among them most of her best. The year 1861 was rather important, also, in American history; but the proportion of Dickinson's letter
given over to the start of the Civil War gives if anything an exaggerated
idea of the importance of that event to her poetry. If any event of the outside world—outside Amherst, Massachusetts—shook the American poet
to the roots of her vocal cords, it was the death in 1861 of Elizabeth Barrett Browning.

"Women, now, queens, now!" means, by Dickinsonian compression,
many things: that Mrs. Browning had gone to heaven, where she twinkled
like a heavenly body, mere woman no longer; that the great women writers, like Browning and Sand, were queens in their genius but women in the
restrictions and repressions of their domestic lives. Dickinson had been
reading about Mrs. Browning in Kate Field's memorial tribute to the English poet, which appeared in the September 1861 *Atlantic Monthly;* just
as, earlier that year, she had read Julia Ward Howe's skillful abridgment of
George Sand's autobiography, from which Dickinson drew the quotation
about Sand's grandmother. "Women, now, queens, now!" is also one of
hundreds of phrases by Emily Dickinson that suggest she had the whole of
Aurora Leigh almost by heart. She thought of its author as "the world's
Aurora," as Mrs. Browning has someone say of Aurora Leigh in Book VII
of the poem:

> Because she was a woman and a queen.
> And had no beard to bristle through her song,
> My teacher, who has taught me with a book. . . .

Emily Dickinson made no secret of her admiration for either the book
or the poet—and why should she? In the mid-century, Mrs. Browning was
one of the most famous and most loved of poets, in America at least as
much as in England; and *Aurora Leigh* was one of the best-selling poems
of all times. Dickinson named Mrs. Browning as a mentor; she referred
often in her letters to her poems, and to the portraits that friends had sent
her. To a friend abroad, she wrote asking that if he visited Mrs. Browning's Italian grave, he should "put one hand on the Head, for me—her unmentioned Mourner—" Why she should still be the "unmentioned

Mourner"—why her love for Mrs. Browning's poetry should be so little mentioned, still today, is a puzzle, for Emily Dickinson also recorded it in a form many people surely know, after Mrs. Browning's *Last Poems* appeared posthumously in 1862:

> Her—"last Poems"—
> Poets—ended—
> Silver—perished—with her Tongue—
> Not on Record—bubbled other,
> Flute—or Woman—
> So divine—
> Not unto its Summer—Morning
> Robin—uttered Half the Tune—
> Gushed too free for the Adoring—
> From the Anglo-Florentine—
> Late—the Praise—
> 'Tis dull—conferring
> On the Head too High to Crown

By today, of course, there has been a reversal of heights and a redistribution of crowns. Mrs. Browning is little read, while Emily Dickinson, who was unknown during her lifetime because virtually unpublished until the 1890s, has achieved what appears to be a permanently high place in American literature. She is regarded as a pivotal pre-Modern in the line that runs "from Baudelaire to Surrealism": "a member in good standing," as R. P. Blackmur puts it, "of the intellectual movement of modern poetry." Dickinson's debt to Elizabeth Barrett Browning would therefore contribute much prestige to the latter's faded reputation, but the Browning scholars, though many are Americans, do not mention it.

Among the Dickinson scholars, those few who have actually read Mrs. Browning's poetry (notably Jack Capps and Rebecca Patterson) have discussed the association between the two women poets with critical seriousness. Among most Dickinsonians, however, perhaps because both poets are women, the literary relationship is treated with embarrassment, even with shocked prurience. To a writer in the latter mode, John Evangelist Walsh, I am personally indebted; for without his 1971 study, called *The Hidden Life of Emily Dickinson,* I would probably never have read, with unwavering attention and delight, the whole of *Aurora Leigh.*

Half the Walsh book is devoted to Emily Dickinson's hidden love life. The other half, intended to be even more shocking, is devoted to her reading, or using, or quoting, or borrowing, or stealing, or, in fine, plagiarizing Mrs. Browning and other women writers. Mr. Walsh provides what he calls "a complete list of Emily's borrowings from *Aurora Leigh* as I have so far been able to identify them": a parallel list of about seventy different Browning passages and somewhat fewer different Dickinson poems (not

many, in fact, against the total number [1,775] that Dickinson wrote).
What I did as a result—and I recommend the procedure—was mark up
my copy of *Aurora Leigh* with the *numbers* of the Dickinson poems on
Walsh's list. (Since she provided no titles, Dickinson's poems must be
referred to by what are in effect the opus numbers supplied by her editor,
Thomas H. Johnson.) And whenever I came to such a number, I made
myself stop, close my *Aurora Leigh,* and faithfully turn to Dickinson's
poems; and read, slowly savoring, the little American verses.

For example: "Therefore come" says Aurora Leigh to Marian Erle,
whom she has just unearthed in Paris, and whose lurid sexual misadven-
tures she is about to hear from the girl's own lips:

> —"I think
> We dare to speak such things and name such names
> In the open squares of Paris!"
> Not a word
> She said, but in a gentle humbled way
> (As one who had forgot herself in grief)
> Turned round and followed closely where I went,
> As if I led her by a narrow plank
> Across devouring waters, step by step;
> And so in silence we walked on a mile.

Eager as I was by then to discover just what had happened to break up
Marian Erle's marriage to Romney Leigh, I dutifully put down my Mrs.
Browning and opened my Emily Dickinson.

> I stepped from Plank to Plank
> A slow and cautious way
> The stars above my Head I felt
> About my Feet the Sea.
>
> I knew not but the next
> Would be my final inch—
> This gave me that precarious gait
> Some called Experience.

Or again, I let the pounding, ringing cadences of that superb Dickinson
poem, "I felt a Funeral, in my Brain," break up my reading of Aurora
Leigh's long journey to Italy, which begins with the roaring of trains and
the clanking of bells, and subsides at last into the hush of funeral solemnity:

> Those marriage-bells I spoke of sounded far,
> As some child's go-cart in the street beneath
> To a dying man who will not pass the day,
> And knows it, holding by a hand he loves,
> I too sat quiet, satisfied with death. . . .

Read in this fashion, the Dickinson poems serve almost as arias in rhyme to break up the onrushing blank verse recitative of *Aurora Leigh;* and I rather suspect that Emily Dickinson sometimes wrote a verse or two with just that complementary function in mind—that is, to underline and elaborate the emotional content of something that happened in *Aurora Leigh,* rather than in her own life. The operatic association is not new; Emile Montégut described Mrs. Browning's unusual approach to narrative poetry as closer to that of an opera libretto than a novel. And Emily Dickinson made the same association with opera in the most beautiful of the poems she wrote about the effect of reading *Aurora Leigh.* "I think I was enchanted/When first a sombre Girl—/I read that Foreign Lady—" it begins,

> And just the meanest Tunes

> That Nature murmured to herself
> To keep herself in Cheer—
> I took for Giants—practising
> Titanic Opera—

The trouble with *Aurora Leigh* is not that it is slow reading, but the reverse; it reads too fast, it's too much fun to read. "Speed and energy, forthrightness and complete self-confidence—these are the qualities that hold us enthralled," wrote Virginia Woolf of *Aurora Leigh,* "this swift and chaotic poem about real men and women." The rush of it all—or the "dash" of it, to use the word the poet Alice Meynell offered and then withdrew, as too vulgar for the occasion—is exactly what Mrs. Browning wanted. "My chief *intention,*" she wrote Robert Browning about her plan for *Aurora Leigh,* ". . . is the writing of a sort of novel-poem . . . running into the midst of our conventions, and rushing into drawing-rooms and the like, 'where angels fear to tread'; and so, meeting face to face and without mask the Humanity of the age, and speaking the truth of it out plainly. That is my intention."

Aurora Leigh is in fact a pretty good novel—not the best Victorian novel you have ever read, not quite on the level where Woolf placed it (with Trollope and Gaskell); but its heroine interests, its love story moves, its melodrama agitates, its settings and conversations and human vignettes amuse, interest, and inform the reader. "As we rush through page after page of narrative in which a dozen scenes that the novelist would smooth out separately are pressed into one, in which pages of description are fused into a single line, we cannot help feeling," Woolf went on, "that the poet has outpaced the prose writer. Her page is packed twice as full as his." But that is exactly the problem. The reader is likely to forget that Mrs. Browning was a poet first of all, and that the reason to read *Aurora Leigh* is not for the good second-rate novel in it, but for the poetry. We want to read it slowly, as Emily Dickinson did, for lines like "I too sat quiet, satisfied with death"; or phrases—remarkably Dickinsonian phrases—like "forgot herself in grief" or "changes backward rang" or "each emerging sense." We need to slow down, to stop running up against conventions and rushing into drawing rooms, to avert our face for a moment from Humanity and plain truth. We want to retreat into solitude, silence, decorum, and rhymed obscurity with Emily Dickinson. In all seriousness, I recommend that someone bring out an edition of *Aurora Leigh* broken up with selected verses by Emily Dickinson. Both poets would profit by the association.

As to Mr. Walsh, indebted as I am to his comparative labors, I must admit to final disappointment with his results, for many of the pairings he makes seem to come down to nothing more than a single word—flood, sphere, pain, lava, fly, cobweb, dust—appearing in both poets' work; and plagiarism is *never* in question. Dickinson's use of Mrs. Browning is a case of tradition in the best T. S. Eliot sense, and were the two poets men rather than women even Mr. Walsh would never discuss their relationship in so coarse a tone; he treats the whole business of Emily Dickinson's reliance on a woman's literary tradition as a dirty secret.

Was "Sue . . . entirely aware," he asks—referring to Mrs. Austin Dickinson, Emily Dickinson's first important reader—"of how these poems . . . were being produced . . . ? In the face of questioning, Emily would hardly have dissembled, in fact would have had no reason to do so, since she probably began the whole operation merely as a means of sharpening her technique, not until later coming to regard the resulting poems as legitimately her own. Did Sue in fact know what her sister-in-law was doing?" That is rather like asking, in reference to the reliance of the second generation of English Romantics upon the first, "Did Percy Bysshe suspect that John pored over Samuel?" or "Did George Gordon ever know that Percy cribbed from William?"

It must be said that Emily Dickinson supplies a unique excuse for this common species of critical rudeness toward women. Her passion for women's literature stands out oddly against the background of the rest of her reading, which was surprisingly skimpy, especially for someone from her sort of prosperous New England family, and for a writer with her sort of long, leisurely life. She was the first major writer of her sex to enjoy access to higher education, an opportunity she threw away after a single year of residence at Mount Holyoke, the oldest women's college in America. She never learned French, never willingly read any language but her own, and in English her literary culture was about as thin as Jane Austen's—who had enjoyed, as the Victorians put it, none of Dickinson's advantages.

The real hidden scandal of Emily Dickinson's life is not the romances

upon which biographers try vainly to speculate, but her embarrassing ignorance of American literature. She knew Emerson's poetry well, and perhaps a little Thoreau and Hawthorne; but she pretended, at least, not to
have read a line of Whitman, no Melville, no Holmes, no Poe, no Irving;
and none of the colonial New England poets. Instead she read and reread
every Anglo-American woman writer of her time: Helen Hunt Jackson
and Lydia Maria Child and Harriet Beecher Stowe and Lady Georgina
Fullerton and Dinah Maria Craik and Elizabeth Stuart Phelps and Rebecca
Harding Davis and Francesca Alexander and Mathilde Mackarness and
everything that George Eliot and Mrs. Browning and all the Brontës wrote.
"Mrs. Hunt's poems," Dickinson wrote in an astonishing letter of 1871,
"are stronger than any written by Women since Mrs — Browning, with the
exception of Mrs Lewes. . . ." Who but Emily Dickinson cared so much
for rating women poets? or cared to read anything by Helen Hunt Jackson
other than *Ramona?* or cared for George Eliot's poetry? or took care to
call her Mrs. Lewes?

Emily Dickinson was self-consciously female in poetic voice, and more
boldly so than is often recognized. It was here, I suspect, that Mrs. Browning meant the most to Dickinson, in her confident use of female experience
and female accessories—the clothes, the looks, the domestic chores of a
woman—for universal purposes. "Because I could not stop for Death,"
Emily Dickinson's most famous poem, manages to be at once grotesque
and ominous, coy and profound, because it is a girlish imagining of seductive death, the gentleman caller. And its source, or rather flying-off point,
seems clearly to be the enforced journey to corruption taken by Marian
Erle in Book VI of *Aurora Leigh.*

Aurora Leigh is a first-person novel poem, told by a heroine who is a
poet proudly absorbed with the significance of her own life as a woman,
and with its effect on her language. "I'm plain at speech, direct in purpose," Aurora says;

> . . . when
> I speak, you'll take the meaning as it is,
> And not allow for puckerings in the silk
> By clever stitches. I'm a woman, sir —
> I use the woman's figures naturally. . . .

And many of these "woman's figures" did indeed find their way from
Aurora Leigh to Dickinson's poetry: grief worn as a tipped hat with a
feather; virtues kept on a high shelf, like the best silver; the malice that
sugars a neighbor's cup of "bohea"; the dust and the fly and the cobweb
that impinge on domestic and spiritual order; the girl's blushes, headaches,
tremors, and stumblings that stand for ideas and emotions of wider than
girlish purview. But the more parallel metaphors one finds in the two

women poets, the more striking appear their differences in temperament and aesthetic.

All that one loves in Elizabeth Barrett Browning—all that Alice Meynell itemizes as her "fruitful genius, her passion for good, her abundance, her nobility, her tenderness, and her strength"—must be put in the negative to produce a likeness of Emily Dickinson. Dickinson was no realist, no feminist, no reformer, no agitator, no daughter of the epic age. Time and again she seems to have abstracted a metaphor from Mrs. Browning and rejected the sense of the passage from which it came. The famous credo of realism from Book V of *Aurora Leigh,* where Mrs. Browning joins together ideas of volcanic lava and of a heaving, throbbing, full-veined, double-breasted woman to suggest the Age toward which the poet should be "unscrupulously epic"—none of the spirit of the passage suited Emily Dickinson's temperament or appears in her poetry. But all the metaphors in the passage can be found there, reassembled for her own purposes. The poem which begins "Rearrange a Wife's affection!" suggests that the rearrangement was of the nature of a surgical operation, for there Dickinson puts a woman's body on the table, dislocates its brain, amputates its "freckled bosom," makes it "bearded like a man," pulls love like a bone from its socket, applies anodyne to pain, bandages a secret, and pulls the whole thing together into a crucifixion metaphor with a crown of thorns. Dickinson's jumble of association is even more "unscrupulous" than Mrs. Browning's, but the result is a love poem, not a battle cry.

It is primarily because of her boldly compressed metaphorical linkings between girlish intimacies and spiritual abstractions that we compliment Emily Dickinson on being a "metaphysical." While in Mrs. Browning's poetry, because of her commitment to write of the "pewter age" she lived in, plain truths about nineteenth-century realities are clamped with earnest, Carlylean fierceness to wild imaginings of spirituality—a great whirring of angels with the paint fresh on them, a swirl of faith and aspiration in the calico empyrean. As a poet-novelist she careened from gritty fact to grand ideal, from chitchat to rapture, from puckered silk to the crucifixion. "The most heterogenous ideas are yoked by violence together"—Dr. Johnson's formula for the wit of the metaphysicals can hardly be applied to a poet so thoroughly Victorian in procedures and temperament as was Mrs. Browning. The jumble of metaphors in *Aurora Leigh* was meant to be and succeeds in being witty, but not "metaphysical." Like the clutter of objects on a Victorian table top, it contributes liveliness, warmth, intensity, and charm to her poetry, but none of the profundity of Emily Dickinson.

. . .

There is no single female tradition in literature; there is no single literary form to which women are restricted, not the novel or the letter or the poem or the play. All that is required to create a productive tradition for women in any of these forms is one great woman writer to show what can be done; and in the case of all those forms the ground was broken for women long ago. It is right for every woman writer of original creative talent to be outraged at the very thought that the ground *needs* to be broken especially for her, just because she is a woman; but it is wrong for the literary scholar and critic (creatures by definition devoid of creative talent) to omit paying their humble toll of tribute to the great women of the past who did in fact break ground for literary women.

There is no such thing as *the* female genius, or *the* female sensibility; although it is extremely interesting to collect the definitions that women writers have provided of such things, because they provide, all unconsciously, self-assessments of considerable fascination. George Eliot, for instance, once got off a theory about female creativity which, for elaborate pseudo-scientific nonsense, has hardly been surpassed even by the psychologists of our own time. In "the Gallic race," she wrote in an article called "Woman in France,"

> the small brain and vivacious temperament . . . permit the fragile system of woman to sustain the superlative activity requisite for intellectual creativeness; while, on the other hand, the larger brain and slower temperament of the English and Germans are, in the womanly organization, generally dreamy and passive. . . . Our theory is borne out by the fact, that among our countrywomen, those who distinguish themselves by literary production, more frequently approach the Gallic than the Teutonic type; they are intense and rapid rather than comprehensive. The woman of large capacity can seldom rise beyond the absorption of ideas; her physical conditions refuse to support the energy required for spontaneous activity; the voltaic-pile is not strong enough to produce crystallizations; phantasms of great ideas float through her mind, but she has not the spell which will arrest them, and give them fixity.

Well! This period piece shows the writer was up on the latest psychological fad, Positivism, which she liked to discuss with Herbert Spencer and George Henry Lewes. But its true interest is self-revelation. Marian Evans, as "George Eliot" was in 1854, perceived in herself the capacity to digest philosophical and religious ideas, but not a shred of what we today call "creative talent"; she had no idea then that she would someday prove her own talent as a writer of fiction. She also saw herself as dreamy, indolent, slow-moving, and heavy-jawed; and probably worried about being overweight.

There is no single female style in literature, though in every country and every period it has been wrongly believed that a female style exists. And many writers, notably Samuel Richardson, have attempted to give the impression that they wrote as women write. If they have genius, as Richardson did, they will convince the world, including the women writers in it: for a good fifty years after *Pamela* English literary circles assumed that what Richardson called the "familiar style," that is, the style of Pamela's letters, was the way women naturally did and always would write. As Clara Reeve said very shrewdly—she was a post-Richardson novelist herself—his novels had "taught many young girls to wire-draw their language, and to spin away long letters out of nothing." But there were, she went on to suggest, worse apprenticeships: "Let the young girls . . . copy *Richardson,* as often as they please, and it will be owing to the defects of their understandings, or judgments, if they do not improve by him."

As early as Fanny Burney, the first important woman novelist in England, it is possible to see how expectations shaped the female style, in her case expectations of breathless, disorganized, "artless" informality. Fanny Burney's epistolary mentor, when she was a girl, was the kindly, sophisticated family friend she called "Daddy" Crisp (and made into a character in her first novel: the tutelary spirit and principal recipient of Evelina's letters). "If once you set about framing studied letters, that are to be correct, nicely grammatical, and run in smooth periods," Crisp wrote her, "I shall mind them no otherwise than as newspapers of intelligence. . . . Never think of being correct when you write to me. . . . if your letters were to be fine-labour'd compositions that smelt of *the lamp,* I had as lieve they travelled elsewhere. So no more of that, Fanny, and thou lov'st me. Dash away, whatever comes uppermost. . . ." And the *dashaway* or *familiar* style, though not the only one Fanny Burney used, undoubtedly became the medium of her best letters and her best fiction. Was this because she was a woman, or because she was a woman writer following Richardson?

It must be said, however, that in every generation since Fanny Burney's there has been some woman writer to convince the pundits that there is a single female style (and that any woman writer who does not use it is a beast). In our time, that role seems to be filled by Anaïs Nin, whose "special way of using available language" inspires the following unguardedly sexy tribute from Professor Harry T. Moore, bless him:

> Miss Nin, delicately petite and delicately beautiful, is a pronouncedly feminine type of woman. To characterize her work we might best use the elemental word female, for Anaïs Nin is not one of those women authors who write like men. Her work is subtle and complex, sensuous, and with soundless depths. It takes the reader in and out of dreams.

What then would the professor say about Gertrude Stein, who also had her "special way of using available language"? Was it because Miss Stein bobbed her hair, and went to medical school, and indulged, as far as we know, in peculiar sexual practices, that she wrote so queer? Is the Stein style to be explained as an effort to "write like men"? Is there anything at all of importance to be said about Gertrude Stein as a woman writer?

When I first began the work on this book, I would have said probably not to the last of these questions, and laughed at the rest. But Gertrude Stein, who always surprises, has taught me many things, especially about the way women learn from reading other women—even a Gertrude Stein, even a writer so intellectual and sophisticated, even a modernist at the head of the avant-garde in painting, music, psychology, and literature.

When Gertrude Stein was a student at Radcliffe in 1894, specializing in experimental psychology, she wrote a theme for Freshman English called "In the Red Deeps"—the earliest writing we have by Stein that indicates true literary gifts. The theme is a first-person account of a hallucination experienced by a young woman afraid of madness and aware of strong sado-masochistic tendencies within herself. Perhaps to be expected as characteristic of the period—the 1890s—are the morbidity, perversity, and decadence of Stein's theme; but wholly unexpected is its title—for "In the Red Deeps" is George Eliot. It is the title she used for Chapter 1, Book V of *The Mill on the Floss*. When I went back to George Eliot's chapter and reread it through Stein's eyes I found nothing at all like Stein's work, early or late, but I did find something that not hundreds of pages in Helene Deutsch or Sigmund Freud himself could have convinced me was true. I found evidence for a single female metaphor which turns out to be so significant in women's literature that it has spawned a whole chapter, the final chapter of this book. Quite unlike the female metaphors exchanged between Emily Dickinson and Mrs. Browning, which reflect the surface of women's life in a particular era, this one metaphor lies deeper, where Freud found destiny, in the one thing about a woman that does not change: her anatomy.

I also learned from Gertrude Stein to listen as women writers do to each other's voices in literature—many voices of different rhythms, pitches, and timbres to which they have always listened with professional sensitivity for an echo to answer their own. So did Victorian women listen to the new and dramatic female voice of *Jane Eyre, an Autobiography*. It was not simply that the unknown author had put certain basic female experiences and emotions into words for the first time; there was something even more intimately, more eerily true to felt female reality. The language of hallucination was often drawn on to express such reactions to *Jane Eyre*. "When I read it," said Harriet Martineau, the least irrational of women, "I was convinced that it was by some friend of my own, who had portions of my childish experience in his or her mind." While Charlotte Brontë, when they finally met, told Miss Martineau that she had read some of the latter's autobiographical writings "with astonishment. . . . It was like meeting her own fetch. . . ." And acid-tongued Jane Carlyle, least enthusiastic of women, recorded even more sharply the same sense of *déjà-entendu*. "If she have not kept *company* with *me* in this life," said Mrs. Carlyle after reading Brontë's *Shirley*, "we must have been much together in some previous state of existence. I perceive in her Book so many things I have said myself, printed without alteration of a word."

Each of these gifted writers had her distinctive style; none imitated the others. But their sense of encountering in another woman's voice what they believed was the sound of their own is, I think, something special to literary women—perhaps their sense of the surrounding silence, or the deaf ears, with which women spoke before there was such an echo as women's literature.

As to Gertrude Stein's peculiar style in prose, of course her experiments with syntax, repetition, word order, and the rest grew essentially from her philosophical and psychological views of the nature of language. But anyone who thinks no one else ever wrote as Stein did, and especially no woman, simply does not have all of women's literature in mind. Take a look at Queen Victoria and St. Teresa, two great ladies who also wrote queer. Stein read Victoria's letters aloud to Alice Toklas; and her enthusiasm for Teresa of Avila was yet another bond between herself and George Eliot. St. Teresa's autobiography in particular (at least in English translation, as Stein read it) is full of echoes of what Gertrude Stein called "the sound inside," when she reminisced about her literary beginnings:

> When I first wrote my first story when I was at Radcliffe I called it Red Deeps out of George Eliot, one does do that, and since well since not, it is a bad habit, American writers have it, unless they make it the taken title to be a sounding board to send back the sound that they are to make inside, that would not be too bad.

MONEY, THE JOB, AND
LITTLE WOMEN: FEMALE REALISM

> There are so many ways of earning a living, and most of
> them are failures.
>
> —Gertrude Stein: *Ida*

I

All of Jane Austen's opening paragraphs, and the best of her first sentences, have money in them; this may be the first obviously feminine thing about her novels, for money and its making were characteristically female rather than male subjects in English fiction. The wonderfully rude blare that starts *Emma*—"Emma Woodhouse, handsome, clever, and rich"—is as it happens imitating Mme de Genlis (the French novelist who meant much to Jane Austen), but the particular Austen touch is precision. While the Genlis heroines, like Richardson's and Fanny Burney's, are merely vaguely, gloriously rich, Emma has precisely 30,000 pounds. From her earliest years, Austen had the kind of mind that inquired where the money came from on which young women were to live, and exactly how much of it there was. In *Love and Freindship,* her classic spoof of the hippie heroine who scorns parental support (written for the ages when Austen herself was fifteen), the money comes from stealing, although Sophia is "most impertinently interrupted" as she is "majestically removing the 5th Bank-note from the Drawer to her own purse."

Marriage makes money a serious business in Austen's fiction; her seriousness about money makes marriage important, as in fact it was in the England of her day. In the last decades of the eighteenth century and the first of the nineteenth, England moved from an aristocratic to a middle-class orientation without any of those vulgar revolutions that convulsed the Lesser Nations of the Continent. New people, with new money and new kinds of power, engaged in that remarkable British enterprise of grafting themselves onto the old aristocratic stock, essentially through intermarriage—Austen's subject. A title like *Pride and Prejudice* denotes less of her conformity to the old eighteenth-century way of thinking in personalized abstractions than of her nineteenth-century concern with social fact: social class, social values, and money. "It is a truth universally acknowledged," runs the celebrated opening sentence of the novel, "that a single man in possession of a good fortune must be in want of a wife." Of all its crystalline phrases, the one about money can least be dispensed with; it conveys the sharp point of Austen's very feminine wit.

Hard facts, with Austen, come first and are swiftly stated. Most of what we need to know about Mr. Bingley, for example, the single man about whom Mrs. Bennet is bursting to tell Mr. Bennet (so that he may get down to the serious business of matchmaking on behalf of their five daughters), is conveyed in her gossipy rattle on the first page of the novel. "Mrs. Long says that Netherfield is taken by a young man of large fortune from the north of England." That is, Bingley resides on an estate he has not inherited but merely "taken," or rented, and his wealth comes out of the North, region of industry and commerce; it is new money. This is the point of the whole comedy of snobbery that Austen spins out of Bingley's hateful sisters: "they were of a respectable family in the north of England; a circumstance more deeply impressed on their memories than that their brother's fortune and their own had been acquired by trade."

The Bingley girls are bitterly opposed to their brother's marriage to Jane Bennet, not because of her relative poverty but because of her middle-class connections. For what the Bingley family needs is not more wealth but aristocratic shadings to what they have; only land ownership, that sign of old money, can remove the stain of trade. That is why Bingley's sisters are desperate for him to purchase an estate, as their self-made father had intended but "did not live to do." And they have cause to fear that Bingley may have inherited dilatoriness and indecision, as well as a fortune, from their father: "it was doubtful to many of those who best knew the easiness of his temper, whether he might not spend the remainder of his days at Netherfield, and leave the next generation to purchase." Happily for all, marriage to Jane Bennet, and her aversion to remaining in the neighborhood of her vulgar mother, force Bingley at the end of the novel to purchase land himself, in another county.

Austen placed Bingley and all the other characters of *Pride and Prejudice* on a financial scale arranged with geometric precision. Her hero Darcy is at the top of the scale, with an income of 10,000 pounds a year, and a fortune twice the size of that of his friend Bingley, who has inherited "nearly an hundred thousand pounds" from which he derives an income of four to five thousand. Each of the Bingley sisters has a fortune of 20,000 pounds, or five times the sum that Mrs. Bennet brought in marriage to her husband. Mr. Bennet's income is 2,000 pounds a year, a fifth of Darcy's and somewhat less than half of Bingley's. He should be thought of as a rich man, nonetheless, by the standard provided by what we know of the novelist's own circumstances: the Austens managed with precarious gentility on about 600 pounds a year.

The Bennet family's socioeconomic position is complicated, however, and not only by that business of the entail which, as Mrs. Bennet is too stupid to understand but Jane Austen is not, deprives the children, simply because they are daughters, of a share in their father's estate. Mr. Bennet's fortune is in land, but Mrs. Bennet's is of less respectable provenance. Her father was a country attorney, and her sister, Aunt Phillips (whose indiscretion begins Lydia Bennet's ruinous course), married their father's clerk, who took over the law business. Mrs. Bennet's brother Gardiner, the girls' uncle, is a more significant figure in the novel; though kept to the background, he serves to point the moral of Austen's economic design. Mr. Gardiner is first mentioned in a shadowy way as "settled in London in a respectable line of trade"—but these shadows cast a smoky pall over the Bennet girls' prospect for social advancement. The Bingleys and Darcy have heard that their uncle "lives somewhere near Cheapside," revolting name; this alone—something like having relatives in the Bronx—"must very materially lessen their chance of marrying men of any consideration in the world."

When Mr. and Mrs. Gardiner take solider shape in the second half of *Pride and Prejudice,* they turn out to be the most sympathetic adults in the novel, the only ones in fact who combine intelligence, style, character, and fortune; not coincidentally, they are also the only happily married adult pair and the only good parents. The Bingley girls never get over their snobbish difficulty in "believing that a man who lived by trade, and within view of his own warehouses, could have been so well-bred and agreeable," but Darcy conquers both pride and prejudice where Gardiner is concerned.

Darcy himself, Austen's earliest conceived and most glamorous hero, is the least precisely imagined character in the novel. With his Norman name and accompanying ancient credentials (his first name is Fitzwilliam); with his splendid estate complete with ancestral portraits, Darcy is actually an improbable close friend for such as Bingley, and an even less probable catch for Elizabeth Bennet. Austen seems to have lifted Darcy, in all his stiff elegance, from Fanny Burney's *Cecilia,* one of her favorite novels; and he stands alone in her work (she would never do such a character again) as a reminder of her eighteenth-century formation. Like Richardson's Sir Charles Grandison, Darcy personifies the benefits that stream down, a sort of gilded rainfall, from landed wealth and power when held by a man of high moral character who, past the age and perils of libertinage, marries the right girl.

"How many people's happiness were in his guardianship!" Elizabeth ponders as she tours Pemberley, the Darcy estate. "—How much of pleasure or pain it was in his power to bestow!—how much of good or evil must be done by him!" These are the old ideas about aristocracy of the century of Austen's birth and juvenile reading, ideas emanating from a society securely ruled by a landed aristocracy; but Austen herself belonged to another era, of shifting class values and alignments. The happy ending of *Pride and Prejudice*—Elizabeth's marriage to Darcy—brings together the uppermost and the shabbiest elements of the country gentry, as they were brought together in Austen's own family history. But not part of her family experience, and not, so far as I can tell, part of the stock of ideas she drew from novel-reading, is her original breeding of old Norman blood with new commercial money from Cheapside, which Elizabeth's marriage also represents. Her uncle and aunt Gardiner are revealed finally to be, in Austen's design, the new kind of people whose benevolent power smooths the working of society, and gilds the happy ending comedy guarantees. The last paragraph of *Pride and Prejudice* is given to them:

> With the Gardiners they were always on the most intimate terms. Darcy, as well as Elizabeth, really loved them; and they were both ever sensible of the warmest gratitude towards the persons who, by bringing her into Derbyshire, had been the means of uniting them.

"Now I will try to write of something else," Austen wrote in a letter announcing the publication of *Pride and Prejudice* in 1813, "& it shall be a complete change of subject—ordination": that is, the taking of clerical orders, the decisive step by which an Englishman enters upon a life's work in the church. No one has ever been happy with this statement of intention —the only one of such sharpness that Austen wrote down—and few have been able to eke out its application to the novel in question, *Mansfield Park*. In the best criticism of the novel that we have, Lionel Trilling looks seriously at "the ideal of professional commitment" as a moral, a religious, and a cultural phenomenon, and what he writes goes far to dignify Austen's intention. But Professor Trilling's relative lack of interest in Austen's concern with the economic aspect of a man's professional choice—to put it bluntly, the question of his income—is, if I may say so, a sign of the masculinity of the critic; it certainly bypasses the feminine quality of Austen's realism.

Because she cared deeply and primarily about young women, because she suffered from a rooted disrespect for parents, especially fathers, because she saw the only act of choice in a woman's life as the making of a marriage upon which alone depended her spiritual and physical health, Austen turned a severe and serious eye (for here she was rarely satirical) on the economic life of her heroes. Heroes were potential husbands, a momentous role. What I am suggesting is that Austen's realism in the matter of money was in her case an essentially female phenomenon, the result of her deep concern with the quality of a woman's life in marriage.

Of all the novels by Jane Austen's female predecessors, Fanny Burney's *Cecilia* is the one most worth rereading as a work of woman's realism—probably the reason why Austen paid *Cecilia* the compliment of lifting the phrase "pride and prejudice" from its last chapter. While in the other Burney novels of manners (*Evelina* and *Camilla*) an all-wise elderly gentleman directs the heroine's marital destiny and corrects her mistakes (a conventional figure Austen dispensed with, for she did not believe in its reality), Cecilia, orphaned at the start of the novel, must search for a proper husband on her own. Indeed the plot of her novel is the story of her dispensing with her three legal guardians, one after the other, for they are all wrongly, even wickedly motivated; and all impede rather than advance the course of Cecilia's courtship.

Courtship is, however, a dreadful word for the subject of Burney's second novel (and for all of Jane Austen's), for it implies something a man does to a woman, and can include adultery. Austen's subject is actually marriageship: the cautious investigation of a field of eligible males, the delicate maneuvering to meet them, the refined outpacing of rivals, the subtle circumventing of parental power (his and hers), and the careful management, at the end of the story, which turns idle flirtation into a firm offer of marriage with a good settlement for life. All this must be carried on in such a way that the heroine maintains her self-respect, her moral dignity, her character as daughter, sister, friend, and neighbor, and her youth; it must be done swiftly, in a year or two, before her bloom fades. (*Persuasion* is the exception—Austen's heart-rending final fantasy of the second chance.) Marriageship was not easy in Austen's time and is not in our own. The major difference between Austen's heroines and the young ladies of today is that the former had a somewhat more realistic sense, from an early age, of the permanent effect on a woman's life of any marriage she makes.

Marriageship is one of those literary subjects that must be read imaginatively from the woman's point of view, which here differs from the man's. And there are certain literary works of indubitable genius which simply fail if they are read in the wrong way. *Pamela,* for example, which of course began the whole subject, is an offensive and irritating portrait of a girl who is a cheat, a hypocrite, a flirt, and a tease unless the reader takes Pamela's side, and wants her, as much as Richardson wants her, to achieve a decent and permanent position in life instead of rotting away on the dunghill of prostitution. Austen's young women face no such melodramatic disasters, but she is just as serious as Richardson, and a more profound moralist, when she weighs from a woman's point of view the three alternatives available to her heroines: the right marriage, the wrong marriage, or spinsterhood.

The two women novelists who followed Austen's lead in taking marriageship seriously were Mrs. Gaskell and George Eliot. In both cases, realism about work and money—man's work and man's money—was the consequence, although in Mrs. Gaskell's most profound novel, *North and South,* a woman's choice of a husband means an even more poignant commitment to the *place* of money-getting (the industrial city) than to the way. In *Middlemarch,* all the issues of marriageship that Austen raised are fully explored in terms of their effect on a man's working life: Lydgate's career in science, destroyed by the terrible Rosamond Vincy, and Fred Vincy's fortunate escape from the church, because of the wonderful Mary Garth. If only one could believe in Dorothea's reformation at the end, *Middlemarch* would be a thoroughgoing triumph of women's realism; if only Dorothea did not say in her "sobbing childlike way" to Ladislaw, "We could live quite well on my own fortune—it is too much—seven hundred-a-year—I want so little—no new clothes—and I will learn what everything costs."

Both Jane Austen and George Eliot are harsher on women who ignore financial realities, for good or evil reasons, than they are on those who think of nothing else. "There was nothing financial, still less sordid in her previsions: she cared about what were considered refinements, and not about the money that was to pay for them." George Eliot's cold irony there, on the subject of Rosamond Vincy, could do as well for Mary Crawford in *Mansfield Park,* who is particularly disagreeable when she expresses astonishment that Edmund Bertram is to be a clergyman: "there is generally an uncle or a grandfather to leave a fortune to the second son." "A very praiseworthy practise," Edmund replies, "but not quite universal. I am one of the exceptions, and *being* one, must do something for myself."

Doing something for oneself, economically speaking, is hard for Edmund and Miss Crawford to conceive; it was also hard for Jane Austen. To the genteel classes of her time, a man should ideally be something and have something, but not *do* anything in order to be or to have. The point of Edmund's taking orders is in fact to place him in a position for someone to give him *a living,* that special British term familiar to readers of Austen and Trollope, signifying a clergyman's benefice: at once the sphere of his responsibility and the attached means of his livelihood—his income. ("And I see no reason why a man should make a worse clergyman," as Edmund sensibly says, "for knowing that he will have a competence early in life.") A *living* was something one inherited, or was given, or took, or bequeathed, according to ancient and complicated systems of secular and clerical ownership of the land. The familiar modern phrase, *to make a living,* may have been, for all I know, in origin an Americanism. The idiom was clearly well established in mid-century America. "I never thought on 't," says slave trader Haley of the work he does in *Uncle Tom's Cabin.* ". . . I took up the trade just to make a living; if 't ain't right, I calculate to 'pent on 't in time, *ye* know."

Even today the Oxford English Dictionary takes as little notice of *to make a living* as it does of the word *job,* in the sense of a man's major, daily, serious employment. I am not suggesting that Jane Austen concerned herself with Edmund Bertram's getting, holding, or executing anything that could remotely be called a job; that subject waited on the later generation of Charlotte Brontë. But I think we must take seriously her intention to write in *Mansfield Park,* however unsuccessfully, a book about a man's practical and active choice of his life's work, and the role that women play in that choice. I think we must believe in her concern here with man's field.

Certainly the subject dominates, and far more brilliantly and successfully, her next published novel, *Emma.* Mr. Knightley is more than the hero of the book, in the sense of the man the heroine marries; he represents, as his name intentionally does, Austen's ripe thinking on the ideal of English manhood. Mr. Knightley has great wealth in the form of ownership of vast and ancient lands—the sole form, for he is short of the cash which marriage to Emma is to provide. But the quality of the man lies not in his mere "possession of a good fortune," but in his active work to preserve it. In his rough gaiters and long stride, his loud, forthright voice, his industrious outdoor life, and his interminable colloquies indoors (to Emma's irritation) on crops and prices, Mr. Knightley is, and is proud to be, a working farmer. Only as such has he been able to preserve in fruitful prosperity and ever-widening extent the beautiful green and spreading lands of his estate. Austen calls it Donwell Abbey to underline her view of Mr. Knightley as the English Knight who has Done Well.

Mr. Knightley is an unusual male character in Austen, not only in his responsible discharge of the landlord's obligations to his society, but also in his free and unencumbered possession of the land: no living parent to await the death of, no indigent brothers or sisters to support, no distant relative to truckle to. More typical, and closer to the reality Austen knew, in her own family, is Frank Churchill in the same novel, who cuts himself off from his amiable father, Captain Weston, dropping even his name, in order to attach himself to his maternal relations, the hateful but rich and childless Churchills. What is a man to do, what can a man do in Austen's world? Austen seems strongly to have disapproved a man's establishing himself by marriage to an heiress, but she appears not to have been much troubled by the scramble after patronage. Any amount of servility, embarrassment, and dependence within the family circle seems in her novels to be worth the hero's prize: to end "in possession of a good fortune."

That Frank Churchill or Henry Tilney or Edward Ferrars (the last two the heroes of *Northanger Abbey* and *Sense and Sensibility*) should defy domestic tyranny, strike out on his own, and take a job seems beyond Austen's imagining. So rare indeed is the subject in nineteenth-century English fiction generations after Austen that one might think—what is not true—that job-holding simply did not exist as a viable possibility for the middle classes: that is, hiring one's services out for money, performing set tasks during fixed hours, surrendering control of the major share of one's waking hours to an employer in return for the means of existence. The shadow of Great Expectations, long after the idea had become a myth, blackened out for even Victorian novelists the subject of the job.

Dickens is the case in point, as George Orwell pointed out: "What he does not noticeably write about is work," said Orwell. And, "One cannot point to a single one of his central characters who is primarily interested in his job." Yet Dickens himself began his adult life with a job: he was employed by a newspaper as a parliamentary reporter, expert in shorthand. This matter barely figures in Dickens's self-portrait as David Copperfield, who sets out in a professional apprenticeship in the law, to which he has access, as Dickens did not, through family patronage. Though superior to Dickens, in Orwell's view, for knowledge about "the way things really happen," Anthony Trollope devoted his dozens of novels to the patronage-ridden professions of the church and the law, to politics and inherited wealth, but not to the civil service, though Trollope himself worked most of his life in the Postal Service, starting out as a clerk. Johnny Eames, Trollope's one attempt to "do" the small clerk (*The Last Chronicle of Barset, The Small House at Allington*), is among those male characters who justify Bradford Booth's comment that "too many of Trollope's heroes [are] indefatigably concerned with who is going to give him some money"—as someone does for Johnny at the last.

Orwell should actually have made an exception for Thackeray, for among the male Victorian novelists he stands out as unusually honest about his own early fall from genteel status: in *Pendennis* Thackeray tried to capture something of the working life of the hack writer that, from necessity, he had been himself as a young man. But posterity better remembers the comic brilliance of the chapters of *Vanity Fair* in which Thackeray wrote of living on Nothing a Year. For the real target of Orwell's complaint about English fiction is English gentility, the blinder of gentility which justified French complaints about the hypocrisy of that "nation of shop-keepers." It was gentility that kept money-getting, Balzac's great subject, out of English fiction, not access to experience, and certainly not the sex of the novelists. Indeed, it is only against the background of national disdain for "the way things really happen" that the English and also the American woman writer's adventurous engagement with the subjects of work and money-making can be appreciated; it was exceptional, and most worthy of remark in Jane Austen, who was the greatest spokesman England ever had for the positive virtues of gentility.

Most of Austen's young men follow a profession, that uncertain mid-path between servile dependence and independent industry, for success in all the professions in Austen's day (as to a degree in our own) began with access to patronage: for example, that "living" in the church, in the gift of family or near acquaintance. The army was in the same sense a profession: witness Darcy's purchase of a commission for Wickham, which raises the latter in social class and readies him for marriage to an heiress.

Medicine was not, in Austen's day, an established middle-class profession. (When it became one, later in the century, women novelists seized on its possibilities for the men in their fiction: the doctor husband in Harriet Martineau's *Deerbrook,* the doctor father in Mrs. Gaskell's *Wives and Daughters,* as well as Lydgate in *Middlemarch.*) For a country novelist like Jane Austen, the law was truly a profession only when practiced mysteriously in far-off London, by someone like Mr. Knightley's brother John. Geographical limitations may also have deprived Austen of the subject of politics and place-hunting. That she had heard of the new class of commercial entrepreneur, and was inclined to admire it, we know from her sketch of Mr. Gardiner in *Pride and Prejudice,* but she did not show anything of the working life of a man engaged in industry, manufacture, commerce, business—all summed up, in nineteenth-century parlance, as "trade." Austen did, however, provide a good deal of information about independent industry, risk-taking, and financial success in the navy, the profession she knew best: it claimed two of her brothers, who rose to be admirals.

The navy and trade might seem worlds apart; *Persuasion* tells us otherwise. The last of Austen's novels, and the most unguarded in social attitudes as well as feelings, *Persuasion* begins with the driving of Sir Walter Elliot from his ancestral estate, for he is a merely ornamental snob who provides neither benevolent leadership nor sound economic management for the county in which he is a principal landowner. Sir Walter's improvidence makes his residence at Kellynch-hall impossible, and its rental necessary to Admiral Crofts and his wife, simple, unfashionable navy people of sterling worth and patriotic ultility but no refinement, who represent Austen's final ideal.

To Sir Walter, who is stupid, nasty, and wrong, the naval career is "offensive," for it is "the means of bringing persons of obscure birth into undue distinction, and raising men to honours which their fathers and grandfathers never dreamt of." Austen's own view, as presented by her heroine Anne, is otherwise: "she could not but in conscience feel that they were gone who deserved not to stay, and that Kellynch-hall had passed into better hands than its owners'." Only when one considers that Kellynch is Anne's own beautiful and beloved home, and its dispossessed owner her father, can one gauge the depth of Austen's revulsion against the idle and worthless landlord, and the height of her admiration for "new people" in the navy. But then *Persuasion* is entirely, as the other Austen novels are only partly, the story of a daughter's moral, emotional, and socioeconomic rejection of her own family.

Austen's account of the naval profession, from which Anne Elliot at last takes a husband, includes little about danger and war (though the navy she knew defeated Napoleon under Nelson) but a great deal about the possibilities it offers of middle-class domestic felicity and middle-class economic success. The plot of *Persuasion* hinges on the economic fact that capture of an enemy vessel, a "prize" in naval parlance, meant direct financial reward to the naval captain of Austen's day. It is the foundation of Captain Wentworth's self-made success. Anne Elliot when young (before the novel opens) had been persuaded not to accept Wentworth as a suitor, because, though a fine and intelligent young man, he had "nothing but himself to recommend him, and no hopes of attaining affluence, but in the chances of a most uncertain profession." Anne follows at a distance Wentworth's rise to captain in the navy: he "must now, by successive captures, have made a handsome fortune. She had only navy lists and newspapers for her authority, but she could not doubt his being rich."

The great names of Trafalgar and St. Domingo echo in the background of *Persuasion,* but what one hears in the foreground is naval reminiscence perhaps only a woman novelist would write, for it is full of money rather than glory. "Ah, those were pleasant days when I had the *Laconia!*" sighs Captain Wentworth. "How fast I made money in her.—A friend of mine, and I, had such a lovely cruise together off the Western Islands.—Poor Harville, sister! You know how much he wanted money—worse than myself. He had a wife.—Excellent fellow!"

. . .

The vulgarity of Jane Austen, a phrase which would hardly occur to us today, is the theme of much of the adverse criticism she received from her Regency contemporaries and Victorian followers. When Mme de Staël pronounced her fiction *vulgaire,* she was perhaps complaining of the absence of the aristocracy from her novels and their setting in dull country places, as well as the want of poetic grandeur which troubled Charlotte Brontë. But

Emerson's famous diatribe against Austen as "vulgar in tone" makes clear that it was her forthright association of marrying with money-getting that primarily offended him. "The one problem in the mind of the writer," he wrote, ". . . is marriageableness. All that interests in any character introduced is . . . , Has he or she the money to marry with, and conditions conforming?" Surely outraged masculinity as well as outraged gentility prompted Emerson's final outburst: "Suicide is more respectable."

Pin-Money is the appropriate title of the novel Catherine Gore wrote in the tradition of Jane Austen's feminine realism: it was an "attempt," she said in her preface, "to transfer the familiar narrative of Miss Austin to a higher sphere." Mrs. Gore happens to be my personal favorite (though she is regrettably less well-known than Ada Leverson and Nancy Mitford) of the many women writers who have made high comedy out of the elegance, the wit, and the nastiness of high society. The period she wrote about (with a backward glance) was essentially Jane Austen's Regency England; their approach as novelists to Regency exclusivism was quite dissimilar. But in *Pin-Money* (1831) Mrs. Gore seized on the one exclusive subject that belongs with Austen's concerns: the arrangements whereby an aristocratic wife (whose husband proposes at the door of Almack's) pays her own bills, and the way these arrangements affect her marriage.

It is a subject not without interest to women today. Though our own approach tends to be more grimly legalistic than comic, we can easily understand why Mrs. Gore said *Pin-Money* was a novel "addressed by a woman to readers of her own sex." Had *Pin-Money* found its way into Emerson's hands, he would surely have found murder more respectable.

A concern with precise sums of money and a feel for the physical lump of the sum persist in twentieth-century women's literature in the work of two distinguished writers entirely different in aesthetic from Jane Austen, and from each other. The coin symbolism pervasive in Virginia Woolf's books—the shilling that Mrs. Dalloway throws into the Serpentine, the coppers that Eleanor alternately clutches and fumbles through *The Years* —carries both feminine and feminist connotations, as readers of *Three Guineas* have observed. Virginia Woolf purposely directs our attention to the minute sums, physically represented by change in the purse and pocket, which to a woman as to a child can mean the difference between freedom and its reverse.

Lillian Hellman's theater brings live money to the stage with a quirky persistence that might almost be considered obsessional; but the presence of money contributes a crackling realism to her family melodramas. Eighty-eight thousand dollars' worth of Union Pacific bonds are contained with difficulty by a safe-deposit box in *The Little Foxes;* forty thousand dollars in cash peep out of an envelope in *Another Part of the Forest;* twenty-three thousand dollars have a walk-on part, locked into a suitcase, in *Watch on the Rhine;* a bankbook recording twenty-eight hundred and forty-three dollars in savings is brandished center stage in *Toys in the Attic;* and even in Hellman's early proletarian play, *Days to Come,* when the first-act curtain goes up, a "five-dollar somebody" predictably makes a bow:

"Did you get your wages this morning? . . . Then hand it over."

"I was going to. But Hannah, I got to keep five dollars out of it because I owe somebody the five dollars."

"Is the five-dollar somebody in this town?"

Such a curtain raiser announces the sex of the playwright as clearly as the opening paragraphs in Jane Austen announce that the novelist is a woman, and to her money is very real.

II

> . . . something unromantic as Monday morning . . .
> —Charlotte Brontë

"Miss Austen being . . . without *poetry,* maybe is sensible, real (more *real* than true), but she cannot be great." So wrote Charlotte Brontë to George Henry Lewes after reading *Pride and Prejudice* because Lewes had urged her to make the acquaintance of her female predecessor. "Nevertheless I will, when I can," she added more mildly, ". . . diligently peruse all Miss Austen's works, as you recommend."

As far as temperament can enter into these matters, Jane Austen was certainly born a realist, while Charlotte Brontë was a romantic of passionate strain. Brontë wrote as a realist, however, and well before she read any Austen; she did so against temperamental inclination, but with deliberation and from conviction. As a Christian; as a modern (that is, a Victorian); as a native of industrial Yorkshire; as an adult—a status only painfully won by the children of her family; finally as a woman, she committed herself to the sober portrayal of the realities of everyday modern life at the outset of her career as a novelist. The results were interestingly original. "I had adopted a set of principles," she later wrote of her first novel. "I said to myself that my hero should work his way through life as I had seen real living men work theirs—that he should never get a shilling he had not earned— . . . that whatever small competency he might gain, should be won by the sweat of his brow. . . ."

She held so firmly to these principles, and discharged so scrupulously her portrait of a man with a job—a middle-class man working routinely for a living—that no one would publish the book. "Indeed," she added drily, "until an author has tried to dispose of a manuscript of this kind, he can never know what stores of romance and sensibility lie hidden in breasts he would not have suspected of casketing such treasures. Men in business are usually thought to prefer the real"—but publishers, she had found, harbor a "passionate preference for the wild, wonderful, and thrilling." The latter preference any Brontë could easily satisfy; and so, against her principles but forced by commercial necessity as well as led by inclination, Charlotte Brontë wrote her second novel, the romance called *Jane Eyre,* and so entered history.

Charlotte Brontë's first novel, *The Professor,* was published only after her death, and barely entered history at all except as a literary curiosity to those concerned with the genesis of the Brontë masterpiece *Villette,* which deals wholly, as *The Professor* deals in part, with Brontë's experience as a teacher in a Brussels school. In *Villette,* her last novel, she provides one of the best literary accounts ever written of what it is like to work in a classroom with the disagreeable, stupid, and intractable young. But her first novel, especially the opening six chapters, has an interest of its own, for *The Professor* is truly the sober, unromantic story of a man intended as a hero, and as at least the social equal of the reader, who works for a living. I do not know any previous work of English fiction carried out upon such principles.

William Crimsworth is well-born and well-educated but penniless, and driven by various exigencies to forget family patronage and consider "engaging in trade." He works as second clerk in a textile-manufacturing establishment in ——shire, charged with translating and copying the firm's foreign correspondence. (Clerk then meant secretary, man's work before the late-Victorian invention of the typewriter, and the ensuing opening of office employment to women, though the only novel I know which makes literature out of secretarial work is *The Deserted House* by Lydia Chukovskaya.)

No exciting incident, no upsweep of fortune, no romance, no amusement other than reading and walking, and very few social encounters break the routine of Crimsworth's office life. He lives on his meager salary in lodgings, a rented bedroom where the sluttish servant regularly lets the fire go out. The interest of the opening chapters of *The Professor* is the peculiar atmosphere Brontë evokes—a kind of sooty, acrid coldness—and the peculiar character of her hero. For sensibility, refinement, youth, and individuality, the qualities with which he is endowed at birth, are swallowed up by the character of the job-holder.

Crimsworth is dry, bitter, and taciturn. He is punctual, diligent, tidy in his work, austere and thrifty in habit. He is obsessed with neatness, and a teetotaler who drinks a good deal of coffee as well as tea in the novel. In appearance he is "only a counting-house clerk, in a grey tweed wrapper." He likes to look at women, but has strong views about what might be called the "single standard." When threatened with violence by his insufferable employer (his brother, whose unnatural hatred underlines the absence of the theme of patronage from the novel), Crimsworth in return merely threatens to summon the magistrate. Altogether, Brontë's hero has a very good hold on his passions and his imagination—something which distinguishes him from the Brontë heroines.

Crimsworth hates his job, in fact hates working. His refusal to romanticize his employment is one of the more original touches in the character. And when a fight with his employer ends the job, and throws Crimsworth loose in the wide world, he reacts very differently from Jane Eyre or Lucy Snowe: they revel in being free spirits, they dream of independence and mysteriously new experience, while Crimsworth grimly faces the fact of job-hunting. "I, a bondsman just released from the yoke, freed for one week from twenty-one years of constraint, must, of necessity, resume the fetters of dependency. Hardly had I tasted the delight of being without a master when duty issued her stern mandate: 'Go forth and seek another service.'" Subservience and self-denial are here the essentials of the white-collar working character. Whatever the defects of *The Professor*—whatever its conscious drabness of atmosphere, which I for one like to savor—the novel does not belong to the self-improving, success-worshiping genre of popular fiction.

The only burst of enthusiasm for work that Brontë permits herself is, interestingly enough, in her delineation of the happy marriage that ends the novel. For an essential ingredient in its happiness is the working wife: it is she (a lace mender turned schoolteacher) who craves employment for its own sake, she who finds fulfillment in work for pay. Crimsworth accedes to his wife's need, though at the end his income (amassed through school-managing and careful investing) makes her earnings a spiritual rather than an economic necessity.

> I put no obstacle in her way; raised no objection; I knew she was not one who could live quiescent and inactive, or even comparatively inactive. Duties she must have to fulfil, and important duties; work to do—and exciting, absorbing, profitable work; strong faculties stirred in her frame, and they demanded full nourishment, free exercise; mine was not the hand ever to starve or cramp them. . . .

Here and throughout the elaboration in the last chapters of *The Professor* of the ideal of work for married women—something of a landmark in that area, I imagine, for 1846—Brontë lets down her guard and reveals herself a woman novelist, whistling in the Victorian dark.

Charlotte Brontë's most important propaganda for work for women makes a strong feature of *Shirley* (1849), the ambitious, brilliant, and also seriously flawed novel set in industrial Yorkshire that she wrote after *Jane Eyre,* with conscious intention to bridle the latter's melodrama and dampen its romance. These violent alternations between romance and realism mark all of her published work and fill her correspondence with George Henry Lewes. Between them, Brontë and Lewes carried on the most important of Victorian debates about Realism, not in the theoretical terms familiar to us from Continental criticism, but in sexual terms both expressed and misunderstood.

Whenever Lewes thought about women's literature, as he often did, the Real to him meant mainly the passions. While to Charlotte Brontë, whose passions fed on her imagination, the Real meant what it meant to all Victorian women: the workaday world. The issue of working for a living was always present in her thinking about the literary Real. "If you think . . . that anything like a romance is preparing for you, reader," she wrote at the start of *Shirley* with Lewes very much in mind, "you never were more mistaken. Do you anticipate sentiment, and poetry, and reverie? Do you expect passion, and stimulus, and melodrama? Calm your expectations; reduce them to a lowly standard. Something real, cool, and solid, lies before you; something unromantic as Monday morning, when all who have work wake with the consciousness that they must rise and betake themselves thereto."

What immediately follows in *Shirley* is a chapter of professional chatter among curates, the one kind of "workingman" Charlotte Brontë knew well, at first hand, because her father was a clergyman. Lewes heartily disliked the beginning and most of the rest of *Shirley,* because it was not so Real, in his sense, as *Jane Eyre.* When he reviewed *Shirley,* his tactless discussion of womanliness in literature, apropos of the Currer Bell he identified as a woman, elicited a famous Brontë outburst: "I can be on my guard against my enemies, but God deliver me from my friends!"

And, as to *Shirley,* "Mr. Lewes," she wrote her publishers, "does not like the opening chapter. . . . Is the first chapter disgusting or vulgar? *It is not, it is real.*"

. . .

When I try to think of a recent American novel of quality which presents the ultimate rewards of a man's life as deriving from his working days and not his sexual nights, I come up with a very moving book called *The Monday Voices,* a title which recalls Charlotte Brontë's definition in *Shirley* of the workaday real: "something unromantic as Monday morning." The author is a woman, Joanne Greenberg (better known for

I Never Promised You a Rose Garden, signed Hannah Green), and her subject is the job of finding jobs for the virtually unemployable, which also recalls the obsession with the job that in the Brontë era consumed the unemployable sex. "Don't you wish you had a profession—a trade?" Brontë's Shirley asks her friend Caroline; who replies, "I wish it fifty times a-day." The wish resolves the paradox: why money, work, and fact have to a significant degree been women's specialties in Anglo-American literature.

And the paradox reopens that vexed question of access to experience, the worst limitation, it is always assumed, that society has imposed upon the woman writer. Virginia Woolf, for example, lamented that many of the greatest Victorian novels "were written by women without more experience of life than could enter the house of a respectable clergyman." But Woolf forgot that such respectable gentlemen of the cloth as the Reverend Mr. Brontë, the Reverend Mr. Gaskell, and the Reverend Mr. Beecher sub- scribed to the newspapers and the quarterlies; and that clergymen's daughters early acquired the habit of reading for fact. Charlotte Elizabeth, the precocious daughter of the Reverend Mr. Browne (she grew up to be Mrs. Tonna), remembered "poring over a newspaper as big as myself" at age five, the same age from which Charlotte Brontë dated her own passion for newspapers and periodicals.

True, the more serious quarterlies reached provincial homes at consid- erable expense and some delay, and they were often reserved for a first reading by father, brother, or husband. It was all the more avidly, there- fore, that the women of the family seized upon these visitors from the larger world. "With a struggle and a fight I can see all Quarterlies 3 months after they are published," wrote Mrs. Gaskell wryly; "till then they lie on the Portico table, for gentlemen to see. I think I will go in for Women's Rights."

It was by reading, of course, that women writers acquired the remarkable quantity and quality of information about workaday realities that they brought to literature. Charlotte Brontë, for example, when she set out to write in *Shirley* about industrial strife in Yorkshire in the Luddite days, simply sent for a file of back issues of the Leeds *Mercury,* from which she worked up the background she required. Any man might do the same; indeed, a respectable clergyman named Charles Kingsley made good use of Mayhew's reporting on the London poor for the novel (*Alton Locke*) Kingsley published the year after *Shirley.* But the disproportionate number of women writers who extended their grasp on fact by hard research ap- pears at first paradoxical. These were deep-bonneted, full-skirted Victorian women—women housebound and chaperoned—women sent away from table after dinner when men talked masculine matters—women denied experiential access to industry and commerce.

All writers are limited in experience. By definition deskpeople rather than workingmen or businessmen, writers who wish to extend their experience beyond the edges of their desks must rely on the method we call research. It is true that the invalid Miss Barrett never worked in a factory —she hardly left her bedroom—but to write "The Cry of the Children" she needed only read R. H. Horne's official report on child labor in the factories. It is true that Mrs. Stowe never was a slave, and that her many children kept her close to home in the North; but to write *Uncle Tom's Cabin* all she needed was to read the documents of slavery by black men and white, journalists and lawyers—writings so numerous that she made a whole book out of them, called *A Key to Uncle Tom's Cabin,* to show the solidity of her documentation.

Harriet Martineau was sickly and deaf, and as a girl rarely went farther from home than the Unitarian chapel, but "the method" by which she produced her *Illustrations of Political Economy* is recorded in several gleeful chapters of her *Autobiography:* the reading of "standard works," the noting of "leading ideas," the consulting of library books for information about "any part of England with which I was not familiar." Later, when the series proved a wide success in educating a nation generally ignorant of economics, "Members of Parliament sent down blue-books through the post-office," in recognition of Miss Martineau's ability to digest and explicate a mass of complicated fact.

In *The Two Cultures* C. P. Snow has written the most influential of all denunciations of "literary intellectuals" for ignoring the realities of the industrial and technological society in which they live. "Natural Luddites" is Snow's term for the machine-hating writers of the Victorian age, but oddly enough he seizes upon the production of buttons as prime example of the kind of technical information which he believes intellectuals require but disdain. And that is odd, because "What There Is in a Button" is the title of the article Harriet Martineau wrote for *Household Words* about the manufacture of metal, pearl, needle-wrought, engraved, and cloth-covered buttons as it was carried on in Birmingham in 1852. The article was part of a successful series on a variety of manufacturing processes that Dickens commissioned, for no one wrote that sort of thing more clearly and thoroughly than Harriet Martineau.

Denial of access to the Real made it fascinating to women. Simple curiosity—that great motivating force all the more powerful for its simplicity—drove literary women to overachievement in their quest for fact, just as it drove their non-literary sisters: Florence Nightingale, who made herself an authority on public health by mastering statistical tabulations from her sickbed; Beatrice Potter, who went from her wealthy home to the London docks to interview the laboring poor; Jane Addams, who discovered the colors and smells of immigrant America through settlement work.

Woman's curiosity, which has been celebrated for millennia in world mythology, deserves an important place in modern history as well.

The Bible teaches that it is extremely risky to tell a woman any kind of knowledge is forbidden fruit. In the days when the Bible was still read seriously, literary women found there what we unbelievers call a "role model" in the person of Mother Eve, that disobedient, adventurous lady who made trouble for everyone because, in Anne Bradstreet's words, "she lost her bliss, to be more wise." The refinements, if such they be, that Milton contributed to Eve's story particularly exercised women writers after his time. Hannah More pondered Eve's being sent away from table while Adam talked astronomy with the angel Raphael. And in *Shirley* the extraordinary chapter Charlotte Brontë gives to a revisionist fantasy of Milton's Eve is called "The First Blue-Stocking."

George Eliot in *Middlemarch* shows Dorothea Brooke's justified "annoyance at being twitted with her ignorance of political economy, that never-explained science which was thrust as an extinguisher over all her lights." Today that science is as freely explained to women as it is to men; enforced ignorance no longer makes literary women especially hungry for fact. Gone too are their illusions about masculine wisdom, and the emulation of masculine example which, as well as curiosity, drove women to master the unexplained Real. "A man's mind—what there is of it—" wrote George Eliot a few pages further on, "has always the advantage of being masculine . . . —and even his ignorance is of a sounder quality." With that crack in (or perhaps crack at) feminine illusion George Eliot in the 1870s shows the gulf already widening between herself and early-Victorian womanhood; and narrows the distance separating her from the modern views of Gertrude Stein: "they are men, and men, well of course they know that they cannot either see or hear unless I tell them so, poor things said Susan B. I do not pity them."

· · ·

American writers, in their attitudes toward work as in much else, appear beside their English contemporaries to be at once childishly naïve and world-wearily sophisticated, both behind and ahead of the times. For bred into the American bone were those "habits of independence and industry" that Charlotte Brontë thought it "most advisable that both sons and daughters should early be inured to"—and sons, in the person of her brother Branwell, were most in her mind. In America, religion, history, and continental destiny all conduced to a native faith in hard work as the practical foundation of personal worth. American literary intellectuals, therefore, were by the mid-nineteenth century already sick of the work ethic and disgusted with money-making.

While Charlotte Brontë was nervously exploring the new subject of genteel man at work for his living, in *The Professor,* Henry David Thoreau was living at Walden Pond, to which he moved on the Fourth of July, 1845, to declare his independence of his hard-working, money-making Concord neighbors. "I am convinced," Thoreau wrote, "that to maintain one's self on this earth is not a hardship but a pastime, if we will live simply and wisely. . . . It is not necessary that a man should earn his living by the sweat of his brow, unless he sweats easier than I do." It was a maiden aunt who paid those taxes in defiant non-payment of which Thoreau went to jail in "Civil Disobedience."

Transcendental improvidence we now know to have been a source of much literary industry on the part of American women. The father, brother, or husband who could not or would not work, and left the entire or major support of a large household to his womenfolk, was responsible for the writing of many best sellers by American women, and a few masterworks.* The literally thumb-crushing labors of Louisa May Alcott were mostly, in this sense, her father's doing; Margaret Fuller derived some spur to literary industry from the marriage into her family (for which she had financial responsibility) of the unemployable Ellery Channing; and there might never have been an *Uncle Tom's Cabin* had the Reverend Calvin Stowe been a better provider for his wife and many babies.

Realism about money is not the least important of the many ways in which Mrs. Stowe's novel deviates from the norm of male-written fiction of her day. In the first chapter, surprising for its domestic and level tone, Uncle Tom is chosen for sale to trader Haley, over the Shelbys' dinner table, because of all their slaves he "will bring the highest sum." The Shelbys are a respectable Kentucky couple whose treatment of their slaves is remarkably civilized. Mr. Shelby is neither a vicious man nor a tyrant but an ordinary husband who, unbeknownst to his wife, has gone seriously into debt. He must raise money quickly to pay for the amenities of their plantation establishment, amenities which include Mrs. Shelby's piety, her high moral code, her tender care of her slaves.

Harriet Beecher Stowe's point, here at the beginning of the novel, is that Mrs. Shelby's genteel ignorance of the financial realities of her married life is, just as much as the sinister trade that Haley plies, a cause of the perpetuation of slavery. "How can I bear," the wife cries when she learns the truth of Tom's sale, "to have this open acknowledgment that we

---

* Helen Papashvily tells the best-seller story in detail, in *All the Happy Endings* (1956), as an American phenomenon. Among non-working Englishmen, however, at least Branwell Brontë requires a place in the economic history of women's literature. "Branwell stays at home and degenerates instead of improving," Charlotte Brontë wrote of her brother's deterioration into alcoholism and drug addiction at the time she began *The Professor.* "He refuses to make an effort; he will not work . . . he is a drain on every resource. . . ."

care for no tie, no duty, no relation, however sacred, compared with money?" That bitter lesson is for the benefit of the readers Mrs. Stowe addressed as "mothers of America"; for them too she wrote the story of Milly, a tragedy of money mixed with motherhood, in her second novel, *Dred*. Milly is a slave woman whose fourteen children are sold away to pay not for the luxuries of plantation life but for the necessities her white mistress is hard put to provide for her own children.

The success of Harriet Beecher Stowe's attack on slavery derives from her associating the "peculiar institution" with the not at all peculiar cash nexus of mid-century America. Without benefit of the statistical sophistications of "cliometrics," which have recently attracted much attention to the economics of slavery, she demonstrated that the true horror was not the inhumanity of slavery but its very human, easygoing alignment with the normal procedures of the marketplace. "Human property is high in the market; and is, therefore, well fed, well cleaned, tended, and looked after, that it may come to sale sleek, and strong, and shining." You shall find, Mrs Stowe went on, as she reached for items to quote from her many documents of the New Orleans slave warehouse,

> an abundance of husbands, wives, brothers, sisters, fathers, mothers, and young children, to be "sold separately, or in lots, to suit the convenience of the purchaser;" and that soul immortal, once bought with blood and anguish by the Son of God, . . . can be sold, leased, mortgaged, exchanged for groceries or dry goods, to suit the phases of trade, or the fancy of the purchaser.

· · ·

Of all the transcendentals no man made so much female literary history, in terms of sheer pages, as the philosopher of improvidence Bronson Alcott, for he had a daughter to support him named Louisa May, who to that end wrote forty books in about thirty years. Besides *Little Women,* she wrote dozens of "juveniles," many thrillers, and a few books intended in all seriousness for adult readers. In the last category, the one I have read that strikes me as most interesting is her first long fiction. Louisa May Alcott began to work on it only fifteen years after Charlotte Brontë wrote *The Professor,* but, for reasons similar to those that hindered publication of Brontë's first novel, it was not published till long afterward, in 1873. It is called *Work: A Story of Experience.*

Alcott's novel opens with a reference to American Independence very different from any to be found in *Walden:*

> "Aunt Betsey, there's going to be a new Declaration of Independence."
> "Bless and save us, what do you mean, child?"

"I mean that, being of age, I'm going to take care of myself, and not be a burden any longer. . . . I don't intend to wait . . . but, like the people in fairy tales, travel away into the world and seek my fortune. . . . I'm old enough to take care of myself; and if I'd been a boy, I should have been told to do it long ago."

Under the jaunty tone, which came naturally to Alcott (it is all over her journals as well as her juvenile fiction), she is quite in earnest. The fairy tale which underlies *Work* is actually *The Pilgrim's Progress,* most revered of Puritan fantasies, and it makes a structure far too solid for this unpretentious tale of a middle-class girl who waits on table, runs after children, and sews seams for her livelihood. Yet there is something impressive, too, about Alcott's attempt to make a latter-day Christian, a pilgrim on the dangerous journey to the desired country, out of the heroine she calls Christie, the working-girl.

Closely modeled after Alcott herself, Christie goes out into the world to make what turns out to be a very scanty fortune. Too poorly educated to be a governess, she goes to a Boston employment agency to apply for a job as housemaid. "I'll begin at the beginning, and work my way up. I'll put my pride in my pocket, and go out to service. Housework I like, and can do well. . . . I never thought it degradation to do it for [Aunt Betsey], so why should I mind doing it for others if they pay for it? It isn't what I want, but it's better than idleness, so I'll try it!" And a live-in housemaid she becomes, in cap and apron, at $2.50 a week, in an establishment where the cook, soon Christie's fast friend, is black.

All this is quite extraordinary for an American or English girl of Christie's type in the 1860s. Like everything else in *Work*—sewing for pay, or working as an actress—it was based on Alcott's real experience, but that did not make it less out of the run of normal American experience. Louisa May Alcott was of the "Brahmin" class, her father from a good if decayed old New England family, her mother a member of the distinguished, prosperous Boston clan of the Mays. The March girls in *Little Women* are presumably month-named for that reason.

A special gift Alcott had, accounting I think for much of her charm as a writer, was her ability to see her own experience—her weird father, her poverty-line childhood, the strange Concord ambiance, her unique working life—as the sunshiny norm, which it was not; and to so transform what she knew into a practical ideal. One result is the curious modernity of Alcott's fiction. It is hard to believe, when reading *Little Women,* that it was written in the 1860s, while Dickens and George Eliot were still writing; or that the War which conveniently abstracts the father from the female household of *Little Women* (and even more conveniently kills off Christie's husband in *Work*) is the contemporary Civil War. For the working girls in Alcott, Jo and Meg as well as Christie, seem more like the college girl of today, working at menial pickup jobs without loss of respectability or class status, than like the Lucy Snowes and Maggie Tullivers who were their near contemporaries.

Also oddly modern is the salute to a special kind of women's solidarity with which Alcott brings *Work* to a close. Widowed almost immediately after marriage, and the mother of a little girl, Christie at the end is forty and wealthy, but still occupied; she is an activist of working-class feminism. She goes among working women to shake their hands ("roughened by the needle, stained with printer's ink, or hard with humbler toil") and arouse their enthusiasm for "the new emancipation" with the sort of simple, earnest speech that only she among the feminists can make, "for I have been and mean to be a working-woman all my life." The novel ends with a scene of hand-clasping all around the table, charmingly illustrated in the Victorian edition I have at hand: Mrs. Wilkins the fat motherly laundress, Bella the elegant young society matron, Letty the fallen woman, Hepsey the black cook, Mrs. Powers the elderly Quaker lady, Christie, and her daughter Ruth—who "spread her chubby hand above the rest: a hopeful omen, seeming to promise that the coming generation of women will not only receive but deserve their liberty, by learning that the greatest of God's gifts to us is the privilege of sharing His great work."

The religion is Protestant, the voice that of nineteenth-century New England womanhood, but in the commitment to work as an act of faith, and in the insistence on humble work, there is a faint presage of the modern philosopher of work, Simone Weil—Jewish, French to the core, a Catholic thinker. Weil was of the first generation of women to have access to the best education and the most interesting work in France. In 1935 she left her normal career as *professeur agrégé* of philosophy to spend most of a year as an assembly-line worker in a factory—brutal and brutalizing work in those days, for which she was physically as well as mentally illadapted, and for which she received the lowest possible wages in the lowest status, that of woman worker. Manual work for Simone Weil was a willed martyrdom of disgust.

"What have I gained through this experience?" Weil asks in *La Condition ouvrière,* the collection of her powerful writings about that factory year, which many consider the most profound study of the working condition produced in this century. Comradeship is one of Simone Weil's answers; moral self-sufficiency another; and in the old tradition of women's realism, "direct contact with life." Finally, humiliation: "to live in this perpetual state of latent humiliation without being humiliated in my own eyes."

Humble work, lower in intellectual content and social prestige than the family ambiance from which her various little women come, is the kind of work that Louisa May Alcott describes with most spirit and conviction. Her first success, *Hospital Sketches,* deals with the unskilled, backbreaking work she herself did as a nurse in a Washington hospital during the Civil War. In *Little Women,* Meg works as a governess, Amy as a companion; Jo does child care and sewing for the mistress of a New York boarding-house. All the girls are unfitted for the work they do, and dislike doing it as much as they dislike the housework—cooking, sewing, cleaning—that, just as much as games, romances, and dreams, makes up the texture of a girl's life in *Little Women.* Work is handled playfully by Louisa May Alcott, but it is not confused with play. It is something real, lasting, serious, necessary, and inescapable as Monday morning, to be shouldered manfully —by women, little and big.

Indeed, the importance of work in America's favorite girl-child's classic is worth pondering. A very different message, for boys, can be found in *Tom Sawyer,* published in the following decade. There work is presented as something to be avoided at all costs and with all ingenuity, whether through the swindle, the ruse, or flight.

▩ 5

FEMALE GOTHIC

A baby at birth is usually disappointing-looking to a parent who hasn't seen one before. His skin is coated with wax, which, if left on, will be absorbed slowly and will lessen the chance of rashes. His skin underneath is apt to be very red. His face tends to be puffy and lumpy, and there may be black-and-blue marks. . . . The head is misshapen . . . low in the forehead, elongated at the back, and quite lopsided. Occasionally there may be, in addition, a hematoma, a localized hemorrhage under the scalp that sticks out as a distinct bump and takes weeks to go away. A couple of days after birth there may be a touch of jaundice, which is visible for about a week. . . . The baby's body is covered all over with fuzzy hair. . . . For a couple of weeks afterward there is apt to be a dry scaling of the skin, which is also shed. Some babies have black hair on the scalp at first, which may come far down on the forehead. . . .

—Dr. Spock: *Baby and Child Care*

What I mean by Female Gothic is easily defined: the work that women writers have done in the literary mode that, since the eighteenth century, we have called the Gothic. But what I mean—or anyone else means—by "the Gothic" is not so easily stated except that it has to do with fear. In Gothic writings fantasy predominates over reality, the strange over the commonplace, and the supernatural over the natural, with one definite auctorial intent: to scare. Not, that is, to reach down into the depths of the soul and purge it with pity and terror (as we say tragedy does), but to get to the body itself, its glands, muscles, epidermis, and circulatory system, quickly arousing and quickly allaying the physiological reactions to fear.

Certainly the earliest tributes to the power of Gothic writers tended to emphasize the physiological. Jane Austen has Henry Tilney, in *Northanger Abbey*, say that he could not put down Mrs. Radcliffe's *Mysteries of Udolpho:* "I remember finishing it in two days—my hair standing on end the whole time." According to Hazlitt, Ann Radcliffe had mastered "the art of freezing the blood": "harrowing up the soul with imaginary horrors, and making the flesh creep and the nerves thrill." And Mary Shelley said she intended *Frankenstein* to be the kind of ghost story that would "curdle the blood, and quicken the beatings of the heart." Why such claims? Presumably because readers enjoyed these sensations. For example, in a work the Shelleys knew well, Joanna Baillie's verse play on the theme of addiction to artificial fear, the heroine prevails upon a handmaiden, against the best advice, to tell a horror story:

> . . . Tell it, I pray thee.
> And let me cow'ring stand, and be my touch
> The valley's ice: there is a pleasure in it.
> Yea, when the cold blood shoots through every vein;
> When every pore upon my shrunken skin
> A knotted knoll becomes, and to mine ears
> Strange inward sounds awake, and to mine eyes
> Rush stranger tears, there is a joy in fear.
>
> *Orra: A Tragedy* (1812)

At the time when literary Gothic was born, religious fears were on the wane, giving way to that vague paranoia of the modern spirit for which Gothic mechanisms seem to have provided welcome therapy. Walter Scott compared reading Mrs. Radcliffe to taking drugs, dangerous when habitual "but of most blessed power in those moments of pain and of languor, when the whole head is sore, and the whole heart sick. If those who rail indiscriminately at this species of composition, were to consider the quantity of actual pleasure which it produces, and the much greater proportion of real sorrow and distress which it alleviates, their philanthropy ought to moderate their critical pride, or religious intolerance." A grateful public rewarded Mrs. Radcliffe by making her the most popular and best-paid English novelist of the eighteenth century. Her preeminence among the "Terrorists," as they were called, was hardly challenged in her own day, and modern readers of *Udolpho* and *The Italian* continue to hail her as mistress of the pure Gothic form.

As early as the 1790s, Ann Radcliffe firmly set the Gothic in one of the ways it would go ever after: a novel in which the central figure is a young woman who is simultaneously persecuted victim and courageous heroine. But what are we to make of the next major turning of the Gothic tradition that a woman brought about, a generation later? Mary Shelley's *Frankenstein*, in 1818, made the Gothic novel over into what today we call science fiction. *Frankenstein* brought a new sophistication to literary terror, and it did so without a heroine, without even an important female victim. Paradoxically, however, no other Gothic work by a woman writer, perhaps no literary work of any kind by a woman, better repays examination in the light of the sex of its author. For *Frankenstein* is a birth myth, and one that was lodged in the novelist's imagination, I am convinced, by the fact that she was herself a mother.

Much in Mary Shelley's life was remarkable. She was the daughter of a brilliant mother (Mary Wollstonecraft) and father (William Godwin). She was the mistress and then wife of the poet Shelley. She read widely in five languages, including Latin and Greek. She had easy access to the writings and conversation of some of the most original minds of her age. But nothing so sets her apart from the generality of writers of her own time, and before, and for long afterward, than her early and chaotic experience, at the very time she became an author, with motherhood. Pregnant at sixteen, and almost constantly pregnant throughout the following five years; yet not a secure mother, for she lost most of her babies soon after they were born; and not a lawful mother, for she was not married—not at least when, at the age of eighteen, Mary Godwin began to write *Frankenstein*. So are monsters born.

What in fact has the experience of giving birth to do with women's literature? In the eighteenth and nineteenth centuries relatively few important women writers bore children; most of them, in England and America, were spinsters and virgins. With the coming of Naturalism late in the century, and the lifting of the Victorian taboo against writing about physical sexuality (including pregnancy and labor), the subject of birth was first brought to literature in realistic form by the male novelists, from Tolstoy and Zola to William Carlos Williams. Tolstoy was the father of thirteen babies born at home; Williams, as well as a poet and a Naturalist, was a small-town doctor with hundreds of deliveries to his professional credit, and thus well equipped to write the remarkable account of a birth that opens *The White Mule*. For knowledge of the sort that makes half a dozen pages of obstetrical detail, they had the advantage over woman writers until relatively recent times.*

---

* Two very popular women novelists (and Nobel laureates), Pearl Buck and Sigrid Undset, were probably responsible for establishing pregnancy, labor, and breast feeding as themes belonging to twentieth-century women's literature. The miscarriage is a powerful new theme in the hands of Jean Rhys and Sylvia Plath, and the unwed mother's labor inspires a spirited obstetrical chapter ("Don't Have a Baby Till You Read This") in the memoir of the young poet Nikki Giovanni, who has a fine sense of the incongruity of the experience. "'A BABY? BUT I DON'T KNOW ANYTHING ABOUT HAVING A BABY! I'VE NEVER HAD A BABY BEFORE.' And I started crying and crying and crying. What if I messed up? You were probably counting on me to do the right thing and what did I know? I was an intellectual. I thought things through. I didn't know shit about action."

But Colette's note of skepticism is most worth recalling, because she was the first

Mary Shelley was a unique case, in literature as in life. She brought birth to fiction not as realism but as Gothic fantasy, and thus contributed to Romanticism a myth of genuine originality: the mad scientist who locks himself in his laboratory and secretly, guiltily works at creating human life, only to find that he has made a monster.

> It was on a dreary night of November, that I beheld the accomplishment of my toils. With an anxiety that almost amounted to agony, I collected the instruments of life around me, that I might infuse a spark of being into the lifeless thing that lay at my feet. . . . The rain pattered dismally against the panes, and my candle was nearly burnt out, when, by the glimmer of the half-extinguished light, I saw the dull yellow eye of the creature open; it breathed hard, and a convulsive motion agitated its limbs. . . . His yellow skin scarcely covered the work of muscles and arteries beneath; his hair was of a lustrous black, and flowing . . . but these luxuriances only formed a more horrid contrast with his watery eyes, that seemed almost of the same color as the dun white sockets in which they were set, his shrivelled complexion and straight black lips.

That is very good horror, but what follows is more horrid still: Frankenstein, the scientist, runs away and abandons the newborn monster, who is and remains nameless. Here, I think, is where Mary Shelley's book is most interesting, most powerful, and most feminine: in the motif of revulsion against newborn life, and the drama of guilt, dread, and flight surrounding birth and its consequences. Most of the novel, roughly two of its three volumes, can be said to deal with the retribution visited upon monster and creator for deficient infant care. *Frankenstein* seems to be distinctly a *woman*'s mythmaking on the subject of birth precisely because its emphasis is not upon what precedes birth, not upon birth itself, but upon what follows birth: the trauma of the afterbirth.

Fear and guilt, depression and anxiety are commonplace reactions to the birth of a baby, and well within the normal range of experience. But more deeply rooted in our cultural mythology, and certainly in our literature, are the happy maternal reactions: the ecstasy, the sense of fulfillment, and the rush of nourishing love which sweep over the new mother when she first holds her baby in her arms. Thackeray's treatment of the birth of a baby in *Vanity Fair* is the classic of this genre: gentle Amelia is pregnant when her adored young husband dies on the field of Waterloo, a tragedy which drives the young woman into a state of comatose grief until the blessed

---

to pick and choose for literature among all the ramifications of female sexuality. In *La Maison de Claudine* she tells of fainting away in horror when, as a young girl, she first came upon a gruesome birth scene in Zola. "Oh, it's not such a terrible thing, the birth of a child," she has her mother comment. ". . . The proof that all women forget it is that it's never anybody but men—and what business was it of his, that Zola?—who make stories about it."

moment when her baby is born. "Heaven had sent her consolation," writes Thackeray. "A day came—of almost terrified delight and wonder—when the poor widowed girl pressed a child upon her breast . . . a little boy, as beautiful as a cherub. . . . Love, and hope, and prayer woke again in her bosom. . . . She was safe."

Thackeray was here recording a reality, as well as expressing a sentiment. But he himself was under no illusion that happiness was the only possible maternal reaction to giving birth, for his own wife had become depressed and hostile after their first baby was born, and suicidal after the last; at the time of *Vanity Fair,* Thackeray had already had to place her in a sanitarium, and he was raising their two little girls himself. So, in *Vanity Fair,* he gives us not only Amelia as a mother, but also Becky Sharp. Becky's cold disdain toward her infant son, her hostility and selfishness as a mother, are perhaps a legacy of Thackeray's experience; they are among the finest things in the novel.

From what we know about the strange young woman who wrote *Frankenstein,* Mary Shelley was in this respect nothing like Becky Sharp. She rejoiced at becoming a mother and loved and cherished her babies as long as they lived. But her journal, which has set the tone of most of the discussion of the genesis of *Frankenstein,* is a chilly and laconic document in which the overwhelming emphasis is not on her maternity but on the extraordinary reading program she put herself through at Shelley's side. Mary Shelley is said—and rightly—to have absorbed into *Frankenstein* the ideas about education, society, and morality held by her father and her mother. She is shown to have been influenced directly by Shelley's genius, and by her reading of Coleridge and Wordsworth and the Gothic novelists. She learned from Sir Humphry Davy's book on chemistry and Erasmus Darwin on biology. In Switzerland, the summer she began *Frankenstein,* she sat by while Shelley, Byron, and Polidori discussed the new sciences of mesmerism, electricity, and galvanism, which promised to unlock the riddle of life, and planned to write ghost stories.

Mary Shelley herself was the first to point to her fortuitous immersion in the literary and scientific revolutions of her day as the source of *Frankenstein.* Her extreme youth, as well as her sex, have contributed to the generally held opinion that she was not so much an author in her own right as a transparent medium through which passed the ideas of those around her. "All Mrs. Shelley did," writes Mario Praz, "was to provide a passive reflection of some of the wild fantasies which were living in the air about her."

Passive reflections, however, do not produce original works of literature, and *Frankenstein,* if not a great novel, was unquestionably an original one. The major Romantic and minor Gothic tradition to which it *should* have belonged was to the literature of the overreacher: the superman who breaks through normal human limitations to defy the rules of society and infringe upon the realm of God. In the Faust story, hypertrophy of the individual will is symbolized by a pact with the devil. Byron's and Balzac's heroes; the rampaging monks of Mat Lewis and E. T. A. Hoffmann; the Wandering Jew and Melmoth the wanderer; the chained and unchained Prometheus: all are overreachers, all are punished by their own excesses—by a surfeit of sensation, of experience, of knowledge and, most typically, by the doom of eternal life.

But Mary Shelley's overreacher is different. Frankenstein's exploration of the forbidden boundaries of human science does not cause the prolongation and extension of his own life, but the creation of a new one. He defies mortality not by living forever, but by giving birth. That this original twist to an old myth should have been the work of a young woman who was also a young mother seems to me, after all, not a very surprising answer to the question that, according to Mary Shelley herself, was asked from the start: "How I, then a young girl, came to think of, and to dilate upon, so very hideous an idea?"

Birth is a hideous thing in *Frankenstein,* even before there is a monster. For Frankenstein's procedure, once he has determined to create new life, is to frequent the vaults and charnel houses and study the human corpse in all its loathsome stages of decay and decomposition. "To examine the causes of life," he says, "we must first have recourse to death." His purpose is to "bestow animation upon lifeless matter," so that he might "in the process of time renew life where death had apparently devoted the body to corruption." Frankenstein collects bones and other human parts from the slaughterhouse and the dissecting room, and through long months of feverish and guilty activity sticks them together in a frame of gigantic size in what he calls "my workshop of filthy creation."

It is in her journal and her letters that Mary Shelley reveals the workshop of her own creation, where she pieced together the materials for a new species of romantic mythology. They record a horror story of maternity of the kind that literary biography does not provide again until Sylvia Plath.

As far as I can figure out, she was pregnant, barely pregnant but aware of the fact, when at the age of sixteen she ran off with Shelley in July 1814. Also pregnant at the same time was Shelley's legal wife Harriet, who gave birth in November "to a son and possible heir," as Mary noted in her journal. In February 1815 Mary gave birth to a daughter, illegitimate, premature, and sickly. There is nothing in the journal about domestic help or a nurse in attendance. Mary notes that she breast-fed the baby; that Fanny, her half sister, came to call; that Claire Clairmont, her stepsister, who had run off with Mary, kept Shelley amused. Bonaparte invaded France, the journal tells us, and Mary took up her incessant reading

program: this time, Mme de Staël's *Corinne*. The baby died in March.
"Find my baby dead," Mary wrote. "A miserable day."

In April 1815 she was pregnant again, about eight weeks after the birth
of her first child. In Janury 1816 she gave birth to a son: more breast-
feeding, more reading. In March, Claire Clairmont sought out Lord Byron
and managed to get herself pregnant by him within a couple of weeks.
This pregnancy would be a subject of embarrassment and strain to Mary
and Shelley, and it immediately changed their lives, for Byron left England in April, and Claire, Shelley, Mary, and her infant pursued him to
Switzerland in May. There is nothing yet in Mary's journal about a servant,
but a good deal about mule travel in the mountains. In June they all
settled near Byron on the shores of Lake Geneva.

In June 1816, also, Mary began *Frankenstein*. And during the year of
its writing, the following events ran their swift and sinister course: in October Fanny Imlay, Mary's half sister, committed suicide after discovering
that she was not Godwin's daughter but Mary Wollstonecraft's daughter by
her American lover. (The suicide was not only a tragedy but an embarrassment to all. Godwin refused even to claim Fanny's body, which was
thrown nameless into a pauper's grave.) In early December Mary was
pregnant again, as she seems to have sensed almost the day it happened.
(See her letter to Shelley of December 5, in which she also announced
completion of Chapter 4 of her novel.) In mid-December Harriet Shelley
drowned herself in the Serpentine; she was pregnant by someone other
than Shelley. In late December Mary married Shelley. In January 1817
Mary wrote Byron that Claire had borne him a daughter. In May she finished *Frankenstein,* published the following year.

Death and birth were thus as hideously intermixed in the life of Mary
Shelley as in Frankenstein's "workshop of filthy creation." Who can read
without shuddering, and without remembering her myth of the birth of a
nameless monster, Mary's journal entry of March 19, 1815, which records
the trauma of her loss, when she was seventeen, of her first baby, the little
girl who did not live long enough to be given a name. "Dream that my little baby came to life again," Mary wrote; "that it had only been cold, and
that we rubbed it before the fire, and it lived. Awake and find no baby. I
think about the little thing all day. Not in good spirits." (*"I thought, that
if I could bestow animation upon lifeless matter, I might in process of time
renew life where death had apparently devoted the body to corruption."*)

So little use has been made of this material by writers about *Frankenstein* that it may be worth emphasizing how important, because how unusual, was Mary Shelley's experience as a young woman writer. Though
the death of one of their babies played a decisive role in the literary careers of both Harriet Beecher Stowe and Elizabeth Cleghorn Gaskell, two
of the rare Victorian women writers who were also mothers, both were

about twice Mary Shelley's age when their babies died; and both were respectably settled middle-class women, wives of ministers. The harum-scarum circumstances surrounding her maternity have no parallel until our time, which in its naïve cerebrations upon family life (and in much else, except genius) resembles the Shelley era. The young women novelists and poets of today who are finding in the trauma of inexperienced and unassisted motherhood a mine of troubled fantasy and black humor are on the lookout for Gothic predecessors, if the revival of *The Yellow Wallpaper*—Charlotte Perkins Gilman's macabre post-partum fantasy—is any indication. The newborn returns again to literature as monster.

> At six months he grew big as six years
> . . . One day he swallowed
> Her whole right breast . . .
> . . . both died,
> She inside him, curled like an embryo.
> —Cynthia Macdonald: "The Insatiable Baby"

Behind them all stands the original fantasy and the exceptional case of Mary Shelley. She hurtled into teen-age motherhood without any of the financial or social or familial supports that made bearing and rearing children a relaxed experience for the normal middle-class woman of her day (as Jane Austen, for example, described her). She was an unwed mother, responsible for breaking up a marriage of a young woman just as much a mother as she. The father whom she adored broke furiously with her when she eloped; and Mary Wollstonecraft, the mother whose memory she revered, and whose books she was rereading throughout her teen-age years, had died in childbirth—died giving birth to Mary herself.

Surely no outside influence need be sought to explain Mary Shelley's fantasy of the newborn as at once monstrous agent of destruction and piteous victim of parental abandonment. "I, the miserable and the abandoned," cries the monster at the end of *Frankenstein,* "I am an abortion to be spurned at, and kicked, and trampled on. . . . I have murdered the lovely and the helpless. . . . I have devoted my creator to misery; I have pursued him even to that irremediable ruin."

In the century and a half since its publication, *Frankenstein* has spawned innumerable interpretations among the critics, and among the novelists, playwrights, and filmmakers who have felt its influence. The idea, though not the name, of the robot originated with Mary Shelley's novel, and her title character became a byword for the dangers of scientific knowledge. But the work has also been read as an existential fable; as a commentary on the cleavage between reason and feeling, in both philosophical thought and educational theory; as a parable of the excesses of idealism and genius; as a dramatization of the divided self; as an attack on the stultifying force of social convention, including race prejudice, for Stephen Crane's *The Monster* must surely be counted among the most powerful descendants of *Frankenstein*.

The versatility of Mary Shelley's myth is due to the brilliance of her mind and the range of her learning, as well as to the influence of the circle in which she moved as a young writer. But *Frankenstein* was most original in its dramatization of dangerous oppositions through the struggle of a creator with monstrous creation. The sources of this Gothic conception, which still has power to "curdle the blood, and quicken the beatings of the heart," were surely the anxieties of a woman who, as daughter, mistress, and mother, was a bearer of death.

Robert Kiely's suggestive study of *The Romantic Novel in England* includes one of the rare serious discussions of *Frankenstein* as a woman's work. For Professor Kiely does more than interpret; he also responds, as one must in reading *Frankenstein,* to what he calls the "mundane side to this fantastic tale."

> In making her hero the creator of a monster, she does not necessarily mock idealistic ambition, but in making that monster a poor grotesque patchwork, a physical mess of seams and wrinkles, she introduces a consideration of the material universe which challenges and undermines the purity of idealism. In short, the sheer concreteness of the ugly thing which Frankenstein has created often makes his ambitions and his character—however sympathetically described —seem ridiculous and even insane. The arguments on behalf of idealism and unworldly genius are seriously presented, but the controlling perspective is that of an earthbound woman.

The "mundane side" to *Frankenstein* is one of its most fertile and original aspects. Mary Shelley comes honestly to grips with the dilemma of a newly created human being, a giant adult male in shape, who must swiftly recapitulate, and without the assistance of his terrified parent, the infantile and adolescent stages of human development. She even faces squarely the monster's sexual needs, for the denouement of the story hangs on his demand that Frankenstein create a female monster partner, and Frankenstein's refusal to do so.

But more than mundane is Mary Shelley's concern with the emotions surrounding the parent-child and child-parent relationship. Here her intention to underline the birth myth in *Frankenstein* becomes most evident, quite apart from biographical evidence about its author. She provides an unusual thickening of the background of the tale with familial fact and fantasy, from the very opening of the story in the letters a brother addresses to his sister of whom he is excessively fond, because they are both orphans. There is Frankenstein's relationship to his doting parents, and his semi-incestuous love for an abandoned, orphan girl brought up as his sister. There is the first of the monster's murder victims, Frankenstein's infant brother (precisely drawn, even to his name, after Mary Shelley's baby); and the innocent young girl wrongly executed for the infant's murder, who is also a victim of what Mary Shelley calls that "strange perversity," a mother's hatred. (Justine accepts guilt with docility: "'I almost began to think that I was the monster that my confessor said I was. . . .'") The material in *Frankenstein* about the abnormal, or monstrous, manifestations of the child-parent tie justifies, as much as does its famous monster, Mary Shelley's reference to the novel as "my hideous progeny."

What Mary Shelley actually did in *Frankenstein* was to transform the standard Romantic matter of incest, infanticide, and patricide into a phantasmagoria of the nursery. Nothing quite like it was done in English literature until that Victorian novel by a woman which we also place uneasily in the Gothic tradition: *Wuthering Heights.*

• • •

The first readers of *Wuthering Heights* were struck as we are still today by the perverse aspects of the novel. "A disagreeable story" about "painful and exceptional subjects," said *The Athenaeum,* ". . . dwelling upon those physical acts of cruelty—the contemplation of which true taste rejects." Much as that assessment misses—the strength, the solidity, the moral wisdom of the novel—it still sums up a side of *Wuthering Heights* that cannot be argued away. Emily Brontë's acceptance of the cruel as a normal, almost an invigorating component of human life sets her novel apart, from its opening pages to its close. Her first narrator, Lockwood, the foppish London visitor to Wuthering Heights who establishes our distance from the central Brontë world, falls asleep at the Heights at the start of the novel and dreams that Catherine—the dead Cathy, Heathcliff's love—is a child ghost outside the casement window, begging to be let in. "Terror made me cruel," says Lockwood; "and, finding it useless to attempt shaking the creature off, I pulled its wrist on to the broken pane, and rubbed it to and fro till the blood ran down and soaked the bedclothes. . . ."

"Terror made me cruel . . ." Is Emily Brontë a "Terrorist," as the first Gothic novelists were called? Is *Wuthering Heights,* which Robert Kiely places at the end of a study largely devoted to Gothic novels as "the masterpiece of English romantic fiction," part of the Gothic tradition? Kiely bypasses the question by his use of the term romantic, but, like virtually every other critic of Emily Brontë's work, he is struck by its successful and almost seamless stitching of mystical eloquence, metaphysical profundity, shrewd realism, and moral dignity to the faded paraphernalia of the

Gothic mode. For there are the graveyard lusts and wandering ghosts; the mysterious foundling and tyrannical father; the family doom, repeated generation after generation; the revenge motif; and the aroma of incest that persists from the introduction of the bastard Heathcliff to the family at the Heights, and to the bed he shares with the girl-child Catherine, his playmate, his sister, his torment, his victim, his beloved, but never his wife.

The Gothic vice of sadism is an extreme and pervasive feature of *Wuthering Heights,* though handled by Emily Brontë with a sobriety that Jacques Blondel aptly describes as "cette dignité dans la violence." Nevertheless, sadism of a particularly horrid kind, child torture and child murder, fills the novel with what Wade Thompson has called "a multitude of insistent variations on the ghastly theme of infanticide."

In 1847 *The Athenaeum* summed up all this material as "the eccentricities of 'woman's fantasy.'" We are more familiar with Victorian clichés about women being by nature (and women writers, therefore, being by right) gentle, pious, conservative, domestic, loving, and serene. That sort of comment was received wisdom among the Victorians and is still, rather thoughtlessly, repeated in our own day. But to confront the long engagement of women writers with the Gothic tradition is to be reminded that its eccentricities have been thought of, from Mrs. Radcliffe's time to our own, as indigenous to "woman's fantasy." In *Wuthering Heights* those female "eccentricities" must be called by a stronger name: perversities.

Thinking about *Wuthering Heights* as part of a literary women's tradition may open up a new approach to a faded classic of Victorian poetry by a woman who was in fact, as Emily Brontë certainly was not, gentle, pious, and conservative: Christina Rossetti's *Goblin Market.* In 1859, twelve years after the Brontë novel, Rossetti wrote her own contribution to the literature of the monster in the form of a narrative poem. Published in 1862, *Goblin Market* quickly became one of the most familiar and best-loved Victorian poems, and was given to little children to read in the days when children had stronger stomachs than they do today. Perhaps the last generation to grow up with *Goblin Market* was that of Willa Cather, who published her first book of short stories a decade after Rossetti's death, called it *The Troll Garden,* and gave it an epigraph from *Goblin Market:*

> We must not look at Goblin men,
>   We must not buy their fruits;
>   Who knows upon what soil they fed'
>   Their hungry thirsty roots?

The roots of Christina Rossetti's goblins are themselves mysterious. In its modest way, her fable was as original a creation as *Frankenstein;* that is, as a maker of monsters Rossetti swerved as sharply from her sources in literary and folk materials as did Mary Shelley. There seems little doubt that particularly female experiences, in both cases, contributed to the disturbing eccentricity of the tale.

Two little girls, two sisters Laura and Lizzie, seem to be living alone together as *Goblin Market* opens, and running their own household without parents. Their relationship is one of spiritual and physical affection:

> Golden head by golden head,
> Like two pigeons in one nest
> Folded in each other's wings,
> They lay down in their curtained bed . . .
> Cheek to cheek and breast to breast
> Locked together in one nest.

Into their neighborhood come goblin men known to all the maids round about as dangerous tempters: they sell fruit which intoxicates and then destroys. One feast upon the goblin fruit and girls turn prematurely gray, sicken, fade, and die young. In verses that seem unquestionably to associate goblin fruit with forbidden sexual experience, Rossetti cites the case of one goblin victim,

> Jeanie in her grave,
> Who should have been a bride;
> But who for joys brides hope to have
> Fell sick and died. . . .

The goblins themselves are monstrosities of a special kind that Emily Brontë, too, worked with in *Wuthering Heights*. Like Heathcliff, who is set off from the norm by animal metaphors ("a fierce, pitiless, wolfish man," or a tiger, a serpent, a mad dog that howls "like a savage beast" or prowls like "an evil beast [between the sheep] and the fold"), Rossetti's goblins are animal people:

> One had a cat's face,
> One whisked a tail,
> One tramped at a rat's pace,
> One crawled like a snail,
> One like a wombat prowled obtuse and furry,
> One like a ratel tumbled hurry scurry.

The sinister music here, one of the numerous auditory variations played by Rossetti's apparently simple verse, establishes that these goblins are not lovable little hobbits, but true monsters.

What are monsters? Creatures who scare because they look different, wrong, non-human. Distortion of scale was the first visual effect employed by Gothic novelists in creating monsters, particularly gigantism: well before Frankenstein's outsize monster, Walpole had filled the *Castle of Otranto* with specters of giant stature. But the classically Victorian device to create monsters was the crossing of species, animal with human. I am thinking of the sneezing pigs, smiling cats, preaching caterpillars, and gourmandizing walruses of Lewis Carroll's *Wonderland;* of Kingsley's *Water Babies,* and Jean Ingelow's Pre-Raphaelite fairy tales; of Melville's *Moby-Dick* and H. G. Wells's *Island of Dr. Moreau*—all fantasies in the Gothic or other modes, with monsters that are animaloid humans.

But there is something more to Christina Rossetti's goblins that suggests to me a specifically feminine Victorian fantasy: that is, that they are brothers. They are not, in so many words, brothers to the sisters Laura and Lizzie in the poem, but a separate breed:

> Leering at each other,
> Brother with queer brother;
> Signalling each other,
> Brother with sly brother.

The brothers stand opposed to the sisters as tempters of clearly double intention: to intoxicate them with forbidden fruit, and also to harass, torture, and destroy them. One of the sisters, Laura, succumbs to the goblin song. She buys their fruit with a lock of her golden hair:

> Then sucked their fruit globes fair or red. . . .
> She never tasted such before. . . .
> She sucked and sucked and sucked the more
> Fruits which that unknown orchard bore;
> She sucked until her lips were sore.

"Suck" is the central verb of *Goblin Market;* sucking with mixed lust and pain is, among the poem's Pre-Raphaelite profusion of colors and tastes, the particular sensation carried to an extreme that must be called perverse. I am suggesting not that *Goblin Market* belongs to the history of pornography as a Victorian celebration of oral sex, but that Christina Rossetti wrote a poem, as Emily Brontë wrote a novel, about the erotic life of children.

Gorged on goblin fruit, Laura craves with all the symptoms of addiction for another feast, but craves in vain, for the goblins' sinister magic makes their victims incapable of hearing the fruit-selling cry a second time. However, the other sister, Lizzie, who through strength of character has resisted the temptation to eat the goblins' fruit, can still hear their cry. Lizzie sets out to buy of the goblins in order to save her fallen sister, who, "dwindling,/Seemed knocking at Death's door."

Lizzie's venture in redemption opens up the question of the spiritual implications of *Goblin Market,* for it is, of course, as a Christian poet that Christina Rossetti is best known. In the view of C. M. Bowra and others, she is one of the finest religious poets in the language, and, until recognition came to Gerard Manley Hopkins (who read her with admiration), she was widely accepted as the greatest religious poet of the nineteenth century. Most of her poems (there are about a thousand) are Christian poems of remarkable fervor and orthodoxy, but not all of them—not, in my opinion, *Goblin Market,* which, if it were in conception a Christian work, would surely be resolved by an act of piety. Rossetti would have Lizzie save her sister through some ceremony of exorcism, a prayer, at least an act symbolizing her own essential purity. What Rossetti does give us at the end is something quite different, for it is in a spirit of heroism rather than of sainthood that Lizzie engages fully with the goblin experience:

She goes to trade with the goblins:

> At twilight, halted by the brook:
> And for the first time in her life
> Began to listen and look.

The goblins rush to greet her:

> Hugged her and kissed her:
> Squeezed and caressed her.

They force their fruit upon her, urging her to "Pluck them and suck them." But when Lizzie makes clear her intention to buy and carry off the fruits to save her sister, without tasting them herself, the goblins become enraged and attack her:

> Grunting and snarling. . . .
> Their tones waxed loud,
> Their looks were evil.
> Lashing their tails
> They trod and hustled her,
> Elbowed and jostled her,
> Clawed with their nails,
> Barking, mewing, hissing, mocking,
> Tore her gown and soiled her stocking,
> Twitched her hair out by the roots,
> Stamped upon her tender feet,
> Held her hands and squeezed their fruits
> Against her mouth to make her eat.

But Lizzie keeps her mouth clenched tightly shut. Though the goblin attack turns even nastier and crueler, she resists, survives, and runs home to Laura to offer herself physically—it is the most eloquent, most erotic moment in the poem—to her sister. For Lizzie bears away not only cuts and bruises from her battle with the goblin brothers; she is also smeared with the juices of their fruit. "Laura," she cries,

"Did you miss me?
Come and kiss me.
Never mind my bruises,
Hug me, kiss me, suck my juices
Squeezed from goblin fruits for you,
Goblin pulp and goblin dew.
Eat me, drink me, love me;
Laura, make much of me;
For your sake I have braved the glen
And had to do with goblin merchant men."

Laura responds: "She kissed and kissed her with a hungry mouth." The effect is at first disastrous (loathing, bitterness, feverish fires in the blood) but at last Laura's cure is complete and permanent. Rossetti concludes with a sober *envoi:* "Days, weeks, months, years/Afterwards . . ." Both sisters, she says, grow to a maturity which includes marriage and motherhood. In reality Christina Rossetti remained a spinster, and her sister Maria, to whom *Goblin Market* was dedicated, became an Anglican nun.

That some kind of biographical fact or event lies behind *Goblin Market* has been a matter of general agreement among Rossetti scholars, starting with William Michael Rossetti, who edited his sister's poems. I find the usual biographical speculations ingenious but not wholly satisfying; I can also go only part way with the standard reading of *Goblin Market* as a poem about the divided self, for it makes too little of the two sisters theme that Rossetti handled with particular intensity. Not only in *Goblin Market* but in many other poems Christina Rossetti presents symbolic oppositions by means of a pair of sisters; sometimes, as in "Noble Sisters" or "Sister Maude," they are rivals in love or hostile to each other's passion.

Who told my mother of my shame,
Who told my father of my dear?
Oh who but Maude, my sister Maude,
Who lurked to spy and peer.

Rossetti brings a special, hissing vigor to the sisters-in-opposition theme which, not surprisingly, is pervasive in women's literature, at least from *Sense and Sensibility* to *Middlemarch.* Its most neurotic variation can be found in Harriet Martineau's *Deerbrook;* its most dramatically symbolic presentation in *Lélia,* where George Sand opposes a sister courtesan to her intellectually frigid heroine.

Laura and Lizzie, in *Goblin Market,* may very possibly symbolize profane versus sacred love, or weak sensuality versus strong reason. But to say that as criticism is no more illuminating than to say (as has been said) that Heathcliff is the Id, and Catherine the Ego. A purely symbolic interpretation of *Wuthering Heights* and *Goblin Market* makes them out to be a sort of Tennysonian "Two Voices," or something different from what they are in fact: perverse and also realistic works in the Victorian Gothic mode. It was a mode to which I suspect both Emily Brontë and Christina Rossetti had access through fantasies derived from the night side of the Victorian nursery—a world where childish cruelty and childish sexuality come to the fore.

In one important respect their formation was similar: both women grew up in a family of four siblings male and female, bound together in a closed circle by affection and by imaginative genius, as well as by remoteness from the social norm. Several Victorian women writers—the Brontë sisters and Christina Rossetti among them—derived a valuable professional leavening from starting out as infant poets, dramatists, or tellers of tales with an audience of enthusiastic and collaborating siblings. That not only much of the technical expertise but also some of the material of their adult work derived from the nursery circle should not surprise us. Quentin Bell's recent biography of Virginia Stephen, a girl in another family of talented, like-minded sisters and brothers, allows us at least to speculate openly on the sexual drama of the Victorian nursery. (Though Mr. Bell does not, for me at least, settle the question of the factual component in Virginia Woolf's memories of fraternal incest, to the reality of a sister's incest fantasy he brings important evidence, if evidence be needed.)

Every reader of Dickens knows the importance of a sister to a brother struggling to resolve the extreme Victorian separation between the purity and the desirability of womanhood. But to Victorian women the sister-brother relationship seems to have had a different and perhaps even greater significance—especially to those women, so commonplace in the intellectual middle class, who in a sexual sense never lived to full maturity. The rough-and-tumble sexuality of the nursery loomed large for sisters: it was the *only* heterosexual world that Victorian literary spinsters were ever freely and physically to explore. Thus the brothers of their childhood retained in their fantasy life a prominent place somewhat different in kind from that of the father figures who dominated them all.

Little sisters were briefly and tantalizingly the equals of little brothers, sharers of infant pains and pleasures that boys quickly grew out of, but that girls—as Maggie Tulliver bitterly tells us—clung to despairingly at an inappropriate age. Women authors of Gothic fantasies appear to testify that the physical teasing they received from their brothers—the pinching, mauling, and scratching we dismiss as the most unimportant of children's games—took on outsize proportions and powerful erotic overtones in their adult imaginations. (Again, the poverty of their physical experience may have caused these disproportions, for it was not only sexual play but *any* kind of physical play for middle-class women that fell under the Victorian ban.)

I was recently reminded of Christina Rossetti's goblins while reading two very different documents: Freud's lecture on symbols, where he says that small animals often appear in dreams to symbolize little brothers and sisters; and *The Diary of Alice James.* This last is a witty, poignant, and distinctively American document by the sister of Henry James the novelist, William James the philosopher, and also of Garth Wilkinson and Robertson James. "I wonder what determines the *selection* of memory," Alice James wrote in 1890, near the end of her life:

> . . . why does one childish experience or impression stand out so luminous and solid against the, for the most part, vague and misty background? The things we remember have a *first-timeness* about them which suggests that that may be the reason of their survival. I must ask Wm. some day if there is any theory on the subject. . . .

Alice James then went on to record her memory of being conscious for the first time "of a purely intellectual process": her brother Henry, when he was about thirteen (and she was seven or eight) said something witty and original which delighted and stimulated her. The James children, in Europe for the summer, had taken an excursion with their governess: a boring, dusty, and non-memorable trip, except for Henry's *mot* and the drive that began the day. "A large and shabby calèche came for us into which we were packed, save Wm.; all I can remember of the drive was a never-ending ribbon of dust stretching in front and the anguish greater even than usual of Wilky's and Bob's heels grinding into my shins." Not only intellectual but also physical stimulus of a surprisingly trivial kind lodged her brothers in a sister's adult memory.

In his introduction to the diary, Leon Edel comments on the teasing that Alice James knew as a girl, on the "usual petty indignities small boys have in reserve for baby sisters." He cites the phrase "greater even than usual" from this passage as one that "sums up whole chapters of childhood history." Chapters perhaps as well of women's writings, for even the civilized James boys, in their role as kicking, pinching, scratching little brothers, are potential goblins, perhaps potential Heathcliffs in their rough and uninhibited physicality.

The puzzles of *Wuthering Heights* may best be resolved if the novel is read as a statement of a very serious kind about a girl's childhood and the adult woman's tragic yearning to return to it. Catherine's impossible love for Heathcliff becomes comprehensible as a pre-adolescent (but not pre-sexual) love modeled after the sister-brother relationship. The gratuitous cruelties of the novel thus are justified as realistic attributes of the nursery world—and as frankly joyous memories of childhood eroticism.

Emily Brontë's view of childhood comprised nature and freedom, but not innocence; this may well be the particularly female component of her romanticism. The children in her novel are brutes, little monsters of cruelty and lust, like Christina Rossetti's goblins; but they are to her, nevertheless, the most real, the most fascinating of creatures. The wonderful childhood journal of the dead Catherine that Lockwood stumbles on at the start of the novel opens to us a world of mean brutality, but also palpitating vitality; it shocks us as it shocks Lockwood into his dream of Catherine's ghost outside his window, the ghost of a child begging to be let in. It is as a child that Catherine first appears in the novel, and as a child that she prays to return to earth when she is dying.

Critics of *Wuthering Heights* have wondered why Catherine should want to return to such a childhood as she experienced at the Heights, for it seems to have been made up of hatred, brutality, and random cruelty. Yet in her dying delirium she cries out against her adult state, against being "Mrs. Linton, the lady of Thrushcross Grange, and the wife of a stranger; an exile, an outcast . . . from what had been my world. . . . I wish I were a child again," she cries, "half savage and hardy, and free . . . and *laughing at injuries, not maddening under them!* Why am I so changed?"

To make my point about the female imagination, and its delight in the remembered brutishness of childhood, I have taken the liberty not only of adding italics but of tampering with that quotation. For what Catherine actually cries is not "I wish I were a child again," but "I wish I were a girl again, half savage and hardy, and free. . . ."

. . .

The savagery of girlhood accounts in part for the persistence of the Gothic mode into our own time; also the self-disgust, the self-hatred, and the impetus to self-destruction that have been increasingly prominent themes in the writing of women in the twentieth century. Despair is hardly the exclusive province of any one sex or class in our age, but to give *visual* form to the fear of self, to hold anxiety up to the Gothic mirror of the imagination, may well be more common in the writings of women than of men. While I cannot prove this statistically, I can offer a reason: that nothing separates female experience from male experience more sharply, and more early in life, than the compulsion to visualize the self.

> All my walls are lost in mirrors,
>   whereupon I trace
> Self to right hand, self to left hand,
>   self in every place,
> Self-same solitary figure, self-same
>   seeking face.
> —Christina Rossetti: "A Royal Princess"

From infancy, indeed from the moment of birth, the looks of a girl are examined with ruthless scrutiny by all around her, especially by women, crucially by her own mother. "Is she pretty?" is the second question put to new female life, following fast upon the first: "Is it a boy or a girl?" Whatever else may have changed in the experience of women, Maggie Tulliver is in this respect still with us, and George Eliot's memories of the ugly intellectual's girlhood still give us the horrors, Gothic or otherwise. I am reminded of something she told Edith Simcox late in life, in explanation of her preference for men over women: "When she was young, girls and women seemed to look on her as somehow 'uncanny' while men were always kind."

Women writers have, in any case, continued to make monsters in the twentieth century, but not so often giants or animaloid humans as aberrant creatures with hideous deformities or double sex: hermaphrodites. "Freaks" is in fact a better word than monsters for the creations of the modern female Gothic: "a horrid sideshow of freaks," to use the phrase T. S. Eliot hoped would *not* be applied to *Nightwood,* for he considered Djuna Barnes's novel of 1936 a masterpiece, rather "Elizabethan" than Gothic in its "quality of horror and doom." *Nightwood* no longer seems so impressive a work, but Djuna Barnes's material—macabre fantasy interlacing lesbians, lunatics, Jews, spoiled priests, artists, noblemen, transvestites, and other masqueraders—has remained attractive to women writers. It reappears in the tales which Isak Dinesen called Gothic, with a special quality recognized by Carson McCullers as a "freakish brilliance."

No writer of our time worked more seriously with Gothic forms or created more haunting monsters of ambivalence than Carson McCullers herself. Sometimes, like Dinesen, whose work she admired, McCullers put distance between herself and the freakish by means of folk-tale fantasy, as in *The Ballad of the Sad Café.* It tells of the love of a huge man-woman, hairy-thighed and muscled like a prizefighter, who loses her heart to a greedy little hunchback of uncertain age and mysterious provenance.

Sometimes, in short stories and in her best-known novel, *The Member of the Wedding,* McCullers cloaks with humorous tenderness her unsentimental perception of the freakish self as originating in female adolescence. McCullers is at her best with creatures poised on a sharp, thin line between opposites: of sex, of race, of age. Her finest work is her second novel, *Reflections in a Golden Eye* (1941), which interweaves in a kind of dance of doom a small group of officers, servants, soldiers, and wives. They are also lovers and murderers, impotent homosexuals and gentle perverts, gluttons, idiots, artists, and nymphomaniacs. McCullers' cast of characters here are as humdrum and as horrifying as their setting: that numb nightmare of the void, an army post located somewhere in the South.

It has long been a critical commonplace to explain the Gothic strain in Carson McCullers, who came from Georgia, as belonging to the Southern American Gothic school of which William Faulkner is the notorious advertisement. But there is abundant evidence of McCullers' participation in a tradition at least as feminine as regional. In *Reflections in a Golden Eye* she seems to have drawn from Isak Dinesen ideas for the relationship between Alison and her Filipino servant Anacleto: between a woman who is wife, mother, and queen (yet has neither husband, child, nor subjects) and a grotesquely devoted servant of another race, perhaps a homosexual, certainly a gifted, sensitive, ridiculous, mad, dwarflike creature, as diminutive as a monkey or a child. (Compare the Kamante material in Dinesen's *Out of Africa*.) More recently, this recognizably feminine theme has surfaced again in the grotesque love triangles of Penelope Gilliatt: the treatment of the male homosexual as an object of frustrated maternal love.

It was at the Museum of Modern Art's retrospective Diane Arbus exhibition that the Female Gothic aspect to Carson McCullers' work struck me most forcibly. For Arbus's photographs of freaks—her drag queens, lesbians, circus people, adolescents, lunatics, dwarfs, and the rest —look as if they might have been designed to illustrate McCullers' fiction. Not only the subject matter, but the tone of Arbus's work recalls McCullers: the cold intimacy, the fear which suggests, in objective terms, the haunted and self-hating self. There is that visit to the circus in *The Member of the Wedding* where the girl stands riveted before the booth of the Half-Man-Half-Woman, with the fascinated horror of the Arbus camera eye: "she was afraid of all the Freaks, for it seemed to her that they had looked at her in a secret way and tried to connect their eyes with hers, as though to say: we know you."

No reference either to women writers or to their monstrous creations was made by Freud in his study of Gothic horror, called in English "Freud on the Uncanny." But Freud does refer there to the perception of the female genitals as monstrous—an idea used by Robin Morgan in the title poem of her recent collection, called *Monster* (1972). Freud locates this perception not in female but in male fantasy, or more precisely, as the Morgan poem indicates, puerile fantasy: she presents a little boy's view (presumably the poet's infant son) of the naked female body. The poem seems to me to have nothing to do with the long and complex traditions of Female Gothic, where woman is examined with a woman's eye, woman as girl, as sister, as mother, as self. Robin Morgan's gifts lie elsewhere, in polemical verse, as for example the crackling "Arraignment" in the same collection: her "J'accuse" directed toward the men in the life, in the suicide, and in the afterlife of Sylvia Plath.

It was Plath herself, with her superb eye for the imagery of self-hatred, who renewed for poets—Anne Sexton, Adrienne Rich, Erica Jong, and

many others—the grotesque traditions of Female Gothic. Her terror was
not the monster, the goblin, or the freak, but the living corpse:

> O my enemy.
> Do I terrify?—
>
> The nose, the eye pits, the full set of teeth?
> The sour breath
> Will vanish in a day.
>
> Soon, soon the flesh
> The grave cave ate will be
> At home on me
>
> And I a smiling woman.
>   —Sylvia Plath: "Lady Lazarus"

PART II
⊞ HEROINISM

❊ 6

HEROINISM:
A NECESSARY INTRODUCTION

> If men could see us as we really are, they would be a little
> amazed; but the cleverest, the acutest men are often under an
> illusion about women: they do not read them in a true light:
> they misapprehend them. . . . If I spoke all I think on this
> point; if I gave my real opinion of some first-rate female
> characters in first rate works. . . .
>
> —Charlotte Brontë

> One generally finds in the writings of even ingenious men that
> they take up the characters of women too easily . . . the
> two sexes are too much considered as different species. He or
> she who soars not above simplicity is most likely to under-
> stand the human heart best in either sex, especially if he can
> make allowance for different modes of education, constitution,
> and situation.
>
> —Samuel Richardson

There seems to be nothing but truth to the familiar legend of Samuel
Richardson's beginning as a novelist. Richardson was a man already fifty,
a successful printer, citizen, and family man with nothing very special
about him, as far as his friends were aware, except a gift for letter writing.
In 1739 two of those friends, two booksellers, asked him to write for
publication a series of Familiar Letters to be used as models by people less
gifted than he. Richardson tossed off several dozen such letters—they are
splendid, lively productions—but stuck fast at Number 138: *A Father to a
Daughter in Service, on hearing of her Master's attempting her Virtue.*
"Consider, my dear child, your reputation is all you have to trust to. And

. . . come away directly (as you ought to have done on your own motion) at the command of *Your grieved and indulgent Father*."

Excellent advice (duly taken by the girl in Number 139) but supposing —just supposing, Richardson must have thought, such a girl had *more* than reputation to trust to, had in fact what I have: a gift for letter writing. Suppose then that she does not "come away directly," as prudence and morality both dictate, but instead finds some pretext to remain (those accounts to finish? that waistcoat to stitch?)—isolated, penniless, unprotected in her master's house, a mere servant girl of fifteen, with nothing but her pen and paper. . . . How far may she not go, wheedling, teasing, faking, charming, testifying, arguing, writing her way to prosperity and power? Richardson put aside the Familiar Letters, and in the space of two months wrote two volumes of *Pamela* letters.

He subtitled the novel *Virtue Rewarded,* meaning by virtue precisely what he meant in the heading of Familiar Letter 138: the intact preservation of physiological virginity. A silly, a narrow subject, Richardson's readers have often, perhaps thoughtlessly complained; Fielding, indeed, showed how brusquely that little matter could be handled in *Shamela,* his parody of Richardson's first novel, where "crosslegged is the Word, faith, with *Sham*." But it was not so much Pamela's merely negative defense of her virtue that seems to have fired up Richardson's imagination, as her positive self-assertion through letter writing. Pamela's good looks first attract her master, "but they were the beauties of her mind," says Mr. B, "that made me her *husband*."

That mental beauties are best developed, exercised, and displayed through the writing of letters is Richardson's insistent lesson in *Pamela.* It begins with Mr. B's complimenting Pamela on her spelling and handwriting, and ends with Pamela triumphant, now Mrs. B, thanking honest Mr. Longman for his help to her in time of trouble: "you don't know how much of my present happiness I owe to the sheets of paper, and pens and ink, you furnished me with." The acquiring of these necessary articles, the secreting of them, the writing with and upon them, the storing and concealing of the written papers, the delivery of them and their return, the reading and rereading, the passing of them about to strangers, the reading aloud in company, and the commenting upon their style and content—all this takes up an enormous amount of space in the novel. Pamela's letters, the very objects, provide Richardson with a subject for melodrama and a theme for pathos ("I cannot hold my pen—How crooked and trembling the lines!"). They outshine her virtue and crowd out her devotions—on her wedding night, an often mocked example of Richardson's obsession, when she first thanks God on her knees but then, "the pen and paper being before me, I amused myself with writing thus far."

Most fascinating is the growing sexuality of Pamela's letters as the novel nears its climax. The pile of written papers rises thicker and higher (hundreds of pages of script to fill up the printed pages we have before us), and Pamela grasps them ever more firmly, more closely to her body, a very pregnancy of letters. "I begin to be afraid my writings may be discovered; for they grow large:" she says; "I stitch them hitherto in my undercoat, next my linen." And Mr. B, after failing at ordinary rape (in a scene famous for its silliness), addresses himself with greater masculine verve to the rape of the letters:

> Now tell me where it is you hide your written papers, your saucy journal? . . . for I *will* know, and I will *see* them. —This is very hard, sir, said I; but I must say, you shall not, if I can help it.
>
> We were standing most of this time; but he then sat down, and took me by both hands, and said, Well said, my pretty Pamela, *if you can help it!* But I will not let you help it. Tell me, are they in your pocket? . . . Are they not, said he, about your stays? No sir, replied I. . . . Artful slut! said he. . . . I never undressed a girl in my life; but I will now begin to strip my pretty Pamela. . . .
>
> I fell a crying. . . . Pray, sir, said I, (for he began to unpin my handkerchief,) consider! Pray sir, do! —And pray, said he, do *you* consider. For I *will* see these papers. But may be, said he, they are tied about your knees, with your garters, and stooped. . . .

This marvelous business comes to a close with Mr. B's capitulation. He is brought round less by Pamela's tears than by her writing yet another letter, direct to him. Pamela's final victory is marked by what she calls her "opening" of her letters to him in her own time and on her own terms. "So I took out my papers; and said, Here, sir, they are. But if you please to return them, without breaking the seal, it will be very generous. . . . He broke the seal instantly, and opened them"—but Pamela has nothing more to fear. Mr. B finds that the reading of her "very moving tale" has "rivetted" his affections upon her, and offers marriage. Never has literary criticism been turned to more direct, more practical account: "You are very happy, said he, my beloved girl, in your style and expressions."

Clearly Richardson was obsessed with the power of the letter to change the world, and with the imperative need for the unprotected, imprisoned female to express herself in letter form. Why the writing *woman* was at the center of his concern can I think be best explained as a matter of only half-conscious subversion on Richardson's part. Of humble origin and little formal education, and lacking the education in the classics that then was the foundation of all correct literary accomplishment, Richardson seems to have identified himself as an outsider and upstart with women as a class. His genius at "incorrect" writing, or what he called the "familiar style" in the shapeless, run-on letter form, dealt a permanent blow to classicism in literature that immediately struck Henry Fielding, who had had the education of a gentleman.

As to the talented women of Richardson's time, the subsequent history of the epistolary novel and of novel-writing women in general suggests that they read the moral of *Pamela* as *Writing Rewarded*. In the novel, Richardson certainly made the reward for Pamela's letters a splendid one: vast wealth and estates, a house in town, fashionable clothes, trips to Europe, a carriage, and a handsome young husband, as amorous as he is adored.

I don't think there was anything odd about Richardson's personal preference for the company and the correspondence of the charming, attractive, and witty women he gathered about him in the years of his post-*Pamela* celebrity; on the contrary, that seems yet another proof of the good sense that characterizes everything else we know about the man. But his active encouragement of literary professionalism among his women friends is worthy of comment. He urged them to put their words on paper and nagged them when they did not—when "afraid, lovely dastards," as he wrote Margaret Collier, "of shewing themselves capable of the perfections they are mistresses of." Several members of Richardson's female circle wrote fiction of some importance: Sarah Fielding, Charlotte Lennox, Frances Sheridan, Hester Chapone. Several more published letters and memoirs, like his clever friend Mrs. Delany, who would sponsor Fanny Burney in the next generation.

Richardson actively trained these women to literature in several ways. He made them privy to his own creative processes, starting with his second novel, *Clarissa*. He stimulated their criticism, debated their ideas, encouraged their writing, and sometimes printed it. When it came to his third novel, *Sir Charles Grandison,* Richardson indulged in an active collaboration with his gifted female friends—the "Pigmalionesses," as Catherine Talbot called them, after finding herself head over heels in love with the ideal hero she and the rest had helped to form. And Richardson's abortive project for a *Grandison* continuation was to be entirely a collaborative effort: a collection of letters by different female hands, which he actively solicited in his last years among the women he called his "daughters" and "sisters."

There would be granddaughters as well. Frances Sheridan wrote, at Richardson's urging, one of the liveliest epistolary fictions; her son was the playwright Richard Brinsley Sheridan; and her great-granddaughter was Caroline Norton, the poet and feminist, who had her partial portrait drawn (to carry the story down to the end of the nineteenth century) as *Diana of the Crossways,* Meredith's neo-Richardsonian heroine.

But Richardson's true literary granddaughter was Fanny Burney, the first thoroughly professional woman of letters, whose career illustrates many of the turnings, right or wrong, that literary women would take after her. She was born with an extraordinary gift for remembering and evoking spoken dialogue, as every reader of the Burney diaries knows. She also happened to be born in 1752; and by the middle of the century, because of Richardson, the epistolary novel already seemed the "natural" choice for women writers, and epistolary fiction is what she set out to write.

I am not the only admirer of Fanny Burney's talent to suspect that her choice of literary form may have been a mistake. Her dazzling but not wholly comfortable first novel-in-letters, *Evelina* (1778), led Sheridan to invite her to write a comedy for him to produce at the Drury Lane theater, which she did. Burney's first play, *The Witlings,* is very funny and quite stageworthy. I shattered the calm of the splendid chamber in the New York Public Library which houses the Berg Collection by laughing aloud when I read the manuscript of the play, which is among the Berg treasures. Manuscript is, however, all that came of the play. Because of the opposition of her father, the musicologist Charles Burney, *The Witlings* was never produced or published. Instead, Fanny Burney wrote a second novel, *Cecilia.*

Dr. Burney's intervention appears at first sight to be the original case of the thwarting by a "patriarchal society" of female talent. But in this case, at least, his prohibition rested not so much on the impropriety of a woman's writing for the stage as on his daughter's tactless choice of subject for her first play. *The Witlings* is a satire on the most literary of literary ladies, the bluestockings, to whose much-sought-after society the success of *Evelina* had just given Fanny Burney access. The play might even have appeared a dig at Mrs. Thrale, that great lady and friend of Dr. Johnson, who particularly encouraged its writing: "You must set about a comedy and set about it openly; it is the true style of writing for you." Had Dr. Burney allowed *The Witlings* to go on the boards, his daughter would have been convicted of a tasteless gaffe equivalent to, say, the submission by an aspiring young authoress of a nasty satire on Gloria Steinem to *Ms.* magazine.

Of all the doors that Fanny Burney's exemplary career opens and shuts on the history of literary women, the one she closed on the theater is the most tantalizing, for it was a very near miss. She completed *The Witlings* in every detail, even to the stage directions; and so strong was her bent for playwrighting that, in the course of her long career as published novelist and diarist, she wrote seven more plays. Four were tragedies, for neo-Shakespearean tragedy was the kind of play all writers, male and female, then most wanted to write; their doing so is principally what killed the nineteenth-century theater. But it is her three additional comedies that I hope to read in manuscript someday and even see produced, especially *A Busy Day,* the last of them, which has been called "an unpublished masterpiece." And I cannot help speculating what might have happened to the English theater had Jane Austen followed in Fanny Burney's footsteps as a playwright rather than as a novelist.

The idea is not entirely farfetched. Many early women writers known to Austen, including the ultra-respectable Hannah More and Joanna Baillie, wrote for the stage—alas, verse tragedies; and *Lovers' Vows,* the romantic comedy Jane Austen has her amateur actors produce in *Mansfield Park,* was the work of Mrs. Inchbald, a highly successful playwright whom someone has called the Neil Simon of her day. But Mrs. Inchbald was no Fanny Burney; and Fanny Burney was no Jane Austen. Think of the comedies Austen might have written—silvery romantic comedies somewhere between Congreve and Alfred de Musset in their delights.

It was not to be. Instead, the success of the novel *Cecilia* brought Fanny Burney the closest female equivalent of high masculine honors that her society could devise—and here again Burney's career predicts the possibilities and the pitfalls awaiting literary women. For, being a woman, she could not be given a ministerial office, or a bishopric, or an academic chair, or a diplomatic post; instead Fanny Burney was appointed Second Keeper of the Robes to Queen Charlotte. To make a lady novelist a lady in waiting was a lovely idea which turned out to be an absolute disaster, and which would not be repeated in the after-history of rewards for women's literature. Waiting on a lady, even as nice a lady as Queen Charlotte, was to enter upon a state of servitude more stifling even than governessing, soon to be the principal, dreaded resource of intelligent women.

"Now began a slavery of five years," wrote Macaulay of this period of Fanny Burney's life, when she gave up "a wide and splendid circle" and "intellectual pursuits in which she was qualified to excel" for the court life: "five years taken from the best part of life, and wasted in menial drudgery . . . under galling restraints. . . ." "Men, we must suppose," Macaulay continued, "are less patient than women; for we are utterly at a loss to conceive how any human being could endure such a life, while there remained . . . a crossing in want of a sweeper. . . ." It is a rare case of a male critic trying to take the literary woman's point of view and see her special problems, but even Macaulay forgot that women were not hired as crossing sweepers.

Fanny Burney, in any case, had the strength to say that her lady-in-waiting post was killing her, to leave it, and to go after what she wanted: a husband. She found a penniless, aristocratic French émigré to adore and be adored by, and in her choice of husband forecasts the numerous non-Anglo-Saxon gentlemen (whose names include Ossoli and Belloc and Woolf and Goudeket) who would make loyal and supportive husbands for middle-aged literary ladies of the future, as Signor Piozzi was already doing for Mrs. Thrale.

Fanny Burney, now Mme d'Arblay, became pregnant at forty-one and ground out a novel—*Camilla* is her most lifeless production—to support her family. For once in her life, she made the economics of publishing work for her (they were just beginning to be organized to favor the independent author) in the one way that mattered: the acquisition of enough money, all at once, to pay for a house on a little piece of land in the country, which she called Camilla Cottage.

The episode once again is instructive, and shows why novel-writing became the profession of choice for literary women, and even for not particularly literary women whose intelligence and talent might have led them to different kinds of work. Only the novel offered the reward of capital endowment, that lump of money without which middle-class women, whatever their charms, would for long be virtually unmarriageable. Fanny Burney's court post had paid her 200 pounds a year, a wretched sum as Macaulay complained, but probably the highest salary a woman had ever received for respectable work, or would receive for generations to come. *Camilla* made her more than 2,000 pounds, or at least $50,000 in today's money.

The career of journalism, while never so important to English literary women as to French or American, began to open up to a few rare women in England fairly early in the eighteenth century, perhaps because it was so ill paid (almost as poorly paid as translating, which women of George Eliot's caliber would do for a pittance for generations to come). In the nineteenth century Harriet Martineau, for example, held an editorial post for which she received 15 pounds a year; but her first fiction, the *Political Economy* tales which took Martineau not much over two years to write, earned her more than 2,000 pounds.

Charlotte Brontë was dazzled by the first payment from her publishers for *Jane Eyre:* it was 100 pounds, the largest sum of money she had ever seen. There would be five such payments for the novel (probably an unfairly small slice of her publisher's profits) as opposed to the 20 pounds a year Brontë had been earning as a governess. ("My salary is not really more than £16 p.a.," she wrote a friend in 1841, "though it is nominally £20, but the expense of washing will be deducted therefrom." Thus, to arrive at a sense of the real value of a governess' salary, we know that it was five times as much as the cost of laundering a governess' not very extensive wardrobe; we also know that it was about eleven times as much as the price of *Jane Eyre*. Governesses could not afford to buy three-volume novels, or almost anything else.)

The same 20 pounds, on the other hand, was the munificent sum Mrs. Gaskell was paid for a mere short story in 1850. "I stared," she wrote, "and wondered if I was swindling them but I suppose I am not; and Wm has composedly buttoned it up in his pocket." Through Mrs. Gaskell's letters can be traced the subtle and subtly changing attitudes of a successful literary woman to her husband's absolute control, in principle, over her earnings. Married life, however, as we all know, is a matter of practice as well as principle. By the late 1850s Mrs. Gaskell was paying for her own trips abroad out of the proceeds of her fiction, and in 1865 "I did a terribly grand thing! and a secret thing too!" she wrote Charles Eliot Norton. "Only you are in America and can't tell. I bought a house . . . for Mr. Gaskell to retire and for a home for my unmarried daughters." Including furnishings, the house would cost her 3,000 pounds or so, all to be paid for in the style of Camilla Cottage, by a literary woman's fiction.

The economic system that made novel-writing look particularly attractive to Fanny Burney was subscription publishing: that is, soliciting payment in advance of a guinea and a half direct from readers, whose names were printed at the head of the first edition. Among the three hundred subscribers to *Camilla* were some of the greatest names of the day. And there were three names on the list even better known to posterity than to Fanny Burney, for they were those of the leading women novelists, which is to say the leading novelists, of the next generation: Mrs. Radcliffe, Miss Edgeworth, and Miss Austen of Steventon.

Jane Austen was only twenty when she subscribed to *Camilla,* but then, she was also only twenty when she began "First Impressions," the first version of *Pride and Prejudice,* and she had already, in her teens, done a good deal of brilliant apprentice writing in imitation of or satirical reaction to the work of her female predecessors. When *Pride and Prejudice* finally appeared in 1813, women's literature came of age and with it the English novel, for in pure artistry no work in the form has ever surpassed it. It was a remarkable accomplishment of female professionalism, in the mere seventy years or so since *Pamela,* and the mere thirty years or so since *Evelina.** Nor can the two phenomena be separated: the rise of the novel and the rise of women to professional literary status. And ever afterward the makeshift novel, last-born of literary genres, has dominated the literature of the world.

What have women to show for it, besides the money and the prestige? "Men have had every advantage of us in telling their own story," wrote Jane Austen. "Education has been theirs in so much higher a degree; the

---

* Whose author was still alive, still writing fiction. Fanny Burney lived to almost ninety, and the posthumous publication of her diaries almost spanned the Victorian age; in the case of her longevity, her life was not characteristic of literary women after her. But her last exemplary act as a woman writer produced yet another manuscript treasure for the Berg Collection: a dozen densely written pages about the operation she underwent for breast cancer in 1811, before the invention of anesthetic.

pen has been in their hands." Now women seized the pen; and female self-consciousness brought heroinism to literature. As literary women themselves have always been grateful to say, it all went back to the first heroine of letters, Richardson's Pamela, not because of her virtue but because, as she says herself, "I have got such a knack of writing, that when I am by myself, I cannot sit without a pen in my hand."

TRAVELING HEROINISM: GOTHIC FOR HEROINES

> The life of woman rolls forth like a stream from the fountain, or it spreads out into tranquillity like a placid or stagnant lake. In the latter case, the individual grows old among the characters with whom she was born . . . moves in the same circle . . . influences the same class of persons by which she was originally surrounded. The woman of mark and adventure, on the contrary, resembles, in the course of her life, the river whose mid-current and discharge into the ocean are widely removed from each other . . . ; violent changes of time, of place, and of circumstances, hurry her forward from one scene to another, and her adventures will usually be found only connected with each other because they have happened to the same individual.
>
> —Walter Scott

Feminism is one thing, and literary feminism, or what I propose to call heroinism, is another. Take someone like Mary Wollstonecraft, if there ever was anyone else like Mary Wollstonecraft. Here is what she sounds like as a feminist: "Strengthen the female mind by enlarging it, and there will be an end to blind obedience; but as blind obedience is ever sought for by power, tyrants and sensualists are in the right when they endeavour to keep woman in the dark, because the former only want slaves, and the latter a plaything." That splendidly vigorous sentence of agitation, explanation, and denunciation is from Wollstonecraft's *Vindication of the Rights of Woman* (1792).

And here is the sound of literary feminism: "In delineating the Heroine of this Fiction, the Author attempts to develop a character different from those generally portrayed." It is Mary Wollstonecraft's voice as a self-consciously female novelist, at the start of her preface to her first novel, *Mary, a Fiction,* published in 1788. "This woman is neither a Clarissa, a Lady G——, nor a Sophie," she goes on.

> It would be vain to mention the various modifications of these models, as it would to remark, how widely artists wander from nature, when they copy the originals of great masters. They catch the gross parts; but the subtle spirit evaporates. . . .
>
> Those compositions only have power to delight, and carry us willing captives, where the soul of the author is exhibited, and animates the hidden springs. Lost in a pleasing enthusiasm, they live in the scenes they represent; and do not measure their steps in a beaten track. . . .
>
> These chosen few, wish to speak for themselves, and not to be an echo—even of the sweetest sounds. . . . The paradise they ramble in, must be of their own creating. . . .

That is a ramble into the literary imagination, not a stride into polemics. Wollstonecraft's preface is a very early, but hardly unique case of the woman writer's stated intention to create a heroic structure for the female voice in literature, and of her encounter with an order of reality perhaps more intractable than social fact—the literary. Matters of literary form affect her intentions, for the work at hand is to be a novel; matters of tradition, for the novel had already been imprinted with the compelling genius of two masters, Richardson and Rousseau (who made the heroines named Clarissa, Lady G——, and Sophie); matters of readership, for her concern is with captivation and delight; matters of inspiration, for she is an Author already lost to enthusiasm, drunk on hidden springs, and conscious of belonging to the "chosen few"; and matters of language. Those dreadful, sexist little words, the pronouns, have always bedeviled the English writer at moments of heightened awareness that I the Author is a She.

The stammer of incoherence comes into Wollstonecraft's prose as she tries to avoid either male or female forms in her preface. This is especially marked in the pronouns of her remarkable final paragraph:

> In an artless tale, without episodes, the mind of a woman, who has thinking powers is displayed. The female organs have been thought too weak for this arduous employment; and experience seems to justify the assertion. Without arguing physically about *possibilities*—in a fiction, such a being may be allowed to exist; whose grandeur is derived from the operations of its own faculties; not subjugated to opinion; but drawn by the individual from the original source.

A more celebrated document of heroism is George Eliot's Prelude to *Middlemarch,* written almost a century later. "Who that cares much to know the history of man," George Eliot begins, ". . . has not dwelt, at least briefly, on the life of Saint Theresa . . . ?"—a question to which the only possible answer is, lots of people. Carlyle, for example, in his lectures on heroism did not dwell at all on that strong-minded, adventurous, efficient, saintly heroine of the Spanish Counter-Reformation, though he might well have done so had it occurred to him to refer to *any* woman as a type of heroism. But George Eliot, like Gertrude Stein after her, was the kind of writer "Fortunately to be interested in Saint Therese," as Stein put it. To get *Middlemarch* underway, she seized on an episode of the saint's legend of particular meaning to her own feminine self-awareness: "the little girl walking forth one morning hand-in-hand with her still smaller brother, to go and seek martyrdom in the country of the Moors."

> That child-pilgrimage was a fit beginning. Theresa's passionate, ideal nature demanded an epic life: what were many-volumed romances of chivalry and the social conquests of a brilliant girl to her? Her flame quickly burned up that light fuel; and, fed from within, soared after some illimitable satisfaction, some object which would never justify weariness, which would reconcile self-despair with the rapturous consciousness of life beyond self. She found her epos in the reform of a religious order.

Between Mary Wollstonecraft's Advertisement and George Eliot's Prelude lies much of the range of aspiration toward heroinism in women's literature, and much of the failure as well. Wollstonecraft's intention was to make an intellectual heroine, the "woman who has thinking powers"; but the thinking heroine is not the subject of the fumbling, tortured sketch of virginal sexuality that *Mary, a Fiction* turned out to be. Where Mary Wollstonecraft did make a sizable contribution to imaginative literature, it was not with the intellectual but with the passionate heroine—the woman in love, the fully sexual being.

George Eliot seems to have had in mind the heroine as leader and reformer, with a great cause toward which to adventure, in which to absorb her epic energies. But for reasons some of which she gave further on in the Prelude, she hardly made such a figure out of Dorothea Brooke in *Middlemarch*. There was to be "no epic life" for Dorothea, no "constant unfolding of far-resonant action"; instead she was indeed to be, as George Eliot said herself, "a tragic failure" as a heroine. Heroism is always an awkward focus of the literary imagination, whether the author is male or female, and never was more so than in the age when women first found their literary voice, as Mario Praz has pointed out in his studies of "The Hero in Crisis" and "the Romantic Agony" in the nineteenth century. For all writers, female and male, the clash between intention and realization is the drama of literary creation itself. And where *heroinism* is concerned, the by-products of the struggle—changes in literary form and language, in tone, imagery, setting—are often more interesting and more important than the particular heroines it has produced.

As a massive force for change in literature, heroinism was born, like so much else that was revolutionary, in the last decades of the eighteenth century and the first of the nineteenth. We still have an imperfect idea of the numbers and quality of the women writers at work in that period, one which resembles our own in the sense that what Gina Luria calls "The Feminist Controversy" was present in the consciousness of every writer, whatever his or her "sexual politics." Professor Luria's reprint series for Garland Publishing of forty or so volumes by Catharine Macaulay, Mary Hays, Helen Maria Williams, Amelia Opie, Jane West, and others; and Pierre Fauchery's massive new study of *La Destinée féminine* in European fiction of the eighteenth century; and Philippe Séjourné's staggering tabulations of the hundreds of novels written by women at the end of the century in England alone—all indicate that Mary Wollstonecraft was not the only, just the most brilliant of turn-of-the-century feminists in England, America, and on the Continent.

Wollstonecraft's radicalism, however, makes only one end of the spectrum of opinion that colors the writings of the self-conscious women of her day. In the 1780s, 1790s, and 1800s, feminism touched them all, from those who supported to those who opposed its doctrines, with all the range of possible attitudes (including apparent indifference to controversy) that lie between: the elitism of Mme de Staël, the Evangelicalism of Hannah More, the conservatism of Maria Edgeworth, the cautious prudery of Fanny Burney, the pedagogical hauteur of Mme de Genlis, the Americanism of Susanna Rowson, the escapism of Mrs. Radcliffe, the irony of Jane Austen.

Hannah More, who was called the She-Bishop in petticoats, pronounced herself "invincibly resolved" never even to read Wollstonecraft's *Vindication,* because she herself strongly favored female "subordination"; and Miss More wrote her *Coelebs in Search of a Wife* to correct Mme de Staël's dangerous ideas about the woman of genius. But Mme de Staël recognized a fellow spirit when she gave *Coelebs* one of the best reviews it received, in *Le Constitutionnel;* and the clever and spirited Mary Berry, whose journals and letters reflect the ideal female reader of the period, found it "amazing" how close Hannah More came in her views on female education to those of Mary Wollstonecraft. "H. More will, I dare say, be very angry when she hears this," chuckled Miss Berry.

Jane Austen turned twenty in 1795. In the brilliant spoofs and whimsical parodies that make up her early writings, there can be found a satirical response to every kind of literary feminism that Austen encountered in her predecessors and contemporaries. *Northanger Abbey* is the best-known because the most fully developed of such Austen responses. There she mocks the Gothic heroine, and "the author," who, she writes at the end, "must share in the glory she so liberally bestows"—a choice of pronoun indicating how far Austen took it for granted that the author of

novels was a she. Gothic novels in particular are the target of Austen's satire in *Northanger Abbey,* where she points to the Gothic as a woman's
self-conscious creation.

Ann Radcliffe, the greatest practitioner of the Gothic novel, was the
most popular writer of her day and, in her moral views, among the most
conventional. She is surely the last of turn-of-the-century writers from
whom we would expect the promulgation of feminist doctrine. Nevertheless, the Gothic fantasies of Mrs. Radcliffe are a locus of heroinism which,
ever since, women have turned to feminist purposes. Feminism and heroinism can often be seen to touch in women's literature, but they are not
the same.

• • •

Ann Radcliffe began to write fiction at almost the same moment as
Mary Wollstonecraft, and she too had an idea of female selfhood. But it
was not the thinking woman, not the loving woman, but the traveling
woman: the woman who moves, who acts, who copes with vicissitude and
adventure. For Mrs. Radcliffe, the Gothic novel was a device to send
maidens on distant and exciting journeys without offending the proprieties.
In the power of villains, her heroines are forced to do what they could
never do alone, whatever their ambitions: scurry up the top of pasteboard
Alps, spy out exotic vistas, penetrate bandit-infested forests. And indoors,
inside Mrs. Radcliffe's castles, her heroines can scuttle miles along corri-
dors, descend into dungeons, and explore secret chambers without a
chaperone, because the Gothic castle, however much in ruins, is still an indoor and therefore freely female space. In Mrs. Radcliffe's hands, the
Gothic novel became a feminine substitute for the picaresque, where
heroines could enjoy all the adventures and alarms that masculine heroes
had long experienced, far from home, in fiction.

Charlotte Brontë, with characteristic clarity, discerned the traveling
heroine in Mrs. Radcliffe's work. In *Shirley* she has a young woman
named Caroline Helstone walk into a room in Yorkshire and find there an
extraordinary little girl named Rose Yorke, who is reading *The Italian* by
Mrs. Radcliffe. Without waiting to be asked, the girl volunteers her view of
the novel: "in reading it, you feel as if you were far away from England—
really in Italy—under another sort of sky,—that blue sky of the south
which travellers describe."

> "You are sensible of that, Rose?"
> "It makes me long to travel, Miss Helstone."
> "When you are a woman, perhaps, you may be able to gratify your
> wish."
> "I mean to make a way to do so, if one is not made for me. I
> cannot live always in Briarfield. The whole world is not very large

compared with creation: I must see the outside of our own round planet at least."

"How much of its outside?"

"First this hemisphere where we live; then the other. I am resolved that my life shall be a life: not a black trance like the toad's, buried in marble; nor a long, slow death like yours in Briarfield Rectory."

"Like mine! What can you mean, child?"

"Might you not as well be tediously dying, as for ever shut up in that glebe-house—a place that, when I pass it, always reminds me of a windowed grave? I never see any movement about the door; I never hear a sound from the wall; I believe smoke never issues from the chimneys. What do you do there?"

"I sew, I read, I learn lessons."

"Are you happy?"

"Should I be happier wandering alone in strange countries, as you wish to do?"

"Much happier, even if you did nothing but wander . . . if you only went on and on, like some enchanted lady in a fairy tale, you might be happier than now . . . you would pass many a hill, wood, and watercourse, each perpetually altering in aspect. . . . Nothing changes in Briarfield Rectory. . . ."

"Is change necessary to happiness?"

"Yes."

"Is it synonymous with it?"

"I don't know; but I feel monotony and death to be almost the same."

That marvelous passage is the finest of all critical responses to the particular kind of heroinism, traveling heroinism, in the Radcliffean Gothic.

The travel motif in women's literature seems, however, to require separating into its two distant kinds: indoor travel and outdoor travel. Outdoor travel is imaginary planetary travel of the kind familiar to someone like Mrs. Radcliffe from the old romances. (We would be justified in surmising, if she did not tell us herself, that a "favourite volume" in the "little library" that the heroine carries about with her in *The Mysteries of Udolpho* is Ariosto's *Orlando Furioso*.) For outdoor travel the Radcliffe heroine becomes, in Brontë's phrase, "the enchanted lady in the fairy tale," who flies through the air independent of the laws of gravity, time, perspective, and, certainly, of real travel. So Emily in *Udolpho* "travels several leagues" in the whisk of a phrase; sleeps one night "in a town on the skirts of Languedoc" and the next morning "enters Gascony." Without apparent effort she "ascends the Apennines," and from their heights easily espies the waves of "the distant Mediterranean."

The naïveté of her landscape painting makes one of the lingering, mysterious charms of Mrs. Radcliffe's fiction, which we moderns welcome as a touch of the surreal. It originated, as does so much of value to the literary imagination, in ignorance and inexperience. For when she wrote *The Mysteries of Udolpho* Ann Radcliffe had never been out of England, had hardly been anywhere but London and Bath. The marvelous Italy she wrote about came from paintings, theater backdrops, and travel books by men who had made the grand tour closed to her by reason of her sex and social class. Women were only beginning to be travelers in the eighteenth century, especially highly placed women like Lady Mary Wortley Montagu. Most important to Mrs. Radcliffe was the unconventional, distinctly female travel book that Mr. Thrale's widow wrote about Italy, once marriage to Signor Piozzi made her own first journey to Italy possible.

The reader of Mrs. Radcliffe's novels "is invited to share in a transport," writes Karl Kroeber, "to cross over into a new kind of experience." Outdoor travel in the Gothic is exactly that transport, "travel combined with rapture," through an exotic, impossible landscape, ever changing, ever delightful to the senses. Many a woman writer after Radcliffe has responded to the restrictions of her life with the same kind of romance, as the titles alone of some of their books testify: *The Wanderer* (Fanny Burney), *Lettres d'un voyageur* (George Sand), *The Wide, Wide World* (the American best seller, by Susan B. Warner), *The Voyage Out* (Virginia Woolf). A recent example is *Jerusalem the Golden* by the clever English novelist Margaret Drabble, where the Jerusalem of her title is London, and her heroine is spun loose from hideous midlands suburbia by that magic carpet of modern youth, the state scholarship. At the end, Drabble's heroine dreams of "a tender blurred world" ahead, "thick with starry inhabitants, where there was no ending, no parting, but an eternal vast incessant rearrangement. . . ."

George Eliot's Saint Theresa is the patron saint of literary transport for her addiction as a girl to the reading of romances of chivalry, as well as for the legend of her venturing forth, with a brother in tow, to the country of the Moors. A similar dream of girlhood is the theme of the opening poem of *April Twilights* (1903), Willa Cather's first published book. There Cather invokes the twilight romancing she shared with her brothers "On an island in a western river"; an invocation

> To the memory of our vanished kingdom,
> To our days of war and ocean venture,
> Brave with brigandage and sack of cities;
> To the Odysseys of summer mornings,
> Starry wonder-tales of nights in April.

* * *

Indoor travel, however, is a more serious affair, because more possible for women; and Mrs. Radcliffe's inventive use of the Gothic setting for indoor travel produced a richer literary tradition. For indoors, in the long, dark, twisting, haunted passageways of the Gothic castle, there is travel with danger, travel with exertion—a challenge to the heroine's enterprise, resolution, ingenuity, and physical strength. Indoors is where Consuelo, George Sand's superheroine,

> courageously descended the steep and winding stairs . . . had sufficient coolness to look down toward the opening in the subterranean passage . . . descended fifty steps, with that address and agility which young ladies educated in drawing-rooms can never attain, but which the children of the people acquire in their sports and pastimes. . . .
>   She continued to advance in the midst of a thousand obstacles. . . . Enormous stones blocked up her path; gigantic bats came striking against her lantern . . . she felt her courage increase with each fresh danger. . . when on turning a sharp angle . . . petrified by surprise and frozen with terror, she came face to face with . . .

Mrs. Radcliffe was a more gifted writer of that sort of heroinism—and a few pages further on in *Consuelo,* George Sand cites her as model.

The Castle of the Giants section of *Consuelo* is in fact the weakest part of George Sand's longest, most variable, most ambitious novel. More interesting is what she does with Gothic travel in its long finale, the *Countess of Rudolstadt* volumes. They provide a mystical-humanitarian fantasy of Masonic ritual (for one of Sand's themes is the early history of secret societies). They are also a story of initiation, of testing-through-trial, with enough music in the background to suggest a novelistic *Magic Flute. La Comtesse de Rudolstadt* powerfully affected nineteenth-century writers as disparate as Dostoevsky and Whitman, among many others. The whole of *Consuelo* appears today, in the opinion of the editors of the recent Garnier edition, to reflect George Sand's ambition to provide for French literature a *Bildungsroman,* a novel of formation and apprenticeship to life equivalent to Goethe's *Wilhelm Meister*—only "the hero would not be Man, but Woman."

The mysterious maze of traps and hazards through which Consuelo is led at the end by her benign but frightening captors, *les Invisibles,* is a Gothic interior; and insofar as Consuelo proves herself through courage and self-control in the face of physical dangers, she is a Gothic heroine. When I think of the distance covered, in only half a century, between Consuelo of Rudolstadt and Emily of Udolpho, I cannot quite, though I should, resist the temptation to quote "You've come a long way, baby" from that ad which sells cigarettes to the liberated woman.

It was *only* indoors, in Mrs. Radcliffe's day, that the heroine of a novel could travel brave and free, and stay respectable. Today young women make headlines by hijacking planes and carrying machine guns to bank robberies, but quite impossible for the Emilys and Evelinas of early women's fiction were the moderately adventurous outdoor activities by

which, say, a Tom Jones could establish himself as a hero: blacking an
eye, climbing a tree, fighting a duel, joining a regiment, poaching, roister-
ing, and tramping. For heroines, the mere walking was suspect. "Whither
have you been rambling so early?" asks Emily's aunt of Emily in the garden, near the start of *The Mysteries of Udolpho.* "I don't approve of these
solitary walks." As late as the high-Victorian years there would still be
aunts to censure heroines like Aurora Leigh, who in celebration of her
twentieth birthday,

> bounded forth
> At early morning, —would not wait so long
> As even to snatch my bonnet by the strings,
> But, brushing a green trail across the lawn
> With my gown in the dew, took will and way
> Among the acacias and the shrubberies,
> To fly my fancies in the open air
> And keep my birthday, till my aunt awoke
> To stop good dreams.

A whole history of literary feminism might be told in terms of the metaphor of walking*—how much of a metaphor, all Book II of *Aurora Leigh*
makes clear. Mrs. Browning's heroine rejects her lover's proposal because
she chooses "to walk another way than his," and her aunt scorns Aurora's
"groping in the dark," her childlike incapacity "to choose a way to walk."
Country walking is Jane Austen's principal symbol for the joys of independent womanhood; and city walking is Charlotte Brontë's somber evocation of its fears. We do not need to read the scene of Lucy Snowe's night-
time arrival in Villette to know that street-walking is, still today, something
different for women than for men.

The prohibitions on outdoor female activities must account for the
proud place of the tomboy in women's literature. For in every age, whatever the social rules, there has always been one time of a woman's life, the
years before puberty, when walking, running, climbing, battling, and tumbling are as normal female as they are male activities. As Mary Wollstonecraft put it, "a girl will always be a romp"; we say *tomboy,* in some
derision, but the figure looms large, and as more than a comic diversion, in
the heroine-creating imagination. George Eliot's Maggie Tulliver and Mrs.
Gaskell's Mollie come first to mind, but for its complexity of spiritual,
social, and racial implications there is no rival to the figure of Topsy in
Uncle Tom's Cabin—the first great portrait of the Bad Boy in American
fiction, only she happens to be a girl.

* I have offered the merest footnote to that history, some speculations on Dickens's response to women's literature, in an article on *Bleak House* (*The Dickensian,*
January 1973). A whole chapter would have to be given to the transformation of
George Sand's brilliant *Lettres d'un voyageur* from a wanderer's reverie, on the
open road, to a woman's exploration of the world, at home.

Mrs. Radcliffe's heroines, as far as I know them, do not begin life as tomboys, but Jane Austen made up the deficiency in *Northanger Abbey*. Catherine Morland is the only Austen heroine—but, because of her taste for Gothic adventure, she is certainly the right one—to begin life preferring cricket to dolls. "She was moreover," writes Austen, "noisy and wild, hated confinement and cleanliness, and loved nothing so well in the world as rolling down the green slope at the back of the house."

The celebrated chapters of George Sand's *Histoire de ma vie* where she tells of her school years are a classic of tomboy literature. As a girl, George Sand was virtually incarcerated in a convent school (under British nuns) which in her autobiography she makes look very much like a Gothic castle: the sprawling old buildings, complicated passageways, mysterious garrets and subcellars, and high walls. But far from being repressed by confinement, Sand discovered during her school years the delights of indoor adventure. She tells of taking leadership of a group of the hardiest girls, who called themselves the *diables;* she tells of exploring subterranean passages, entering forbidden gardens, scrambling along rooftops, jumping from windows, and carrying on a fantasy chase, that lasted several years, for a non-existent buried victim of Gothic villainy (all mock-Gothic experiences of life in a girls' school which Charlotte Brontë was writing about, at almost the same moment, in her novel *Villette*). And it is appropriately in this context that George Sand digresses most substantially to pay tribute to the influence upon her of Ann Radcliffe's fiction.

The Victorian woman writer's interest in Mrs. Radcliffe, long after her kind of mannered and genteel Gothic fiction had vanished from the literary mainstream, is a minor but interesting sign that women's literature flourished on its own traditions. More significant is the whole thrust in women's writings toward physical heroics, toward risk-taking and courage-proving as a gauge of heroism, long after male writers had succumbed to the prevailing antiheroic, quiescent temper of the bourgeois century, and admitted, with whatever degree of regret or despair, that adventure was no longer a possibility of modern life. Latecomers to literature as they were, and still bedazzled with the strengths of feminine self-assertion, women writers of the nineteenth century were long reluctant to succumb to the ennui, the spleen, the *tedium vitae* of the *mal du siècle*. "Qu'est-ce que l'audace?" cries Lélia, "et qui n'en a pas?" at the start of one of the extraordinary aria-like passages in George Sand's most Romantic work. Here she puts in question the possibility of bravery in modern life.

"Who loves life, in our time? We speak of courage, when recklessness serves to further some good end, but when it simply risks a destiny without value, then should we not call it inertia?

"Inertia, Sténio! that is the sickness of our hearts, that is the great scourge of this age. Only negative virtues remain; we are brave only because we can no longer feel fear. Alas, yes! everything is used up, even the weaknesses, even the vices. . . .

"When there was still energy on earth, men fought with prudence, with calculation, with deceit. Life was a perpetual combat in which the bravest drew back incessantly from danger, for to be most brave was to live the longest in the midst of perils and hostility. Since civilization has made life easy and calm for everyone, everyone finds it monotonous and without savor. . . .

"Alas! Sténio, we are become nothing, we are no longer good or bad, we are not even cowards, we are inert. . . ."

But the very pulse of the prose (which my translation hardly captures) belies George Sand's theme, and makes *Lélia* a work of a different kind from Senancour's *Obermann* (that early plaint of the *mal du siècle* which George Sand helped bring to the attention of her contemporaries, including Matthew Arnold). In *Lélia* (1833) George Sand was claiming all of Romanticism for women, its guilty frenzy, its warped sexuality, its despair. But by her willful creation of *une enfant du siècle*—a *girl*-child of the century—she showed the countervailing force of heroism in an antiheroic age. The very context of Lélia's outburst on inertia (cited above) is a locus of heroism. "I have brought you to the valley of the desert," says Sténio to Lélia—

"I have led you, Lélia, over the precipices. You have braved without fear all the dangers of the journey; with a tranquil eye you have measured the glacial crevices . . . and traversed the cataracts. . . . You have not once trembled, Lélia; and I, how I have been shaken . . . my heart's blood frozen, and my heart stopped in its beating to see you pass over the abyss, reckless, indifferent, glancing at the sky and careless of where you placed your narrow feet. You are very brave and very strong, Lélia! When you say your soul is worn out, you lie; no man is possessed of greater confidence and greater bravery than you."

"—What is bravery?" replied Lélia. . . . *Qu'est-ce que l'audace?*

Bravery survives, even today, as an anachronistic ideal of literary feminism; but novelists like Carol Hill and Erica Jong who lay claim to reviving the picaresque make the mistake of sending their heroines out of doors for not very brave adventures with prostitution and adultery (and with a complaisant cuckold of a husband to write their traveler's checks). I suspect that Gothic heroism at its strongest still survives in the indoor setting, and in one more somber than the girl's school, more real than the castle: the insane asylum. A phenomenon of literary feminism in the early 1960s was the near-simultaneous appearance of three novels by three gifted writers, very different in tone, yet all dealing with madness in the institutional setting. Sylvia Plath's *The Bell Jar* is the best-known, but of at least equal quality are *I Never Promised You a Rose Garden* by Hannah Green and *Faces in the Water* by the New Zealand novelist Janet Frame.

That women as well as men go mad and women too commit suicide is, alas, a feminist assertion. But I mention these three novels here mainly to suggest that their setting, the asylum itself, becomes for these writers an elaborated, enclosed, and peculiarly feminine testing ground for survival. There are the large, spreading, mysteriously complicated buildings; the harsh guards and strange rules; the terrifying inmates; the privations, restraints, and interrogations; the well-meant, but indubitable torture of electric shock treatment. The last is evoked in Anne Sexton's 1960 book of poems, reflecting a similar institutional experience, called *To Bedlam and Part Way Back:*

> Black arms of thunder strapped
> upon us; . . .
> . . . and that suddenly inadequate stain
>
> of lightning belling around our skin.
> > "The Exorcists"

It is at least a certainty that long ago, when women's literature was beginning, the first novel by a woman to use the asylum as a setting belonged to the Gothic tradition and drew directly from it. That was Mary Wollstonecraft's idea, in the extremely interesting novel called *The Wrongs of Woman, or Maria* on which she was working when she died in the aftermath of childbirth, at the age of thirty-eight. (Godwin published the two volumes she had completed among her posthumous works, in 1798.) The year before, in the *Analytical Review,* Wollstonecraft had reviewed Mrs. Radcliffe's *The Italian* with an enthusiasm perhaps unexpected from a feminist. Mrs. Radcliffe had an "uncommon talent," she wrote, "for exhibiting . . . the vague and horrid shapes which imagination bodies forth"; and her "spell, by which we are led, again and again, round the same magic circle, is the spell of genius."

In the opening sentences of *Maria,* Wollstonecraft pointed to her Gothic source with similar imagery:

> Abodes of horror have frequently been described, and castles, filled with spectres and chimeras, conjured up by the magic spell of genius to harrow the soul, and absorb the wondering mind. But, formed of such stuff as dreams are made of, what were they to the mansion of despair, in one corner of which Maria sat, endeavouring to recal her scattered thoughts!

The real "mansion of despair" is an asylum, for Maria, though far from mad, has been forcibly imprisoned by her tyrant husband. As a setting, Wollstonecraft's asylum is detailed in reference to the Gothic castle model —the iron gates and grated dungeon windows, the manacled arms and

ruthless jailers, the desolate walks and ruined turrets, and especially the
"groans and shrieks" of Maria's fellow inmates, which "were no unsub-
stantial sounds of whistling winds, or startled birds, modulated by a romantic fancy . . . ; but such tones of misery as carry a dreadful certainty
to the heart."

For Mary Wollstonecraft, the terrors, the restraints, the dangers of the
Gothic novel were not the fantasies but the realities of a woman's life.
"Was not the world a vast prison," she wrote further on in *Maria,* "and
women born slaves?"

. . .

We know next to nothing about Mrs. Radcliffe's life and personality,
but we can be certain that she was never a feminist in any of the ways
associated with Mary Wollstonecraft. She was married young to a journalist, an Oxford man; she was childless; she was shy, and sensitive about
her respectability as woman and author. It was an extreme sensitivity, like
Fanny Burney's, and I would guess from the same source: an awkwardly
ambiguous social position. Fanny Burney's father gave music lessons to
the aristocracy, and thus stood somewhere between the servant class at the
bottom and, because of his genius (he was the leading musical scholar of
the age), the top of English society. Ann Radcliffe's father, whose name
was Ward, was a petty shopkeeper, but he dealt in the most aristocratic of
eighteenth-century goods, Wedgwood pottery. We shall never know exactly why Mrs. Radcliffe shaped the Gothic novel as a structure for
heroinism, but how she did so is at least worth a closer look.

In her best-known work, *The Mysteries of Udolpho* (1794), the narrative as a whole is designed to accord with the rhythms of a woman's life.
Little critical attention has been paid to this shaping aspect of her Gothic,
because the critics' attention, like that of Mrs. Radcliffe's vast popular audience, has been distracted by the isolated episodes of terror that make up
the bulk of her *Mysteries:* the black veil, the burned manuscript, the mysterious nun, the ghostly musician, the living corpse, and so on. But she
blocks out the narrative in terms of female childhood, youth, and faded
maturity. *Udolpho* begins as an idyl—somewhere out of England, sometime in the past—the details are nothing, only the atmosphere matters: a
muted, gentle, or—Mrs. Radcliffe's favorite meaningless word—a pensive
serenity full of groves, streams, and vistas.

Emily's birthplace is in the valley—called La Vallée—where, after her
brothers have conveniently died in infancy, and her mother has conveniently slipped away into a pensive death, Emily is left an only child, alone
with her father, the perfect man: wise, kind, tender, indulgent, noble in
birth and mind, a former ornament of the "gay and busy scenes of the

world" to which he wisely prefers "the forms of pastoral simplicity." Emily's father also dies early in the novel, but his influence persists as a moral force forever. It is the father who first warns Emily against the *dangers* of sensibility, a theme which pervades all Mrs. Radcliffe's fiction, to the surprise of her readers—for what is her Gothic novel, with its groans, shrieks, and tremors, but a subspecies of sensibility fiction? It is sensibility, however, with a difference. "Above all, my dear Emily," says the father, "do not indulge in the pride of fine feeling, the romantic error of amiable minds. . . . Beware of priding yourself on the gracefulness of sensibility. . . . Always remember how much more valuable is the strength of sensibility." The strength of sensibility is in fact what Mrs. Radcliffe's heroinism is all about.

Emily's father returns to play an important negative role, I rather suspect, in the person of the villain Montoni—one of those sinister Italian gentlemen that Ann Radcliffe found in the writings of her favorite English author (Shakespeare) but that she transformed into what looks very like a shattered mirror image of the impossibly good father of her imagination. Thus she seems to provide Emily with a father who is at one moment gentle, kind, and indulgent, and the next moment is whisked off the stage to be replaced by the father who is severe, demanding, nasty, and perverse. Montoni is of course not officially Emily's father; he plays the bad father role in his capacity of uncle by marriage. (Schedoni, the most splendidly sinister of Radcliffe's villains, in *The Italian,* is related to the fatherless heroine there by closer ties: he is her father's wicked brother and her mother's dreadful second husband.)

One critic of Mrs. Radcliffe, William Ruff, is so strongly impressed by her feminine bias that he wonders whether she should be considered a Gothic novelist at all, but rather a novelist of taste; and much closer in attitude than we have suspected to her apparent satirist, Jane Austen. They both wrote for a feminine audience, Professor Ruff writes, "and their point of view toward decorum is feminine." Decorum, or taste in manners, is what he sees as the central issue of Mrs. Radcliffe's *Udolpho:* "no matter how often her story threatens to be about horrid deeds, her heroine stands in the foreground of her books, pure, tender-minded, elegant, and conscious of the etiquette each situation demands." Leaving Jane Austen aside for the moment, I would suggest that where Ann Radcliffe writes about the horrors of a woman's life with a woman's sense of decorum, there she is very close to Fanny Burney, whose career as a novelist began over ten years before and ended over ten years after Mrs. Radcliffe's.

Fanny Burney's principal gift, as diarist and novelist, was for comic dialogue, and Mrs. Radcliffe, as far as we know, never cracked a smile, yet the real relationship between them has emerged more clearly with the passage of time. This is not merely because *The Mysteries of Udolpho* reads much less frightening today, more down to earth (and, all unconsciously, much funnier); while *Evelina* (and *Cecilia* and *Camilla* as well) reads much less funny than Burney intended, much more strained, extreme, fantastic, and even frightening in the impossible trials to which the heroine is subjected. The perils that threaten *A Young Lady's Entrance into the World* (the subtitle of *Evelina*) seem to issue from the same grim realities of eighteenth-century girlhood that inspired Mrs. Radcliffe's Gothic: the same unjust accusations and uncaused severities; the same feminine malice and masculine cruelty; the restraints on her freedom, all the way to actual imprisonment; the mysterious, unexplained social rituals; the terrible need always to appear, as well as always to be, virtuous; and, over all, the terrible danger of slippage from the respectable to the unrespectable class of womanhood. If Burney and Radcliffe both traffic in real female fears, there is however an important difference between them beyond the presence or absence of the comic spirit: that is, their different sense of a woman's main guarantee of her security in the respectable class. For Fanny Burney, that guarantee was the social circle in which the heroine fixed herself, through marriage or other means; while for Ann Radcliffe it was property.

Here I would differ with Professor Ruff, when he writes that "two-thirds" of *The Mysteries of Udolpho* "is about the course of true love and not about gothic horrors at all"—for property seems to loom larger than love in *Udolpho*. The end of Emily's childhood idyl in The Valley is not her father's death, but an event which precedes it: his ruin. Through no fault of his own, but the collapse of some financial gentleman offstage, the family suddenly loses its money, its property, its valley of pastoral simplicity. This is the real start of Emily's adventures, not her meeting with her lover. A lover is of course provided; his name is Valancourt; Emily will duly marry him at the distant end of all her trials. But property interests dominate the second half of the novel, and account for the curiously delayed end of the love story.

In chapter 29, the death of her aunt makes Emily an heiress; in most of the ensuing chapters, she is engaged gently, pensively, yet firmly in the consolidation of her property. Her struggle with the villain Montoni is essentially legalistic, concerns her property rights, and "instead of overcoming her with despondency," the struggle

> roused all the latent powers of her fortitude into action; and the property which she would willingly have resigned to secure the peace of her aunt, she resolved that no common sufferings of her own should ever compel her to give to Montoni. For Valancourt's sake also she determined to preserve these estates, since they would afford that competency by which she hoped to secure the comfort of their future lives. . . .

It is lovely of Emily to think of Valancourt; but she seems to enjoy her legal debates with Montoni, and certainly relishes "the day devoted entirely to business" that she spends in chapter 48, when at last she starts to play the châtelaine.

Emily comes through all her horrors, and comes face to face at last with Valancourt, not on the final page of *Udolpho* but a good fifty pages from the end. That leaves enough time for Emily to resolve her prudent doubts about her lover's character, which significantly center on the rumor that he is a gambling man. The rumor is, happily, unjustified, and the marriage takes place in the final chapter, the last page of which is given over to legacies, estates, marriage portions, and, of course, the moral of the story: "that innocence, though oppressed by injustice, shall, supported by patience, finally triumph over misfortune!" To those who have never quite made it to the end of *The Mysteries of Udolpho,* it is a pleasure to report that Emily ends her days in the pastoral serenity of The Valley, pensively musing on her father's memory, and confident that his injunction—to demonstrate the strength of sensibility—has been obeyed.

If this hasty sketch of the heroine of *Udolpho* as a kind of Capability Emily sounds like a travesty of the familiar Gothic heroine, that is because of what was done with the figure by the male writers who followed Mrs. Radcliffe. For most of them—an interesting exception is the American novelist Charles Brockden Brown—the Gothic heroine was quintessentially a defenseless victim, a weakling, a whimpering, trembling, cowering little piece of propriety whose sufferings are the source of her erotic fascination. The Marquis de Sade, for example, is known to have admired Mrs. Radcliffe's work. But that the sadistic ramifications of the Gothic were not at all her intention emerges from the one piece of almost certain information that we have about her literary development. She seems to have been dismayed by Matthew Lewis's avowed imitation of her work in his shocking novel called *The Monk;* and in defense of her genre she then wrote *The Italian,* a work which is at once a borrowing from and a severe corrective to "Monk" Lewis's erotic fantasy. *The Italian* proved to be Mrs. Radcliffe's last novel, though she lived a quarter of a century after its publication in 1797. It contains her best villain and best writing; its heroine, who spends many of the early scenes as a genteel but self-supporting needlewoman, is somewhat closer to Frances, the little lace-mender in Charlotte Brontë's *The Professor,* than she is to the garroted, raped, and debauched ladies in Lewis and de Sade. Whatever use was made of her fiction, the erotic flame burned very feebly in Mrs. Radcliffe.

The best formulation I have seen of the pressure of heroinism on the Gothic novel is something Elliot Gose writes in his study of *The Irrational in the Nineteenth Century Novel*. There Gose opposes what he calls "Mrs. Radcliffe's concern with the stability of her heroine's identity" to Monk

Lewis's "revelling in the disintegration of his hero's identity." Stability and integrity are indeed the major resources of the Radcliffe heroine; her sensibility and her decorum never falter; and however rapid or perilous her journeys, the *lares* and *penates* of proper English girlhood travel with her. She always manages to pack up her books, her sketching materials, and her lute, no matter how swiftly she is abducted from, say, Venice to the Castle of Udolpho. Locked up in a gloomy, haunted chamber high in a castle tower, Emily "arranged her little library . . . took out her drawing utensils, and was tranquil enough to be pleased with the thought of sketching the sublime scenes beheld from her windows." No mean-minded, authoritarian older man (the source of most of Emily's troubles) can be a match for such a young lady. "She opposed his turbulence and indignation," writes Mrs. Radcliffe in a sentence that is my choice for Emily's epitaph, "only by the mild dignity of a superior mind, but the gentle firmness of her conduct served to exasperate still more his resentment, since it compelled him to feel his own inferiority."

No matter what happens, Emily is always correctly employed, correctly behaved, God knows correctly spoken—and of course correctly dressed. One particularly tight corner of *The Mysteries of Udolpho* sticks in my mind: a moment of great confusion at the castle, when Emily effects a rapid escape with the help of the faithful Ludovico. Down the castle staircase she flies, along the vaulted passage, through the gates, over the broken road. They travel in breathless silence through the Apennines, in the "feeble light which a rising moon threw among the foliage," until they come to a little town where, in the "morning light now glimmering on the horizon," Emily at last appears to the rustic inhabitants. "Her appearance excited some surprise," Mrs. Radcliffe tells us, "for she was without a hat." It is with relief that we learn on the next page that Emily can cope, even with this emergency: she has "purchased a little straw hat, such as was worn by the peasant girls of Tuscany. . . ."

This kind of novel-writing deserves being laughed at. The author plays with her heroine, dresses and undresses her, transports and arranges her, much as a girl plays with her doll; there is indeed a witty passage in the letters of Mary Brunton, a novelist of the generation following Radcliffe's, where Mrs. Brunton describes her own heroine-making in terms of playing with dolls. Mary Brunton's *Self-Control* was the novel that Jane Austen read more than once, making fun of it each time, because the heroine has some extraordinary adventures hurtling down Canadian rapids in a canoe.

But there are two points worth making about traveling heroinism that are not funny. There is something very English about Mrs. Radcliffe's doll heroines (just as there is something very Scottish about Mrs. Brunton's); and something of perhaps solider historical than literary significance. They

remind us of all the British ladies who in point of fact did set sail for
Canada and India and Africa, with their bonnets, veils, and gloves, their
teacups and tea cozies—ill-equipped for vicissitudes of travel, climate, and
native mutiny, but well-equipped to preserve their identity as proper Englishwomen. Emily in her straw bonnet, in flight from Udolpho, should be
played by Katharine Hepburn in the style of that proper but heroic
spinster on the decks of the *African Queen*. The dauntless British spinsters
who carried British decorum around the planet were real people, and one
of them was in Charlotte Brontë's mind when she wrote her celebration of
the traveling heroism in Mrs. Radcliffe's *The Italian*. Her friend Mary
Taylor had just emigrated to New Zealand; and little Rose Yorke in
Shirley, who dreams of travel to another hemisphere, was no fantasy but a
portrait of the Yorkshire child that Mary Taylor had been. She became
one of the leading early New Zealand settlers, the founder and manager of
an important Wellington business, and she was also the most radical
feminist Brontë knew. In her letters from New Zealand she wrote Charlotte
that she approved her portrait in *Shirley,* found the Yorkshire scenes true
to memory, but she denounced her friend's hesitant feminism and never
excused Charlotte Brontë's failure to emigrate to the other side of the
planet.

The domination of the English novel by women at the turn of the
eighteenth century came to an end for a while at least when Walter Scott,
rather late in life, put aside poetry for fiction. In many critical statements
Scott paid his debt in full, and with characteristic graciousness, to all the
women novelists, Mrs. Radcliffe among them. To her he owed not only
much of his atmosphere, much of his handling of the excitements of adventure, but also much of his way with heroism, for Scott, too, played with
dolls, though they were masculine. The heroes of the Waverley novels, as
Scott himself was the first to say, were a "very amiable, and very insipid
sort of young men." In Scott's famous phrase for Waverley, "the hero is a
sneaking piece of imbecility." Yet Scott's defense was that he used the
hero as a transparent medium through which to show the heroic deeds and
romantic scenes of the past. Surely no one has ever accused Scott of weak-
minded effeminacy because he made Waverley a model of British legality
and gentlemanly decorum.

In an important way, however, the Radcliffe heroine differs from the
Scott hero: though stable in her identity, she changes in a woman's way, as
Waverley does not. In a word, she ages. All those vicissitudes, transports,
and perils of Emily's adventurous life take their toll. "The bloom of her
countenance was somewhat faded," writes Mrs. Radcliffe, "but . . . it was
rendered more interesting than ever, by the faint expression of melancholy
that sometimes mingled with her smile." In fact, melancholy is closing in

on Emily, and at the end the adjective "drooping" begins to replace "pensive" in Mrs. Radcliffe's favor.

"It was a grey autumnal evening," she writes;

> heavy mists . . . and a chilling breeze, that sighed among the beech
> woods, strewed her path with some of their last yellow leaves . . .
> foretelling the death of the year. . . . She walked mournfully on, . . .
> watching the swallows tossed along the wind. . . . The afflictions and
> vicissitudes of her late life seemed portrayed in these fleeting
> images. . . .

Such images from the end of *Udolpho* bring to mind the atmosphere of
Persuasion, last and most autumnal of Jane Austen's novels, and, in its
vista opening toward the sea and the sailor's life, also the most adventurous. It is perhaps in *Persuasion,* rather than in *Northanger Abbey,* that
Radcliffe's influence on Austen can most clearly be perceived. At least the
faded Anne Elliot, victim of a woman's life, is closer than that silly goose
of a Catherine Morland to Emily in *The Mysteries of Udolpho.*

What is officially called a happy ending—that is, marriage—brings
Persuasion to a close, as well as all the Radcliffe novels. But I don't think
my reaction is eccentric when I sense a specially female melancholy and
weariness toward the close of the books that women writers have struc-
tured around the heroism of travel and adventure—from Radcliffe to
Austen to Sand to Cather. Charlotte Brontë recorded a similar reaction
when she brought to a close the dialogue in *Shirley* about Mrs. Radcliffe's
fiction. "I fear a wanderer's life, for me at least" (says Caroline Helstone), "would end like that tale you are reading,—in disappointment,
vanity, and vexation of spirit." "Does 'the Italian' so end?" asks little
Rose Yorke. "I thought so when I read it."

But Rose of course has the last word. "Better to try all things and find
all empty, than to try nothing and leave your life a blank."

8

LOVING HEROINISM:
FEMINISTS IN LOVE

> Ah! my friend, you know not the ineffable delight, the ex-
> quisite pleasure, which arises from an unison of affection and
> desire, when the whole soul and senses are abandoned to a
> lively imagination. . . . These emotions . . . appear to me to
> be the distinctive characteristic of genius, the foundation of
> taste, and of that exquisite relish for the beauties of nature, of
> which the common herd of eaters and drinkers and *child-*
> *begetters* certainly have no idea.
>
> —Mary Wollstonecraft

*It is Midsummer over Thornfield, with skies so pure and suns so radiant
. . . as if a band of Italian days. . . . The hay is in, the trees in their dark
prime, the fields green and shorn, the roads white and baked. . . . It is
the sweetest hour of the twenty-four, sunset at meeting with moonrise. . . .
Honeydew falls . . . a nightingale warbles . . . I walk into the garden . . .
into the walled orchard, sheltered and Eden-like. . . . The trees are laden
with ripening fruit. . . . Sweet-brier and southernwood, jasmine, pink, and
rose . . . and a new scent, neither of shrub nor flower; it is—I know it
well—it is Mr. Rochester's cigar. . . . I step into the ivy recess. . . . He
strolls on . . . he lifts a branch of the gooseberry-tree, and the fruit large
as plums . . . he takes a ripe cherry . . . he stoops to the flowers . . . in-
hales their fragrance . . . the dew-beads on their petals. . . . A great moth
goes humming by. . . .*

    "Jane, come and look at this fellow."
    I had made no noise: he had not eyes behind—could his shadow
feel? I started at first, and then I approached him.

"Look at his wings," said he; "he reminds me rather of a West
Indian insect; one does not so often see so large and gay a night-rover
in England. . . ."

•   •   •

I need not and could not define what love is, but I know a love scene
when I read one; so did the Victorians. That a love scene was underway
they knew at once when they first read the above material in *Jane Eyre,*
which they were given to memorizing in snatches, much as I have printed
it. The word they used, however, was not love but passion, because of the
unblushing sensual component of the scene: the fruit ripe for plucking, the
heavy scents, the dewy warmth of Currer Bell's garden of Eden. Our
ancestors were not so quick as we are, of course, to see the phallus in the
cigar, but they retained a sensitivity to the exotic in the scent of tobacco.
Cigar-smoking, not altogether commonplace in England in the 1840s, was
probably a habit that Mr. Rochester, that dangerous night-rover, had
brought back with him from the West Indies, along with a mad wife.

William Makepeace Thackeray, who was a cigar-smoker himself,
caused Charlotte Brontë the greatest embarrassment of her life when he
met her in London and, forgetting his promise to keep the secret of her
identity with Currer Bell, quoted at her from memory, in a roomful of
people, the sentence that begins "Sweet-brier and southernwood, jasmine,
pink, and rose . . ." The throb of Brontë prose, like the pulse of Brontë
passion, was quite new to English fiction and caused a great stir. For a
long time after the identity of the Brontë girls became known, and something about their background, it was the fashion to explain the un-English
treatment of love in their novels by the fact that they were Celts—their
father an Irishman (whose name had probably once been spelled Brunty).

That English fiction was weak in the area of passion was a complaint
almost as characteristic of the Victorian age as that French fiction was in-
decently full of lust. Much of the critical rapture with which people like
George Henry Lewes and Matthew Arnold greeted George Sand's work is
informed with their sense of a lack in English fiction which Sand made up,
without the blatant indecency of Balzac—a writer to whom she was always
compared in the mid-century, routinely to her advantage.

The same theme is sounded in the early critical reception of the Brontës'
fiction, and it continued sounding down to the time of Henry James, who
put it best. George Sand, he wrote, "has the advantage that she has portrayed a *passion,* and those of the other group [the writers of her own class
who present virtuous love] have the disadvantage that they have not. In
English literature . . . we do not 'go into' the matter, as the phrase is."
James explained he was talking only of the novelists, and he mentioned

Austen, Scott, Dickens, Thackeray, Hawthorne, and George Eliot as writers who "have omitted the erotic sentiment altogether." He might have included himself; he could not have included the Brontës—who, though exceptions to the rule, did not occur to him.

They did occur to Thomas Wentworth Higginson, the American critic who, when he wrote in 1870 about "Americanism in Literature" complained that his compatriots had merely followed instead of corrected the English weakness in the area of literary passion, and he extended the discussion to poetry. "In looking over any collection of American poetry," Higginson wrote, "one is struck with the fact that it is not so much faulty as inadequate. Emerson set free the poetic intuition of America, Hawthorne its imagination. Both looked into the realm of passion, Emerson with distrust, Hawthorne with eager interest; but neither thrilled with its spell, and the American poet of passion is yet to come." From such a source the comment is particularly interesting, for Higginson was uniquely placed in 1870 to know that the American poet of passion had come, though she had not published, for he was Emily Dickinson's principal literary advisor, had read her poems in manuscript—and advised her against publication.

The same sort of push-pull relationship emerges from the Lewes-Brontë correspondence, whenever her passion as a writer and its source in her experience are at issue. For it was an article of faith with Lewes—only he would have called it science—that the greatest literature issued from real experience; the proof, for him, was the passion in the work of George Sand, for her love affairs were well, if imperfectly, known to him. "Sand, in her rich experience of life, knows passions because she has felt them," Lewes wrote. ". . . Balzac has felt less and observed more. . . . The passionate experience contained in the works of George Sand, is greater than in those of any writer of the epoch."

In no area of literature have women writers been subjected to such earnest, constant, and contradictory advice as in the literature of love. Women are the passionate sex, they are always told, and therefore love is their natural subject; but they must not write about it. If they avoid love, that proves they are mere women, inferior to men, next to whom women are always told they are cold, narrow, childish. If they dwell on love they are doing what is expected of the worst of women, who are said to be stupid, sentimental, hysterical creatures incapable of thinking of anything else. And, by the ladies on my left, the radical feminists, they are berated as traitors to their sex, for love is the snare by which women are made the slaves of men.

If women write pornography, that proves they are trying to write like men, for everyone knows women do not read pornography and never write it. Many a publisher today, now that the production of pornography has become an open industry, could give the lie (wiping the tears of laughter from his eyes) to the latter statement. In earlier times, the women whose sexual experience was varied enough to permit them to write effortlessly of its permutations either were too well off to bother, or were illiterate. (As older works of pornography clearly show, whores were almost by definition unable to read, and maidservants were regularly seduced by means of *illustrated* editions of *Fanny Hill*.)

The earliest women romancers, of the Restoration or early eighteenth century, of whom Aphra Behn is the best-known, are instructive in this connection, for they offer a combination of circumstances unique in the history of literary women until our day: they were sexually experienced, highly literate, short of money, and indifferent to respectability. Mrs. Manley, in her lightly fictionalized autobiography of 1714, proclaimed herself a writer who had "so peculiar a genius" for love, and had "made such notable discoveries in that passion," that the erotic scenes in her fiction "carried the passion farther than could be readily conceived":

> such representations of nature that must warm the coldest reader; it raises high ideas of the dignity of human kind, and informs us that we have in our composition wherewith to taste sublime and transporting joys. After perusing her enchanting descriptions, which of us have not gone in search of raptures which she everywhere tells us, as happy mortals, we are capable of tasting.

That is an excellent self-advertisement for the kind of erotica Mrs. Manley went on serenely writing till, rich and unrespectable, she died in 1724—too early to read Richardson. But her successor, Mrs. Haywood, who wrote salacious fiction in the early years of the century and rushed into print with an indecent *Anti-Pamela* (1741) as soon as Richardson's novel appeared, was nevertheless quite shrewd enough to perceive that henceforth there would be bigger royalties in virtue than in vice, and ended her career turning out creditable samples of epistolary fiction in the respectable Richardson manner.

But historical data have never inhibited the promulgation of theories about women—or literary women—or women and the literature of love. If women writers do succeed with the expression or the dramatization of passion, if they do create an attractively erotic male character, their real-life experience at once becomes the only subject of critical discussion. Their biographies are assiduously examined for evidence of scandal or romance, and if nothing is forthcoming their scenes or poems of love are reassessed, to be pronounced untrue to life, unsatisfying, imitative.

Then criticism invades the literary woman's life. If the woman who writes warmly about love is alive, she is subjected to insulting gossip, rude proposals, and obscene phone calls. If she is dead, the worst scandals are put about under the respectable heading of literary scholarship: the absence of an identifiable lover proves her a lesbian; a taste for handsome young men proves her a harpy; a predilection for distinguished older men proves her a neurotic. Only an early and lasting marriage to a suitable young man her own age is proof against scandal, for it is pronounced too boringly uninteresting to have anything to do with literature (though the extreme rarity of the happy marriage in the lives of writers of either sex should give it the status of a mystery). If she is George Sand, and handles the acquisition and dispatch of a series of distinguished lovers with efficiency, then she is denounced as a "transvestite" and attacked for her "technique of games-playing"—the points made in a bitterly warped recent study of Sand by Anthony West, who, since he is a male writer, is exempt from *ad hominem* criticism centering on his being the product of the love affair between Rebecca West and H. G. Wells.

The Charlotte Brontë/Thackeray relationship is the prime example history offers of the hazards facing the woman who writes of passion, for that "relationship," which consisted of hardly more than a few hours of awkward formal converse, was expanded into a scandal revolting in its overtones, and it invaded their work. *Jane Eyre* appeared with the imprudent subtitle *An Autobiography* in October 1847; its success was such that a second edition was printed in January 1848. Meanwhile, Thackeray's first novel, *Vanity Fair,* was appearing in monthly numbers throughout 1847, and Charlotte Brontë was so impressed by what she read of the beginning of the novel, which she took to be a work of social satire directed against "the great ones of society," that she included an outburst of praise for Thackeray in her preface to the second edition of *Jane Eyre:* "I regard him as the first social regenerator of the day, as the very master of that working corps who would restore to rectitude the warped system of things." The radical tone of this language was imprudent; but the danger of allowing a coupling of her name with Thackeray's was such as Charlotte Brontë, in the wildest flights of her imagination, could never have conceived.

For *Jane Eyre, An Autobiography* is about a governess who falls in love with her master, who is already married to a wife who is mad. And Thackeray had a governess in his employ to look after his two daughters, and he had a mad wife, suicidal after the birth of her last child, who was confined in a sanitarium—none of this, of course, known to Miss Brontë. Furthermore, the most interesting character in *Vanity Fair,* as became ever clearer as the novel continued to appear in parts throughout 1848, was Becky Sharp, a wicked young woman, poor and orphaned like Jane Eyre, who takes a post as a governess and plays her seductive wiles on both her master and her master's son, managing a secret marriage with the latter. Indeed, the innumerable details that make up Thackeray's wonderful Becky which are like satirical refractions of bits of the character of Jane Eyre are among the most fascinating coincidences of literary history; mere coincidence they in fact were, but that was not the way they appeared to readers and reviewers of 1847 and 1848.

That some sexual relationship tied the original of Jane Eyre to Thackeray—that there was spite in the affair, on both sides—seemed all too clear. The gossip was irritating to Thackeray but not distressing, for he was a man of the world, with his clubs, his cigars, and his discreetly managed private existence. But as to the author of *Jane Eyre*—the defenseless Currer Bell—"if we ascribe the book to a woman at all," said the *Quarterly Review*, "we have no alternative but to ascribe it to one who has, for some sufficient reason, long forfeited the society of her own sex." *Jane Eyre, An Autobiography* was a novel of passion by a woman, and so had to reflect the woman novelist's real experience of passion. There had to be a "real" Rochester, and the woman novelist had to be the "real" Jane Eyre.

"Evidence of life?" inquires Erica Jong in the Prologue to *Half-Lives*. "My dreams," she answers. "The dreams which I write down." "Evidence of love?" she inquires again; and then, addressing "you" the lover:

> Do you exist?
> Evidence:
> these poems in which
> I have been conjuring you,
> this book which makes your absence palpable,
> these longings printed black.
>
> I am exposed.
> I am a print of darkness
> on a square of film.

That there are hazards and conflicts which confront the woman writer on love may explain the striking correlation between strong-mindedness and love-writing in the history of women's literature, for on the whole it is the feminists who have written most urgently and insistently about love, from Mary Wollstonecraft to Erica Jong, by way of Flora Tristan and Margaret Fuller. The unguarded demand for passionate fulfillment that Margaret Fuller made—"I shall always reign through the intellect, but the life, the life! O my God! shall that never be sweet?"—sounded through the convention-bounded lives of Victorian women like George Eliot, who quoted that line from memory and commented, "I am thankful, as if for myself, that it was sweet at last."

Women in love have in fact been a subject of irresistible fascination to writers for centuries, long before there were women novelists to tackle it, or D. H. Lawrence to kick it around. Whether a woman's way of loving is significantly different from a man's is open to question; but that the *expression* of love by a woman must be different in kind and literary consequence from the expression of love by a man was the literary challenge to which Jean-Jacques Rousseau responded when he wrote *La Nouvelle Héloïse,* and so began the great landslide of modern sensibility that we call the Romantic movement. He also began a lesser but hardly unrelated literary enterprise, loving heroinism, by which I mean the woman writer's heroic resolve to write herself, as men for centuries had tried to do, the love story from the woman's point of view.

There came a time in the writing of this book when I grew as sick of the word heroinism as the reader is about to become—a word I had invented, in spite of myself, because I could find nothing else in English to serve for the feminine of the heroic principle; and a word which sounds, I am well aware, more like an addiction to drugs than a seal on literary accomplishment. Just about that time I had lunch with a medievalist friend, Marcelle Thiébaux of St. John's University, told her what I was working on, and that I called it by the ugly title of loving heroinism. Professor Thiébaux stopped me and asked why I had bothered to invent a term at all, when Ovid had already provided exactly what I wanted with his *Heroides.*

The more I began to learn about the poetry Ovid wrote with conscious intention to give tongue to the heroine of love; and about the literary tradition Ovid began, which extended well into the eighteenth century, in fact laps at the feet of the infant novel and then is born anew in women's literature of the nineteenth century, the less I worried about the word heroinism. For had that noun or the adjective heroinical been allowed to creep into our language, the poetry that John Donne and Alexander Pope wrote in imitation of Ovid's *Heroides* would be known to us not incorrectly as Heroical Epistles but as *Heroinical* Epistles—the versified letters of the woman in love. *Heroides,* therefore, is an excellent term for the love poems women began to write in the nineteenth century and are still writing today. These are the most important literary residue of loving heroinism; the letter form, verse or prose, is central.

* * *

When the final word is said on Mary Wollstonecraft, she will appear to us, I suspect, as one of the great prose writers of the language, and as one of the few writers of whom it can reasonably be said that, had she lived beyond the age of thirty-eight, she would have made a major literary contribution, perhaps in the novel. Though there are splendid passages in her *Vindication of the Rights of Woman* (1792), the work by which she is best-known today, it is as boring as are all polemics which have been answered in the affirmative by history; for all that Mary Wollstonecraft there cried for—education, employment, legal and political rights for women—has come about.

A Vindication is an historical document of major interest, but for the living Wollstonecraft one must turn to her fiction, her reviews, especially her letters. Her contemporaries and immediate followers read this material, but until only a few years ago none but the scholars (particularly the Shelley scholars) were familiar with it. From the best of Mary Wollstonecraft, now slowly coming back into print, a slim but dazzling volume of prose will be found worthy of selection and preservation; and the best of that will be found to be about love, a subject on which she wrote only during the final five years of her short life.

"Love is a want of my heart," she wrote,

> I have examined myself lately with more care than formerly, and find that to deaden is not to calm the mind. Aiming at tranquility, I have almost destroyed all the energy of my soul—almost rooted out what renders it estimable. . . .

And again:

> I have looked at the sea, and at my child, hardly daring to own to myself the secret wish, that it might become our tomb; and that the heart, still so alive to anguish, might there be quieted by death. At this moment ten thousand complicated sentiments press for utterance, weigh on my heart, and obscure my sight.
>
> Are we ever to meet again?

There is a sound to Wollstonecraft's language that becomes unmistakable. The closest equivalent, but it is not the same, is in Jane Austen:

> "I can listen no longer in silence. I must speak to you by such means as are within my reach. You pierce my soul. I am half agony, half hope. Tell me not that I am too late, that such precious feelings are gone for ever. I offer myself to you again with a heart even more your own, than when you almost broke it eight years and a half ago. Dare not say that man forgets sooner than woman, that his love has an earlier death. I have loved none but you. Unjust I may have been, weak and resentful I have been, but never inconstant. . . ."

The Austen letter—it is the one Captain Wentworth addresses to Anne Elliot at the end of *Persuasion*—is very beautiful, but it is a shade too dry, too clipped. Wollstonecraft's prose is all liquidity under severe compression. There is a slow, formal deliberateness about the way each of her words sits separately on the page; and a musical swell and fall rocking the Georgian balance; and a silvery resonance to her sounds. It must be read aloud; somewhere in this prose there is a speaking voice of remarkable musicality.

"Now by these presents," she wrote in her rarer, radiant mood,

> let me assure you that you are not only in my heart, but my veins, this morning. I turn from you half abashed—yet you haunt me, and some look, word or touch thrills through my whole frame —yes, at the very moment when I am labouring to think of something, if not somebody, else. Get ye gone Intruder! though I am forced to add dear—which is a call back—
>
> When the heart and reason accord there is no flying from voluptuous sensations, I find, do what a woman can—Can a philosopher do more?

The biographical occasions behind these letters have often, and lately very rudely, been told. Less often said is that these letters stand perfectly well alone as literature, though they were not written to be published. In the literature of love, from the beginning of time, whatever the sex or nationality of the writer, the letter is the central form—real letters, hoax letters, letters in novels, verse letters, secret letters, sung letters, spoken letters, letters that stand or fall not by the test of truth to fact, but by the test of truth to love.

In 1793 Mary Wollstonecraft the strong-minded feminist fell in love with love. Before then, her two *Vindications,* her *Thoughts on the Education of Daughters,* her *Original Stories from Real Life,* most of her criticism for the *Analytical Review,* and the other work she did between 1787 and 1792 belong to what can be bluntly, because accurately, called her virginal period. *Mary, a Fiction* (1788), her first novel, is the startling text from that earlier time: a cold, gnarled fantasy of the virgin mind. It ends with the heroine's marriage to a man who disgusts her: "when her husband would take her hand, or mention anything like love, she would instantly feel a sickness, a faintness at her heart, and wish, involuntarily, that the earth would open and swallow her." In the last lines of the novel the girl dwindles toward death and a virgin's dream of heaven: "a gleam of joy would dart across her mind—She thought she was hastening to that world *where there is neither marrying,* nor giving in marriage."

Mary, a Fiction is not a successful novel, but it is extremely interesting for what it shows of the pressure of female self-consciousness on literary goals and forms. Thoughtful about fiction, as her criticism in the *Analytical Review* reveals, Mary Wollstonecraft brought the force and originality of her thinking as a feminist to bear on the transformation of the novel and the heroine by the "chosen few," as she put it in her preface, who "wish to speak for themselves."

The work which best shows her potential as a novelist is *Maria,* the novel fragment William Godwin published among her posthumous works in 1798. Wollstonecraft (who in the last months of her life became Mrs. Godwin) died giving birth to a daughter before she could complete or revise the very rough though long fragment that *Maria* is. Had she been able to perfect it, that novel might have made a landmark of English Romanticism—as *Frankenstein,* the book her daughter wrote, would do twenty years later.

The Wrongs of Woman; or, Maria, to use its full title, contains Wollstonecraft's most radical feminism and most powerful writing on a woman's passion; there seems no way or need to separate these two aspects of the work. The story centers on the brutality and bestiality of a husband, and attacks marriage laws. It celebrates an unhappy wife's adulterous love affair, and argues for divorce. It includes background vignettes of sexually exploited lower-class women, and raises the issue of prostitution. (Included in *Maria* are an abortion scene and an adultery trial; Wollstonecraft planned to include a miscarriage.) But most remarkable as contrast to *Mary, a Fiction* is its celebration of passion from the point of view of a woman who has not only a mind, a tongue, and a sensibility, but a body capable of sensation and impregnation. (Pregnancy, she once wrote dryly to Godwin, was that "inelegant complaint, which no novelist has yet ventured to mention as one of the consequences of sentimental distress.")

Not the "wrongs of woman," then, but the right of woman to passion is the most interesting theme of *Maria.* "When novelists or moralists praise as a virtue, a woman's coldness of constitution, and want of passion," writes Maria in the novel, in a letter to her daughter, "and make her yield to the ardour of her lover out of sheer compassion, or to promote a frigid plan of future comfort, I am disgusted. They may be good women . . . and do no harm; but they appear to me not to have those 'finely fashioned nerves,' which render the senses exquisite. They may possess tenderness; but they want the fire of the imagination, which produces *active* sensibility, and *positive* virtue." Maria's letter goes on to discuss the relationship between truth, heartlessness and female virtue; to demand that men please women as much as women please men; to call the morality which rests on the idea of female frigidity a fabrication in masculine interest. Polemical in part, the whole novel explores the literary consequences—in terms of sensibility, imagination, language—of female truths about female passion. Wollstonecraft writes these truths with the freshness of personal discovery, for until she fell in love herself, in 1793, with an American she met in France named Gilbert Imlay, she had no idea that "Love is a want of my heart."

The Imlay affair brought Mary Wollstonecraft nothing but trouble, one might think, in the form of an illegitimate child, poverty, abandonment, attempted suicide. But the burden of her Imlay letters, as of *Maria,* is not Wollstonecraft's suffering so much as her rejoicing at the discovery of love.

"I have the sincerest esteem and affection for you," she wrote Imlay, "but the desire of regaining peace (do you understand me?) has made me forget the respect due to my own emotions—sacred emotions, that are the sure harbingers of the delights I was formed to enjoy—and shall enjoy, for nothing can extinguish the heavenly spark." Mary Wollstonecraft would indeed enjoy heavenly, albeit short-lived delights with the philosopher William Godwin, who had also, before he met her, recorded his disbelief in the passion of love. Their story makes a partly ludicrous, partly moving footnote to the disintegration of philosophical rationalism in the waning years of the eighteenth century; and to the rise of the Romantic ideal of love. Mary Wollstonecraft, as a legendary woman and a writer, meant a great deal to Shelley, as did William Godwin; and to their daughter Mary.

. . .

No one will ever be able to make sense out of Rousseau's place in the history of feminism, a subject now being worried over in scholarly circles, until they see Rousseau's work through the eyes of the feminists, and grasp the close connection between feminism and loving heroinism. There was good reason for feminists like Mary Wollstonecraft to be furious with Rousseau, for in the *Émile,* his pedagogical treatise, he promulgated the most benighted view of female education, or, more properly, non-education. Woman to Rousseau the pedagogue was a charming but mindless creature, and as such he represented her in the character of Sophie, Émile's female counterpart; her only functions were to serve and to please man, her only necessary training that which conduced to those ends. "Indignation" and "the rigid frown of insulted virtue" were Mary Wollstonecraft's attitudes as she attacked Rousseau's pedagogy throughout her *Vindication of the Rights of Woman.* She was even more wrathful, in the early 1790s, with those of her own sex who praised Rousseau, of whom the most important was Mme de Staël.

Mme de Staël was very much a presence in the great decade of English feminism, the 1790s, not only because she lived in England (an émigrée in 1793, when she was in her twenties) but because of her *Lettres sur les ouvrages et le caractère de Jean-Jacques Rousseau* (1788), her first publication, translated and widely read in English from 1789 onward. The excitement this little book caused among English women leads me to suspect that it was received as the first full-fledged, formal critical study of a literary man ever published by a woman. To read it today is to recognize with a smile the kind of writing that young women are most likely to produce in our time, for it is really a term paper, quite creditable work any professor would be happy to give a high mark to at the end of a term's study of Rousseau. But from what Mary Wollstonecraft wrote of de Staël's *Rous-*

seau in the *Analytical Review* and the *Vindication,* she clearly would never have given it more than a C.

The trouble was that Mme de Staël, who was at least as strong-minded as Wollstonecraft, and had at least as much reason, as the most intelligent woman of her time, to denounce Rousseau's pedagogy, regarded him first and foremost as the author of *La Nouvelle Héloïse,* for which, as a literary woman, she would forgive him anything. It was a work, Mme de Staël shrewdly perceived, written not for men but for women, and women would take from it profit or harm: "Son ouvrage est pour les femmes; c'est pour elles qu'il est fait; c'est à elles qu'il peut nuire ou servir." The nub of Wollstonecraft's outraged reaction to de Staël's view of Rousseau was this: "He denies woman reason, shuts her out from knowledge, and turns her aside from truth; yet his pardon is granted, because" (here she quoted de Staël) " 'he admits the passion of love.' "

Indeed, the particular opinion that Mme de Staël protested in Rousseau was not pedagogical but literary, his view that the subject of passion was not one women were capable of expressing for themselves. She was willing to grant Rousseau, she wrote—and from such a source it was an extraordinary submission—that women lacked strong intellects, or purely literary talents, or what is called genius, but she would not grant their inability to write of love. "Women can at least express what they feel," wrote Mme de Staël in the most eloquent passage in her *Rousseau;* ". . . and that sublime abandon, that melancholy grief, those all-powerful sentiments by which they live or die—these will perhaps stir more emotion in the reader's heart than all the transports born from the exalted imagination of the poets."

Prescient as always, Mme de Staël there predicted the coming tradition of loving heroinism among literary women, the first of whom was to be the transformed Mary Wollstonecraft, feminist in love. Along with Wollstonecraft's personal and literary discovery of the power of a woman's passion came a corresponding change in her attitude toward the founding father of the new tradition, Jean-Jacques Rousseau. "I have always been half in love with him," she admitted as early as 1794, in a letter to Imlay.

A passion for Rousseau will be found characteristic of the great women writers of the ninetenth century, and in despite of logic. "I might admit," George Eliot wrote, ". . . that Rousseau's views of life, religion, and government are miserably erroneous—. . . and it would be not the less true that Rousseau's genius has sent that electric thrill through my intellectual and moral frame which has awakened me to new perceptions. . . ." (From *La Nouvelle Héloïse,* as it has often been pointed out, came the pattern for Maggie Tulliver's drift down the waters of illicit romance at the end of *The Mill on the Floss.*) And George Sand, whose particular reason for revulsion against Rousseau was his abandonment of his illegitimate children, wrote in her own fragmentary "Letter on Rousseau," "Yes, I remain faithful to him; or rather I have come back to him. . . . Shall I tell

you why and how I have undergone these alternating reactions of veneration, of terror, and of love?"

So it was with Mary Wollstonecraft. An early scene in *Maria* shows the
heroine, imprisoned by her tyrant husband in an insane asylum though far
from mad, reading *La Nouvelle Héloïse*. "She had read this work long
since," writes Wollstonecraft; "but now it seemed to open a new world to
her—the only one worth inhabiting." It was the woman's world of love—a
new literary terrain to which Rousseau, honored be his name, threw wide
the gate.

Julie; or the New Heloise is Rousseau's enormously long novel in letters published in 1761: the fruition of Richardson's inventive accomplishments in the 1740s and 1750s. It is an overblown, boring, infuriating,
pompous, silly, eloquent, brilliant fiction which establishes Rousseau as the
founder (while Richardson was only a precursor) of the Romantic movement.

By means of letters exchanged (as Rousseau's subtitle puts it) between
two lovers living in a little town at the foot of the Alps, Rousseau tells the
romance between Julie d'Étanges, a girl of noble birth, and her tutor, a
commoner named Saint-Preux. They fall in love; they cannot marry; they
have sexual relations; they part. Julie then marries an older man, the husband of her father's choice, M. de Volmar, and wholeheartedly espouses a
virtuous life as wife and mother. The husband Volmar, a noble-minded
gentleman, trusts so absolutely in Julie's virtue that he brings Saint-Preux
back into their household (though he knows Saint-Preux to have been,
before marriage, his wife's lover) as tutor to their children. The love story
between Julie and Saint-Preux is thus reopened, recapitulated, redoubled
in passion and poignancy, this time without sexuality, but still by means of
letters exchanged between two lovers living at the foot of the Alps. The
novel ends with Julie's death (in letters): a saint of virtue and of love, the
perfect wife and mother but still, in spirit, the passionate mistress of Saint-
Preux.

If I can dare to sketch crudely, and in a few paragraphs, what *La
Nouvelle Héloïse* meant to literary women, I would say first that Rousseau
gave tongue by means of the letter form to the woman in love: the woman
who loves consciously, willingly, with the full force of her moral and intellectual being, and has the brains and the verbal facility to express her love.
Julie is a woman who sins for love, and knows what sin is; but she is not
destroyed by what for centuries was called a woman's fall; quite the contrary. Julie rises to her apotheosis as a moral being *after* surrendering to illicit sexual passion. Her surrender is total and voluntary; she is neither
raped nor is she truly seduced. She chooses Saint-Preux for his qualities of
mind and heart, and never afterward swerves from her initial assessment
of her lover, whom she would always have wished to marry, had the laws
of family, class, and society not prohibited their union. Julie's suffering is

great, for she loves Saint-Preux and not, so far as passion goes, her husband. But she survives to tell that suffering in her own words—thousands of them, in letter after letter after letter.

Women writers also drew from Rousseau a new lease on the old subject of adultery; as old a theme as literature itself, adultery had already inspired remarkable fiction by women, from the eleventh-century Japanese classic *The Tale of Genji* to the seventeenth-century French classic *La Princesse de Clèves*—the first by Lady Murasaki, the second by Mme de La Fayette. But Rousseau's adultery was not the time-honored courtly theme, but modern adultery newly seen from the woman's point of view— that is, part of a feminist outburst against the institution of marriage as created not in heaven but on earth, by unjust, man-made laws. The adultery novel after Rousseau became the woman writer's vehicle of attack on the economic and social-class realities that make a mockery of love; as well as a vehicle of demonstration that woman has a capacity to think, feel, and act for herself.

George Sand has always had the reputation, among people who don't read her, for writing about nothing but adultery, which is in fact the subject of her earliest novels—and *Valentine* in particular makes out the feminist case against marriage through its strong-minded heroine. But there is much less impetus to adultery in Sand's fiction, much less unbridled passion in fact, than in that of her English contemporaries. The observation is hardly a new one: George Henry Lewes, in 1844, pointed to "the hundreds of English novels in which adultery is either the subject of tragedy or farce," and said there was nothing in Sand's fiction "half so revolting as the love of a man for his wife's sister, who is living under the same roof with him . . . , the subject of a much applauded novel by a much admired authoress of the day"—a reference, I assume, to Harriet Martineau's *Deerbrook*.

George Eliot, for example, hardly wrote a fiction that was not an adultery novel, though tricks of the cautious novelist's trade have tended to obscure this fact. It is hard to name a George Eliot heroine who is not either a woman who loves a man belonging to another woman, or a wife who loves a man not her husband. *Middlemarch* would be a pure version of the adultery novel had George Eliot not, with signal impurity of intention, killed off Casaubon at around the age of fifty, and thus allowed Dorothea to run off with her handsome young lover without offending English proprieties or hurting the novelist's reputation as a moralist. In *Daniel Deronda*, George Eliot lets Gwendolen Harleth get rid of her dreadful husband by pushing him out of a sailboat on the Mediterranean; of course, it all happens offstage—we cannot be sure what really transpires —but the reader is allowed at least to hope that Gwendolen had a share in Grandcourt's drowning.

Jane Eyre and *Wuthering Heights,* and in a more guarded way even *Villette* are all adultery novels; but the strongest work by a Brontë on the marriage question is *The Tenant of Wildfell Hall* by Anne Brontë, who has the reputation, among people who don't read her, for being the most timid of the sisters. Anne Brontë's heroine is a woman who marries impulsively for love and suffers terribly for her mistake in judgment. She runs away from her brutal husband, raises her child alone and on the money she earns herself; she grows through suffering, and falls more passionately and more maturely in love with another man.

French critics have been struck by a parallel here to the marriage-question fiction of George Sand, and it is quite possible that Anne Brontë thought as highly of Sand as did her sister Charlotte; I find the parallel to Wollstonecraft's *Maria* even more striking.* The interesting point to make is that neither Anne Brontë nor Wollstonecraft before her nor Virginia Woolf after her had any reason to complain, as their heroines do with great vigor, of being trapped by an unhappy marriage. The modern adultery novel has simply been a compelling vehicle for heroinism. "Gallantry and intrigue are sorry enough things in themselves, but they certainly serve better to arouse the dormant faculties of woman than embroidery and domestic drudgery"—so wrote George Eliot in "Woman in France," where, as in all her anonymous criticism, she allowed herself to speak with the unguarded sophistication of a man of the world on such sensitive matters as the positive consequences of adultery.

Anne Brontë is wholly forthright, in *The Tenant of Wildfell Hall,* about the woman writer's resolve to discuss love, sex, and marriage in her own terms. A conversation at the start of the novel attacks the different styles in moral education then prevailing for boys and girls. Boys are to be armed like heroes against temptation, and strengthened by a thorough experience of life; while girls are to be raised like hothouse plants, "taught to cling to others for direction and support, and guarded . . . from the very knowledge of evil. . . . It must be . . . that you think she is essentially so vicious, or so feeble-minded that she cannot withstand temptation. . . ."

"I would not," concludes the heroine, speaking for Anne Brontë and all the literary women who wrote on passion for the benefit of their own sex, "I would not send a poor girl into the world, . . . ignorant of the snares

---

* There is no evidence that the Brontës read Wollstonecraft. However, the often repeated "fact" that Wollstonecraft was completely forgotten by the Victorians is untrue: there is firm evidence that Harriet Martineau, Elizabeth Barrett, Margaret Fuller, and George Eliot read her work (and probably more than the *Vindication*), though none was so enthusiastic about her feminism as Flora Tristan. Wollstonecraft was not a unique early example of the feminist in love. Pierre Fauchery, who knows more about the literary feminism of the 1790s than anyone else, cites French and German parallels to Wollstonecraft's fiction, and writes that "at the end of the [eighteenth] century, rejection of the sexual neutrality of woman was an important article in the credo of female radical intellectuals."

that beset her path; nor would I watch and guard her, till, deprived of self-respect and self-reliance, she lost the power or the will to watch and guard herself. . . ." The same heroic resolve to open the forbidden, abandon discretion, and consider woman as an active and conscious participant in the affairs of love can be paralleled in texts by other Victorian spinsters—notably Charlotte Brontë's *Shirley*. And from literary women of fuller sexual experience—from Gaskell and Browning and Colette and Woolf—have come similar assertions of the obligation as well as the right to speak as a woman about love. "I'm a woman and know womanhood," cries Aurora Leigh for them all; and female sexuality is treated very boldly in Mrs. Browning's novel-poem. (Marian Erle in *Aurora Leigh,* like the heroine of Mrs. Gaskell's *Ruth,* is an unwed mother who glories in raising her child—a note of defiant independence which nowhere appears in the treatment of the fallen woman by male Victorians.)

As to adultery in marriage, Mrs. Browning had her say on the literary woman's right to that subject in a letter to Thackeray, when, in his capacity as an editor, he rejected one of her poems for its dangerous frankness.

> Has paterfamilias [she wrote], with his Oriental traditions and veiled female faces, very successfully dealt with a certain class of evil? What if materfamilias, with her quick sure instincts and honest innocent eyes, do more towards their expulsion by simply looking at them and calling them by their names?

. . .

Women writers also appropriated from Rousseau the species of lover that he provides in *La Nouvelle Héloïse* for his noblehearted Julie to love. Saint-Preux is not a lord, not a soldier, not an *élégant,* not a prince, not a rake, but a teacher. He wins Julie's heart, which he enters in tutorial guise, through his intellectual and moral prestige. How many heroes of the same species—mature men, wise and learned—have women writers given their heroines to love: Austen gave Mr. Knightley to her Emma, Brontë gave M. Paul Emanuel to her Lucy Snowe,* Gaskell gave a brilliant scientist to her Mollie, Louisa May Alcott gave Dr. Bhaer to Jo. Perhaps only coeduca-

---

* Austen's and Brontë's hero may look odd side by side, for Mr. Knightley entirely lacks M. Emanuel's learning; but at least one woman reader (with whom I would agree) wrote Charlotte Brontë that she considered the two gentlemen to be aspects of the same ideal of a lover. In real life, the clever Geraldine Jewsbury announced herself willing to make do with maturity in a man, and pass up intellect. "I wish I had a good husband and a dozen children!" she wrote her friend Jane Carlyle (who had married intellect). "Only the difficulty is that 'women of genius' require very special husbands—men of noble character, not intellect, but of a character and nature large enough, and strong enough, and wise enough to take them and their genius too, without cutting them down to suit their own crotchets, or reprobating half their qualities because they don't know what to do with them, or what they are intended for."

tion ended this long tradition of teacher-lovers, when women found, given half a chance at schooling, they were better learners than men; George Eliot, early on, gave it the kick of derision with Casaubon.

It is a mistake—often committed—to see only modesty in the woman writer's worshipful attitude, presented through her heroine's upraised, adoring eyes, to the man above her in wisdom and educational acquirements. On the contrary, this is the feminist's fantasy of perfect love—foolish perhaps, but the result of pride rather than humility. The heroine of all these books, Rousseau's included, is ambitious. She intends to improve herself spiritually by association with the superior male—improve herself spiritually but not socially, and that is important. For another originality of *La Nouvelle Héloïse,* striking to literary women, was that Rousseau made his heroine rich and noble, her lover poor and common; only thus was it possible for the heroine of a novel to give herself voluntarily to the lover of her choice. For the poor girl must wait, and ordinarily in silence, to be chosen.

The difference between Richardson and Rousseau, and the different traditions of women's literature that they fathered, might here be simplified by pointing to the single fact decisive to the love story in fiction: Pamela is the poor girl who wants a rich man, and Julie the rich girl who wants a poor man. The latter situation was seized upon by every woman writer who was a feminist in love, because it gave her a chance to do the scene of choice: the heroine choosing and demanding her love, as Catherine demands Heathcliff; the heroine giving herself freely and, throwing Jane Austen's prudence to the winds, declaring her passion. In *Méphis* Flora Tristan identified this sort of scene as a plank in her utopia. "In the future," she wrote,

> when woman is conscious of her power, she will free herself from the need for social approval, and those little tricks which today aid her to deceive men, will become useless; when that time comes, woman will say:—"I choose this man for my lover, because my love will be a powerful force on his intelligence, and our happiness will be reflected on others'." . . . To love one's fellow-man is rational self-love.

Emma, alone among Jane Austen's heroines, has self-love, according to Lionel Trilling, and this astonishes him: "The extraordinary thing about Emma is that she has a moral life as a man has a moral life"—and he does not see the simple reason why. "Women in fiction," he goes on,

> only rarely have the peculiar reality of the moral life that self-love bestows. Most commonly they exist in a moon-like way, shining by the reflected moral life of men. . . . They seldom exist as men exist—as genuine moral destinies. It is only on the rare occasions when a female character like Emma confronts us that the difference

makes us aware of the usual practice. Nor can we say that novels
are deficient in realism when they present women as they do: it is
the presumption of our society that women's moral life is not as
men's. No change in the modern theory of the sexes, no advances
in the status that women have made, can contradict this. The self-
love that we do countenance in women is of a limited and passive
kind, and we are troubled if their self-love is as assertive as man's
is permitted, and expected to be. Not men alone, but women as
well, insist on this limitation. . . . But there is Emma, given over
to self-love. . . .

All that Professor Trilling had to note about Emma's uniqueness as a
Jane Austen heroine—and it would have saved him the disgrace of that
paragraph—is that she is the only one who is an heiress. Emma is rich
enough to have a wide choice among any number of men over whom to
make a fool of herself, with whom to make or unmake her moral life.

Similarly, male critics have damned Charlotte Brontë for creating the
all-time castrating heroine in Jane Eyre because, at the end of the novel,
she brings back a broken Rochester for Jane to love. But it is only
catastrophe that gives Jane Eyre the chance to play Julie as well as
Pamela. It is only a Rochester reduced from glory—impoverished, crip-
pled, and blinded—that Jane can give herself to, in the pride of her soul,
saying: "My dear master. . . . I am Jane Eyre: I have found you out—I
am come back to you."

* * * *

There is no reason to be reluctant, as literary women have never been
reluctant, to pay tribute to the tutelary male, in this case Jean-Jacques
Rousseau, the tutelary genius they were "half in love with." But fidelity to
historical fact compels me to correct the impression I may have given by
saying that Rousseau opened the woman's world of love; a reopening or a
renewal of a tradition was his own intention, as the title of *La Nouvelle
Héloïse* implies. For there was an *old* Héloïse behind the new one, to whom
Rousseau deferred: a real woman, and one of the earliest great writers in
France. Her contribution to the heroinism of love goes back to the twelfth
century.

Héloïse was a Parisian girl of good family and remarkable endowments;
in an age when literacy was a rare accomplishment in either sex, she had a
reputation for being the most learned woman of her time. She fell in love
with her tutor, a theologian named Abélard, and entered upon a passionate
sexual relationship. The lovers were separated by her irate family (who
castrated Abélard) and during their separation Héloïse wrote Abélard a
series of love letters (in Latin) which are among the glories of medieval,
indeed world literature.

The legend of Héloïse was never forgotten. "If the sexes be really to live in a state of warfare, . . . let them act nobly" wrote Mary Wollstonecraft, ". . . when, like Heloisa, a woman gives up all the world deliberately for love." Margaret Fuller and George Henry Lewes claimed Héloïse for the Victorians. To Lewes, who had personal reasons to worship her legend,* she was "a great heroic woman. . . . She had not only *endurance*—that is a feminine virtue—she had courage of the highest sort, she had firm and steady *will*."

More important than her legend to literary history, Héloïse's letters were read, translated into every modern language, for centuries. Scholars who have studied the pre-history of the modern novel point to a rising vogue for Héloïse's letters in the early years of the eighteenth century—of which Pope's versified version, "Heloisa to Abelard," is the best-known evidence. Before Richardson created Pamela out of fictional letters which he pretended were the work of a real woman, there were innumerable collections of letters, pretend and real, printed for the eager public for which Richardson wrote. Nine editions of the Héloïse/Abélard correspondence appeared in England in the years just before *Pamela,* and about twenty editions, translations, and reworkings of the most popular female love letters of the day, the *Lettres portugaises.*

These so-called Portuguese Letters, or, as they were more fully known in England, *The Letters from a Portuguese Nun to a Cavalier,* have recently reemerged from the modest obscurity of scholarly research to the spotlight of literary and political scandal, with the publication of the so-called New Portuguese Letters. Three sophisticated, professional Portuguese women (Barreno, Horta, and da Costa), who all have the first name Maria, collaborated on an erotic farrago of letters, poems, and stories they called *Novas Cartas Portuguesas.* The work was banned for its mixture of pornography and feminism, and the three authors arrested. Their drawn-out trial became an international scandal credited with a share in the collapse of the oppressive Portuguese regime; the three Marias have become heroines of political as well as female liberation.

The English edition, published in America in 1975, is called *The Three Marias: New Portuguese Letters,* and includes a translation of the *Lettres portugaises* of old—thus proving the eternal vitality of that literary artifice, loving heroinism. The fact is that there never were any Portuguese Letters

---

* Reasons which had nothing to do with Marian Evans (George Eliot), whom Lewes had not met when he wrote in the *Foreign Quarterly Review* in 1846 that "we are so much in love with" Heloise. Lewes's wife Agnes, a beautiful and very intelligent young woman (she translated and wrote for publication), was of a social class superior to his own, her father a Member of Parliament who hired Lewes as secretary. In that post he met and, perhaps, played Abelard with the lovely Agnes. (It was she who later brought their at first very happy marriage to an end, through her adultery with Thornton Hunt.)

or any scribbling nun to begin with. The whole thing was a literary fabrication by a Frenchman, a hack who for once showed he had a touch of genius, named G. J. Lavergne de Guilleragues, who brought out in French, in 1669, what he pretended were translations of real letters some unnamed Portuguese nun had written to some French soldier who had seduced her, awakened her to the joys of passion, and abandoned her. The eighteenth century swallowed the hoax and elaborated it; the nineteenth century obligingly supplied a name for the nun and her cavalier; and the twentieth century, thanks to the three Marias, has now given the imaginary nun a full life story, and a battery of relatives and descendants, all of which will surely become a part of the "fact" of the literary legend.

With love letters, of course, it matters not in the least whether they are true or false; readers can read the *New Portuguese Letters* with the delight or distaste they deserve. As the three Marias put it in their first letter, "what is of interest is not so much the object of our passion, which is a mere pretext, but passion itself"; and as they add in their third letter, with an even more sophisticated sense of their literary tradition, "Ponder the fact, my sisters, as our flesh today is warmed by this gentle sun shining down on everyone and bringing in flocks of tourists, that this literary novelty of ours is going to sell well."

Loving heroinism—the challenge to tell the woman's side of the love story in her own words—knows no sex or age in the history of literature; women writers have claimed their right to it from every motive, the personal, the feminist, or the pecuniary (though none, perhaps, with so warped a motive as Philip Roth, who made a fantasy of loving heroinism by turning his hero into a female breast). Whatever the motive, the literary challenge fascinates the writer, because the words of a woman in love must be different from those of a man. In the central form of love, the letter, what occasion can set the correspondence going, if the writer is the woman in the affair? The three Marias have cleverly exploited the sororial atmosphere of our current feminism and have addressed their principal letters to each other. But normally, lovers write letters to lovers, which implies their separation—and in the rare love letters of poetry where married love is at issue, the travels of the male are the occasion for the versified tears of the female. "Weep me not dead in thy arms" cries John Donne, and Anne Bradstreet:

> Even thus doe I, with many a deep sad groan
> Bewail my turtle true, who now is gone,
> His presence and his safe return, still wooes,
> With thousand dolefull sighs and mournfull Cooes.

When the lovers are not married, however (which is what most of us mean by love), from a woman's point of view separation implies abandonment; from a man's, seduction, a subject from which women are barred. A woman cannot write "Come live with me and be my love, and we will all the pleasures prove"—for if she did so, that would mean, if not *la fin de l'histoire,* certainly the end of her letters. There is nothing out of which to make literary heroinism in the passionate woman who woos. (The calculating woman, bent on power rather than love, is something else.)

They tell me that, in what passes for real life in our time, teen-age girls go wooing all the time, en masse, to popular singers; but literary history offers only the sorry spectacle of a teen-age girl named Claire Clairmont, throwing herself by letter and in person at Lord Byron. (When one comes to think of it, Byron supplied for his time reasonable equivalents for the enticements of rock 'n' roll.) And the only letter worth preserving from that affair is Byron's. "You know that odd-headed girl," he wrote a friend, "who introduced herself to me shortly before I left England; . . . I never loved nor pretended to love her, but a man is a man, and if a girl of eighteen comes prancing to you at all hours, there is but one way—the suite of all this is that she was with *child*—and returned to England to assist in peopling that desolate island. . .—the next question is, is the brat mine?"

Charlotte Brontë tried her hand at the exercise of writing wooing letters, and the proof that it was an exercise is that they are in French—very careful, delicate explorations of the different resources of the French language by a gifted English writer. These letters in fact show that Brontë was more in love with the language of the letters than she was with the man to whom she wrote them—her Belgian *professeur,* a married man, named Constantin Heger. It is coming to be the reprehensible fashion to print these Brontë letters in English, a language in which they never could have been written and do not in fact exist. Doubters should examine the end of *Villette,* where Brontë similarly experiments with a word like *ami,* enchanted with the fact that it can mean both friend and beloved in French, as no word can in English, and that it can be used by timid girls, shrewish wives, and kindly older men, as well as by lovers.

There is nothing, however, that a woman writer cannot do if she puts her mind to it; and if she has a mind that is both ingenious and tender, subtle and coarse, that is, if she is Colette, she can find the one occasion which makes a wooing woman into loving heroinism. The result was Colette's *Mitsou* (1919), which Proust rightly pronounced exquisite, and which all alone proves that the epistolary novel gaily survived, against all odds, into the twentieth century.

The wooing letters that make up Colette's novel are written by a little tramp from the Parisian gutter, a semi-illiterate, semi-prostitute called Mitsou by the middle-aged man who keeps her: M.I.T.S.O.U. are the initials of his flour business. She is a music-hall star who bubbles along in disreputable comfort, but without love, until the day she falls head over heels in love with a young man she meets backstage, and proceeds to woo by let-

ter. They finally share a night of love, which is not very satisfactory, and
the young man saves himself, as the French say—he disappears. Nevertheless, Mitsou is utterly charming, a true heroine, all because of the
unique occasion: it is wartime. The letters are sent to a nameless French
soldier stationed at the front, Mitsou's "Lieutenant Bleu." *Mitsou* was
Colette's contribution, and that of loving heroinism as well, to the war
effort.

II

> Illa novavit opus.
> —Ovid

Just after Virgil's *Aeneid* was published—or whatever they did with
best sellers in the first century B.C.—Ovid set himself the task of rewriting
some of the great heroic love stories of Greek and Roman antiquity from
the woman's point of view. Virgil had just told the Dido and Aeneas story
very grandly, as a tragic moment in a national epic about the hero who
founded Rome; Ovid would tell the story, very cleverly, from Dido's
standpoint. So he imagined Dido in the act of writing a love letter to
Aeneas as he sails away, leaving her on the shores of Carthage: a Dido
mournful, furious, eloquent, and passionate by turns, but always scribbling
—*scribentis imago;* a Dido hopeful of her lover's return in response to her
letter, and hoping she is not pregnant. In the latter respect, Ovid's Dido is
quite the opposite of Virgil's tragedy queen.

But everything is topsy-turvy and fresh in the women's love letters
Ovid wrote in verse, called the *Heroides.* Helen writes to Paris—no, I am
a respectable wife and can't even consider the shocking relationship you
have proposed—and yet . . . Hero writes to Leander—what a pother over
a little swimming—if you really loved me. . . . Penelope writes to Ulysses
—I'm still faithful to you, of course—but I wonder if you'll be put out to
find how I've aged—you know I'm not exactly the girl you left behind—

> Certo ego, que fueram te discendente puella,
> protinus ut venias, facta videbor anus.

"Ovid contrives," writes the classicist W. S. Anderson, "to let the woman
speak every line of the poem [by resorting] to the fiction of a letter. We are
reading the letter, or, to be more accurate, we are peeking over the
woman's shoulder as she is writing it." He goes on to say that "total spontaneity" is the principal originality resulting from Ovid's adoption of the

woman's point of view. But everything that Professor Anderson writes
about the effect on Ovid's poetry of his decision to make heroines rather
than heroes is of interest to modernists, for it is just what we say about the
transformation of the modern sensibility that resulted from—was it
perhaps caused?—the rise of the epistolary novel in the eighteenth century. We find in the novel of letters the same fresh realism, for the lovers
appear not as conventional abstractions, as in the old romances, but as a
real woman addressing a real man. We see the same fresh immediacy, not
so much to the events of the love story as to the act of expression, of literary creation itself. We mark the same subtilized psychology; the same
twists and turns, starts and stops of language itself, as if a real voice is
speaking as the hand writes. We also talk of spontaneity.

What Willa Cather writes of Ovid's *Heroides* might well be said of
Richardson's *Pamela.* "He read the *Heroides* over and over," she says
through the eyes of Niel Herbert, the narrator of *A Lost Lady,*

> and felt that they were the most glowing love stories ever told.
> He did not think of these books as something invented to beguile
> the idle hour, but as living creatures, caught in the very behavior
> of living, —surprised behind their misleading severity of form and
> phrase. He was eavesdropping upon the past. . . .

The spontaneous, the instinctive, the natural, the informal, the anticlas-
sical, and the artless: all these terms of art have been associated with the
woman's voice in literature from the beginning of time. They are also applied to the start of modern literature that we call Romanticism, and that
cannot be separated from the raising of the woman's voice in letters.
Where literary women themselves are concerned, spontaneity is a term of
terrifying ambivalence. For it can be read as a challenge to genius—or as
an excuse for failed work. It can characterize the art that springs from the
richest and deepest reaches of the imagination—or the art that clearly
lacks and clearly requires more control.

The letter form, in any case, is spontaneity formalized, and it travels
through the history of women's literature with a momentum all its own.
From Richardson to Fanny Burney, and the long imposition of the "familiar style" on female fiction; in Mme de Staël's *Corinne,* where the art form
in which female genius expresses itself is the *improvisation,* the spontaneous spoken threnodies by which that superheroine holds the world in
thrall; in George Sand's *Lélia,* where chapter-long monologues alternate in
a formal pattern which bares only the faintest trace of its origin in the
epistolary exchange—and end by veering, as so much Romantic writing by
women does, toward the operatic. It is in reading George Sand that we are
especially reminded that the aria of nineteenth-century opera is a musical

monologue closely related to the literary letter, for it is designed to serve as both self-assertion and conversational interchange.

When the philosopher-critic Alain began the revival of George Sand early in this century, two aspects of her art engaged his attention: her musicality, and her treatment of love. Like Walt Whitman, Alain was struck by the relationship between her writing and the art of singing, the art, he wrote, "so profoundly visceral, and yet which carries us so high. . . . Power and reason, those enemy sisters, who does not wait for, hope for the rare occasions when they are reconciled? . . . I imagine George Sand seated before her clavier, improvising, understanding that the instrument, however well-tempered, is not enough to regulate the redoubtable heart."

. . .

Verse letters of love that a woman writes to a man is the proper Ovidian sense of *"Heroides";* and when women poets set out to write them they created some of the most powerful poetry in the language.

> And wilt thou have me fashion into speech
> The love I bear thee . . . ?
> . . . .
> Nay, let the silence of my womanhood
> Commend my woman-love to thy belief,—
> Seeing that I stand unwon, however wooed. . . .

And:

> Belovèd, dost thou love? or did I see all
> The glory as I dreamed, and fainted when
> Too vehement light dilated my ideal,
> For my soul's eyes? Will that light come again,
> As now these tears come—falling hot and real?

And:

> If I leave all for thee, wilt thou exchange
> And be all to me? Shall I never miss
> Home-talk and blessing and the common kiss
> That comes to each in turn. . . .

And:

> How do I love thee? Let me count the ways.
> I love thee to the depth and breadth and height
> My soul can reach, when feeling out of sight
> For the ends of Being and ideal Grace.
> I love thee to the level of everyday's
> Most quiet need, by sun and candle-light. . . .

These are lines from a few of the forty-four poems called *Sonnets from the Portuguese* by Elizabeth Barrett Browning, or, more precisely, from the love letters in verse that Elizabeth Barrett wrote to Robert Browning when he was courting her. She showed them to him for the first time only after they were married, and she finally published them, at Browning's urging, under the title devised to conceal the intimate love-letter quality of the sonnets. "From the Portuguese" was meant to suggest a translation from another language, in the time-honored tradition of loving heroinism; but the reference was not to the abandoned "Portuguese" nun and her cavalier. Instead it was a reminder of an early Barrett poem that Browning was particularly fond of, called "Catarina to Camoens," which is a pure, if not distinguished, sample of the *Heroides* tradition.

Elizabeth Barrett, who read Portuguese, knew all about Camoens, the Renaissance poet and national bard of Portugal. Like Renaissance poets everywhere, he wrote a series of love sonnets, the occasion for which was apparently his unhappy love for a young noblewoman named Catarina, whom he could not marry. Banished from Lisbon, and sent to fight in Portugal's colonial wars, Camoens dispatched from another hemisphere a sonnet series celebrating the beauty of his beloved and the splendor of his love. Elizabeth Barrett, as a beginning poet, decided to rewrite the love story from Catarina's point of view—a love letter in verse, written by the girl when she is dying, about the dimming of her eyes that the poet called "Sweetest eyes were ever seen. . . ."

Behind Elizabeth Barrett's love poems, and all the other love poetry that women wrote in the mid-nineteenth century, was the conscious intention to reverse the ancient tradition of love poems all by men. In poetry as in fiction, the creation of the woman in love was an enterprise of heroinism—and the result was the love poems written by Emily Brontë, Emily Dickinson, and Christina Rossetti, as well as by Mrs. Browning. I have been reading them over, all together, and the effect is like uncorking a bottle of rare wine, like an explosion of sealed sensation and intoxication. This sudden outbreak of love in the verse of women—proper Victorian women—is a phenomenon; it is as if that lady in Shakespeare who never told her love got down off her monument, where she had been sitting like patience all those centuries, and began to speak like this:

> "Love me, for I love you"—and answer me,
> "Love me, for I love you": so shall we stand
> As happy equals in the flowering land
> Of love, that knows not a dividing sea.

Or like this:

> I wish I could remember that first day,
> First hour, first moment of your meeting me,

> If bright or dim the season, it might be
> Summer or winter for aught I can say;
> So unrecorded did it slip away,
> So blind was I to see and to foresee,
> So dull to mark the budding of my tree
> That would not blossom yet for many a May.
> If only I could recollect it, such
> A day of days! I let it come and go
> As traceless as a thaw of bygone snow;
> It seemed to mean so little, meant so much;
> If only now I could recall that touch,
> First touch of hand in hand—Did one but know!

These poems are from Christina Rossetti's late sonnet sequence called *Monna Innominata,* meaning Unnamed Lady. Each sonnet is preceded by a line in Italian from Dante and Petrarch, the greatest male lovers in Italian poetry, whose work Rossetti knew well in the original language. That she thought of the love poem as normally a male province, its traditional form the sonnet; that as a woman poet Christina Rossetti was consciously writing *Heroides,* purposely reversing tradition to give the loving woman her own poetic voice, her own love sonnets, are not matters of speculation, for she said so herself.

In the head-note Christina Rossetti supplied for the *Monna Innominata* sequence, she wrote that Dante's Beatrice and Petrarch's Laura "have come down to us resplendent with charms, but (at least to my apprehension) scant of attractiveness." There must have been many more such heroines, she goes on, whose names we don't know, but "one can imagine many a lady as sharing her lover's poetic aptitude. . . . Had such a lady spoken for herself, the portrait left us might have appeared more tender, if less dignified." That rather dry animadversion then gives way to a poet's boast. "Or had the Great Poetess of our own day and nation only been unhappy instead of happy, her circumstances would have invited her to bequeath to us, in lieu of the 'Portuguese Sonnets,' an inimitable 'donna innominata' drawn not from fancy but from feeling, and," Rossetti concludes, "worthy to occupy a niche beside Beatrice and Laura." After 1850, when Mrs. Browning's love sonnets were published, women poets everywhere wrote *Heroides* with a sense that they were working within a woman's literary tradition. On the other side of the Atlantic, Elizabeth Barrett Browning's most gifted disciple, Emily Dickinson, began around 1861 or 1862 to write her own love poems, among the finest written in English during the Victorian age.

As Christina Rossetti pointed out, Mrs. Browning was happy in her love, the other Victorian women poets not; but they were all virgins, I believe, when they wrote their love poetry. The many differences among them—of religion, education, temperament—are certainly not to be minimized. But it is time, perhaps, to read them all together as women poets of love, in order to inquire into the literary differences between women's love poetry and men's, a question of great interest to the poets themselves, and of greater interest than the biographical snoopery such poetry commonly elicits. The subject is enormous; and while it can begin with consideration of Victorian women poets (whose work mainly inspires the few suggestions I have to make myself) it should include a backward glance (based upon an unprejudiced rereading) of the annuals and news-paper poetesses of the early nineteenth century, and a forward look to the turn-of-the-century years, when, according to Louise Bogan, the task of reconstituting "warmth of feeling" in American poetry "was accomplished almost entirely by women poets." The American women poets Bogan discusses, as well as the English poet Alice Meynell, at least deserve a rereading.

Not all women poets write love poetry; Amy Lowell and Edna St. Vincent Millay did, Marianne Moore did not, and neither did Sylvia Plath—hate poems being her more characteristic form. Women's poetry of the 1960s and 1970s is triumphantly concerned with love, and once again, I think, from a feminist impetus. But whoever wants to take the subject of women's love poetry seriously must know many languages, for the subject must carry them from Sappho to the saints, in the days when the poetry of spiritual love reveled in the imagery of marriage with Christ. There are French, Italian, and Spanish women poets to be read seriously; and Russian would be absolutely essential, for Anna Akhmatova used love poetry as her principal vehicle for ideas of a philosophical and historical cast. That Akhmatova had many followers who wrote *Heroides* in Russian, and that she lived to regret it, is suggested by her little "Epigram" that Stanley Kunitz translates:

> Could Beatrice have written like Dante,
> Or Laura have glorified love's pain?
> I set the style for women's speech.
> God help me shut them up again!
> (1960)

* * *

Women's love poetry seems to me to be I-You poetry, not I-He poetry on the whole; the effect is verse letters directed by a woman to the specific man she loves, and not about him; women poets do not celebrate *his* eyes, *his* hair, *his* smile; they mostly write about Me. Oddly enough, a certain realism results: the lover seems to be a real man, because he is You; we usually put this adversely, saying that women are too sentimental in their love poetry, too responsive to their own emotions (which we deduce from the poems alone). On the other hand, we criticize male love poetry as being too abstract, too conventional, for the beaming eyes, golden tresses, snowy bosom, and blushing cheeks of the lady seem interchangeable from a Beatrice to a Laura; and the experience of love behind men's poetry tends to seem unreal.

Women poets do not complain of the power of love, the poison on Cupid's dart. On the contrary, they rejoice in love, and boast of the transformation in themselves resulting from what Kate Chopin called "The Awakening" and Emily Dickinson called a Glory, a Sumptuousness, a Resurrection, a "Title Divine—is mine!" Dickinson and the others can be quite shameless as they exult in the revelation love has brought:

> Blush, my spirit, in thy Fastness—
> Blush, my unacknowledged clay—
> Seven years of troth have taught thee
> More than wifehood ever may.

There seems to be more fire than ice in women's love poetry. Men always have to draw on the imagery of cold, because their beloved's resistance, denial, and betrayal are the principal occasions dramatized in their poems. But lightning bolts and volcanic eruptions are as useful to Emily Dickinson as to *Jane Eyre;* Edna Millay makes clever use of a burning cigarette, as well as a candle; and in the *Sonnets from the Portuguese* pure fire stirs the red flame of passion in the ashes of life before love. Elizabeth Barrett imagines the overturning of a burial urn at her lover's feet:

> Behold and see
> What a great heap of grief lay hid in me,
> And how the red wild sparkles dimly burn
> Through the ashen grayness.

Then she adds a very neat compliment to Browning:

> . . . those laurels on thine head,
> O my Belovèd, will not shield thee so,

And she concludes with a line in the imperative voice, for which women love poets have a marked weakness: ". . . Stand farther off then! go." Similarly, in Christina Rossetti: "Come back to me, who wait and watch for you." But the ultimate in order-giving can be found in the wifely love poems of Anne Bradstreet, such as her charming "Phoebus" poem, where she hurls a series of contradictory commands at the sun-god employed to carry her message to her absent husband, starting with "Phoebus make haste," moving on to "But stay this once," and ending with "Now post with double speed, mark what I say,/By all our loves conjure him not to stay." The effect of all these love commands in verse is deftly summed up by Bradstreet's couplet:

> And if he love, how can he there abide?
> My Interest's more than all the world beside.

In women's love poetry, just as in men's, the convention holds that the beloved must be placed high above the lover, a divine or royal object on a superior plane. But women poets seem to devote a special ingenuity to imagining the lovers as high/low and, simultaneously, on a plane of equality. Angels are terribly useful to women poets, for they are at once sexy, of no particular sex, and independent of gravity. "What thing is this?" asks Edna Millay in *Fatal Interview:*

> beneath
> My winged helmet and my winged heel.
> What sweet emotions neither foe nor friend
> Are these that clog my flight? . . .
> . . . .
> Up, up, my feathers!—ere I lay you by
> To journey barefoot with a mortal joy.

Elizabeth Barrett Browning imagines her lovers as two wonderful pre-Raphaelite angels who "spread wing and fly in the outer air," and "look surprise/On one another, as they strike athwart/Their wings in passing." All the *Sonnets from the Portuguese* are filled with images of rising and falling and dropping and lifting and flying and swooping, often in conscious reversal of the norms of male/female sexual imagery. For example, I expect Mrs. Browning knew just what she was doing with her angels in sonnet xxii:

> When our two souls stand up erect and strong,
> Face to face, silent, drawing nigh and nigher,
> Until the lengthening wings break into fire
> At either curvèd point,—

A fondness for disembodied angels does not imply an avoidance of physicality in women's love poetry; on the contrary. While so much male love poetry celebrates the glance of an eye, women's love poems thrive on the touch, which is sometimes violent. There is that splendid, distinctly female image in the first of Mrs. Browning's sonnets, where she imagines herself bending and weeping over the grave when suddenly

> a mystic Shape did move
> Behind me, and drew me backward by the hair;
> And a voice said in mastery, while I strove,—
> 'Guess now who holds thee?'—'Death,' I said. But, there,
> The silver answer rang,—'Not Death, but Love.'

All of which is pretty energetic work for a mystic Shape.

In Christina Rossetti it is the "First touch of hand in hand" that makes her bud burst into blossom; in Emily Dickinson—

> He touched me, so I live to know
> That such a day, permitted so,
> I groped upon his breast—

It is all so real, so true to life, so immediate (did I hear someone say so artless and spontaneous?). The exact moment, the specific occasion that gave rise to woman's love is so precisely recorded that when we read

> Of all the Souls that stand create—
> I have elected—One—

we are sure that a few thousand more pages of industrious research will turn up the name of Emily Dickinson's One, as they never will. What a chase the women poets of love have sent their biographers scurrying on, to pinpoint the exact occasion, the hour of the day, the one man who touched, pulled, whispered, kissed the woman in love!

It used to be the fashion to say that literary spinsters were specialists in renunciation. Now it is the fashion to say that they were all in love with a married man, and had fate not intervened in the shape of an officious relative or a mortal illness, they would all have behaved very wickedly indeed. Curiosity about their love life will surely continue, whatever I or anyone else may write about loving heroinism. May I suggest, therefore, that a rich untapped field remains to yield a fortune in scholarly dissertations, and that is the animals in the lives of literary women. George Sand had a horse, by a delicious coincidence named Colette; Christina Rossetti had a wombat; Colette had all those cats; Virginia Woolf was positively dotty, as her unpublished papers will reveal, about all sorts of animal creatures. But it is their dogs who will serve the purpose best—Elizabeth Barrett's spaniel named Flush; Emily Dickinson's "dog as large as myself," as she coyly wrote Thomas Higginson, "that my father bought me"; and Keeper, that ferocious canine without whose company Emily Brontë would not stalk the moors. With their rough, shaggy coats, their deep, senseless voices, their stupid affection, and their dirty habits, surely dogs supplied the want for all that is precious in masculinity to literary spinsters.

It was in vain that Charlotte Brontë tried to explain to the well-meaning but obtuse George Henry Lewes that it is a species of critical stupidity, as well as critical rudeness, to deny the woman writer her access to that divinity of all literature, the imagination. When Lewes, stunned by the disparity he discovered between the real life of Charlotte Brontë and the passion in *Jane Eyre,* warned her to keep to the Real, Miss Brontë wrote him as follows—a justly famous passage. "Imagination is a strong, restless fac-

1. Fanny (Austen) Knight, Jane Austen's favorite "neice," sketched by her sister Cassandra Austen. There is no acceptable Jane Austen portrait.

2. Elizabeth Barrett in 1843 (before her marriage to Robert Browning),
sketched by her brother Alfred Moulton-Barrett.

3. Harriet Martineau in 1833; by Daniel Maclise for *Fraser's Magazine*.

4. Kate Chopin in 1899.

5. Willa Cather as managing editor of *McClure's Magazine*, around 1910.

6. Harriet Beecher Stowe during her trip abroad in 1853; by George
Richmond.

7. Elizabeth Cleghorn Gaskell in 1851; by George Richmond.

8. Christina Rossetti in 1877; by her brother Dante Gabriel Rossetti.

9. Emily Dickinson at Mount Holyoke in 1847–48.

10. Anne, Emily and Charlotte Brontë around 1838; by their brother Branwell Brontë.

11. Fanny Burney by her cousin Edward Francesco Burney, who was her "trusted agent" during the publication of *Evelina*.

12. Stéphanie Félicité Ducrest de Saint-Aubin, Comtesse de Genlis, during her early social triumphs in Paris; by Deveria.

13. George Sand in 1834; by Delacroix.

14. George Sand — her
self-caricature from the
same period.

15. Gertrude Stein in 1906; by Picasso.

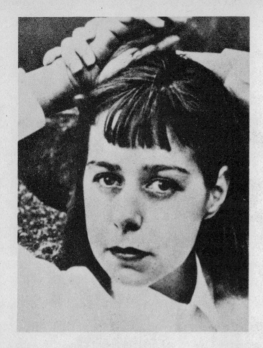

16. Carson McCullers.

17. Simone Weil.

18. Louisa May Alcott around 1862.

19. Madame de Staël as a girl: Germaine Necker at about thirteen; by Carmontelle.

20. Madame de Staël posed as Corinne; by Élisabeth Vigée-Lebrun.

21. Mary Wollstonecraft in 1797; by John Opie.

22. Mary Shelley in 1841; by Richard Rothwell.

23. Virginia Stephen in 1908 (before her marriage to Leonard Woolf); by Francis Dodd.

24. George Eliot in 1872; by L. C. Dickenson.

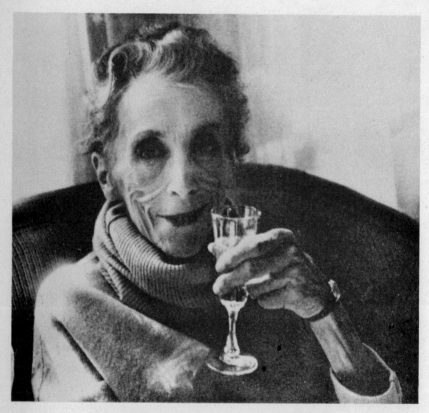

25. Isak Dinesen — the last portrait by Cecil Beaton.

26. Colette in 1924.

27. Sylvia Plath.

ulty. When she shows us bright pictures, are we never to look at them, and try to reproduce them? And when she is eloquent, and speaks rapidly and urgently in our ear, are we not to write to her dictation?"

Because of the posthumous publication and brilliant editing in our own time (by Fannie Ratchford and others) of the Brontës' private fantasies, we see more clearly than Lewes ever could the "bright pictures" they carried in their minds; we know the source of Rochester and Heathcliff. These Brontë legends of Gondal and Angria are unique in literary history (as the Brontës were unique) because they were family fantasies, shared openly among the girls and their brother, nourished and developed from early childhood to advanced adulthood, and written down in miniature imitations of the magazine literature of the day. Other women's fantasies we can only guess at, but one similarity to those of the Brontës recurs: the *stability* of the fantasy, its continuous, scenario-like quality featuring the same characters and their descendants over a long stretch of time, through slowly developing adventures and gradually changing settings.

So Fanny Burney wrote *Evelina,* her first published novel, out of the fantasy materials which persisted after the writing of her true first novel, which she was forced to burn; Evelina was literally the descendant of the pair of lovers whose story Burney had brought to a happy conclusion years before. Jane Austen amused herself (and her family) with inventing marriages and after-histories for all the Bennet girls in *Pride and Prejudice.* George Sand had a running religious fantasy, well into adulthood, surrounding the worship of a palpable deity of indeterminate sex named *Corambé;* it inhibited her novel-writing at first, she wrote: "j'aimais mieux me taire et poursuivre intérieurement l'éternel poëme de *Corambé,* où je me sentais dans le vrai de mes émotions." Mary Shelley perhaps spoke for them all, when she wrote in her preface to the third edition of *Frankenstein:*

> As a child I scribbled. . . . Still I had a dearer pleasure than this, which was the formation of castles in the air—the indulging in waking dreams—the following up trains of thought, which had for their subject the formation of a succession of imaginary incidents. My dreams were at once more fantastic and agreeable than my writings. In the latter I was a close imitator— . . . but my dreams were all my own; I accounted for them to nobody; they were my refuge when annoyed—my dearest pleasure when free.

How familiar to their own experience as child and woman is this ceaseless scenario-making in the waking mind, I leave it to my women readers to decide. And to the psychologists among them, whether this kind of stable imaginative play is more characteristic of women than of men seems a subject worthier of investigation than most.

We know at least that all the Brontë virgins, Charlotte, Anne, and
Emily, loved with brute passion, committed adultery and incest, bore illegitimate children, moldered in dungeons, murdered, revenged, conquered,
and died unrepentant in the imaginary kingdoms they called Gondal and
Angria. To the power of their imagination, and the woman's passion that
drove their fantasies, we owe not only the fiction but the love poetry of
Emily Brontë:

> Cold in the earth, and the deep snow piled above thee!
> Far, far removed, cold in the dreary grave!
> Have I forgot, my Only Love, to love thee,
> Severed at last by Time's all-wearing wave?
> . . . .
> Sweet Love of youth, forgive if I forget thee
> While the World's tide is bearing me along:
> Sterner desires and darker hopes beset me,
> Hopes which obscure but cannot do thee wrong.
> No other Sun has lighted up my heaven;
> No other Star has ever shone for me:
> All my life's bliss from thy dear life was given—
> All my life's bliss is in the grave with thee.

We now can say, with both assurance and relief, that it was not some uninteresting ordinary man, some pawky, consumptive Yorkshire curate,
who inspired that operatic effusion. It is the lament of Rosina Alcona,
otherwise Augusta Geraldine Almeda, Queen of Gondal, over the grave of
Julius Brenzaida, Prince of Angora, King of Almedore, and Emperor of
Gaaldine.

9

PERFORMING HEROINISM: THE MYTH OF CORINNE

I The Myth

> [*Corinne*] is an immortal book, and deserves to be read three score and ten times—that is once every year in the age of man.
>
> Elizabeth Barrett (age 26)

> The hour of agony and revolt . . . passes away and does not return; yet those who, amid the agitations . . . of their youth, betook themselves to the early works of George Sand, may in later life cease to read them, indeed, but they can no more forget them than they can forget *Werther*. George Sand speaks somewhere of her "days of *Corinne*." Days of *Valentine*, many of us may in like manner say,—days of *Lélia*, days never to return!
>
> Matthew Arnold (age 55)

Let us try to take *Corinne* seriously; it was *the* book of the woman of genius. At least a few chapters and scattered passages, as well as the complex scheme of the novel that Mme de Staël had the brilliance but not the talent to write, should be familiar to anyone pretending to an interest in the traditions of women's literature; they are already familiar to historians of Romanticism.

Published in 1807, *Corinne, ou l'Italie—Corinne, or Italy*—was the work of a woman already known in Europe and America as the author of *De la littérature*, which established Mme de Staël's name forever as the one which "still rises first to the lips," in George Eliot's words, "when we are asked to mention a woman of great intellectual power." To take *Corinne* seriously is to perceive its place in Mme de Staël's thought about literature and culture, but to read the novel itself is also to encounter a predecessor of those "Silly Novels by Lady Novelists" which George Eliot so wittily demolished. *Corinne* stands alone in Mme de Staël's *oeuvre*, in its silliness as in its enormous influence upon literary women. For them, the myth of Corinne persisted as both inspiration and warning: it is the fantasy of the performing heroine.

Let us try to take *Corinne* seriously, in order to comprehend George Eliot's expressed and unexpressed conceptions of heroinism in such a scene as this, from *The Mill on the Floss:*

> "Take back your *Corinne*," said Maggie. . . . "You were right in telling me she would do me no good; but you were wrong in thinking I should wish to be like her."
>
> "Wouldn't you really like to be a tenth Muse, then, Maggie?" said Philip. . . .
>
> "Not at all," said Maggie, laughing. "The Muses were uncomfortable goddesses, I think—obliged always to carry rolls and musical instruments about with them. . . ."
>
> "You agree with me in not liking Corinne, then?"
>
> "I didn't finish the book. . . ."

At this point of *The Mill on the Floss*, the reader is just as surprised as Philip Wakem to discover that Maggie Tulliver, whom we have known up to now as a sensitive, misunderstood child, is not to turn into a mature woman of intellectual distinction and wide ambition—a *femme supérieure*, like Mme de Staël or George Eliot herself—but instead into a merely pretty and dangerous flirt who steals a rich, good-looking suitor away from her cousin Lucy. Swinburne could not bear it. No such "abyss of cynicism" on the subject of female character had been sounded by the wickedest of French novelists—not by Stendhal, Mérimée, or Laclos. "My faith will not digest at once," he wrote, "the first two volumes and the third volume of 'The Mill on the Floss'; my conscience or credulity has not gorge enough for such a gulp."

The myth of Corinne bridges the abyss in *The Mill on the Floss*, even though Maggie Tulliver is not allowed to say whether she likes the heroine of Mme de Staël's novel, which George Eliot read in her adolescence or early twenties. *Corinne* served as a children's book for a special kind of nineteenth-century child: girls of more than ordinary intelligence or talent, and rising ambition to fame beyond the domestic circle. Reading *Corinne* made an event of their youth—for some, a catalyst to their own literary development—which in later years they could not wholly reject unless willing also to deny their own enthralling, painful awakening as women of genius—their own "days of *Corinne*," in Matthew Arnold's phrase. For the aspiration to glory which is a happy and a wholesome thing in the development of a gifted young man was very different then (perhaps still is today) for an exceptional young woman. For her, noble ambitions cut cruelly across the normal process of female maturation; for her, as Mme de Staël put it in *De la littérature,* the desire for fame stimulates her mind, but reason counsels obscurity. That is the dilemma of Corinne as Mme de Staël, with daunting lucidity, expounded it; and she left it unresolved.

"I didn't finish the book," Maggie Tulliver continues—

> "As soon as I came to the blond-haired young lady reading in the park, I shut it up, and determined to read no further. I foresaw that the light-complexioned girl would win away all the love from Corinne and make her miserable. I'm determined to read no more books where the blond-haired women carry away all the happiness. . . ."

The business of dark hair versus light is not at all trivial in *The Mill on the Floss,* where much of Maggie's childhood anguish is represented by her inability to manage her unruly mop of dark hair; and the inhibiting forces of conventional femininity are represented by the hatefully neat blond curls of her cousin Lucy. In *Corinne,* hair color is momentous: Corinne represents the passionate exuberance of dark-haired Latin culture, and Lucile, her blond rival, stands for the subdued and inhibited sensibility of Nordic culture, along with all that is implied by the home, the wife, and the private virtues in English society.

Maggie goes on to mention Rebecca in *Ivanhoe* and other dark-haired non-Anglo-Saxon heroines in Scott (who knew all about *Corinne*) as examples of "the dark unhappy ones" that "I want to avenge." Philip takes her light words seriously:

> "Well, perhaps you will avenge the dark women in your own person, and carry away all the love from your cousin Lucy. She is sure to have some handsome young man of St. Ogg's at her feet now; and you have only to shine upon him—your fair little cousin will be quite quenched in your beams."
>
> "Philip, that is not pretty of you, to apply my nonsense to anything real," said Maggie, looking hurt. "As if I, with my old gowns and want of all accomplishments, could be a rival of dear little Lucy."

Pretty or not, Philip has made a fair summary of the rest of the novel, except that Maggie's convenient death in a flood is designed to smooth over, both practically and morally, her ugly revenge on blondes in the person of "dear little Lucy." Corinne, incidentally, also dies at the end, making her faithless lover and her blond rival wretched with regret, after subversively coaching their little daughter to carry on her own tradition of feminine genius. Mme de Staël's is a funnier revenge of feminine spite, but perhaps preferable to George Eliot's.

For literary women, Corinne was the female Childe Harold, and Byron owed something, as he and his contemporaries recognized, to Mme de Staël. Thanks to Lady Blessington, there is a record of the hilarious debate between Lord Byron and Mme de Staël over which had done more harm through their hero and heroine. And just as the Byronic hero became a myth wider than any single literary creation because Byron's own life entered into its making, so the legend of Mme de Staël's life blended with the myth of her heroine. (For her contemporaries, the single name denoted them both, for after the publication of the novel in 1807 Mme de Staël was everywhere known as Corinne.)

In the eyes of literary women, hers was a woman's life unique in history for its great public swath. Mme de Staël was the first woman of middle-class origins to impress herself, through her own genius, on all the major public events of her time—events political, literary, in every sense revolutionary. Her position and wealth came initially from her father, who was Jacques Necker, citizen banker of Geneva and finance minister to Louis XVI. But after her marriage to a Swedish diplomat (the only trivial event of her life), she became a power in her own right. Gibbon, Napoleon, Jefferson, Schlegel, Sismondi, Constant, Narbonne, Goethe, Talleyrand—the extraordinary gallery of great men who pass through her life story, as friends, colleagues, lovers, enemies, correspondents, were drawn to Mme de Staël by her mind, her talk, and her writings.

She was indeed one of the greatest talkers ever to dominate a salon—but there were so many talking women in the history of the French salon; more important, Mme de Staël was a professional writer, whose books changed the world. Her studies of Rousseau, of Peace, of Fiction, of the Passions in the 1790s; of Literature Considered in Its Relations to Social Institutions, in 1800; of Germany, of Suicide, of the French Revolution in the 1810s brought her persecution by an emperor and "a degree of homage never before paid to any woman who was not a queen." So wrote Lydia Maria Child, the New York writer, who wrote one of the early biographies of Mme de Staël and was herself under the spell of the myth of Corinne, which associates queenship with literary glory.

As early as the 1790s, when she was in her twenties, the rarity of Mme de Staël's accomplishment entered the consciousness of literary women, as Fanny Burney, Hannah More, Mary Berry, and Maria Edgeworth testify. Her presence in England (an émigrée in 1793) provided an impetus to the feminist ferment of that remarkable decade, as well as, in the person of a minor member of her entourage, a husband for Fanny Burney. But it was only with Corinne, in 1807, that the myth floated free—the myth of the famous woman talking, writing, performing, to the applause of the world.

As early as 1808, Jane Austen was recommending "Corinna" (in one of the quickly available English translations) to a gentleman of her acquaintance who was stone deaf—with what accents of irony one can only imagine. Mary Godwin picked up *Corinne* as soon as her first illegitimate baby (by Shelley) was born. Catharine Sedgwick, the American novelist, made a pilgrimage to Mme de Staël's grave at Le Coppet, and was rather surprised to find that the author of *Corinne* had actually been silenced by her death in 1817.

The poetesses of the 1820s, in England and America, were identified by their large public with Corinne, and for good reason. "That book," wrote Felicia Hemans, "has a power over me which is quite indescribable; some passages seem to give me back my own thoughts and feelings, my whole inner being, with a mirror more true than ever friend could hold up." The poet Maria Jewsbury wrote an imitation of *Corinne* called *The History of an Enthusiast,* in which the heroine proclaims her enthusiasm for fame because "it would make amends for being a woman."

In distant Scotland Jane Welsh was being urged to write an essay on the author of *Corinne* by her suitor Thomas Carlyle: "If I do not live to see you by far the most distinguished female I ever knew I shall die disappointed," he wrote. She wrote that Fame attracted her, "but I feel clearly that I wish to be loved as well as admired," and did not write the essay; Carlyle married her, and did not die of the disappointment.

By the early 1830s young Elizabeth Barrett had already read *Corinne* three times over, and George Sand was writing *Lélia,* and on the American frontier young Harriet Beecher read *Corinne* and a life of its author. "I have felt an intense sympathy with many parts of that book, with many parts of her character," she wrote—and set out on her own literary career.

By the early 1840s Margaret Fuller was being called the "Yankee Corinna" by Emerson and everyone else—and the Victorian apotheosis of the Corinne myth was underway. It would last as long as the century, and spread as far as Maine and Missouri; Kate Chopin, a votary of the myth, would be called the Corinne of St. Louis. "Female Authorship," wrote Margaret Fuller, owed a great debt to Mme de Staël's intellect: "its beams make the obscurest school-house in New England warmer and lighter to the little rugged girls who are gathered together on its wooden bench." On one of those benches decades later, a rugged New England schoolgirl named Sarah Orne Jewett penciled on the flyleaf of her copy of *Corinne* the following warning lines of Victorian verse:

> Be good, sweet maid, and let who will be clever;
> Do noble things, not dream them, all day long:
> And so make life, death, and that vast for-ever
> One grand sweet song.

The Corinne myth was "perilous stuff" to women, to use Bulwer's phrase for Byronism, and like the Byronic hero Mme de Staël's heroine often makes her most significant presence felt by the force of resistance she evokes. So Maggie Tulliver insists that she does *not* want to be a

Corinne, and neither does Lucy Snowe, the supreme antiheroine of Victorian fiction. Charlotte Brontë cast the hero of *Villette* as a Napoleon, in his opposition to intellectual and strong-minded women; for Napoleon, who censored, banned, and exiled Mme de Staël for her writings, entered too into the myth of Corinne. "He resembled the great Emperor," wrote Charlotte Brontë of her Paul Emanuel; ". . . would have exiled fifty Madame de Staëls, if they had annoyed, offended, out-rivalled, or opposed him." Lucy Snowe personally struggles against all the excelling, all the public display that the myth of Corinne implies.

But in Charlotte Brontë's youthful imagination, Corinne herself had stalked untrammeled and unrepressed in the person of Zenobia Percy, Countess of Northumberland. With flashing eyes and raven hair, with her velvets, plumes, and crowning turban, Zenobia is "the prima donna of the Angrian Court, the most learned woman of her age, the modern Cleopatra, the Verdopolitan de Staël." At eighteen Brontë wrote the figure into her Angria tales, those fantasies which served to nourish her mature fiction and also to exorcise from it such perilous stuff as the myth of Corinne.

II *Corinne*

> *Do you want to make an author out of a woman?*—Exactly as if you should announce the project of making your daughter an opera singer when you give her a singing teacher. I say . . . that a woman must never write anything but posthumous works. . . . For a woman under fifty to get into print, is submitting her happiness to the most terrible of lotteries; if she has the good fortune to have a lover, she'll begin by losing him.
>
> —Stendhal: *De l'amour*

There is a hero in *Corinne,* and he is dealt with—actually, set up—in the first of the novel's twenty books. There we find an English nobleman progressing in a distracted and melancholy fashion, during the winter of 1794–95, across the Continent toward Italy, in what is a kind of preromantic ruined fragment of the grand tour which such men made throughout the eighteenth century. He is a Scottish peer called Oswald lord Nevil—an orthography which has always made trouble, though it is a fair representation of what the French ear hears when the name Neville is pronounced. Such trivia as spelling and the distinction between England and Scotland meant little to Mme de Staël, but it was very important to her that her hero be a Briton, an exemplar in emotive and moral tone of the new sensibility and culture then sweeping down like a tidal wave out of the north to engulf the Francophone, Latin civilization of the *Age de Lumières.*

Mme de Staël makes Oswald "interesting" by giving him noble birth, unrevealed past, and unexplained gloom; but she must also make him worthy of such a heroine as Corinne. The matter is efficiently dispatched in Book 1: Oswald steers a ship through a storm, calming both the elements and the spirits of lesser men about him; and then he saves a whole community from destruction by fire. These "scenes" are all the reader has to cling to, later on, when Corinne loses her heart to the hero. Mme de Staël tosses them at us, and later looks back at them, with an air of saying: however weak and vacillating, however dull and priggish is my Oswald, remember that he has demonstrated that physical courage and that proto-military leadership which alone are lacking to the heroism of the woman of genius.

And the fire scene is our first indication that the more stupid the narrative in *Corinne,* the more interesting are the ideas which drive it forward. For no apparent novelistic reason, Mme de Staël sets fire to Ancona, a city she describes as equally divided among people of the Roman Catholic, Greek Orthodox, and Jewish faiths. Lord Nelvil risks his life to save the Jews, barricaded in their quarter at nightfall, and blamed by the Christians of the city for the conflagration that threatens them all. Oswald's indignant and generous rejection of superstition is that of a Briton and a Protestant, as well as a hero. So ends Book 1, called "Oswald," and so ends our interest in that gentleman.

Book 2, the most important of the novel, is called "Corinne au Capitole." It establishes the ultimate fantasy of the performing heroine with a brio, a luster, and a folly beyond the possibility of future novelists to exceed. All this takes place in the Capitol of the capital of the world. Oswald awakens to the brilliant sun of Rome, and to the ringing of bells and booming of cannons which announce that, that very day, there will be carried in triumph to the Capitoline Hill, there to be crowned with the laurel wreath of genius, as Petrarch and Tasso were before her, the most famous woman of Italy: "Corinne, poëte, écrivain, improvisatrice, et l'une des plus belles personnes de Rome."*

---

* In my translations from *Corinne* I have tried to capture the style of the original, which includes some startling modernisms, but this sentence defeats me; who would believe me if I had Mme de Staël call Corinne one of the "beautiful people" of Rome? The prose of the novel seems to me to have all the flat-footed grace and dignity of some sprightly elephant—not perhaps quite what Sainte-Beuve meant, in his 1839 preface, when he praised "la majesté soutenue" of the style of *Corinne.* Here it is the mythmaking of a brilliant writer that interests, not her language; for Mme de Staël's prose at its most eloquent, and for her most serious and powerful feminist statement, see her chapter on women of letters ("Des femmes qui cultivent les lettres") in *De la littérature.*

All of Rome seems to have turned into the streets for the occasion. The babble of the populace arouses Oswald's curiosity about a woman whose nationality, past, and even real name are unknown (but not her age: she is twenty-six, a year older than he)—and predisposes him to admire Corinne before he sees her. "In England he would have judged such a woman very severely, but in Italy he could ignore social conventions and take an interest in the crowning of Corinne similar to that of an adventure in Ariosto." This love affair begins with a clashing of cultures as well as a clanging of bells.

Music sounds. A parade of Roman and foreign dignitaries marches by. Then come the four white horses which draw the chariot mounted with an antique throne, on which, in a noble attitude, sits Corinne. Young girls dressed in white walk by her side, but Corinne herself is no maiden: she is a mature woman of what we would call solid build. Mme de Staël insists on her beautiful arms and asks us to think of Greek statuary, just as George Eliot does with the "large round arm" of Maggie Tulliver at the time of that heroine's apotheosis:

> . . . the dimpled elbow . . . the varied gently-lessening curves down to the delicate wrist . . . the firm softness. A woman's arm touched the soul of a great sculptor two thousand years ago, so that he wrought an image of it for the Parthenon which moves us still. . . . Maggie's was such an arm as that. . . .

Corinne is robed in white like the Domenichino sibyl, with a blue drapery flowing from her shoulder and an Indian shawl wound round her head and through her beautiful black hair. It is an "extremely picturesque" costume, Mme de Staël points out, "but not so far out of fashion as to be liable to the charge of affectation." For an idea of the style, do not look at the Gérard portrait of Mme de Staël in the garb of Corinne, which is simply too depressing, but instead look at Dorothea Brooke in *Middlemarch* as posed by George Eliot in a museum in Rome—

> standing against a pedestal near the reclining marble; a breathing blooming girl, whose form, not shamed by the Ariadne, was clad in Quakerish grey drapery; her long cloak, fastened at the neck, was thrown backward from her arms, and one beautiful ungloved hand pillowed her cheek, pushing somewhat backward the white beaver bonnet which made a sort of halo to her face around the simply braided dark-brown hair.

"Vive Corinne! vive le génie! vive la beauté!" cheers the marvelously responsive Italian crowd: long live genius, long live beauty, long live Corinne. And Oswald loves. Or, to be more precise, he suddenly experiences a transforming shock that runs like a thrill of electrical energy (the image is Mme de Staël's) from this moment to the end of the novel, a

shock to his soul and to his cultural prejudices. All Oswald's British respectability, dignity, impassivity, and taciturnity; all his essentially
religious deference to the sacred idols of *the home*—privacy, discretion,
solitude, patriotism, paternal ancestry—are shaken by a threefold experience: Italy, its climate and culture; applause by the masses of spiritual
rather than military genius; and the woman of genius. As Mme de Staël
puts it, "The admiration of the populace grew ever greater the closer she
came to the Capitol, that place so rich in memories. This beautiful sky,
these enthusiastic Romans, and above all Corinne herself electrified the
imagination of Oswald."

For what Oswald is made to love in Corinne is not the woman in the
genius but, if the expression is pardonable, the whole package: the woman
of genius at the moment and in the place of her greatest public triumph. It
isn't easy, and in fact does not work out very well, but at least it must be
said that what Mme de Staël puts at issue is no simple *amour,* but the total
transformation of cultural attitudes (and perhaps civilization itself) by the
romance of the woman of genius.

At last the procession reaches the Capitol. Senators, cardinal, acad-
emicians are seated, as well as a spill-over crowd. Corinne touches her knee
to the ground before taking her seat and listening to the speeches and odes
recited in her praise. Then she rises to improvise on the theme of "The
Glory and the Happiness of Italy"—almost a chapter-length of throbbing
prose. It is the first of many such improvisations which are dotted through
the novel, and which were rendered into English verse, in the most widely
read translation of *Corinne,* by Letitia E. Landon, herself one of Corinne's
disciples, known as "L.E.L." and as the author of a poem called "The Improvisatrice."

The final chapter of Book 2 deals with the actual crowning. A senator
rises with the laurel wreath. Corinne detaches her turban, letting her ebony
curls flow free, and advances her bare head with a smile of undissimulated
pleasure on her face: no longer a modest woman, for she has just spoken
very well indeed; no longer a fearful woman, but an inspired priestess
dedicated to the cult of genius. Music sounds, the crown descends,
Corinne's eyes fill with tears—and my own emotions are at this point too
strong to permit me to continue with what is almost a literal translation of
the passage. I have been following Mme de Staël's scenario very precisely,
for the steps in Corinne's triumph were very precisely observed not only
by Oswald but by writers after her: first the gossip overheard by a skeptical
stranger, then the fanfare, then the procession, then the distant view—oh
so lovely, so unusual—of the heroine, then the formal praises; only then
the actual performance (very difficult for a novelist to make convincing);
and at last the crown. Reading this material with a woman's eye makes it
hard to keep a straight face; but I am bound to say that *Corinne* is one of

very few works by women which is trivialized rather than honored by being read as a woman's work.

What contemporary readers saw in the triumph of Corinne was not the adolescence of Maggie Tullivers to come, but a remarkably courageous celebration of the rights of spiritual genius and intellectual freedom, in defiance of the spreading imperial rule of a military genius named Napoleon. "Corinne is the sovereign independence of genius even at the time of the most absolute oppression," wrote Sainte-Beuve, "Corinne who has herself crowned in Rome, in the Capitol of the eternal city, where the conqueror who exiles her will not set foot." That Napoleon was a man and Mme de Staël a woman was a matter of historical accident, and did not affect the Emperor's decision to exile the author of *Corinne*. That the claim for art over force, for mind over might was made—in somewhat original and Romantic terms—by a woman, and in a woman's novel, was an historical accident with major literary repercussions. But the politicizing of genius, that is, the demonstration of genius by means of public acclamation, by an actual crowning, was Mme de Staël's principal intention, before self-aggrandizement, before feminism, when she wrote Book 2 of *Corinne*.

Literary women, however, dearly wanted that crown: some formal, palpable, public tribute to female genius. The most charming of all Victorian crowning scenes, because the one which most consciously records a young woman's reactions to *Corinne*, is in *Aurora Leigh*. Mrs. Browning's heroine, an aspiring poet, playfully makes herself a poet's crown for her twentieth birthday: not of bay leaves, the classical laurel ("The fates deny us if we are overbold") but of "that headlong ivy! not a leaf will grow / But thinking of a wreath." In the midst of her solitary play-acting, Aurora finds that she is being observed by "My public!—cousin Romney—with a mouth / Twice graver than his eyes."

The very name of poet, for Aurora Leigh, "Is royal, and to sign it like a queen" is what she yearns to but dares not do, for " 't is too easy to go mad/And ape a Bourbon in a crown of straws." These images of crowns, and queens, and even Bourbons traveled across the ocean to the poetry of Emily Dickinson, who revered Mrs. Browning herself as "the Head too High to Crown" and wrote wistfully, in the accents of the girl poet Aurora Leigh,

> I'm saying every day
> "If I should be a Queen, tomorrow"—
> . . . .
> If it be, I wake a Bourbon
> None on me, bend supercilious—

George Eliot is always trying to put a golden halo on Dorothea Brooke's head, and, in a different mood, she pins a gold star on

Gwendolen Harleth's archery dress in *Daniel Deronda*. She also has a "star of brilliants" descend from the royal box on the brow of Armgart, the prima donna in George Eliot's verse play of that title. When accused of enjoying the "ecstasy" of satisfied ambition, "Why not?" Armgart asks,

> Am I a sage whose word must fall like seed
> Silently buried toward a far-off spring?
> I sing to living men. . . .
>
> . . . If the world brings me gifts,
> Gold, incense, myrrh—'twill be the needful sign
> That I have stirred it as the high year stirs
> Before I sink to winter.

I think it must be said that women writers who have attempted the literary portrait of genius have insisted more than men on showing it off at the moment of public acclaim; and that the literary result is more often raw fantasy than finished art. But the compulsion to write public triumphs, in the nineteenth century, surely resulted from the impossibility of ever having them in real life. The sort of experience that only moderately distinguished women today consider routine—making speeches, chairing meetings, lecturing, arguing in court—was absolutely closed to a Jane Austen, a Brontë, indeed to a Mme de Staël, and was only beginning to be conceivable at the time of a George Eliot or a George Sand. It should not surprise us that women's literature reveals their craving for the *forms* of public recognition, starved for centuries. "Give Thyme or Parsley wreath," Anne Bradstreet had written in her 1650 Prologue; "I ask no Bayes"—but she certainly wanted some kind of wreath.*

. . .

In the performance of Corinne, Mme de Staël apparently intended to summarize all the gifts of genius by which women of her own time and before laid claim to fame—all gifts but one significant by its absence: Corinne is not a novelist. She is an *improvisatrice,* that is, a maker and

---

* The issue of posthumous recognition for women of genius is also raised by Mme de Staël in the scene where Corinne takes Oswald to see the niche reserved for her in the Pantheon; because of Anne Dudley Bradstreet I was reminded of it on my most recent trip to Harvard. I went to look at the Thomas Dudley memorial behind Lamont Library, and found lines from Bradstreet's poetry but not her name. Nothing in Dudley's life which is there extensively recorded—his military career in England, his public posts in the Bay Colony—is so important to history as the fact that he was the father of the first American poet, Anne Bradstreet, who lived in what is now Harvard Square but could not, of course, attend the university which today dishonors her with anonymity. A sense of outrage similar to my own must have inspired those who, in the 1930s, had a plaque to the memory of Charlotte Brontë placed on a wall of the Poets' Corner in Westminster Abbey, where not a single English literary woman is buried.

reciter of spontaneous verses, because Mme de Staël heard Isabel
Pellegrini recite to great applause when on her own Italian tour of
1804–5. Improvisation was an Italian tradition (it referred to poetry
before music) which impressed all eighteenth-century travelers, and particularly one like Mme de Staël, for its romantic spontaneity, its popular
appeal, and its near-domination by women. She herself was no poet, spontaneous or otherwise, but she has her heroine choose a poet's name, that
of Corinna, the Greek lyric poetess reputed to be the teacher of Pindar.
For Mme de Staël's Corinne has the problem professional women have always had with the social implications of a maiden or a married name; her
own real name, which turns out in Book 14 to be "miss Edgermond," simply will not do.

When Mme de Staël herself performed in public, it was as a talker and
provoker of serious talk by others. Her eccentric use of the social institution of the salon as a medium of education or philosophical discussion,
rather than conversation, aroused amusement in France, surprise in England, and consternation in Germany. Much of the fluency, the brilliance,
the intensity, and, alas, the bore of her own manner she did indeed
transfer to her heroine: "I see her, I hear her, I feel her," cried Napoleon
on St. Helena when he attempted to reread *Corinne;* "I want to flee from
her, I throw away the book." Women readers of *Corinne* who attempted
to re-create and to direct in their own person a similarly high-minded level
of social discourse—Margaret Fuller in Boston, George Eliot in her
sibylline mood at the Priory, Kate Chopin in St. Louis—seem to have pat-
terned themselves after this aspect of de Staël's heroine; but intellectual
talk is only a small part of Corinne's performance. She is also a great
tragic actress, midway in the novel acting a scene (in her own translation)
from *Romeo and Juliet;* and Mme de Staël's model here was the great
Mrs. Siddons, whom she had seen act in England, and in the novel sends
Corinne to see for herself.

For Corinne's gifts as a dancer, and for the famous scene in which she
dances a tarantella, Mme de Staël had in mind similar performances by
her beloved friend Mme Récamier and by the novelist Juliette von
Krüdener. Corinne is, like them, a woman of social and intellectual standing who accedes to her admirer's request to dance, in a formal ballroom,
not a minuet or gavotte (not, de Staël writes, one of the French dances remarkable for elegance and intricacy) but a peasant dance of passion and
spontaneous genius. "Corinne made the spectators feel what she was feeling, as if she had improvised, as if she had played on the lyre or done
sketches"—both the latter, incidentally, among Corinne's other talents.
"Everything was language for her . . . and I know not what impassioned
joy, what imaginative sensibility electrified all the witnesses of this magic

dance, and transported them to an ideal existence where one dreams a happiness not of this world."

The tarantella scene in *Corinne* suggests both the glamour and the risk that attend the woman who gives herself spiritually and physically to a wide public, while offending, exciting, and perhaps losing the single lover who awaits her in the privacy that is a romance. George Eliot used just such a dance scene to open *The Spanish Gypsy,* her verse drama about a heroine in the cause of social justice. And Ibsen turned the scene around, for the purposes of feminist rebellion, in *A Doll's House.*

Poet, *improvisatrice,* dancer, actress, translator, musician, painter, singer, lecturer—Corinne is all of these, as well as a published author of various unspecified volumes. That Mme de Staël was primarily concerned with literary genius is clear from her emphasis on the imaginative quality, the spontaneity and depth of soul, rather than the perfection of a craft, conveyed by Corinne with all her gifts. But as a woman writer concerned with the theme of fame, Mme de Staël was impelled to bring her heroine's genius out of the study and into the public eye, where she could be shown in the act of swaying the multitude; and as a novelist, Mme de Staël was perhaps the first to discover that book-writing is an anti-novelistic subject. Many a novelist after her, attempting to make heroism out of literary genius, has discovered that the best way to do it is to exchange his own art for another, one offering more colorful scenes and costumes, more exciting apprenticeships and rivalries, more dramatic public response to turn to narrative purposes.

The poet at least can be made to talk like a poet. (How does a novelist talk? Certainly not like Stephen Dedalus.) The composer's music can be evoked in words, as Proust and Mann have done, and the artist's works can be described, as well as his models, his studio, his Marble Faun. But the successful novelist, as the dreary ending of *David Copperfield* showed long ago, has only royalties, reviews, and second marriages. (The unsuccessful novelists who abound as heroes of second-rate novels in our time bring teaching positions and psychoanalysis to fiction, not works-in-progress.)

"My story is a simple one," Virginia Woolf once said in a lecture—not a novel—about her profession. "You have only got to figure to yourselves a girl in a bedroom with a pen in her hand. She has only to move that pen from left to right—from ten o'clock to one." Woolf made Lily Briscoe in *To the Lighthouse* a painter rather than a novelist, painting being probably the most popular of the mysteries that novelists have always used as substitutes for their own; and women novelists have done so almost from their beginning. The heroine of *The Tenant of Wildfell Hall* is posed before her easel, with brush and smock, for other characters to marvel at; although her dry rejoinder to the hero (when he tries to rhapsodize over her talent) that she paints because she needs the money indicates that Anne Brontë cared more for the feminist than for the artist, and may have been thinking more of the painter-heroine of Mary Brunton's *Self-Control* than of Corinne. But her sister Charlotte worked within Mme de Staël's myth.

Charlotte Brontë makes a serious claim for the imaginative genius of Jane Eyre, and clearly for her own, when she unties her heroine's portfolio of watercolors and spreads them out for Rochester's examination.

> "Were you happy when you painted these pictures?" . . .
> "I was absorbed, sir: yes, and I was happy. To paint them, in short, was to enjoy one of the keenest pleasures I have ever known."
> "That is not saying much. Your pleasures, by your own account, have been few; but I daresay you did exist in a kind of dreamland while you blent and arranged these strange tints. Did you sit at them long each day?"
> "I had nothing else to do, because it was the vacation. . . ."
> "And you felt self-satisfied with the result . . . ?"
> "Far from it. I was tormented by the contrast between my ideas and my handiwork; in each case I had imagined something which I was quite powerless to realise."

All the Brontës had a little painterly talent—Emily, who never wrote about it, most of all. But those familiar with the Brontë story recognize in this dialogue a reference not to painting but to the proto-novelistic activity that filled the sisters' few free hours when in service as governesses or teachers: the imagining of such serial fantasies as could hardly be spread out for Rochester's appraisal. Instead, Charlotte Brontë offers a few extraordinary paragraphs of prose fantasy, which purport to be paintings:

> The first represented clouds low and livid, rolling over a swollen sea. . . . One gleam of light lifted into relief a half-submerged mast, on which sat a cormorant, dark and large, with wings flecked with foam; its beak held a gold bracelet, set with gems, that I had touched with as brilliant tints as my pallette could yield, and as glittering distinctness as my pencil could impart. Sinking below the bird and mast, a drowned corpse . . . a fair arm. . . .
> The second picture contained for foreground only the dim peak of a hill, with grass and some leaves slanting as if by a breeze. Beyond and above spread an expanse of sky, dark blue as at twilight: rising into the sky was a woman's shape to the bust, portrayed in tints as dusk and soft as I could combine. The dim forehead was crowned with a star . . . the eyes shone dark and wild; the hair streamed shadowy, like a beamless cloud torn by storm or by electric travail. On the neck lay a pale reflection like moonlight. . . .

The third showed the pinnacle of an iceberg piercing a polar winter sky: a muster of northern lights reared their dim lances, close serried, along the horizon. Throwing these into distance, rose, in the foreground, a head,—a colossal head. . . . Two thin hands, joined under the forehead, and supporting it, drew up before the lower features a sable veil; a brow quite bloodless, white as bone, and an eye hollow and fixed, blank of meaning but for the glassiness of despair. . . .

No wonder Rochester inquired if Jane Eyre was happy while painting these pictures! But their fantasy content, fascinating as it is, is not so important novelistically as the touches of information about the painter's craft which make this imaginative material workable as pages of a novel. Charlotte Brontë establishes the creativity of her heroine, not just her sensibility, by making her art into a performance—and making her beloved the audience.

* * *

In *Corinne,* the fantasy-transposition of Mme de Staël's own specialty as woman of genius had a curious effect on her novel and reverberations in women's history. The sort of thing she had already done in *De la littérature* (1800), and was already preparing for her study of Germany (1810), was the writing of analytical studies of national traditions, social institutions, and literary culture; but she could not make Corinne, with her drapery, her lyre, and her chariot, into a book-writer huddled over a desk laden with notes and texts. Instead Mme de Staël made her heroine an improviser in motion before a beautiful and changing scene—a veritable tour guide to the sights of Italy. Throughout the novel Corinne delivers a running lecture—those improvisations—as she leads Oswald and the reader past the scenes and monuments of Italian civilization: past "Tombs, Churches and Palaces," or "Vesuvius and the Environs of Naples," as the various tourist-like titles of the books of the novel indicate.

Among lesser fashions set by Corinne's tour was the obligatory visit to the Coliseum by moonlight—Corinne's dramatic farewell to Rome. The episode first provided a *locus romanticus* for the poets (Byron in *Manfred,* 1817, and Lamartine in the *Méditations,* 1820). But its most famous reworking appropriately dramatizes the restless independence of the American girl on tour. "Well, I *have* seen the Coliseum by moonlight!" cries Daisy Miller. "That's one good thing."

The major fashion set by Corinne as tour guide was the opening of the field of art history to women in the days when there were no academic or curatorial posts available to them. The development can be charted through the career of another important Corinne disciple, Anna Jameson, who in the 1840s and 1850s wrote books on art that were immensely successful in both England and America and played a significant share in forming Victorian taste. Mrs. Jameson began in the 1820s as a governess in the employ of a wealthy family that took her along on their Italian tour. Her *Diary of an Ennuyée* (1826) is one of the most charming English imitations of *Corinne:* a hybrid work, part novel, part diary, part guidebook, in which the author suppressed the governess and presented herself as a highly improbable English Corinne, that is, as a husbandless, parentless spinster who most respectably but in independent grandeur tours the sights of Italy and feasts upon its art. (Ironically, Mme de Staël herself was a reluctant tourist in the domain of the plastic arts; the field she insisted should be claimed by women was literary criticism.)

"A wild desire for an existence of lonely independence" was the typical reaction of women readers, in this case young Fanny Kemble, to *Corinne* and its imitations published in England in the 1820s and 1830s. "Mrs. Jameson's 'Diary of an Ennuyée,' which I now read for the first time," Miss Kemble continued,

> added to this desire for isolation and independence such a passionate longing to go to Italy, that my brain was literally filled with chimerical projects of settling in the south of Europe, and there leading a solitary life of literary labour, which, together with the fame I hoped to achieve by it, seemed to me the only worthy purpose of existence.

That reads like a fair summary of the story of *Aurora Leigh,* which recapitulates a good deal of Mme de Staël's novel. But Elizabeth Barrett Browning, a precocious poet, provides less remarkable evidence of the power of the myth of Corinne than does Fanny Kemble, who was a unique case among respectable, educated Victorian women. Miss Kemble had wide fame and public applause within her grasp, from an early age, as an actress. A member of a solidly established theatrical family—her aunt was the Mrs. Siddons that Mme de Staël admired, her father the actor-manager of Covent Garden—Fanny Kemble triumphed on the stage as Juliet at the age of nineteen. But she disliked "the theatrical profession," found everything about the stage "more or less repugnant," and always wanted to be remembered as an author (as she mainly is today).

In the novels women wrote after Mme de Staël, the actress did not become the principal descendant of her performing heroine, and for the reasons one need not turn to Zola's *Nana,* but to Fanny Kemble's *Record of a Girlhood* or to a woman's novel like *Villette.* "It was a marvelous sight: a mighty revelation," Charlotte Brontë wrote in the course of her unconventional tribute to the actress as artist (the chapter given to the performance of Rachel, called Vashti in *Villette*). But she adds immediately: "It was a spectacle low, horrible, immoral." Vashti partakes of the divine fire, she is a woman of genius; nevertheless "Vashti was not good . . . though a spirit, she was a spirit out of Tophet. Well, if so much of unholy force can arise from below, may not an equal efflux of sacred essence descend one day from above?"

The answer to Charlotte Brontë's prayer was the opera singer.

> When the first chords of the orchestra summoned Consuelo to her place, she rose slowly; her mantilla fell from her shoulders, and her face finally appeared to the nervous and impatient spectators. . . . But what a miraculous transformation had taken place in this young girl, a moment before so pale and worn . . . ! Her large brow seemed bathed in a celestial fluid . . . her calm glance spoke of none of those trivial passions which aim at ordinary success. There was instead something grave, mysterious and profound . . . which commanded respect. . . .

From George Sand's *Consuelo* (1842) to Willa Cather's *Song of the Lark* (1915), the prima donna justified the myth of Corinne; the miracle of operatic performance served as could no other to show off a woman's genius. For a great voice does indeed transport an audience to an ideal existence, as Mme de Staël wrote of Corinne's tarantella; and it excuses any degree of hyperbole. There is only one voice like it in a century, as Flora Tristan could write of her opera singer heroine in *Méphis;* and readers cannot quibble with Willa Cather's elitism (though we may be troubled by its vehemence) when she says of Thea Kronborg that "she is uncommon, in a common, common world."

For the feminist, such as Flora Tristan, the opera singer makes a heroine who is strong, willful, and grand; an international traveler; a solitary, but with a subservient entourage in attendance. Men adore her, but there is no other kind of heroine, not even the saint, who can so plausibly be made a chaste as well as a mature and desirable woman. George Sand keeps Consuelo a virgin, even a married virgin, for more than a thousand pages. And George Eliot has her prima donna, in *Armgart,* reject a nobleman's proposal of marriage in coldly elitist terms:

> *Armgart.* . . . Seek the woman you deserve,
> All grace, all goodness, who has not yet found
> A meaning in her life, nor any end
> Beyond fulfilling yours. The type abounds.
> *Graf.* And happily, for the world.
> *Armgart.* Yes, happily.
> Let it excuse me that my kind is rare:
> Commonness is its own security.

Mme de Staël put the matter even more drily in relation to literary women. "Many men prefer," she wrote in the 1814 preface to her *Letters on Rousseau,* "wives who are solely involved with household cares . . . and incapable of understanding anything else. It's a matter of taste; and anyway, as the number of distinguished women is very small, those who don't want one have a wide choice."

Both George Sand and Willa Cather loved the opera and both knew opera singers well; neither novelist had any musical talent. Intimacy without rivalry explains their success with the woman of opera as heroic stand-in for the woman of letters. In the Venetian scenes of *Consuelo,* the Chicago scenes of *The Song of the Lark* (and several Cather short stories), both showed the brutal physical labor, the rigorous technique, and the first-rate training of the singer to be almost as important to her art as the qualities of mind and feeling upon which, as literary artists, they primarily insisted. (Just as did Mrs. Gaskell in her portrait of Margaret, the Manchester folk singer, in *Mary Barton:* though blind and working-class, she is a thorough professional.)

George Sand met Pauline Garcia, the model for Consuelo, in 1839; she became a prima donna almost as important in the history of opera as her older sister Maria Malibran. Pauline Garcia married Louis Viardot, the distinguished journalist with whom George Sand collaborated on the *Revue Indépendante*—where *Consuelo* first appeared in 1842: a literary, political, and musical manifesto, as well as a version of the myth of Corinne.

It was the most famous treatment of the opera singer in nineteenth-century fiction, and every woman of more than ordinary distinction read *Consuelo* or at least knew that it was there. Charlotte Brontë read it; her feminist friend Mary Taylor wrote her from New Zealand that it was worth learning French just to read it. George Eliot read it; her friend Sara Hennell wrote her that *"Consuelo* is the only thing to compare with" *The Mill on the Floss.* Elizabeth Barrett cited it to Robert Browning; Queen Victoria found it *"dreadfully* interesting"; and if there was one reason why Willa Cather kept George Sand's portrait over her mantelpiece as late as the 1930s, it was surely *Consuelo.*

Sand's and Cather's opera singers have education without genteel refinement, distinction without birth, and the manners of a queen, an artist, and a woman of the people, all in one. Like real singers too, and in this way significantly different from real actresses, their heroines did not need to be and were not beauties. Consuelo, illegitimate daughter of a gypsy, studies in Venice under Porpora (a real figure: George Sand was writing a historical novel, including personages from early eighteenth-century musical history); she triumphs at the court of Frederick the Great, and along the way acquires the title which she never uses of Countess of Rudolstadt. Thea Kronborg is a girl from the prairies who studies in Chicago; her teacher is a disciple of Theodore Thomas (the real conductor); she triumphs in New York at the Metropolitan and becomes the great Wagnerian soprano of international reputation that Olive Fremstad was in fact. Fremstad was, as much as Willa Cather herself, the model for the heroine of *The Song of the Lark,* Cather's most realistically documented as well as most autobiographical novel. Cather met the Swedish-American singer as a journalist, worshiped her as a friend, and dreaded her reaction to her portrait as heroine. But the soprano reassured her, when they met in Nebraska after *The Song of the Lark* appeared. It was the only such book, Fremstad said, where she felt "there was something doing" in the artist.

What is Thea Kronborg's secret, someone asks Harsanyi, the piano teacher who first discovers that her musicality is of an operatic nature. " 'Her secret? It is every artist's secret'—he waved his hand—'passion. That is all. It is an open secret, and perfectly safe. Like heroism, it is inimitable in cheap materials.' " That Cather credo, often quoted, says much about her attitude as a writer; but there is more than passion to the heroine of *The Song of the Lark.* Here is the way Cather handles the beginning of Thea's professional career: the discovery by Harsanyi that she has the makings of a great voice.

Thea has been paying her way in Chicago, including her piano lessons, by singing in a church choir. One night in the Harsanyis' shabby parlor, after their lesson, and after the family dinner to which Thea is invited, the teacher on impulse asks her to sing.

> When she finished, Harsanyi sprang from his chair and dropped lightly upon his toes, a kind of *entre-chat* that he sometimes executed when he formed a sudden resolution, or when he was about to follow a pure intuition, against reason. His wife knew from his manner that he was intensely interested. He went quickly to the piano. . . .
>
> "Sing *ah—ah* for me, as I indicate." He kept his right hand on the keyboard and put his left to her throat, placing the tips of his delicate fingers over her larynx. "Again—until your breath is gone. —Trill between the two tones, always; good! Again; excellent!— Now up—stay there. E and F. Not so good, is it? F is always a hard one.—Now, try the half-tone. . . ."
>
> "Now, once more; carry it up and then down, *ah—ah.*" He put his hand back to her throat and sat with his head bent, his one eye closed. He loved to hear a big voice throb in a relaxed, natural throat, and he was thinking that no one had ever felt this voice vibrate before. It was like a wild bird that had flown into his studio on Middleton Street from goodness knew how far! No one knew that it had come, or even that it existed; least of all the strange, crude girl in whose throat it beat its passionate wings. What a simple thing it was, he reflected; why had he never guessed it before?

Everything about her indicated it—the big mouth, the wide jaw and chin, the strong white teeth, the deep laugh. The machine was so simple and strong, seemed to be so easily operated. She sang from the bottom of herself. Her breath came from down where her laugh came from, the deep laugh which Mrs. Harsanyi had once called "the laugh of the people." A relaxed throat, a voice that lay on the breath, that had never been forced off the breath; it rose and fell in the air-column like the little balls which are put to shine in the jet of a fountain.

The rough physicality of the scene (the teacher's hand on Thea's throat)—the inelegant surroundings—the absence of sexual overtones—the twangy Americanisms—all set off the image of the bird and of the fountain, so exquisitely phrased, which Cather uses to make her point about the otherworldly quality of genius, that uncommon thing, which is to take possession of her heroine and command of her public. But just as much as Corinne's, Thea's genius is the kind that demands, that cannot exist without public response, vibrating here for the first time in the fingers of the piano teacher.

• • •

Thea Kronborg is of immigrant family, not of the old Virginia stock of the Cathers; Consuelo is La Zingara, not a Frenchwoman; Corinne is not French or Genevese, but Anglo-Italian. The singers in George Eliot's work (Tina in "Mr. Gilfil's Love-Story," Mirah in *Daniel Deronda,* the prima donna in *Armgart*) are Italian, Jewish, German, anything but Staffordshire ladies nervous about their respectability—but it was George Eliot who dispensed with the safety screen of otherness, and domesticated the performing heroine. No woman writer after Mme de Staël strove harder to spotlight, in the beam of glory, the isolate woman of genius: the "cygnet," in George Eliot's metaphor from the Prelude to *Middlemarch,* "reared uneasily among the ducklings in the brown pond." Her heroines are never silly, whatever other adjective we may wish to apply to them; when they fail, they are painful failures. Much anguish in George Eliot's personal life underlay the pain, but the kind of heroism found in her novels belongs to a tradition of women's literature that stretched long before, and continued long after her.

That the heroine of her first novel is a Methodist preacher rather than an opera singer hardly disguises the fact that Dinah Morris, in *Adam Bede,* is a true descendant of Corinne. She is seen first from a distance, seen to be admired by a skeptical, upper-class stranger who comes riding into *Adam Bede* at the start of the novel for the single purpose of succumbing to the magic of Dinah's performance.

Dinah's clothes are Quaker gray, not sibylline draperies and turbans;

her listeners are yokels and milkmaids, not Roman noblemen; her setting, the Village Green, not the Capitoline Hill; her vehicle, a wheelwright's cart drawn under the maple tree to serve as pulpit, not a chariot drawn by four white horses; her music is not a fanfare but a hymn; her advance praises are given not in formal odes but in the gossip of carpenters and innkeepers; and the subject of her improvisation is not the civilization of Italy but the gospel of Jesus Christ. Nevertheless Dinah fascinates—"for there is this sort of fascination in all sincere unpremeditated eloquence, which opens to one the inward drama of the speaker's emotions." So thinks the stranger, who many early readers of *Adam Bede* must have thought would become an Oswald in the course of the novel—"the stranger, who had been interested in the course of her sermon, as if it had been the development of a drama. . . ." He rides off, however, "while Dinah said, 'Let us sing a little, dear friends'; and he was still winding down the slope, the voices of the Methodists reached him, rising and falling in that strange blending of exultation and sadness. . . ."

My *Times* this week carries a front-page photograph of a woman in clerical robes newly ordained as an Episcopalian minister, though in the teeth of episcopal opposition. No other advance in the current cause of "women's liberation" could be more astonishing to the Protestant women novelists of the past century. For them, preaching was the most familiar career; the one offering the most obvious opportunities for public performance of an inspirational nature; the one most absolutely closed to women. They saw their fathers, brothers, and suitors go into the church as a sexual at least as much as a spiritual prerogative, as Mary Garth points out to Fred Vincy with considerable acerbity, in *Middlemarch*. The Gaskell and Brontë and George Eliot and Harriet Beecher Stowe heroines who speak religious and moral truths to eager, instantly converted listeners are spokesmen of views deeply held and maturely ruminated by the novelists; but they are also fulfillments of a compelling female fantasy.

The most clearly professional of Victorian preaching heroines is little Eva on her deathbed in *Uncle Tom's Cabin:*

> "I sent for you all, my dear friends," said Eva, "because I love you. I love you all; and I have something to say to you, which I want you always to remember. . . . In a few weeks you will see me no more"—Here the child was interrupted by bursts of groans, sobs, and lamentations, which broke from all present, and in which her slender voice was lost entirely. She waited a moment, and then, speaking in a tone that checked the sobs of all, she said,—"If you love me you must not interrupt me so. Listen to what I say. I want to speak to you about your souls. . . ."

The novelist's father was a minister and so were her seven brothers (among them Henry Ward Beecher, the most famous American preacher of the day)—but not Harriet, because she was a girl. Mrs. Stowe called her child-heroine Eva for Evangeline: the girl's destiny, thwarted in the novel by death, was to play the role of evangelist and not, certainly, that of mother Eve.*

Dinah Morris gives up her preaching career at the end of *Adam Bede* with a flutter of glad submission, for George Eliot, as her readers have always been surprised to discover, was no feminist. That is, her aim as a novelist was not to argue for a diminishing of the social inhibitions and a widening of the options that affect the lives of ordinary women; instead, like Mme de Staël, George Eliot was always concerned with the superior, large-souled woman whose distinction resides not in her deeds but in her capacity to attract attention and arouse admiration. Her heroines are not intellectuals (any more than Corinne is centrally an intellectual); they do not enjoy using their minds or working for those acquirements which George Eliot herself so remarkably achieved. Instead, as Lucy marvels at the phenomenon of Maggie Tulliver, for having absorbed "Shakespeare and everything" since she left school, it seems to be the result of "witchcraft . . . part of your general uncanniness." In one way or another, George Eliot's heroines are women of genius noticed by the world.

Dorothea Brooke in *Middlemarch* is the worst kind of product of the myth of Corinne (and the worst sort of influence on novelists like Doris Lessing) for she is good for nothing *but* to be admired. An arrogant, selfish, spoiled, rich beauty, she does little but harm in the novel. Ignorant in the extreme and mentally idle (without feeling any of the guilt of Jane Austen's heroines for their failure to read) Dorothea has little of interest

---

* Little Eva's demise is in part a repeat of that death of Little Nell, in Dickens's *Old Curiosity Shop* a decade earlier, which Oscar Wilde said a man would have to have a heart of stone not to laugh at. But in Stowe's case our laughter is directed not only at her bathos but at her realism, for little Eva effectively dramatizes that child-who-plays-the-preacher who at one time inhabited all churchgoing homes. Young Harriet Beecher's school sermons won prizes and even her father's praise (something, she wrote, "past all juvenile triumphs") and Eva is a self-portrait. By this I mean not that Stowe as a little girl was an angelic spirit like Little Nell —a male fantasy—but that she was an ambitious show-off with the gift of tongues, who in adolescence would go on to read *Corinne*.

"A woman's preaching," Dr. Johnson said, "is like a dog's walking on his hinder legs. It is not done well; but you are surprized to find it done at all." This famous snub has I think been misunderstood: Johnson was not insulting female piety but recording the impossibility of female performance as public speakers in 1763, as George Bernard Shaw's parody of the Johnson line, in 1889, makes clear. "A woman making a speech," Shaw begins his misquotation from Johnson. "Now mark my words," he goes on. "The time is approaching when that story will reverse its genders, and be attributed to some female sage. . . . Public speaking is a despicable art, only fit for women . . . but let Miss Achurch just try her hand at musical criticism and you will soon acknowledge the unassailable pre-eminence of Creation's master-piece: Man." A speech, not a sermon by that lady, inspired Shaw's *mot* (in, of course, a column of music criticism). The occasion was the annual *Doll's House* dinner at a London theater, and it marks a midpoint in the history of performing women between Dr. Johnson's time and our own.

to say, but a magnificent voice to say it in. "What a voice! It was like the voice of a soul that had once lived in an AEolian harp" to Will Ladislaw; and to Caleb Garth, whose musical tastes are less romantic, "Bless me! it reminds me of bits in the Messiah." She also has what must be the most stunning wardrobe in Victorian fiction.

Here is one of Dorothea's typical Corinne-like entrances:

> When the drawing-room door opened and Dorothea entered, there was a sort of contrast not infrequent in country life when the habits of the different ranks were less blent than now. Let those who know, tell us exactly what stuff it was that Dorothea wore in those days of mild autumn—that thin white woolen stuff soft to the touch and soft to the eye. It always seemed to have been lately washed, and to smell of the sweet hedges—was always in the shape of a pelisse with sleeves hanging all out of the fashion. Yet if she had entered before a still audience as Imogene or Cato's daughter, the dress might have seemed right enough: the grace and dignity were in her limbs and neck; and about her simply parted hair and candid eyes the large round poke which was then in the fate of women, seemed no more odd as a head-dress than the gold trencher we call a halo. By the present audience of two persons, no dramatic heroine could have been expected with more interest. . . .

Merely pretty and well-dressed women, in novels by Mrs. Gaskell and Mrs. Stowe, make some of the most attractive heroines in fiction (I would particularly recommend Nina, the charming Southern belle in *Dred*). But in George Eliot as in Charlotte Brontë, prettiness is a focus of anguish, not of heroinism; and in their earliest novels it inspires some moments of malice too strong for anything in their religion or their morality to control. In *Jane Eyre* the venom discharged upon the showy beauty Blanche Ingram, Jane's putative rival for Rochester's affections, is made a trifle more palatable to the reader, rather than less, because envy of the spoiled rich combines with envy of the spoiled beauty in Brontë's mind. But nothing excuses George Eliot's vindictiveness toward Hetty Sorrel in *Adam Bede,* made worse by all the words about tolerant understanding that George Eliot mouths but does not heed herself, as a novelist.

A minor but interesting gauge of the maturity that both George Eliot and Brontë achieved in their last novels is the peace they were able to make with merely pretty women characters, a peace with honor and with irony somewhat equivalent to the one Dickens made in *Our Mutual Friend* with his dandy heroes. Ginevra Fanshawe in *Villette* is a triumph of tolerance carried to the pitch of good humor and affection; she shows Charlotte Brontë's admiration for that particle of grit at the base of every "merely pretty" woman's power to charm. And George Eliot repeated the triumph with her Gwendolen Harleth in *Daniel Deronda,* a character created, I daresay, with a conscious bow to Charlotte Brontë's last novel, a work which George Eliot estimated at its true value.

Both Brontë's Ginevra and George Eliot's Gwendolen are spoiled and shallow beauties, coarse-minded and ignorant flirts, wretchedly brought up to be family tyrants and shameless fortune hunters. Cut loose from religion, morality, and even nationality, they wander the Continental resorts in search of social position, and they teeter not far from the edge of the abyss of high-grade prostitution. Each has just enough intelligence to admire a finer quality of being, as represented by Lucy Snowe or Daniel Deronda. But Gwendolen Harleth is the richer and deeper creation, because George Eliot used her to sound out the sources and test the implications, in the widest sense, of the myth of Corinne.

Gwendolen is and is not a heroine; she is a victim, and also a villainess; she is an irritation as well as a focus of concern in the novel; but the one thing she is not is an idealized self-portrait of the novelist. George Eliot at last, by the 1870s, when she was in her fifties, had lived down her own days of *Corinne*. Yet none of her novels is so imbued as is *Daniel Deronda* (1876) with the idea of performing heroism, with the life given over to the impulsions of genius, with the challenge of the arts and the perils of public admiration. To the ideal of female glory she brought a sense of artistic standards on the one hand, and on the other— for the first time in her work—a realistic and tolerant appraisal of the difficulties of a woman's life.

George Eliot presents Gwendolen Harleth with wry sympathy as "The Spoiled Child," the title of Book I of *Daniel Deronda*. She makes our first sight of Gwendolen a distant one, in the Corinne tradition; places her at the center of a mixed and admiring crowd; has her performance observed by a distinguished stranger—a visitor from another world. But George Eliot's aim is here to criticize female fantasy, not reinforce it. Thus she makes the setting a sordid one, a German casino, and to Gwendolen's showing-off at the gambling table, to her posing and preening, the stranger, Daniel Deronda, responds with pity and disgust, mixed with only a touch of admiration. "The darting sense that he was measuring her and looking down on her as an inferior" is the first lesson in Gwendolen's education to reality.

Gwendolen is not a genius, not even a girl of talent, but representative of a common kind: "The Spoiled Child." She is one of thousands of pretty girls whose idle and selfish youth, whose deferential family and servants, whose school successes and whose early triumphs among the neighbors and suitors in the restricted province of their immediate circle give them a thirst for admiration which they assume will be quenched forever, and by the world at large. And "The Spoiled Child" is not so far from "Corinne au Capitole" as one might assume.

George Eliot directs our attention to a source of the performing fantasies in women's literature more durable and more dangerous even than societal restrictions on women's careers. That is, the admiration on which little girls are fed, in treacly spoonfuls, from their earliest years. Little boys, who also come in for their share, are made to outgrow the poisonous food; but throughout female youth, often to the brink of marriage, girls are praised for cuteness, for looks, for dress, for chatter, for recitations, for jangling rhymes, for crude sketches, for bad acting, for wretched dancing and out-of-tune singing. They are praised, fondled, and petted for giving pleasure with the amateur entertainment girls are required to provide in the domestic circle, just as Corinne provides it for all of European civilization on the Capitoline Hill.

Some time in the future, television may prove to be an invention as liberating for women as was the typewriter, by providing, not jobs, but something to look at in the home other than little girls. But in the past, and as far back as we have biographical records of literary women, the warpage of gifted girls by an excess of domestic admiration is supported by a mass of depressing evidence. Mme de Staël herself sat from the age of six by her mother's side in their Paris salon, and early received praise for her conversational talents; the component of admiration in her father's affection counted for even more. "To see his daughter was his only and dearest relaxation," recorded a girlhood friend. "He never criticized her, let her talk freely, enjoyed the wit she displayed, applauded her enthusiastically, caressed her, and left her content and with refreshed spirits"—and left her, too, not just with an Oedipus complex of such dimensions as to stimulate Napoleon's derision, but also with a lifelong greed, as reflexive as that of a salivating dog, for the food of applause.

A century before her, Lady Mary Wortley Montagu was elected reigning beauty and toast of the year by the Kit-Cat Club, fashionable center of male Whig society. Dressed in her finest clothes, according to contemporary witness,

> she went from the lap of one poet, or patriot, or statesman, to the arms of another, was feasted with sweetmeats, overwhelmed with caresses, and, what probably already pleased her better than either, heard her wit and beauty loudly extolled on every side. Pleasure, she said, was too poor a word to express her sensations; they amounted to ecstasy; never again, throughout her whole future life, did she pass so happy a day.

Lady Mary was then seven years old, and a Corinne in the making. She grew up to be one of the great letter writers of the eighteenth century, and one of the most remarkable of literary amateurs, but from amateur status she never escaped. An excess of early praise for amateur accomplishment may have done more than all the hardships of woman's lot to separate minor from major achievement among literary women.

Much sentimental pity has been expended on Jane Austen, because of the story that she wrote her novels in odd moments in the middle of the family drawing room. (It may have been the ideal place for the working of her genius; and her family gave her just the praise she wanted and of a kind that does not blight: laughter.) But let us instead lay a mournful wreath on the childhood of all those facile women poets of the nineteenth century—like Felicia Hemans, who was fussed over and fondled, a ravishing golden girl of precocious talent, by all who knew her in her earliest years, and, having survived her, lamented that "she did only a partial justice to her powers," as Henry Chorley put it in his tenderhearted memorial to Mrs. Hemans. Girl poets seem to be more susceptible than girl novelists to early spoiling, for their verses lead them into recitation, a performance which brings them the sort of praise that tends to flatter their charms rather than refine their compositions.

How did Elizabeth Barrett escape triviality? Some evidence suggests that her displacement from the center of the adoring family circle by the claims of a younger brother counted for much in the protection of her precocious talent; and Sylvia Plath may have escaped mediocrity for the same reason. For Plath, who was very pretty as well as precociously gifted (a potentially disastrous combination for poets), who had her first poem published when she was eight, who was showered with prizes and scholarships throughout her school years, was a sister under the skin of Felicia Hemans.

Plath's professional career might well have ended where it began, with her selection through nationwide literary competition to serve as an editor of a fashion magazine—and to be dressed up, made up, dined out, danced with, feted, and photographed as the presumed reward for *literary* ability. "I was supposed to be the envy of thousands of college girls all over America. . . . And when my picture came out in the magazine," Plath wrote with self-disgust at the start of *The Bell Jar,*

> Look what can happen in this country, they'd say. A girl lives in some out-of-the-way town for nineteen years, so poor she can't afford a magazine, and then she gets a scholarship to college and wins a prize here and a prize there and ends up steering New York like her own private car.

The shallow and premature glory that is a menace to women's talent has merely been institutionalized, hardly invented, by American ingenuity.

And what of the writer who is gifted and plain, the case of the great majority of the literary women of history? I would guess that the onset of adolescence brings a shock of a specially female kind, for then such a girl discovers that the ecstasy of admiration which was hers as a child, as re-

ward for performance, is now withdrawn from her plainness and given instead, by inexorable right, to the beauty. Beauty alone draws the eyes of
the world, is the grim lesson of female maturity; beauty alone is drawn by
four white horses in triumph to the Capitoline Hill to be crowned as "Miss
Universe"; beauty alone—"this tall dark-eyed nymph with her jet-black
coronet of hair" that Maggie Tulliver so implausibly becomes in adolescence—has a line of partners waiting to dance with her in the brilliantly lit
drawing room at Park House, and draws all the attention to her stall at the
bazaar in the baronial hall of St. Ogg's. That is why "the culmination of
Maggie's career as an admired member of society" is not the day she sings
an aria, or makes a speech, or publishes a book, but "was certainly the day
of the bazaar, when her simple, noble beauty, clad in white muslin of some
soft-floating kind" etc. etc. The gulf in *The Mill on the Floss* that made
Swinburne gag was surely the revenge of female fantasy on the tortures of
female adolescence for the gifted but plain girl. Maggie really does want to
be something other than a Corinne; and she is quite right in her opinion
that "the Muses were uncomfortable goddesses."

Gwendolen Harleth, however, does want to be a Corinne, and thinks it
will be both easy and delightful as a way of life. Her piano playing has
never been criticized in the drawing room. Her face looks exceptionally
pretty when she sings, everyone has told her, and her voice keeps pretty
well in tune. For parlor charades, her acting has always been much in
demand. Brought up to be a lady, she has a beauty and a style which are
beyond question very fine. Therefore, when family reverses make her think
of looking out for herself, Gwendolen decides that she will be an artist—
or rather that, without condescending to try, or certainly to work, she already is one. Note George Eliot's careful switch of tenses in the following
passage from *Daniel Deronda:*

> . . . the dawning smile of self-contentment rested on her lips as
> she vaguely imagined a future suited to her wishes: it seemed but
> the affair of a year or so for her to become the most approved
> Juliet of the time; or, if Klesmer encouraged her idea of being a
> singer, to proceed by more gradual steps to her place in the opera,
> where she won money and applause by occasional performances.
> Why not? At home, at school, among acquaintances, she had been
> used to have her conscious superiority admitted; and she had moved
> in a society where everything, from low arithmetic to high art, is
> of the amateur kind politely supposed to fall short of perfection.
> . . . The self-confident visions that had beguiled her were not of a
> highly exceptional kind. . . .

The Klesmer mentioned here is a German-Slavic-Jewish musician of
unassuming appearance, brusque manners, and funny accent, as well as international reputation. (He was drawn after the composer Anton Rubin-

stein, whom George Eliot admired.) Klesmer comes into the novel to teach Gwendolen* that there are standards other than those of genteel English society, and rewards for the artist other than applause: "the honour comes from the inward vocation and the hard-won achievement." The artist's life is not for spoiled children.

> "You are a beautiful young lady—you have been brought up in ease—you have done what you would—you have not said to yourself, 'I must know this exactly,' 'I must understand this exactly,' 'I must do this exactly' "—in uttering these three terrible *musts,* Klesmer lifted up three long fingers in succession. "In sum, you have not been called upon to be anything but a charming young lady, whom it is an impoliteness to find fault with."

III   *or Italy*

I am not used to Hope—
It might intrude upon—
Its sweet parade—blaspheme the place—
Ordained to Suffering—

It might be easier
To fail—with Land in Sight—
Than gain—My Blue Peninsula—
To perish—of Delight—

—Emily Dickinson

The oddest thing about *Corinne* is that it is a guidebook to Italy just as much as it is a guidebook to the woman of genius. Mme de Staël called the novel *Corinne, or Italy* to signify its double usefulness. The reader who enjoys guidebooks will find much of the Italian matter interesting, some of it brilliant; but he will be puzzled by Mme de Staël's priorities. Did she plot the movement of her love story across the map of Italy in such a way as to cover the principal monuments? Or did her idea of Italian culture evoke the spirit and shape the destiny of the heroine she called Corinne?

And why Italy? She had already written extensively about England and France; she had traveled to Germany in 1803 and was already at work on her study of German culture, which she interrupted to make her first trip to Italy in the winter of 1804–5. She went with the definite intention of finding materials for a novel in her Italian tour. Why Italy? may seem a foolish question, for what northern European needs an excuse to go south

---

* Somewhat as, a generation later, the ugly old pianist Mlle Reisz comes into Edna Pontellier's life, when the heroine of Kate Chopin's *The Awakening* starts to play at being a painter.

in search of sun? to know the land of *Mignonslied* where lemons grow? But this question, like so many others, poses itself differently for a literary woman like Mme de Staël than for a literary man like J. W. von Goethe.

Why did Mrs. Radcliffe set her Gothic novels in Italy, the European country on which the Gothic style (the turreted and moated castles essential to her fiction) made relatively little impress? Her predecessor Horace Walpole knew Italy well when he wrote *The Castle of Otranto;* but if there is one way in which Radcliffe broke with Walpole to demonstrate the Romantic potentialities of the Gothic novel, it was as a writer of strange landscapes—landscapes of an Italy she had never seen. At the turn of the century, her *Udolpho* and *The Italian,* and *Corinne* as well, did at least as much as Goethe's *Wilhelm Meister* to arouse the passion for Italy which, for Byron, Shelley, and Keats, marked high Romanticism in England.

In the history of Victorian Italophilia no name is more prominent than that of Elizabeth Barrett Browning. In her case, ideas about Italy as *the* place for the woman of genius (specifically, Mme de Staël's ideas) figured as largely as reasons of health and finance in her determination to settle in Italy as soon as marriage to Browning made travel possible. As much can be said of Margaret Fuller. Why Italy for women? is a question to which *Corinne, or Italy* provided the most important answer. And I suspect that Mme de Staël's thinking on the subject, when she first planned her novel-guidebook, originated in her response to *Sir Charles Grandison* by a novelist who, like Mrs. Radcliffe, wrote of an Italy he never saw.

When Samuel Richardson set a good portion of his last novel in Italy, he knew only that it was a Catholic country, that Ariosto's marvels took place there, and that people there were somehow different from the norm. "Men—Women—and Italians" was Richardson's way of dividing his huge cast of characters, of which the most important was the hero of the novel. In Sir Charles Grandison Richardson intended to provide for women readers their ideal of the perfect husband: a man not only wealthy, aristocratic, handsome, elegant, and intelligent, but also unfailingly kind, courteous, deferential, and faithful to the female sex. And he succeeded in the case of Mme de Staël, who seems to have had Grandison in mind as the pattern for Oswald, lord Nelvil in *Corinne.*

Like Richardson, Mme de Staël gave her hero a virtuous English bride at the end of the novel and an exotic Italian woman in his past; only she told the story from the point of view of the woman left behind in Italy. Richardson kept his novel going for thousands of pages by sending Grandison back to Italy to try to change his Clementina's mind (she rejects his proposal out of passionate attachment to her Italian homeland and Catholic faith); and also to allay any suspicion among his English friends that he has merely trifled with a lady of foreign fascination encountered on his Italian tour. That such suspicions were commonplace, Corinne herself points out. "Listen to me," she says to Lord Nelvil on the eve of his departure from Italy; "when you get to London they will tell you, the men about town, . . . that all the Englishmen who have ever lived have fallen in love with Italian women met on their travels, and forgotten upon their return; . . . and that, at your age, the whole future course of your life cannot be determined by whatever delight you have found, for a brief period, in the society of a foreign woman."

Oswald protests his troth in all sincerity, for he is not a mere man about town but a Grandison, which is why Corinne loves him in preference to all the brilliant Italian and witty French noblemen who surround and court her. But it is Oswald's British morality that parts him from Corinne, and makes their final separation an affair of state.

Both Oswald's values and the secret behind his melancholy derive from his worship of his dead father, as he explains to Corinne halfway up the slope of Mount Vesuvius, where "all that has life disappears, you enter the empire of death, and only ashes shift beneath uncertain feet." It seems that Oswald had hastened his father's death through a previous cross-cultural *amour,* an entanglement with a scheming Frenchwoman at a time when England and France were enemies; now he is resolved to fulfill every wish of the dead man, especially in regard to his own marriage. And he must leave Corinne and travel back to Britain to learn the reasons why his father wanted him to marry Lucile Edgermond, the young daughter of an old family friend, and why he did not want Oswald to marry Corinne.

These reasons are extremely interesting—more interesting than the tricks of plot whereby Corinne is enmeshed in Nelvil-Edgermond family affairs. For Corinne, it transpires, is only half Italian; her father was Lord Edgermond by his first, Italian wife; she is a half sister of Lucile and a rejected first choice by Oswald's father for his son's bride. "I owe to our friendship a frank statement of my reasons for wishing that their marriage not take place," the senior Lord Nelvil had written to Corinne's father in a letter that Oswald travels home to read.

> "Your daughter is charming, but I seem to perceive in her one of those beautiful Greek women who enchanted and subjugated the world. Don't be offended—of course your daughter has been brought up to possess only the purest of feelings and principles; but she needs to please, to captivate, to impress.
>
> She has more talent than self-love; but talents of so rare a kind necessarily inspire the desire to develop them; and I do not know what stage can contain that activity of mind, that impetuous imagination, that ardent character which one senses in every word she speaks. She would of course take my son away from England, for such a woman cannot be happy here. Only Italy would suit her."

Why Italy? Because Italy is a country—I am now following the analysis Mme de Staël scatters through the novel—where one lives openly, in the open air and sun, and where the populace is always on hand to cheer artistic genius. The Italian past was glorious, the Italian future may be so as well, but "in the present condition of the Italians, artistic glory is the only kind they are permitted." (This bit of offhand social commentary was one of many by which Mme de Staël infuriated Napoleon, part of whose empire Italy had been since 1804.) Life in Italy, she goes on, is free in a way unknown to more advanced, more politically liberated nations, and therefore most suited to women of artistic talent. For in Italy there is no hypocrisy about morals, as in England; no malicious gossip, as in France; no false modesty or artifice; no obsession with rank or convention; but only spontaneity in love and art. If a woman can give delight with her dancing or reciting, in Italy she does so at once, without being begged, without simpering. If a woman loves a man, she can tell him she does so— "a terrible fault in England, but so pardonable in Italy." For married happiness and domestic virtues, England is undoubtedly the place; but for love outside of marriage, go to Italy.

There is simply no way to "compromise" a woman's reputation in Italian society, as Corinne tells a nervous Oswald: women are expected always to be in love in Italy, to speak of love and their lovers. "Thus, in this country, where no one thinks of anything but love, there isn't a single novel, because love is so rapid here, so public, that it doesn't lend itself to any kind of development; to give a true account of love Italian style, you would have to begin and end on the first page."

For Corinne, the result of these special conditions of Italian society is not the possibility of attaining perfect happiness in love (no heroine ever felt more doomed to personal suffering) but that of leading an independent life as a woman of genius, and developing all her talents to the full with the open encouragement rather than the shocked disapproval of society. And in fact, underneath all her lyre-strumming and drapery-shaking, Corinne did illustrate a life-style of such novel fascination that it turned the heads of young women from Yorkshire to New England, and gave them "a wild desire for an existence of lonely independence," as Fanny Kemble put it, along with "a passionate desire to go to Italy."

Corinne lives alone on her own money; she maintains her own establishment, is waited on by her own servants. She uses her own name, an invented one, and like Flora Tristan's heroine, whose theme song is "Ne me demandez-pas d'où je viens," Corinne never refers to her family or true nationality. She goes into society without protector or escort; she has friends and lovers of her own free choosing. She does her own work— publishes, exhibits, performs—and is famous in her own right. She travels everywhere, alone or with a man as she chooses. In every sense, she guides her own life.

So does George Sand's Lélia, and so does Aurora Leigh. The delightful scenes of Aurora's independent literary life in a London flat owed nothing to Miss Barrett's life with father up to the age of forty, and Swinburne—in 1898!—protested violently against this fantasy material as "rather too eccentric a vision to impose itself upon the most juvenile credulity: a young lady of family who lodges by herself in Grub Street, preserves her reputation, lives on her pen, and dines out in Mayfair. . . ." "Genius cannot do everything," Swinburne apologized for Mrs. Browning in conclusion; but female genius very much wanted to do that fantasy of the independent woman's life, called Corinne, which Mme de Staël first located in an Italy of dreamland, that feminine somewhere-else, where people were Men, Women, and Italians. For Emily Dickinson that land was simply "My Blue Peninsula" of hope and dreamed delight, an image which she derived from Mrs. Browning's Italy in *Aurora Leigh*.

Mme de Staël herself knew just as well as her English and American readers what it meant to be raised as a proper young lady in a strict Protestant family. For she was no Corinne but Germaine Necker of Geneva; she had been laughed at and criticized in society for her mannerisms; and married off at the age of nineteen to a man chosen by her family for his title (from the restricted available field of Protestant aristocrats). She carried her heroine's story back to childhood, and this was another important originality of the novel; for when before *Corinne* had the sufferings of the gifted girl been told in fiction?

Corinne puts off the revelation of her early life to Oswald until she can pose with lyre in hand on Cape Miseno. There, inspired by the nearby tomb of Virgil, she makes one of her more famous improvisations on the cruelty of fate toward the elite few: "some unknown force drives genius toward misery . . . : we hear a music of the spheres not caught by ordinary mortals, we feel stronger passions, think higher thoughts, are doomed to greater suffering. . . ." And then she launches into a tale of childhood suffering all too familiar to Victorians who had grown up talented and female.

Her father was an Englishman, Lord Edgermond of Northumberland, a province as close to the edge-of-the-world as Mme de Staël could imagine. He returned there from Italy when her Roman mother died, leaving her in the care of an aunt who kept reminding her that the fear of leaving her native land had made her mother die of grief. Nevertheless, at fifteen Corinne too must leave Italy and live for the next six years in England. She was right to grieve, for her father had married again, and the second Lady Edgermond turns out to be a dignified, cold woman who cares only for English provincial life and domestic virtue, and hates everything Italian, especially the style of womanhood represented by young Corinne.

Corinne suffers terribly in rainy and gloomy England, full of teacups and boring neighbors (who much resemble the good ladies of Highbury in

Jane Austen's *Emma*). The only gleam of happiness is provided by her three-year-old half sister Lucile, who has the whitest skin and the blondest hair that olive-skinned, black-tressed Corinne has ever seen.

Corinne's Italian spontaneity and expansiveness are squelched, her conversation censored and silenced. So shocked is Lady Edgermond when Corinne, at a formal dinner party, quotes a few lines of Italian verse which refer delicately to the subject of love, that she enforces much earlier than usual that dreadful English custom of the after-dinner separation of women from men. (Here Mme de Staël drew on memories not only of her uncomfortable exile year in England, but also of her childhood with a strict mother much like Lady Edgermond.)

All of Corinne's nascent talents, for music, recitation, literature, are repressed and despised—not through active malice or cruelty, but because her stepmother adheres to a cultural standard different from her own. When Corinne spends more time by herself, studying and developing her native gifts, Lady Edgermond protests:

> "What is the good of all that?" she asked; "will it make you happy?"—and the question plunged me into despair. For what is happiness, I asked myself, if not the development of our faculties? Is not mental suicide as bad as physical? And if I must repress my mind and my spirit, what's the use of preserving the miserable rest of my life, which begins to drive me wild?

> But there was no use saying these things to my stepmother. I once tried to, and she had answered that a woman was created to take care of her husband's household and her children's health; all other ambitions led only to trouble, and I should conceal any that I had. And these words . . . left me absolutely speechless; for emulation and enthusiasm, those motive forces of genius, require encouragement, or they fade like withered flowers beneath a cold gray sky. . . .

> Narrow spirits and mediocre people attempt in the name of Duty to impose silence on talent. . . . But is it true that Duty prescribes the same rules for all? . . . Every woman, just like every man, must forge her own path according to her character and her talents.

Little wonder that Harriet Beecher felt "an intense sympathy" with Corinne. "But in America," she wrote, "feelings vehement and absorbing like hers become still more deep, morbid, and impassioned by the constant forms of self-government which the rigid forms of our society demand. They are repressed, and they burn inward till they burn the very soul."

Little wonder that Elizabeth Barrett Browning invented for Aurora Leigh a Florentine mother, an English father, and an Italian homeland to mourn throughout her years of oppressive upbringing in England by her spinster aunt.

> I broke the copious curls upon my head
> In braids, because she liked smooth-ordered hair.
> I left off saying my sweet Tuscan words. . . .

The Corinne that we first encounter in Mme de Staël's novel being drawn by four white horses to the Capitoline Hill was not to triumph born, but to the sufferings of the gifted girl in a strict home and a conventional society. Italy was in her soul—a quality of spirit as much as an actual heritage; to Italy she dreamed of going, there to live the independent life of the woman of genius. And Corinne in fact runs away—from home, stepmother, neighbors, England. What actually happens between her flight to Italy and her crowning on the Capitoline, Mme de Staël does not tell us, except that in some marvelous way it all works out in Italy, the training, developing, publishing, applauding of female genius. For "Italy," as Mrs. Browning wrote in *Aurora Leigh,* "Italy/Is one thing, England one."

It will be noticed that Harriet Beecher's reaction to *Corinne* was to comment on "the rigid forms of our society," not on the strict New England stepmother who, in actual fact, had soured her own childhood. So Miss Ophelia, in *Uncle Tom's Cabin,* provides a subtle criticism of New England values, and a comic counterpoise to the wild spirit of Topsy, rather than an acid portrait etched with remembered pain. In the same way, Miss Leigh, the spinster aunt in Mrs. Browning's novel-poem, is drawn with witty malice but without bitterness. She represents English cultural attitudes toward the raising of women:

> . . . she owned
> She liked a woman to be womanly,
> And English women, she thanked God and sighed
> (Some people always sigh in thanking God),
> Were models to the universe.

Generalizing as well as performing was Mme de Staël's legacy to literary women: the ability to abstract social value and cultural law from domestic fact.

The curious split in form, part novel and part guidebook, that puzzles readers of *Corinne* suggests on a small scale the problem that all students of Mme de Staël must face when attempting to fix her place in the history of thought. Her principal contribution was the extension of the central point of Montesquieu's *Esprit des lois,* that political systems grow out of and are inseparable from social custom and national tradition, to fields other than politics, most of all to literature. Her analysis of the distinct cultural traditions behind European literature made way for Romanticism, a term she was the first to use. She introduced the German Romantics to France, and it was the reading of her *De l'Allemagne* that led Carlyle to study German, and to pay an uncharacteristic tribute to intellectual womanhood when he called Mme de Staël "the loftiest soul of any female of her time."

Irving Babbitt rightly saluted her as founder of the study of comparative literature, and Ian Watt has honored her as precursor of his study of the rise of the novel. But "Madame de Staël was not really a belle-lettrist or a literary critic, nor even a literary historian," as Morroe Berger observes; "today . . . we should call her a social scientist, since she sought to find in social institutions the influences that shaped the ideas and forms of literary expression."

In *Corinne,* Mme de Staël does not argue for an adjustment of marriage to female requirements; the novel is not, in any polemical sense, a feminist work. Instead her point is to show that regional or national or what we call cultural values determine female destiny even more rigidly, even more inescapably than male. For as women are the makers and transmitters of the minute local and domestic customs upon which rest all the great public affairs of civilization—a perception she derived from Montesquieu—so women suffer more, in their daily and developing lives, from the influences of nationality, geography, climate, language, political attitudes, and social forms.

Oswald's father is quite right. Corinne really is not a proper wife for a Nelvil, or for anyone else. She belongs on the open, sunlit stage of Italy, and he in the retired domestic privacy of rainy England. Corinne is a wild spirit, and England, as Mrs. Browning puts it, is a tame place:

> . . . All the fields
> Are tied up fast with hedges, nosegay like;
> The hills are crumpled plains, the plains parterres,
> The trees, round, woolly, ready to be clipped,
> And if you seek for any wilderness,
> You find, at best, a park. A nature tamed
> And grown domestic like a barn-door fowl

—and like the clucking, strutting, pecking barnyard women who are as much a part of the English landscape as are Aunt Pullet and Aunt Glegg in *The Mill on the Floss.*

George Eliot, in her scrupulous attention to the domestic habits of rural England; Charlotte Brontë in *Villette,* a novel which in its title as in its every scene and event is concerned with the power of place; Mrs. Stowe, in the wide geographical and socioeconomic sweep of her novel on slavery; George Sand, in her hundreds of brilliant pages on the clashing values transmitted by the women of her own family; Willa Cather in "Old

Mrs. Harris," the most delicate study that we have in fiction of the cultural determination of women's lives—all belong to the tradition of *Corinne, or Italy.*

I hesitate to name in this connection the distinguished women anthropologists, for fear of suggesting, as I definitely am not, that anthropology is a "woman's field." The reason for Ruth Benedict's and Margaret Mead's success in the new profession, which clearly emerges from their memoirs, was economic opportunity: there were jobs for women in anthropology in the 1920s because half the field work, that half concerned with investigation of female customs in remote societies, simply had to be done by women. (If such assignments had not come their way, both Mead and Benedict might have gone on writing the poetry and fiction that they wrote in college.)

Nor will I affirm the cliché that the delicate sensibility of women to the little ways of home makes them preservers and, in their literature, celebrants of conservative and local values. In some writings by some women, of course, just as in some writings by some men, there can indeed be found conservative views and regional affections, but these are hardly the hallmark of the tradition of Corinne's Italy. For what Mme de Staël passed on to her disciples was a heady sense of cutting loose from custom, an intoxicating awareness of the possibility of otherness in the human condition, resting on an unsentimental perception of its varying forms in various societies. As in anthropological writing at its cautious best, *Corinne* provides no easy choices, no simple prescriptions for ideal happiness under the blue sky of Italian culture.

Indeed, one of the most remarkable things about the novel is Mme de Staël's admiration of England, the enemy nation of women as of France. Here Napoleon was justly furious, and he punished Mme de Staël's literary treason by forbidding her residence in Paris. " 'I leave you the universe to exploit,' " the Emperor remembered telling her; " 'I abandon the rest of the earth to you and reserve only Paris for myself'—but Paris was all she wanted." Paris, its salons and its enlightenment, was her center. Paris was the source of her intellectual values, and the geographical and historical heart of the culture then being undermined, as Mme de Staël well knew, by the North European and Romantic values that sift through the pages of *Corinne.*

Corinne herself worships Oswald because he personifies the English ideal of *home,* a word Mme de Staël used without translating—for there is no French equivalent for what is more a value than a place. And for such a male personification of that ideal, the ideal woman is in fact not Corinne but her blond rival, who personifies English womanhood, English culture, and English Romanticism. Lucile is young, pale, innocent, and silent. She has no personality, no education, no talent, no society but her mother, no thought but Oswald; her very nullity as a person is the source of her charm, a mysterious and subtle charm that Corinne, with all her demonstrative brilliance, does not provide.

Lucile is Oswald's *blanche fiancée,* his *jeune vierge en fleur,* his *still unravish'd bride of quietness,* as Mme de Staël had not the slightest poetic inclination to say. But she did turn her remarkable analytic powers on Oswald's reflections:

> Lucile was on her knees beside her mother, and it was Lucile who was reading first a chapter of the Bible and then a prayer adapted to domestic and rural life. . . . Tears fell from her eyes . . . she covered her face . . . but Oswald saw them. . . . He studied that air of youth which is so close to infancy, that glance which seems to preserve a recent memory of heaven. . . . He reflected upon her austere and retired life, without pleasures, without the homage of the world. . . .
>
> . . . Corinne delighted the imagination in a thousand ways, but there was nevertheless a species of thought and, if one can use the expression, a musical sound which went only with Lucile. Images of domestic happiness were more easily combined with her Northumberland retreat than with Corinne's triumphal chariot. . . .
>
> He fell asleep thinking of Italy; yet during his sleep he thought he saw Lucile passing gently before him in the form of an angel. . . .

Patterns of contrast fill the conclusion of the novel. Lucile is pale and blond, with white plumes in her hat; Corinne is dark, and covers herself with the black Venetian domino. Lucile is the quintessential virgin and Corinne, in spite of Mme de Staël's sporadic efforts to clean up her past and order her present, is clearly a woman who has lived. Lucile in her extreme youth "presents the innocent image of the springtime of life"; and Corinne, while not precisely the spirit of autumn—for Mme de Staël was only a woman—is very ripe.

Lucile has no existence apart from her family, and Corinne has no family. Lucile is a Protestant who prays at home, and Corinne honors all the public rituals and ceremonies of the Catholic church. Corinne is open, spontaneous, talkative, bold, talented, famous; Lucile is silent and shy—a girl for a man to dream of, for a man to worship, for a man to marry. Corinne is the city and civilization, is art and joy; Lucile is melancholy, country retirement, and boredom. For as the epilogue points out—Mme de Staël was only human—Oswald is terribly bored by his marriage to Lucile, which, the reader feels, is just what he deserves. As for Corinne, much as she grieves for Oswald, much as she yearns for domestic happiness, all she gets is what she deserves—Italy.

I rather like the way Mme de Staël ties up the novel, without attempting to resolve any of the cultural dilemmas which face the woman of genius. On the arm of a frivolous French count, who turns out to be a good sort of chap to have around in time of trouble, Corinne staggers back to Italy from Scotland, where she has gone to release Oswald and free him for marriage to Lucile. In Italy she finds that love has destroyed her talents as well as her happiness, and she retreats from the public eye. Years later, Oswald and Lucile, now man and wife, make a trip to Florence and search out Corinne. She stages a final public triumph in the Academy and then expires—finding time, however, to coach their little daughter to be a Corinne of the future and, one assumes, a terrible handful for her strict mama.

All this takes place in northern Italy, the one region of the country not already covered, guidebook style, by the novel. Perhaps Mme de Staël felt that Florence was the only possible locale for the finale of the woman of genius. However, what she actually drew upon in the last chapters, as we know from her letters, was memories of the inauspicious start of her own Italian tour. The surprise and disappointment that she then felt, travelers from the north both before and after her time have shared. For northern Italy is cold, cold as the rest of Europe, "and winter displeases more there than anywhere else, because' the imagination is not prepared for it." The skies are leaden and gray at the end of the novel; the snow falls, the fog thickens, the rivers flood; even the architecture (at least of the cathedral of Milan) is Gothic; one might as well have stayed at home.

"Où donc est votre belle Italie?" Lucile asks her husband—So where is your beautiful Italy?

" 'I don't know,' Lord Nelvil sadly answered, 'when I shall ever find it again.' "

10

EDUCATING HEROINISM:
GOVERNESS TO GOVERNOR

> We come now to the last form of Heroism; that which we
> call Queenship. The Commander over Men; she to whose will
> our wills are to be subordinated, and loyally surrender them-
> selves, and find their welfare in doing so, may be reckoned
> the most important of Great Women. She is practically the
> summary for us of *all* the various figures of Heroism: Priest,
> Teacher, whatsoever of earthly or spiritual dignity we can
> fancy to reside in a woman, embodies itself here, to *command*
> over us, to furnish us with constant practical teaching, to tell
> us for the day and hour what we are to *do.*
>
> —Carlyle

I

At sixteen, a boy raised by a loving mother is a creature
apart. He belongs in a way to no sex; his thoughts are as pure
as an angel's; he does not have that puerile coquetry, that un-
quiet curiosity, that shadowed personality which often mar a
woman's early development. He loves his mother as a daughter does not and will not ever love her. . . . It is the ideal of
love. . . .

I find that poets and novelists have been insufficiently aware
of the subject for observation, the source for poetry offered by
this swift and unique moment in the life of man. It is true
that, in these sad times, the adolescent no longer exists. What
we see today is the ill-kempt and ill-taught student, infected
by some vulgar vice. . . . He is ugly, even if naturally beauti-

ful; he wears disgusting clothes, he doesn't look you straight
in the eye. He devours filthy books in secret, and for all that
the sight of a woman frightens him. His mother's caresses
make him blush—as if he felt himself unworthy. The world's
most beautiful languages, the great poems of humanity are for
him merely a source of indifference, revolt and disgust; . . .
his taste is depraved. . . . It would take years for him to lose
the fruits of this detestable education, to learn his own language by forgetting the Latin which he barely knows and the
Greek that he does not know at all, to form his taste, to acquire a just idea of history, to lose that stamp of ugliness that
the wretchedness and the brutalising slavery of the school
years have imprinted on his brow, to gain the look of frankness and to carry his head high. Only then will he love his
mother. . . .

                                                    —George Sand

Gender in French—in all Western languages, excepting only English—is
free of sexual connotation, purely arbitrary: the female apple, the male
tomato. Or so says the grammatical rule; but not, in my reading at least,
the great women writers of France. My notes are full of significant in-
stances where a Mme de Staël, a George Sand, a Simone Weil will, at a
moment of heightened sexual self-consciousness, choose a word for its
gender, and for the train of adjectives, pronouns, and endings resonant in
sexual consequence that follow after her choice. What a resource the
French woman writer has, denied to her English colleague, when, especially in a love scene, she can choose freely among such words as person,
heart, soul, spirit—a list which alternates between feminine and masculine
gender in the French. No grammarian will ever convince me that it was
not by choice that Colette summed up her final passionate tribute to her
mother's influence by calling her *un personnage:* "il n'a pas fini de me
hanter"—he has never stopped haunting me. Had Colette called her
mother a person—*une personne*—rather than a personage, *she* would
have been the one to haunt. Pronouns can be liberating for the French
women writers; while for the English, from Mary Wollstonecraft to Gertrude Stein, they can impose awkwardness and obscurity on her prose.

The French language, however, imposes one sexual burden on the
woman writer that English does not: in the role-words, such as doctor or
professor. Since no gender normally attaches to such words in English,
one can say and write Dr. Helene Deutsch or Professor Marjorie Nichol-
son without forcible linguistic reminders of whatever sex-typing persists in
English-speaking society. But the women I know in France today who are
doctors and professors are admittedly sensitive to the wisp of irony that

clings to the clash of genders in their titles. "Bonjour, madame le professeur," one says; or, "Merci, madame le docteur." And when an alternate feminine role-word does exist it is far more often pejorative, far more nastily ironic in French than in English—words like *peintresse* or *poétesse* for ladies who play at painting or poetry. A friend of mine who edits a scholarly Romance language journal reacts to the inferior status often implied by a feminine role-word in French when she bridles at being called *l'éditrice* of her journal; she is quite good enough to be known as *l'éditeur*.

In English there is only the word *editor,* which does for either sex, as do singer and dancer. In the latter cases, French has feminine role-words in good standing, without pejorative connotation, surely because for centuries women have sung and danced in France. For the same reason there is a female word for the schoolteacher, *l'institutrice,* she who deals with little children on the lower levels of education. But there is no such female equivalent for the professor, he who deals with older students and deeper subjects; and *"Docteur,"* as the grammarian Maurice Grevisse lugubriously puts it, "when designating a person promoted to the highest grade of a university faculty, has no feminine form."

To browse through the twenty fascinating pages that M. Grevisse gives in *Le bon usage* to feminine gender is to absorb linguistic footnotes to the march of history. For example, in the eighteenth century and earlier *peintresse* was not a silly but a useful word, surely because there were many distinguished women painters in France; and in our own century, journalists have flouted lexicographers in their use of the word *ambassadrice* to refer not to the wife of an ambassador but to a Clare Boothe Luce. Grevisse does not, unfortunately, discuss the role-word of most importance to literary history, that for the male and female people who have written novels. There is a feminine form in French for novelist; but *la romancière* does not appear in the more scholarly dictionaries I have consulted. When I come across the word in a French text I am never sure how much of a pejorative sense clings to the feminine gender (how much indeed to "woman novelist" in English, where "lady novelist" has never recovered from the onslaught of W. S. Gilbert?). I would wager that Nathalie Sarraute is more often *le romancier* while Françoise Sagan is more often *la romancière* in French criticism today; and I doubt if anyone dares call Simone de Beauvoir *une romancière*. When Sainte-Beuve used *la romancière* in his 1850 essay on Mme de Genlis he put the word in italics, thus indicating that it was newer and slangier than *le romancier,* and that the creation of a female form of the word novelist was a response to the crush of women like Mme de Genlis into the field of novel-writing, which marked the latter eighteenth century in France as it did in England.

Sometimes role-gender in French is so far from merely arbitrary, so awash with sexual connotations, that a change in gender wholly transforms the sense of the role it touches. Take *master* and *mistress:* in English these words are still recognizable as male-female variations of the same role; but not in French, especially not to literary people. *Maître, mon maître* is the honorific title which the aspiring man of letters reserves for his literary master, as Maupassant addressed Flaubert; but when a young French writer says he has *une maîtresse,* a mistress, he is hardly referring to his participation in the naturalist movement. So Flaubert himself, when in middle age he turned to that grand old lady of French letters, George Sand, for literary discussion and maternal affection, addressed his wonderful letters *"Ma chère maître"*—my dear-lady master—to Mme Sand. They were both aware of all the warmth and all the cool irony of that form of address. The word *not* spoken between them—*la maîtresse*—carried implications sexual as well as literary, for Flaubert was a son-lover by temperament, and George Sand was a mother-mistress all her life.

· · ·

All this is by way of introduction to an historic event important to literature, to pedagogy, and to heroinism: the official change in title from *la Gouvernante* to *le Gouverneur* which marked the climax of power in the career of Mme de Genlis, the eighteenth-century writer and educator. From *Gouvernante* to *Gouverneur* is a change as momentous in French as it is in English, for *Governess* is in the nursery, and *Governor* rules the world. And the educating heroine, as the writings of Mme de Genlis were among the earliest to show, stands for the heroinism of power.

Because the children that Mme de Genlis taught were of royal blood—one became a king—her title (as well as her method) was a matter of considerable deliberation in her day. Its change to the masculine gender signified in a large sense the establishment of the woman as educator and, in a narrow sense, that she was eminently qualified to govern male princes as well as female princesses. To Mme de Genlis's pedagogical fictions, which are the most severe and the most elegant of the genre that I have read, a whiff of royalty still clings, and the peculiar charm that emanates from her central persona, *la femme enseignante*—Sainte-Beuve's phrase, the teaching woman—is worth trying to define. There is a seductive coldness about her, an amalgam of the stiff unapproachability of the very old with the supple grace of the very young. "Her imagination has remained fresh," as George Sand wrote of Genlis, "under the frosts of age."

The educating heroine is a domestic figure, not a hireling; she teaches in the home, and it looks very like a palace. In her professional capacity, this figure has nothing to do with the weary teachers and exploited governesses of women's literature (from Charlotte Brontë to Sylvia Ashton-Warner). Educating heroinism, from Genlis onward, is more a rank than a profession, and more often than not is embodied in what is the greatest of all the ranks: the Mother. For women writers fascinated by power, the place to look, as feminists are often too rushed to notice, is motherhood; but it is a kind of motherhood that male writers are often too slow to recognize.

In her dazzling array of talents and accomplishments, the educating heroine exhibits none of that thrust toward ceremonial glory and public applause that accompanies the genius of a Corinne. She is in fact the most severe of anti-Corinnes, the proponent of reason over feeling, of prudence over spontaneity, of private influence over public celebrity. ("The *exhibiting,* the *displaying* wife may entertain your company," wrote Hannah More in *Coelebs in Search of a Wife,* "—but . . . you will want a COM-PANION: an ARTIST you may hire.") The educating heroine is not an artist on display. Heard more than seen, and feared as much as admired, she is sometimes anonymous to the point of invisibility, a narrative presence which controls and dominates behind the scene.

In the work of Jane Austen, the author eludes us: that is one of the reasons many have coupled her name with Shakespeare's when saluting Austen's rare quality. But where with Shakespeare we are still searching for clues to his occupations, travels, and acquaintances, with Jane Austen we know quite enough about her life to satisfy our curiosity about her non-literary, non-domestic activities with a single word: none. Instead, our curiosity is all about Austen's temper and mind. When did she laugh, and when grow serious? What did she hold as a moralist? Where did she stand —we want the answer almost in a physical sense—in relation to her characters? It is very difficult to know.

For example, near the end of *Emma,* Mrs. Weston has a baby that turns out to be a girl. Mrs. Weston, the heroine's genteel and now well-married former governess, remains a friend and neighbor to Emma, who rejoices in the sex of the child, for Emma is "convinced that a daughter would suit both father and mother best. It would be a great comfort to Mr. Weston as he grew older . . . to have his fireside enlivened by the sports and the nonsense, the freaks and the fancies of a child never banished from home." Good God! Was Jane Austen so little a feminist that she did not protest her own lifelong imprisonment at home? Is she with Emma here or against her, as her heroine takes the paternalistic view of the spinster daughter's doom? Impossible to know. Emma goes on to think of the daughter's mother, once her own governess:

> and Mrs. Weston—no one could doubt that a daughter would be most to her; and it would be quite a pity that any one who so well knew how to teach, should not have their own powers in exercise again.

"She has had the advantage, you know, of practising on me,"
she continued—"like La Baronne d'Almane on La Comtesse d'Ostalis, in Madame de Genlis' Adelaide and Theodore, and we shall
now see her own little Adelaide educated on a more perfect plan."

Freighted with its awkward French, the sentence is uncharacteristically
out of balance; that is perhaps why we feel that Austen is here, for a frac-
tion of a second, off her guard. We seem to catch her in the act of rueful
self-examination, when her own role as novelist and moralist is at issue—
here, as throughout *Emma,* the role of surrogate mother who engages to
teach "on a more perfect plan." *Emma* is a novel like no other in the
Austen canon, the most abstract, the closest to allegory in its names and
locations; it is the only one to carry the name of its heroine—and that a
heroine Austen was sure "no one but myself will much like." Emma is
uniquely placed, by wealth and social position, to order lives, plan marriages, regulate society, and construct characters through the play of her
lively imagination. She seems to have been ironically conceived as stand-in
for the novelist herself, the arrogant romancer, the woman who arranges
lives in order to teach the world how to go "on a more perfect plan." This
doubling of role, where the narrator-novelist is also the educating heroine
of her own tale, is a visible rather than (as in Austen) an invisible feature
of the Genlis fictions.

But the educating heroine that Jane Austen knew, in Genlis and elsewhere, is always right; while her own Emma is always wrong, her imagination faulty, her arrogance unjustified, her rule meddlesome, for she herself
is the product of bad teaching. *Emma* is a cautionary pedagogical tale in
the Genlis tradition, a tradition which Austen, as was her way, satirized as
she brought it to perfection. The mocking point of the little scene quoted
above is that Mrs. Weston has botched the job of raising Emma; she is no
Baronne d'Almane; she will teach her own daughter no better, whatever
Emma thinks, for having practiced on a surrogate. ("She will indulge her
even more than she did you," says Mr. Knightley, "and believe that she
does not indulge her at all. It will be the only difference.") And so will it
continue to go down through the generations of women, Austen seems to
be saying in a rare mood of self-mockery; so will it go in fiction as in life,
those tight interlacings of women teaching women, their plans ever better,
their results ever faulty.

Surrogate motherhood may seem an odd term to apply to Jane Austen
or any childless writer, but in fact most of the literary women who wrote
of motherhood as a focus of power had no children of their own. They include the spinster, such as Willa Cather; the childless wife, such as Virginia Woolf; and the young woman, such as Mary Wollstonecraft *before*
motherhood descended upon her—a condition of life which perhaps, except in the case of the strongest-minded, blurs the sharp sight and weakens

the firm grasp that educating heroinism requires. "To cure those faults by reason, which ought never to have taken root in the infant mind," wrote Wollstonecraft in the preface to her *Original Stories,* is a task that "requires more judgment than generally falls to the lot of parents." A similar view is reflected in the long gallery of incompetent mothers portrayed by Jane Austen; from Mrs. Bennet in *Pride and Prejudice* to Mary Musgrove in *Persuasion.* "I hope I am as fond of my child as any mother," says Mary to her spinster sister Anne, the heroine of *Persuasion,* "but I do not know that I am of any more use in the sick-room . . . I have not nerves for the sort of thing. . . . You, who have not a mother's feelings, are a great deal the properest person. You can make little Charles do anything; he always minds you at a word."

Surrogate motherhood was the role we know Jane Austen played with greatest relish in real life, as maiden aunt to her beloved nieces. "She shone most brightly as an aunt," writes R. W. Chapman, the great Austen scholar, and he goes on to reflect on her creation of character. "There is something, in the role of the consummate aunt, not unlike her relation to those young people who owed their existence to her genius."

Long before *Emma,* when Austen was still in or barely out of her teens, and just beginning to sport with her nieces and her characters, she made fun of the literary role of "consummate aunt." "My Dear Neice," she wrote to little Fanny Austen in a mock dedication,

> As I am prevented by the great distance between Rowling and Steventon from superintending your Education myself, the care of which will probably on that account devolve on your Father and Mother, I think it is my particular Duty to prevent your feeling as much as possible the want of my personal instructions, by addressing to you on paper my Opinions and Admonitions on the conduct of Young Women, which you will find expressed in the following pages.—
>
> > I am my dear Neice
> > Your affectionate Aunt
> > The Author.

Outside of Jane Austen, there is otherwise not much fun in educating heroinism—certainly nothing to laugh at in the story of and the stories by Mme de Genlis.

* * *

Born in 1746 with a name out of a Radcliffe novel (Stéphanie-Félicité Ducrest de Saint-Aubin), Mme de Genlis was of noble birth—the only woman of that class in this book—and of a very early generation of women professionals. She was six years older than Fanny Burney, thirteen years older than Mary Wollstonecraft, twenty years older than Mme de Staël, twenty-one years older than Maria Edgeworth, twenty-nine years older than Jane Austen, fifty-eight years older than George Sand, all of whom read her. By marriage at the age of sixteen she became a *comtesse* (de Genlis) and eventually a *marquise* (de Sillery). By the age of twenty-one she had two children and was ready to go to work: as mistress to the Duc de Chartres, heir to the house of Orléans; as lady-in-waiting to his wife; as brilliant star of a Paris salon. Of how many Frenchwomen before and after her could a similar account be given, as well as a sketch such as those supplied in abundance by her contemporaries of Mme de Genlis's beauty, charm, and intelligence. But she was something more than a salon woman. She had one marked peculiarity, from youth to death, her mania for teaching. Mania is Sainte-Beuve's word for Genlis as educator: "cette verve de pédagogie poussée jusqu'à la manie."

The house of Orléans to which Genlis was attached was the cadet branch of the ruling Bourbons, and when she resided with the family it was at the Palais-Royal, within walking distance of the Louvre. (In her day, none but the mob walked; today the tourist strolls through the enclosed gardens of the Palais-Royal and tries to spy out the windows of the flat where Colette lived a century and a half later.) There, in the mid-1770s, Mme de Genlis began her fame as an educator: she organized science courses for the court and wrote the first of her educational plays for its entertainment. In 1777 she was named Governess of the duke's infant daughters, given a regular salary, and provided with the secluded rural establishment which her educational theories demanded, a pavilion on the grounds of the convent of Belle-Chasse, just outside Paris.

Eight years and fifteen published volumes later (including her most important pedagogical fictions) Mme de Genlis achieved her ambition: the royal sons were given to her care, their governors dismissed, and she, a woman! (there was much satirical commentary, some of it salacious) was named their Governor. She hired masters for special subjects, and plotted an elaborate educational strategy for the children which turned every moment of the day and evening, every lesson, meal, excursion, and pastime, to the training of intellect, body, and character. She was always in residence, and always in command—a word justified by the published documents of Belle-Chasse, including her letters to her little princes and princesses, written in the evening to assess and reward or punish the behavior of the day.

For this position, Mme de Genlis relinquished her brilliant social existence at the Palais-Royal (and perhaps her sexual activities as well). To maintain her independence, she is said to have refused a chair in the Académie Française; in the same year, 1785, she journeyed to England to be honored by Oxford. Influence over royal children was at the time a matter of more than ordinary public concern. Whether kings were to be men or divinities, whether Bourbons or from the house of Orléans, was about to be decided in France on the scaffold, as well as in the school-room.

On the eve of the French Revolution, the children's father was elevated to Duc d'Orléans. For his role during the Terror he was awarded the title by which he is still best known (but not much honored) of Philippe-Égalité. The duke denied his Orléans blood, voted the execution of the king, and before long went to the guillotine himself, as did a lesser noble-man, the husband of Mme de Genlis. But she survived, sometimes in flight, sometimes in exile, as loyal protector and tutelary genius of the chil-dren of the house of Orléans, one of whom came back to France—after Terror, directory, consulate, empire, Waterloo, and restoration—to rule as the so-called Citizen King Louis-Philippe in the 1830s. Meanwhile, Mme de Genlis lived to the age of eighty-four through four distinct periods of French history, and established herself as a scribbling woman of prolific versatility (she wrote more than one hundred works) and sufficient quality to merit a study of her *Oeuvre* by Sainte-Beuve. His essay remains the best introduction to Mme de Genlis.

She was a woman writer (*une femme-auteur*) like so many others, wrote Sainte-Beuve, but of a special character:

> Charming and brilliant in youth, she did not limit herself to a single taste or talent . . . ; all the arts of pleasing, all the crafts and skills (for she did not omit the *métiers*) made her a living Encyclopedia, who prided herself on being the rival and antagonist of that other *Encyclopédie;* but what gave spirit and life to all her multitudinous occupations was a single vocation which tied them to-gether, gave them order and direction. Mme de Genlis was something more than a woman-writer, she was a woman-teacher (*une femme enseignante*); she was born with that mark on her brow. To some, God says *Sing;* to others, *Preach.* To her He said, *Profess and Teach.* Never was a firmer denial given to the words of the Apostle: *"Docere autem mulieri non permitto"*—or, "I do not permit women to teach," as Saint Paul said to Timothy. Even had she wanted to, Mme de Genlis was simply not at liberty to obey this precept, so powerful and irresistible was her vocation from her earliest years. She man-ifested from infancy an instinct and an enthusiasm for pedagogy, in the best sense of the word. It had been ordained, from her birth, that she would be the most graceful and the most dashing of peda-gogues.

In the history of pedagogy, Mme de Genlis has a distinct place as an innovating follower as well as opponent of Rousseau. (She had some in-teresting ideas, for example, about "living language" training from in-

fancy; about the games with which to introduce children to natural
science; about a regimen of spartan austerity then "revolutionary," in
every sense, to the raising of the aristocratic young, and credited by Louis-
Philippe as contributory to his survival through the years of his exile, a
stretch of which he spent in America.) But in literary history she belongs
with the women writers who created the novel. She wrote what Joyce
Hemlow, the biographer and editor of Fanny Burney, calls "courtesy
books," the elegant portmanteau term Hemlow uses for moral tales, educational fictions, and pedagogical treatises. Insofar as Fanny Burney has
the honor of being the first major woman novelist, so far do the "courtesy
books" of the eighteenth century deserve an honored place, as Hemlow
demonstrates, among the several kinds of writing that in confluence gave
rise to modern fiction.

The term "courtesy books" locates us at once on that point of converg-
ing lines where criticism has fixed the novel as Burney made it and Austen
brought it to perfection, where manners and morals meet. But in their
humdrum guise, they suggest all that can be dreariest in the printed book,
those improving works which conscientious mothers read and force on
their resisting offspring. They have always been written to be read aloud
by parent to child and parsed between them, thus falling somewhere in
that no woman's land between children's books and adult literature. It is
much to the credit of Mme de Genlis, and to her imagination as well as
her style, that more than a flicker of life remains in her pedagogical
fictions, even in translation. (The contemporary Thomas Holcroft translation is unusually fine—perhaps the reason why Maria Edgeworth never
published her own translation.) "What a surprising talent that woman
has," wrote the English rival to Mme de Genlis, Hannah More, "of making everything that passes through her hands interesting! the barrenest and
most unpromising subjects she 'turns to favor and prettiness.'"

Jane Austen probably read *Adèle et Théodore* in translation, for in
Emma she gave the title in English; she read *Les Veillées du Château* in
French. These are the two most important of Mme de Genlis's books,
published one after the other in 1782 and 1784 and meant to be read
together, for the first, subtitled *Letters on Education,* is an epistolary novel
designed to explain the circumstances and theory of Genlis pedagogy; and
the second, always translated as *Tales of the Castle,* is a string of educational tales designed to show her method in action. The Mother writes the
letters, the Mother tells the tales; she is the dominating persona of both
works as both narrator and heroine. For her portrait of the Baronne d'Almane, the mother figure cited by Austen, Mme de Genlis was accused of
inordinate self-esteem, but she did not at all resemble that lady, Genlis
later wrote. Mme d'Almane was a woman grave, serious, and circumspect,

"d'une prudence parfaite," and "I am not at all like that, not even today, when I am twenty years older."

The Baroness d'Almane, whom I shall call "A" for convenience, and because it suits the Genlis style, astonishes her Paris friends, at the opening of *Adèle et Théodore,* by her sudden move with her family to their isolated château in the country. Actually it is mature deliberation, as she proceeds to explain in her letters, which convinces her that four years of rural retreat from "the world" are what she requires for the proper education of her children, Adèle and Théodore. Her principal correspondent is the Comtesse d'Ostalis (or "O"), a young married woman of twenty-one, already the mother of twins and pregnant, at the start of the novel, with what turns out to be a son. The relationship between "A" and "O" to which Jane Austen alludes is interestingly complex: they are friends as well as relatives, teacher-pupil as well as colleagues in the educational enterprise, and also mother-daughter. "A" is thirty-two; married at seventeen, she was an "ornament of the world" for fifteen years, but to her grief long remained childless. At twenty-one, "A's" desire to begin to raise children had grown so strong that she "adopted" her orphan niece, then ten years old, and began to practice upon her those skills as an educator for which "A" possessed a special genius. "O" is that niece, now a countess and a mother in her own right, but still reverent and adoring toward "A," though they are only eleven years apart in age. "O" yearns to join "A" in the country as soon as her condition permits her to travel. By continuing as a daughter and pupil to "A," "O" will learn to be mother and teacher in her own right according to what Austen calls "a more perfect plan."

All the adult correspondents of *Adèle et Théodore* are engaged, with varying degrees of success, in the same pedagogical endeavor. All are voluntary inhabitants of childhood, a timeless time almost without youth and certainly without innocence, which Wordsworth could not recognize. In the Genlis world, adulthood succeeds to childhood, and childhood to the principal function of adulthood—the teaching of children—with an astonishing rapidity due not to fantasy but to fact: the very early marriages of aristocratic women in her day.

For example, the Vicomtesse de Lumours ("L"), an artificial but goodhearted society figure, is already worried, though only thirty-one herself, that she has irrevocably spoiled her older daughter Flora, who is fifteen. By benefiting from "A's" epistolary advice, "L" hopes that she can do well enough with the education of her younger daughter, Constantia, who is four, to make her worthy of becoming "A's" daughter-in-law through marriage to Théodore, who is seven. The son of "A's" country neighbor, thirteen-year-old Charles de Valmont, is being groomed as future husband of "A's" six-year-old Adèle. Meanwhile, "L's" brother, the

Count of Roseville ("R"), corresponds with "A" and her husband about
the education of a young prince, heir to an unnamed throne, whose education has been placed in "R's" governorship for twelve years. The real and
adopted children of "A," "O," "L," and "R"; their friends' and neighbors'
children, who form a fairly thickly populated world for gossip in the background of the novel; all are analyzed, trained, and discussed with their
adult roles in view, especially marriage to each other. The education of
these children is for power and influence in "the world."

If this summary suggests a confusingly intricate fiction, in which educational maneuvers are plotted by letter with the strategy of a chess game,
that is a fair account of *Adèle et Théodore.* And if the reader is reminded
of a better-known work of eighteenth-century fiction, *Les Liaisons dangereuses,* he is one with the contemporaries of Mme de Genlis, for when
the Choderlos de Laclos novel appeared anonymously in the same year
(1782) as *Adèle et Théodore,* it was attributed to her. Mme de Genlis was
horrified, for, whatever her private morals and political maneuvers in real
life, in literature she worked to inculcate virtue and reason in the aristocratic young; and *Les Liaisons dangereuses* is a cynical plotting of sexual
seduction. The seductions and stratagems of maternal power, not of sexual
conquest, were Mme de Genlis's subject. A few years later, she and Laclos
became personal enemies in the battle for influence over the house of
Orléans, when he was appointed personal secretary to Philippe-Égalité.
Les Liaisons pédagogiques, however, would make an excellent subtitle for
Adèle et Théodore.

In *Les Veillées du Château* another atmosphere takes hold. Solitude
closes in on the castle; letter-writing ceases; the world drops away; the
salon gives way to the nursery. Now the children themselves come to the
fore, and they are locked with the Mother in an educational situation
which centers on her telling of a series of moral tales. There are now three
children, of different names and ages, and the Mother too has a different
name: the Marquise de Clémire. But the important change of personnel in
Tales of the Castle is that now the Mother stands alone (backed only by
her own mother, the Grandmother), without male collaboration. The
Genlis castle becomes a domain of absolute matriarchy suffused with what
Colette once called, when describing her own matriarchal childhood, "the
deep peace of the harem." What Genlis does to divest childhood of the paternal influence is send the father off to war:

> The duties of a soldier obliged the Marquis de Clémire to quit his
> family and join the army. He received, at the painful moment of
> farewel, the mournful adieus of his wife, his wife's mother, and
> his three children. Caesar, his little son, bitterly complained because
> he was not big enough to follow his father. . . .
>
>   (Holcroft)

These are the opening sentences of *Tales of the Castle*. They plunge us at once into a female fantasy that is as old as the sex and as lasting as women's literature, as every grown-up American who was once a Little Woman will recognize:

> "Christmas won't be Christmas without any presents," grumbled Jo. . . .
> "It's so dreadful to be poor!" sighed Meg. . . .
> "I don't think it's fair for some girls to have plenty of pretty things, and other girls nothing at all," added little Amy. . . .
> "We've got father and mother and each other," said Beth contentedly, from her corner.
> The four young faces . . . brightened at the cheerful words, but darkened again as Jo said sadly,—
> "We haven't got father, and shall not have him for a long time." She didn't say "perhaps never," but each silently added it, thinking of father far away, where the fighting was.

Louisa May Alcott, in these opening lines of *Little Women*, was sketching her real family during a real American wartime in the 1860s, but fantasy was nevertheless her inspiration. For Alcott's father did not volunteer for service as a Union chaplain, as the father is made to do in *Little Women;* she herself was the only member of her family to "join the army"—as volunteer nurse—during the Civil War. (Reality is instead with Jo, the girl-child who stands in for the author and, much like Mme de Genlis's little Caesar, complains of not being able to go to war.) But the stage of *Little Women* must be set fatherless for the rule of that "noble-looking woman," tall, dignified, efficient, resolute, authoritarian, and supreme in command, the "Marmee" who might just as well be a Baronne d'Almane or a Marquise de Clémire.

Les Veillées du Château means something like Getting-Together-for-Work-and-Play-before-Bedtime in the Château; to translate the title as *Tales of the Castle* is to ignore the importance of the "frame" of the tales, a disciplinary even more than a narrative construct. For the Mother becomes a romancer not only to inculcate rational virtue but to reward it; and woe to the child whose daytime behavior is judged a fall from virtue, for his share in the evening's entertainment (from 8 to 9:30 *precisely*) is withdrawn for a number of *veillées* counted out, like lashes on the convict's back, in precise proportion to the gravity of the offense: Sloth, Greed, Waste, Spite, and Insubordination. The last is the worst, and the largest number of banishments from the *veillées* is assigned to the culprit who dares argue the Mother's interpretation of the tales when she is not by to correct and clarify.

The starts and stops of narration, for the giving of instruction and the administering of law, make much of the fascination of the whole, and it can be a rather cruel fascination:

> "Is that true," interrupted Madame de Clémire, and looking sted-fastly at Caroline—"Is that true, my child? Can you think so?"
>
> Caroline blushed, hung her head, and said nothing.
>
> "And are you sure, Pulcheria, it was not from malice that you laughed? Were you not pleased at the confusion in which you sup-posed M. Frémont? Did you not endeavour to increase it? Examine yourself well, and answer me."
>
> "I am not capable of telling lies, mamma,—I did—I—I am un-worthy—to—to—keep your company—and listen to your stories and —to—to—to—"
>
> Pulcheria's heart was ready to burst.
>
> "But you always merit my tenderness and forgiveness, my child," said Madame de Clémire, kissing her, "when you are sincere and tell the truth."—"And must I be for ever banished from your evening meetings, mamma?"—"No—not for ever; for eight days only."—"Thank you, thank you, my dear, dear mamma—"
>
> (Holcroft)

Justice is summary in the castle, and "evening meetings" is an excellent rendering (Thomas Holcroft was a friend of William Godwin and Thomas Paine) of *les veillées*.

The aristocratic children who are the principal figures in the tales the Mother tells and the aristocratic children who listen at night to her tales are precisely observed and differentiated by Mme de Genlis on pedagog-ical principle. But the effect is an evocation of a world of children with the minute detailing, the fine coloring, the brittle posing of a group of eight-eenth-century *porcelainerie*. They slide chairs around a frozen pond; they go to the opera in a coach with a footman; the children are complete figures—to their dolls, their clothes, their pet birds, their sweetmeats, their harpsichords. "In her details she is truly an artist and a poet," wrote George Sand, whose admiration for the severe pedagogical fictions of Mme de Genlis has caused some puzzled comment.*

The Genlis tales are not, on principle, fairy tales. Their extremes of

---

* *Les Veillées* is the composite name George Sand took over from Genlis for her own *romans champêtres,* and in her autobiography she wrote at length of the place of the Genlis tales in her childhood. She evokes the memory of hearing her mother read Genlis aloud, of letting her own attention wander from the old-fash-ioned moral precepts and settings, and of creating as she listened her own fantasies of an entirely different nature. This striking passage in Sand's *Histoire de ma vie* predicts a similar one in *Du côté de chez Swann*. Proust, whose distaste for Sand did not prevent his learning from her, writes there of listening as a child to his mother reading aloud from the moral fables of George Sand, his mind wandering, his fantasy embroidering everything that was faded and old-fashioned in a country tale like *François le Champi*. In Sand's prose and in her moral idealism, Proust writes, he would ever after hear the maternal and grandmaternal accent.

aristocratic wealth and peasant poverty, their sudden reverses of fortune reflect the real world of the *ancien régime*. For example, the tale called "The Brazier; or Reciprocal Gratitude" deals with a footman's devotion to a general's widow who has lost her pension, and ends with the happy apparition of a beautiful lady who comes to announce that a house has been built, a coach made ready, a pension reinstated, a footman rewarded. She is no fairy godmother, but Mme de P——, who comes straight from Versailles, where she is very close to the *roi*.

"'This story proves,'" the Mother tells the listening children just before bedtime, "'that . . . did men only understand their own interest, they would all be virtuous . . . the most certain method of fixing the attention of the world. . . .' 'Nothing,' interrupted Caesar, 'can be more true; the conclusions are wonderfully just.'" But they are upside-down conclusions to upside-down fairy tales, pointed at the princes who bestow blessings in reality, not at the poor who fantasize receiving them. Caesar and his sisters are being instructed to reward virtue, relieve poverty, and scatter benefactions in their path, like the little princes and princesses, the noble patrons and heroes that in reality they are themselves. "'Benevolence is the best, the greatest, the only true happiness.'" But benevolent princes and princesses begin life as good children, who listen to their Mother.

For example, here is the story of "Delphine, or the Fortunate Cure": the heroine a spoiled girl of nine, the cure both disciplinary and medical. Its opening sentence, in the Holcroft translation, is

> Delphine was an only daughter, and an heiress; her birth was noble, her person handsome, and her heart and understanding good.

But Jane Austen seems to have remembered the original French—

> Delphine, fille unique et riche héritière, avoit une naissance illustre, une jolie figure, de l'esprit, et un bon coeur.

—if the rhythms of the opening sentence of *Emma* are any indication:

> Emma Woodhouse, handsome, clever and rich, with a comfortable home and happy disposition, seemed to unite some of the best blessings of existence;

In *Emma* as in "Delphine" the heroine's many natural advantages are threatened by a faulty education at the hands of an imperfect mother. Emma's governess, who replaces her dead mother, "had fallen little short of a mother in affection," Austen writes, but

> the mildness of her temper had hardly allowed her to impose any restraint; and the shadow of authority being now long passed away, they had been living together as friend and friend very mutually attached, and Emma doing just what she liked. . . .

> The real evils indeed of Emma's situation were the power of having rather too much her own way, and a disposition to think a little too well of herself. . . .

Genlis gives Delphine a widowed mother who "loved her exceedingly, but wanted fortitude and strength of mind to give her daughter a proper education."

> Flattered, caressed and humoured as she was, Delphine soon became one of the most unfortunate children in Paris. Her natural tendency to goodness each day declined. . . . Capricious, vain, and stubborn, she would not endure the least contradiction. Far from being willing to obey, she would command; . . . so fond of flattery that she was unhappy when not praised; full of whimsies, and without any one fixed inclination; devoted to her dolls and playthings . . . she was equally deficient in justice and moderation.
>
> "What a picture!" said Pulcheria.—"'Tis the picture of a spoilt child," said her mamma, "and resembles many a woman of twenty."

How far the portrait resembles that of Emma, I leave it to readers of Austen's most subtle novel to decide. But the narrative tone of both works is that of educating heroinism: it is crisp, it is severe, and it is very wise.

The rest of Delphine's story belongs to the *ancien régime*. Deprived of exercise, fattened on sweets, wearied by evening entertainments and tight lacing, the little girl is attacked in her lungs as well as in her morals. A famous German specialist, Dr. Steinhaussen, is called in by the distracted mother, and he prescribes a severe remedy: Delphine must move to his country house and live for eight months under the eye of the doctor's wife, in a cowhouse—an efficacious remedy, Mme de Genlis explains, for consumption. Carried off in a rage, Delphine encounters strict discipline and spartan conditions for the first time; her hysterical tantrums are to no avail, and neither are her jewels. When she shows them off to the twelve-year-old daughter of the household, Henrietta counters with a display of her collection of fossils, those fascinating little stones imprinted with plants or animals "either by chance, or the sport of nature."

It turns out that nine-year-old Delphine, with a lifetime of Paris balls and theaters behind her, barely reads and cannot write at all. Henrietta teaches her; and Henrietta, who devotes herself to the care of an old blind peasant and his family, also shows Delphine the joys of benevolence. When Dr. Steinhaussen operates successfully for cataract—the wonders of medicine as well as of palaeontology ornament the tale—the old peasant's cure brings on Delphine's. From sullen to sweet, cranky to cheerful, arrogant to humble, idle to industrious, greedy to generous—the transformation of Delphine makes a spoiled child into a benevolent princess: she writes her mother to send no more new playthings from Paris, but to bestow a pension on the peasant's family instead. It is a transformation as satisfying as that of the horrid little girl in *The Secret Garden,* which of all children's books deals most successfully from a woman's point of view with the miseries of spoiling.

. . .

Mme de Genlis was hardly the inventor of either the moral tale for children or the pedagogical treatise. Such works are as old as literacy, and were written in ever increasing quantities as literacy spread through the middle classes. For the whole eighteenth century, in England as well as France, the model treatise was Fénelon's *Télémaque,* designed to guide and to portray the education of the prince who, had he lived, would have succeeded Louis XIV; it was published in the last year of the seventeenth century. Fanny Burney read *Telemachus* when a child in the mid-eighteenth century, and read it again, aloud to her own son, in the early years of the nineteenth century. During that span of years, however, the courtesy books tradition underwent a double transformation, one sudden and sharp, in 1762, with the publication of Rousseau's *Emile,* which made child-raising a subject of intellectual prestige and revolutionary implication; the other almost imperceptibly gradual but nonetheless momentous (it helped produce the novel of manners), which can be called the feminizing of the tradition.

Increasing numbers of literate middle-class women made a widening market for educational works written with the raising of girls in mind. For three quarters of the eighteenth century, these were written almost entirely by men, clergymen like Dr. James Fordyce, whose *Sermons for Young Women* are still being read with "monotonous solemnity" by Mr. Collins to the Bennet girls in *Pride and Prejudice.* But as women moved increasingly into professional writing status in the last quarter of the century, they began to write their own courtesy books for the training of their own sex. Chapone, Macaulay, Pennington, Barbauld, Trimmer, Edgeworth, Delany, as well as Genlis are the women's names which appear with ever greater frequency in Joyce Hemlow's account of the tradition that played so large a share in Fanny Burney's formation. To summarize the sexual shift very crudely, Fénelon's *Télémaque* of 1699 gave way to Hannah More's *Hints Towards Forming the Character of a Princess* of 1805; the latter was written for the improvement of Princess Charlotte Augusta, daughter of the Prince of Wales, who, had she not died in childbirth, would have ascended the English throne in the place of her Uncle William and her cousin Victoria. Unfortunate in many ways, Princess Charlotte as a young girl was made to listen for an hour or two a day to the Bishop of Salisbury's reading aloud to her from Miss More's *Hints* for the forming of her own character. "This, I believe," the princess wrote in her diary, "is what makes me find the hours so long. *I am not quite good* enough for that yet."

No one has ever been quite good enough for the books women wrote
when they first asserted their own claim as pedagogues. If I can venture on
a very hesitant assessment of the changes that came over courtesy books
when they were feminized, severity would head the list. Certainly women
writers were the most severe among the opponents of Rousseau's progres-
sivism. One would assume—were not the testimony of our own mad times
before us—that anyone doomed to the day-long, year-long company of
the young would oppose a permissive attitude to their upbringing. A Rousseau, who dumped his own bastards at the door of a foundling home,
might well expatiate on the attractions of unbridled youth, but a Genlis,
who voluntarily incarcerated herself in a rural retreat with a parcel of little
princes and princesses was necessarily a rigid disciplinarian.

No more absolute insistence on authority can be imagined than that
which pervades the Genlis matriarchy. It is a despotism, "an almost Egyp-
tian bondage," commented Mary Wollstonecraft disgustedly; "one duty,
obedience to parents swallows up all the rest," she wrote, reviewing
Genlis. Wollstonecraft's own childhood experience as daughter to a brutal
father and disagreeable stepmother predisposed her to scornful skepticism
toward any educational writer who insisted on the duty of the young to
pay blind obedience to adult authority. Yet Mary Wollstonecraft was just
such a writer herself when she wrote as surrogate parent; and Wollstonecraft wrote one of the best of all "courtesy books": her *Original
Stories from Real Life; with Conversations calculated to Regulate the
Affections—and Form the Mind to Truth and Goodness* (1788). Mrs.
Mason, the narrator of *Original Stories,* is an awesome figure of at least
equal severity with the educating heroines in Genlis.

All the blessings of life in educating heroinism are vertically aligned.
Mothers condescend to teach their children; children obey their mothers;
heroic deeds are done, and virtues performed at the altar of filial duty.
Marriages are made to please parents, and married children remain well
within the orbit—they normally live on the premises—of parental control.
In a *château* tale such as *Olympe et Théophile,* the miseries of the young
couple, whose marital felicity is destroyed by the bride's imprudence, is as
nothing to the demands of their parents, the satisfaction of which must be
put off until the birth and suitable marriage of the next generation. Such a
display of domestic tyranny is excessively French, and one would expect
an independent-minded Protestant Englishwoman like Jane Austen to
make fun of it, as indeed she did. "I do not think I could even now, at my
sedate time of life, read *Olimpe et Theophile* without being in a rage," she
wrote her niece Caroline, who was reading Genlis the year *Emma* was
published. "It really is too bad!—Not allowing them to be happy together,
when they *are* married.—Don't talk of it, pray." But Austen went on in

the same letter to say she was lending her own copy of *Les Veillées du Château* to another niece, Mary Jane. "It will be some time before she comes to the horror of Olympe"—but come to it, one must expect Mary Jane surely will, in the normal course of female destiny. The happy marriage at the end of *Emma*, after all, is made on the condition, set by Emma herself, that the couple live with Mr. Woodhouse at Hartfield, in order to cater to the selfish whims of Emma's sweet, doddering old tyrant of a father. Who would dare to say how far Austen's icily gentle comedy at the end of the novel calls in question the moral, that the young are put on earth to gratify those who have attained "a sedate time of life"?

Youth is close to age in educating heroinism. In every daughter, struggle as she may against the rule of law, there coexists a mother-figure, a giver of the law that is never broken; and in every mother, a self-perpetuating pedagogue. Educating heroinism thus supplies Anne Bradstreet, who is its bard, with the peculiarly feminine concept of the afterlife in her poem of farewell to her children. Tell your own "young ones," she urges them, that she herself had taught them "what was good and what was ill,/What would save life and what would kill. . . ." For it is less in the biological than in the pedagogical role that the mother lives on:

> Thus gone, amongst you I may live,
> And dead, yet speak, and counsel give.
> Farewel my birds, farewel adieu,
> I happy am if well with you.

And here the Puritan poet is one with the worldly lady in the castle, for the Baronne d'Almane takes leave of her children with a similar gesture:

> After dinner I took Adelaide and Theodore into my closet; and fetching from my bureau two copies of a Work in three thick volumes: This, said I, my children, is all I have left to give you. It is written for you; and intitled, LETTERS ON EDUCATION. . . . It was labouring for your happiness and my own. I am still young enough to flatter myself with the hopes of superintending the education of your children; but if death should rob you of your mother, you will find in these books all the advice she could have given you. . . .

Today it is fashionable to talk of the sisterhood of feminism as paradigm of that strength which issues from equality, but there is more in women's literature about the timeless bond of teaching, which links mother to daughter and teacher to pupil as equal to equal. "Mon enfant—allons chercher ensemble" are the words of dedication in equality that George Sand addressed to her daughter, when in her most feminist mood; and Mary Wollstonecraft has her pedagogue, Mrs. Mason, say "You are now

candidates for my friendship" to the little girls in her charge, when their
"advancement in virtue" has progressed far enough toward that state of female perfection defined as equality of pupil with teacher.

As well as severity and timelessness, isolation too enters into the atmos-
pheric quality of educating heroinism. There must somewhere be a world
apart, remote, serene, and orderly, where feminine authority can reign
supreme. Of all the metaphorical locations for matriarchy, one of the most
elaborate is the entire town created by Charlotte Brontë for the prologue
to *Villette*. It is a place between places, neither Continental nor English, as
its name suggests: "the clean and ancient town of Bretton." And its
presiding deity is the godmother of Lucy Snowe, Mrs. Bretton of Bretton,
a lady not young but handsome and erect, not sentimental but just, not
tender but kind, bright of eye, flawless of health and temper, "though a
commanding, and in grave matters even a peremptory woman."

> When I was a girl I went to Bretton about twice a year, and well
> I liked the visit. The house and its inmates specially suited me.
> The large, peaceful rooms, the well-arranged furniture, the clear
> wide windows, the balcony outside, looking down on a fine antique
> street, where Sundays and holidays seemed always to abide—so quiet
> was its atmosphere, so clean its pavement. . . .
>   Time always flowed smoothly for me at my godmother's side.
> . . . The charm of variety there was not, nor the excitement of
> incident; but I liked peace so well. . . .

Modern writers have gone even farther afield to find the metaphorical
isolation required by female authority: Isak Dinesen to the African highlands, Willa Cather to the Nebraska frontier, Sigrid Undset to the feudal
middle ages. Real experience or careful research of course provides their
details, but their imagination is foremost in shaping these locations for the
exercise of female power. In *Out of Africa,* for example, Isak Dinesen
might well have written a circumstantial account of her life for seventeen
years (from 1914 to 1931) as wife of Baron Blixen-Finecke, the Swedish
owner of a coffee plantation in the hills above Nairobi, in Kenya, where
she was first an excited bride, then a disappointed, ailing, and childless
wife, then a divorcee, then struggling with her brother to prevent the total
economic collapse of their particular venture into colonial exploitation. Instead she wrote a poem in prose, which perhaps should be called a saga, of
the woman as absolute ruler.

"I had a farm in Africa," she begins—for "he" does not exist. (The
single sentence in which the heroine admits her married state, toward the
close of the work, notes the unnamed husband's departure for wartime
service—and "I was then alone on the farm.") "A farm in Africa" is an
equally sublime invention, as is the title *Out of Africa:* an entire continent

is the heroine's place of commanding isolation. And if we must locate her more precisely, it is on her perch in the highlands over the equator, from which the whole of the globe and its sky are commanded by a figure more important than "she," more universal than "I": "Looking back on a sojourn in the African highlands, you are struck by your feeling of having lived for a time up in the air. . . . In the highlands you woke up in the morning and thought: Here I am, where I ought to be."

This heroine is a great hunter, who sups on claret and raisins while lions are skinned at her feet, and then, to complete the epic occasion, makes a poem. She is a regal hostess to heroes who come bearing furs to her highland fastness. She is a breaker of fields, who gets down from her tractor to parley with the High Priest; and when the old Kikuyu chief comes to call, a chair is brought to the verandah for the lady of the house, "and on these occasions Kinanjui sent away everybody, to point out that now the world was going to be governed in earnest." There are no children to rule in Dinesen's Africa, only natives—to doctor, to teach, to judge, to govern. And she is no mere snob of a colonial wife, no tedious bwana-lady, but a ruling queen. In her isolate grandeur high over the equator, her queendom free from masculine intervention, she is very like the Mistress of Husaby, in Sigrid Undset's *Kristin Lavransdatter;* or Willa Cather's empress of the prairie, Alexandra Bergson of *O Pioneers!,* who lives in

> a big white house that stood on a hill, several miles across the fields. There were so many sheds and outbuildings grouped about it that the place looked not unlike a tiny village. A stranger, approaching it, could not help noticing the beauty and fruitfulness of the outlying fields. There was something individual about the great farm, a most unusual trimness and care for detail. . . . Any one thereabouts would have told you that this was one of the richest farms on the Divide, and that the farmer was a woman, Alexandra Bergson.

Can it be mere coincidence that these three moderns are not only novelists by profession but also romancers, spinners of tales: Dinesen, with her *Winter's Tales* and *Gothic Tales* at one here with Cather and Undset, who interpolated folk tales and religious legends into their fictions? They share an antecedent unknown to them in the eighteenth-century Frenchwoman who told tales in the castle, evening after evening, to children under her control. In educating heroinism the telling of tales is an act of seduction and also of power; the tales enslave as they delight. In creating a heroine who is also a severe enchantress, Mme de Genlis was hardly inventing anything new: her Baronne d'Almane looks very like a Scheherazade of the nursery.

II

> The heroic woman is much the same in Greece and England.
> She is of the type of Emily Brontë. Clytaemnestra and Electra
> are clearly mother and daughter, and therefore should have
> some sympathy, though perhaps sympathy gone wrong breeds
> the fiercest hate.
>
> —Virginia Woolf

There is seduction too in educating heroinism, a theme no less erotic in
force for its maternal origin. To severity, authority, timelessness, and isolation must be added for completeness and modernity its peculiar sexual
drama—a sexuality without fulfillment, virtually without kindness. With-
drawal is here the recoil of attraction. The disparities of age; the odd pairings (or triplings or quadruplings) of lovers; the sexual disjunctions outside custom and marriage; the fantasies, sterilities, fetishes—here are all
that we moderns recognize as the normal appurtenances of love, that fated
drive to recapitulate in maturity the parent-child bond.

An easy shorthand way to distinguish the modern from the old-
fashioned in fiction is to note in the former the disappearance of the
courtship motif without which the latter could not function. The girl-
meets-boy story and its adulterous countervariant, married woman meets
lover, rest on Christian marriage and the procreation of heirs as the central facts of a well-run society; toward the end of the nineteenth century,
these stories and these facts began to be avoided or simply ignored by the
novelists. It was Flaubert who here showed the way to modernism: having
written in *Madame Bovary* the greatest of adultery novels, he produced in
his final masterpiece the typos of modern love stories: a twenty-year-long
fantasy of romance (during which French civilization crumbles into disar-
ray) between a sterile young man and a much older married woman he
barely knows. Flaubert called the novel *L'Éducation sentimentale* to signify, among its many bitter and ironic connotations, the inwardness of the
modern love story, which plays itself out inside the observing and feeling
consciousness, not across the gap that separates one mature lover and one
sex from the other.

James, Proust, Mann, Joyce are among the male novelists who pursued
the consequence of Flaubert's sentimental education; and the great women
writers of the early twentieth century, Virginia Woolf, Willa Cather, Gertrude Stein, Colette, belong to the identical modern movement away from
courtship, toward a fictional world where girl never meets boy. But their

feminine access to the theme of maternal seduction made a special contribution to modern literature, during a literary era uniquely hospitable to a very ancient, very female view of the nature of love.

In modern times the mother-daughter relationship which lies at the base of educating heroinism undergoes a characteristic twist: now it is not the parent's but the child's viewpoint which dominates. The controlling literary consciousness is that of the subject of matriarchal authority, its enraged victim, its adoring slave. Someone like Willa Cather's Nellie Birdseye:

> I slipped quietly in at my aunt's front door, and while I was taking off my wraps in the hall I could see, at the far end of the parlour, a short, plump woman in a black velvet dress, seated upon the sofa and softly playing on Cousin Bert's guitar. She must have heard me, and, glancing up, she saw my reflection in a mirror; she put down the guitar, rose, and stood to await my approach. She stood markedly and pointedly still, with her shoulders back and her head lifted, as if to remind me that it was my business to get to her as quickly as possible and present myself as best I could. I was not accustomed to formality of any sort, but by her attitude she succeeded in conveying this idea to me.
>
> I hastened across the room with so much bewilderment and concern in my face that she gave a short, commiserating laugh as she held out to me her plump, charming little hand.
>
> "Certainly this must be Lydia's dear Nellie. . . . And you must be fifteen now, by my mournful arithmetic—am I right?"
>
> What a beautiful voice, bright and gay and carelessly kind—but she continued to hold her head up haughtily . . . partly, I think, because she was beginning to have a double chin. . . . Her deep-set, flashing grey eyes seemed to be taking me in altogether—estimating me. For all that she was no taller than I, I felt quite overpowered by her—and stupid, hopelessly clumsy and stupid. . . . I fastened my gaze upon a necklace of carved amethysts she wore. . . . I suppose I stared, for she said suddenly: "Does this necklace annoy you? I'll take it off if it does."
>
> I was utterly speechless. I could feel my cheeks burning. . . .
>
> "Oh, we'll get used to each other! You see, I prod you because I'm certain that Lydia and your mother have spoiled you a little. You've been over-praised to me. It's all very well to be clever, my dear, but you mustn't be solemn about it—nothing is more tiresome. Now, let us get acquainted. . . ."
>
> *My Mortal Enemy*

· · ·

Willa Cather and Colette were born in 1873; Gertrude Stein a year later; Virginia Woolf eight years after Stein. Different as they were from each other, when considered together they suggest a coming to literary maturity of women writers, a peak of achievement from which our own later time may well seem, if not a falling-away, clearly a descent. In that sense, at least, they are "The Mothers of Us All," to borrow Gertrude Stein's title.

All four enjoyed long careers of literary productivity; they chose their forms, subjects, and settings with brilliant freedom; and they dominated their language—for each of the four did something to the prose of her native tongue from which it has not yet recovered. They traveled widely, in the intellectual as in the geographical sense, for each enjoyed productive relationships with the artists, musicians, and thinkers of their time. They led comfortable, unencumbered lives on the whole, alongside companions (male or female) devoted to their creature comforts. They made a decisive choice for the literary over the lady's life, and the world rewarded them with public ceremonials, pilgrimages, prizes, collected editions, medals, degrees, and honors in an abundance never showered on literary women before.

There is something imposing, even alarming about the four of them. As a company, I can't help visualizing them blocked out together in stone as a sort of Henry Moore grouping—massive sculptural forms, somber, solid, and remote, with heavy shoulders, strongly modeled skulls, and perhaps a hole—in the Moore style—where the heart is. The image of female statuary may come to mind because of Gertrude Stein: not only the way she looked to Picasso in the famous portrait, but because of what she did with the figure of Susan B. Anthony in the last scene of *The Mother of Us All* (1946). At the end of the play (or opera libretto) she turns the feminist leader to stone and puts her on a pedestal at the center of a statuary group celebrating the fight for suffrage. From that vantage point, Susan B. continues to survey and to dominate the world after the winning of the vote for women. One of Stein's male characters comes in to look at the statue, and sighs: "Does it really mean that women are as white and cold as marble does it really mean that?"

Virginia Woolf did much the same sort of thing with the mother-figure at the center of her first novel, *The Voyage Out* (1915). It is not so much the beauty of Mrs. Ambrose, "but her largeness and simplicity, which made her stand out from the rest like a great stone woman." To the girl-consciousness in the novel Mrs. Ambrose conveys an awesome monumental quality—if merely sewing, for example, "her figure possessed the sublimity of a woman's of the early world, spinning the thread of fate." (Girls, however, are different from mature women, thinks Mrs. Ambrose: "There was nothing to take hold of in girls—nothing hard, permanent, satisfactory.")

And in Willa Cather's work nc single image is so compelling, has caused more puzzled debate, than the group of dressmaker forms which dominate the opening section of *The Professor's House* (1925). These are female statuary of another kind: the cloth-covered wire dummies on which women's clothes are fitted by hand. *The Professor's House,* one of Cather's most fascinating, most inchoate works, deals with the retreat from life of an American university professor. He is a distinguished historian who in middle life withdraws in revulsion from everything success has brought—a fashionable wife, two charming daughters, sudden wealth from non-academic sources, an elegant new home—and pulls back from all that is worldly into his own scholarly pursuits; then further back, into boyhood memories, into the aboriginal earth, almost (there is a near-suicide) into death.

The place of the Professor's retreat is the attic of his shabby old house, where he writes his books; there also, at different hours, the German seamstress Augusta comes to sew for the ladies of the family—thus the presence of the dressmaker forms along the walls of the Professor's attic study. He grows strongly, freakishly attached to these forms; won't let them be moved out of his way; he himself won't move to the new home. "You can't have my women, that's final," he says to Augusta, and it is an odd kind of joke, this struggle for possession between the Professor and the uneducated seamstress.

> These "forms" were the subject of much banter between them. The one which Augusta called "the bust" stood in the darkest corner of the room. . . . It was a headless, armless female torso, covered with strong black cotton, and so richly developed in the part for which it was named that the Professor once explained to Augusta how, in calling it so, she followed a natural law of language, termed, for convenience, metonymy. Augusta enjoyed the Professor. . . . Though this figure looked so ample and billowy (as if you might lay your head upon its deep-breathing softness and rest safe forever), if you touched it you suffered a severe shock, no matter how many times you had touched it before. It presented the most unsympathetic surface imaginable. Its hardness was not that of wood, which . . . is stimulating to the hand, nor that of felt, which drinks something from the fingers. It was a dead, opaque, lumpy solidity, like chunks of putty, or tightly packed sawdust—very disappointing to the tactile sense, yet somehow always fooling you again. For no matter how often you had bumped up against the torso, you could never believe that contact with it would be as bad as it was.

What is this form, this horror to Willa Cather? What does she intend it to mean to her youth-seeking, death-seeking Professor? Leon Edel has written a whole essay of biographical speculation on its sources, with particular attention to Cather's attic residence in the home of her most important woman friend, whose marriage came as a shock to Willa Cather shortly before she wrote *The Professor's House*. Cather was a reserved, dignified woman with a gift for both friendship and privacy, and into whose secrets it is both fruitless (we cannot read her letters) and improper to pry. But her image of the lifeless female form, soft-seeming and hard-feeling, seducing and repelling, beautiful and revolting, holds no literary mysteries. It is a brilliant symbolic summary of everything Willa Cather's generation of women writers had to say—and no generation ever said more, or with greater complexity—about Motherhood.

They wrote about the motherhood of their mothers or grandmothers, not, certainly, their own. Cather and Stein never married; Virginia Woolf married but remained childless by design; Colette married (three times) and did finally have a child in middle age, much to her surprise. (She referred to the "accidental quality" of her maternity, and said she was not so much a mother as "un écrivain qui a fait un enfant.") Of the four, it was wicked, sophisticated Colette who wrote most unashamedly of her mother-worship, in the hundreds of pages of her memoirs devoted to the creation she named Sido. There is nothing at all remarkable about Colette's mother-figure; she is middle-aged, middle-class, plump, gray, scarred, dirty from the garden; nothing out of the ordinary except in Colette's eye for her beauty, her wisdom, her strength, her inexhaustible gaiety, her irresistible charm.

They wrote of the power and grandeur of motherhood with an air of finality, as if what they were describing would never come again; as if there would never more be any mothers. They do not write of harassed, frantic, young mothers, but of mature, calm women of still, sculptural beauty. They do not explore the world to which the poetry of Sylvia Plath so often carries us—"here on a visit,/With a goddam baby screaming off somewhere,/There's always a bloody baby in the air." Their mothers are great queens, who impose order on the world. They have the power to create an ambiance, a drawing room, a whole landscape; they give access to the arts of civilization, the life of the senses. Colette's mother is her link to the garden paradise of childhood, its plants and animals; for Sido is a woman who, just as Cather writes of her Ántonia, "could still stop one's breath for a moment by a look or gesture that somehow revealed the meaning in common things." These are mothers who "make of the moment something permanent," as Lily Briscoe says of Mrs. Ramsay in *To the Lighthouse;* they are women who say "Life stand still here."

In spite of, perhaps because of their advancing age, these mother-figures are dangerously seductive, especially to the young. Their beauty seems to grow ever greater after the gray hairs and the wrinkles come, after the double chin that makes Cather's Myra Henshawe hold her head so high, after the thickening neck around which Colette's Léa fastens her choker of pearls. Virginia Woolf's Mrs. Ramsay is adored by all her children, by her philosopher husband, by virginal Lily Briscoe, by middle-aged Mr. Bankes, the widower botanist, even by young Charles Tansley, that wretched species of graduate student (how Woolf despised him, with his working-class snobberies, and radicalism, and sexism!) who stands waiting in the parlor for the chance to walk Mrs. Ramsay home—

> heard her quick step above; heard her voice cheerful, then low
> . . . ; waited quite impatiently, looked forward eagerly to the walk
> home; determined to carry her bag; then heard her come out; shut
> a door; . . . when, suddenly, in she came, stood for a moment
> silent . . . , stood quite motionless for a moment against a picture
> of Queen Victoria wearing the blue ribbon of the Garter; when all
> at once he realised that it was this: it was this:—she was the most
> beautiful person he had ever seen.
>
> With stars in her eyes and veils in her hair, with cyclamen and
> wild violets—what nonsense was he thinking? She was fifty at least;
> she had eight children. Stepping through fields of flowers and taking
> to her breast buds that had broken and lambs that had fallen; with
> the stars in her eyes and the wind in her hair—He took her bag.

That is the language of passion as well as self-mockery; its rhythms fill all of Woolf's writing about Mrs. Ramsay, often called her greatest creation of character because infused with the love she bore her own mother, who died tragically early in the novelist's life. But to see only love in the portrait is to sentimentalize *To the Lighthouse,* and miss the powerfully ambivalent emotional quality of Woolf's art. There are also resentment, envy, the pain of betrayal, the cry of protest—not me, never again—in all her mother portraits, and these are the portraits, oddly enough, which dominate her work. Why are there so many Mrs. Dalloways, Mrs. Ramsays, and Mrs. Ambroses in Woolf's fiction? we should wonder; why all these unintellectual society matrons? who raise their numerous children, run their elaborate homes, protect their husbands from annoying practical concerns, direct their large staff of servants, and are always seen sitting at the head of a long dining table, or entering a crowded drawing room, for they seem to be principally engaged in the giving of parties. *Mrs. Dalloway* is the fine work it is because constructed entirely around an evening party; a house party fills most of the space in *Between the Acts,* Woolf's last novel, dominated by the sexually restless matron Mrs. Oliver.

Sometimes a note of tragedy, sometimes simple boredom comes into Woolf's novels from the bored distaste she felt for the lives these women lead. For she herself rejected their life, refused maternity, pared her domestic obligations down to the slatternly minimum, preferred the dirty work of setting printer's type to the mess of housekeeping. Turning her back on the social and ornamental demands that Edwardian England made on a woman of her class, Woolf herself was a literary intellectual of the reckless Bloomsbury stamp, not a hostess in a drawing room. What anguish, what yearning pain are here; what guilty, unrequited passion.

Most of the passion in Willa Cather's work is in the eye of the narrator, the remembering mind, who, whether male or female (it doesn't matter) is always a solitary, one of the unmated. But the portraits that Cather's memory draws are mainly those of pioneer foremothers, or regal, autocratic wives who dominate their salons: Mrs. Alexander, in Back Bay Boston; Mrs. Henshawe, in her Madison Square drawing room; Mrs. Forrester, hostess to the railroad men who pass through Sweet Water; and Sapphira Dodderidge Colbert, the ante-bellum, slave-owning heiress, who, though swollen with age and dropsy, "sat in her crude invalid's chair as if it were a seat of privilege." In *My Ántonia* (1918), which ends with a moving portrait of the heroine in middle-aged maternity, surrounded by her many sons—"a rich mine of life, like the founders of early races"— the steely point of the tale is Jim Burden's telling of it; for *My Ántonia* is not *mine* at all. To possess her is for the narrator as impossible as the possession of what he calls, in the last line of the novel, "the precious, the incommunicable past." Memory itself is an act of possession in Willa Cather's work: thwarted possession, ruthless in intent. It kills as it brings to life, somewhat like the God imagined by one of Cather's opera singers, a "merciless artist" armed with a pruning knife.

Niel Herbert, the remembering narrator of *A Lost Lady* (1923), actually wills death upon the beautiful and corrupt wife of the title, Marian Forrester. He feels "weary contempt" for her because she is not willing to die with the pioneer period to which she belongs, but instead prefers "life on any terms"—his bitter comment after he spies on her in a rather disgusting scene of adult sexuality. When Knopf reissued *A Lost Lady* in elegant format to celebrate Cather's centennial (for in the opinion of her publishers, as of many others, it is her masterpiece) many of the reactions in the press suggested that criticism has not yet caught up with Willa Cather, who, because she was writing of the West and the past during the frenetic 1920s, gets slotted as a nostalgic old lady of conservative tastes, stuck on the proprieties. *Time* called *A Lost Lady* "typical of the kind of prairie pastoral Cather did best."

Prairie pastoral! *A Lost Lady* is an Electra story, raw and barbarous. Marian Forrester is a queen and a whore as well. She has betrayed the king—that traveler and conqueror of the West, the old, impotent railroad man Captain Forrester. Her various seductions and adulteries both inflame and revolt young Niel, who is as impotent in revenge as he is in lust. Mrs. Forrester is indeed the symbol of an age, worthy of adoration. She is a great teacher—not, certainly, of morality; but of those ideals with which modern educating heroinism seems primarily to concern itself—the civilized standards and aristocratic honor of an age slipping irrevocably into the past.

Marian Forrester brings courage and beauty to her husband; romance and elegance to the magnates who stop at the Forrester house; civilization and style to the crude boys of the town; envy and drama to the women. And to Niel she brings the whole meaning of his life—too much meaning. For Niel is forced to see how it is done, this womanly mythmaking without which there would be no civilization, no "taming of the West." He sees the veils and the jewels, the rouge and the dyed hair, the brandy tippling, the teasing of little boys and old men; most of all, he sees with mingled yearning and rage the woman's fully sexual nature—"life on any terms." "Beautiful women, whose beauty meant more than it said . . ." thinks Niel; "was their brilliancy always fed by something coarse and concealed? Was that their secret?"

All the fiction from Willa Cather's greatest period centers on the death of a mother-figure. There is much reason to regret that Virginia Woolf could not find time in 1926, the year of Cather's *My Mortal Enemy,* to write the article assigned to her on Willa Cather, because she was engaged with the passing of Mrs. Ramsay from *To the Lighthouse.* One would want to read Woolf on the daughter's ambivalent anguish recorded by her American contemporary. In our own time there has been no clearer index to the revival of a specifically female impetus to literature than the return to women's fiction of this crucial scene, the maternal deathbed, and of the character of aging female tyrant. There is nothing more powerful, it seems to me, in all of Simone de Beauvoir, or Tillie Olsen, or Doris Lessing, or Margaret Drabble, or Marie Claire Blais.

Final daughter-mother confrontations are not sentimental occasions in women's literature. Anne Roiphe did one in her first novel, which predicts the black comedy of maternity for which *Up the Sandbox!* has made her famous. In the earlier book, the grown-up daughter returns from her independent, intellectual existence away from home to the Park Avenue apartment of her childhood to see her regal mother die, wasted and paralytic. The old lady sits stiffly in her bed; the daughter, with nothing to say, rummages through a dressing table drawer and idly smears on her mother's cosmetics and ornaments that she remembers having played with as a child years before. Thus grotesquely bedecked, the daughter walks to her mother's bedside, and the old lady peers up at her, reaches up a sharp-nailed hand, and claws her daughter's cheek.

. . .

The creation of great women characters as symbols of civilization is hardly limited to women's literature; Swann's Way is strewn with such figures, Howards End entombs one, and every Rosenkavalier has his

Marschallin. But to see such women both as objects of inspiration and as threats to selfhood; to see them simultaneously afar and near—from within the female mind and body, within the nursery, the kitchen, the dressing table—is the woman writer's gift to modern literature. In Woolf and Cather an agonizing drama results from their own womanly ambivalence, and when the writer is French as well as female high comedy of a uniquely bittersweet variety ensues.

The French say of Colette that she created three great women characters and reworked each of them in various guises in her seventy or more published volumes: first, Colette herself, an artful creation (the name—her maiden last name—is real); second, Sido (short for Mme Adèle-Sidonie Landoy Colette), the mother-figure who dominates the many volumes of memoirs that Colette scattered through her fifty-year-long writing career; and then Léa—

> A quarante-neuf ans, Léonie Vallon, dite Léa de Lonval, finissait une carrière heureuse de courtisane bien rentée, et de bonne fille à qui la vie a épargné les catastrophes flatteuses et les nobles chagrins.

Léa is the most successful of all—successful as a woman, as a prostitute, as a teacher and ruler of men, as a creation of comic genius.

Léa is the *courtisane* pushing fifty at the center of the novel which does not bear her name: Colette's 1920 masterpiece which instead she called *Chéri,* that is, dearie, honey, sweetie, darling—terms of endearment normally used (as Chekhov used the last) for a beloved woman, a *chérie.* Here Chéri is the name given to a twenty-five-year-old gigolo, a mean, greedy, exquisitely beautiful young man, who is Léa's last indulgence. She buys Chéri—pays for his cigarettes and his finery, fattens him up for love on strawberries and country cream; we see her looking over Chéri's naked beauties as he lies in her vast bed, with the eye of a horse-breeder. From her title, from her unforgettable opening scene (Chéri playing with, trying on, begging for the gift of the pearl necklace), in every twist of language and emotion, Colette here reverses with a mocking glee the reader's sexual prejudices and expectations. *Woman's* sensuality, *woman's* honor, *woman's* will, *woman's* power, *woman's* maturity are her subject.

Sordid as it may appear in summary, the relationship between Léa and Chéri becomes in Colette's hands a love story of remarkable delicacy which still has the power to astonish the reader as it astonished André Gide, who wrote Colette, sputtering, of his reaction. The love between Léa and Chéri is real because of the fact—not in spite of it—that they stand as mother and son to each other, as much as rich old mistress and hired young lover. Now Chéri must marry and leave Léa; it is the end of their six years of passion of which Léa is justly proud, and which she sometimes calls an *adoption* rather than a *liaison*—"par penchant à la sincérité." Léa manages their separation (as she manages everything else) in the style of a great lady. Its torture falls mainly on Chéri, whose suicide is the subject of the almost-worthy continuation, *La Fin de Chéri* (1926), which Colette wrote later, in a fully post-war mood.

Léa at fifty is a marvel: a blue-eyed beauty with country-red flesh and firmly curved body, who dyes her blond hair and laces her tight shoes in the style of the age (pre-1914) when to be a rich man's mistress was the most demanding and rewarding profession open to French women. Her life is a model of order and opulence founded on debauchery and exploitation. In the *Chéri* books, and much later, in the popular favorite among her novels, the delightful *Gigi*, Colette took the most hacked-at subject of French fiction, the high-grade prostitution of the *demi-monde,* and told it afresh from the woman's viewpoint, made that half-world a wholly complete domain of matriarchy. *Gigi* is entirely about the educational regimen devised by a family of whores to teach a young girl, their successor, "les principes de convenances élémentaires."

There is nothing shady about Colette's shady ladies; they are nothing like the immature, amateur whores and "superstars" that we meet in contemporary fiction, drugged to indifference. Colette's *courtisanes* are mature, powerful, proud women, who play the stock market shrewdly, collect the best jewels, set the best tables, serve the best wines, live in Paris townhouses with a staff of servants kept under tight control. Everything about these loose women is in fact under control: their bodies tightly corseted, their heads carefully coiffed and powdered from the earliest hours of the day, their underclothing and bed linen of the best quality and washing. They make a fetish of cleanliness, especially between the legs (one's face, in an emergency, says Gigi's grandmother, can be put off till tomorrow morning, "Tandis que le soin du bas du corps, c'est la dignité de la femme"). Whatever happens outside, inside their world they are the guardians of those perfected arts of living which the French, when in their most materialist mood, call civilization.

Colette was no sentimentalist, however, and no fool. Her kept women are vulgar horrors as well as marvels, and her *demi-monde* is a stifling, philistine terrain that one would wish away with a revolutionary wave of the hand. These women, after all, live by exploiting the frailties and the lusts of men, whereas Colette herself was an independent, a *vagabonde,* in spite of her three husbands. She was a writer first of all, a woman who could and did do without men—without their sexuality or their money. "Peace, oh Lord," cries the mime heroine at the end of *La Vagabonde* (1910), as she abandons her settled life and lover for a theater tour and another kind of sexual companionship; "give me peace! I've had about enough of *chichis,* enough of idyls, enough of wasted time, enough of men."

It is instructive to read Colette's *Gigi* (1944) together with Willa Cather's "Old Mrs. Harris" (one of the *Obscure Destinies,* 1932). Both were late returns to early materials. Colette wrote *Gigi* to keep her spirits up the year the Germans took her Jewish husband away to internment; Cather ended her bitterest decade with this most frank and most wise of all her celebrations of her Nebraska family. Both works deal with female adolescence in a matriarchy; neither could be called a domestic tale. In "Old Mrs. Harris" (as in *Gigi*) Cather is concerned with three generations of women locked in a deadly serious, yet also comic skirmish over civilization. Her grandmother is the noblest and wisest; her mother, the most beautiful, the most spoiled, the most helplessly adored; her daughter, the brightest and strongest, but, we are made to feel, only temporarily victorious over the conditions of a woman's life. Cather had none of Colette's comic genius, but she comes closest to the smile of wisdom when she sends Vickie Templeton off to university at the end, with her books, her hard-won scholarship, her cropped hair, full of irritation with her mother for getting pregnant again, and with her grandmother for dying just at the moment " 'when my whole life hangs by a thread,' she told herself fiercely. What were families for, anyway?"

11

METAPHORS: A POSTLUDE

I

> In this same time our Lord shewed me a spiritual sight of His homely loving. . . . He shewed me a little thing, the quantity of an hazel-nut, in the palm of my hand; and it was as round as a ball. I looked thereupon with the eye of my understanding, and thought: *What may this be?* And it was answered generally thus: *It is all that is made.* I marvelled how it might last, for methought it might suddenly have fallen to naught for little. And I was answered in my understanding: *It lasteth, and ever shall for that God loveth it.* And so Allthing hath the Being by the love of God.
>
> —Dame Julian, the Anchoress of Norwich: *Revelations of Divine Love* (c. 1373–93)

> All true histories contain instruction; though, in some, the treasure may be hard to find, and when found, so trivial in quantity, that the dry, shrivelled kernel scarcely compensates for the trouble of cracking the nut. Whether this be the case with my history or not . . .
>
> —Anne Brontë: opening of *Agnes Grey* (1847)

> My little morsel of human affection, which I prized as if it were a solid pearl, must melt in my fingers and slip thence like a dissolving hailstone.
>
> —Charlotte Brontë: *Villette* (1853)

> Indeed, if we look at her a little more closely we shall see that something dark and hard, like a kernel, had already formed in the centre of Christina Rossetti's being. It was religion, of course. . . . everything in Christina's life radiated from that knot of agony and intensity in the centre.
>
> —Virginia Woolf: "I Am Christina Rossetti" (1930)

Perhaps there's an "I" at the middle of it, she thought; a knot; a centre; and again she saw herself sitting at her table drawing on the blotting-paper, digging little holes from which spokes radiated. Out and out they went. . . . She shut her hands on the coins she was holding, and again she was suffused with a feeling of happiness. Was it because this had survived—this keen sensation (she was waking up) and the other thing, the solid object . . . had vanished? Here she was; alive. . . . She hollowed her hands in her lap . . . ; she felt that she wanted to enclose the present moment; to make it stay; to fill it fuller and fuller, with the past, the present and the future, until it shone, whole, bright, deep with understanding.

—Virginia Woolf: *The Years* (1937)

Creation—truth—affection—hatred—the self: these are the great themes of all literature, by men and women both. But what of the metaphor: the little hard nut, the living stone, something precious in miniature to be fondled with the hand or cast away in wrath? Is it a feminine metaphor?

Littleness as a physical fact, though only a relative one, is inescapably associated with the female body, and as long as writers describe women they will all make use of the diminutive in language and the miniature in imagery. In literature by women, especially their poetry, it must however be admitted that the metaphor of littleness is overused. Anne Bradstreet is too often coy—

> Accept O Lord, my simple mite,
> For more I cannot give. . . .

and Christina Rossetti too often demands "the lowest place"; religious women seem all to eager to claim, as if by sexual right, the imagery of Christian humility. And the reader of Emily Dickinson can hardly resist irritation with the look of her poems, hundreds upon hundreds of them, on the page: their visual bitsiness.

I was grateful for the chance to be surprised by the look of Dickinson's manuscripts in the Boston Public Library. She wrote in a large and swirling hand, and her elaborate capitals and broad dashes make each poem fill the manuscript page with a sense of confident power that is drained away in print. Here, for example, in a poem which makes a different use of the recurring metaphor of the pebble in the hand:

> I took my Power in my Hand—
> And went against the World—
> 'Twas not so much as David—had—
> But I—was twice as bold—

> I aimed my Pebble—but Myself
> Was all the one that fell—
> Was it Goliah—was too large—
> Or was myself—too small?

. . .

Of all the creatures—the flowers, the insects, the cats—that women writers use to stand in, metaphorically, for their own sex, it is their birds who have made the most impression on me, probably because of the extraordinary virtuosity with which Charlotte Brontë handles them, as she does all the metaphors, in *Jane Eyre*.

Is the bird merely a species of the littleness metaphor? Or are birds chosen because they are tortured, as little girls are tortured, by boys like John Reed, who "twisted the necks of the pigeons, killed the little peachicks. . . ."? Or because bird-victims can be ministered to by girl-victims —as in the scene where Jane, a prisoner in the nursery, tugs at the window sash to put out a few crumbs from her meager breakfast for the benefit of "a little hungry robin, which came and chirruped on the twigs of the leafless cherry-tree nailed against the wall near the casement"—a metaphor which draws as much on the crucifixion as on country winters. Or is it because birds are beautiful and exotic creatures, symbols of half-promised, half-forbidden sensual delights, like the bird of paradise painted "nestling in a wreath of convolvuli and rosebuds" on the china teaplate which Jane begs to take in her hands and examine closely, but is "deemed unworthy of such a privilege"?

Because birds are soft and round and sensuous, because they palpitate and flutter when held in the hands, and especially because they sing, birds are universal emblems of love.

> My heart is like a singing bird
> Whose nest is in a watered shoot:

proclaims Christina Rossetti in her best-known poem, because "the birthday of my life/Is come, my love is come to me." Indeed, without birds, those patterns of animal monogamy, the Jane Eyre/Rochester love affair could not advance from romantic beginning to marital consummation. They meet on an icy moonlit road: Rochester, fierce and virile on a black horse, but lamed; and Jane—" 'Childish and slender creature! It seemed as if a linnet had hopped to my foot and proposed to bear me on its tiny wing.' " She peers at him through wide, inquisitive eyes "like an eager bird"; she struggles in his arms "like a wild frantic bird"; and when at last they are united, Rochester in his maimed blindness is like "a royal eagle, chained to a perch, . . . forced to entreat a sparrow to become its purveyor."

Not the eagle and the sparrow but the eagle and the dove are the most familiar pair of bird-contrasts. As early as the seventeenth century, that pair of birds was associated with St. Teresa of Avila to point up the contrast she offered between ailing, feminine, mystical saintliness and aggressive, domineering, organizational accomplishment. Perhaps some memory of the Crashaw lines which saluted her favorite saint ("By all the eagle in thee, all the dove") led Gertrude Stein to place "pigeons on the grass alas" at St. Teresa's feet. *The Eagle and the Dove* was Victoria Sackville-West's inevitable title for the book she wrote about the two very different St. Theresas: the great lady of sixteenth-century Spain, and the French Thérèse, the nineteenth-century saint of miniature ecstasies from Lisieux.

Children's literature of a serious kind—that is, books written for adolescent girls—often cuts loose a metaphor from its original context in women's literature and runs with it. Frances Hodgson Burnett is a mine of such female metaphors, and her predecessor among the Victorians, Charlotte M. Yonge, made the paired-bird metaphor a beloved emblem of romance in *The Dove in the Eagle's Nest* (1866), her historical fantasy about a young girl, pure as a dove (and as a Christian young lady should be), who is ensnared in a mountain aerie by robber barons. (The tale reads so much like a chaste revision of *Mauprat* [1837] that one might dare to suspect that even Charlotte M. Yonge looked into George Sand.)

George Sand herself does characteristically witty things with birds and women, for her family heritage included (she tells us) a grandfather who was a Paris bird-seller. Thus the taming of a robin by a woman who has a poet's affinity with Nature is a scene reworked, in various delightful fashions, in her autobiography and fiction; but it is a wild bird of prey that Fiamma, the guerilla-heroine of *Simon* (a Hemingwayesque figure), grapples with and finally subdues. The more feminist the literary conception (if I can dare to generalize), the larger, wilder, and crueler come the birds. I was struck, leafing through Ann Stanford's extremely interesting anthology of *The Women Poets in English,* by the herons and the fish hawks who come swooping, diving, slashing, and killing their way into twentieth-century women's verse. "Hawk Is a Woman" is a marvelous example by a poet new to me, Hildegarde Flanner. It begins:

> I saw a hawk devour a screaming bird,
> Devour the little ounce sugared with song,
> First bent and ate the pretty eyes both out,

And it ends:

> May she, the very she, may that hawk hear
> The ugly female laughter of a hawk.

And as I look along my shelf that holds the books of current feminists, I wonder if I am supposed to think only of Freud (whose ideas on metaphor must figure in this chapter); or may I also imagine the characteristic motions of a wild bird when I read *Flying* (Millett), *Falling* (Schaeffer), *Diving into the Wreck* (Rich), or *Fear of Flying* (Jong).*

For birds are frightening and monstrous as well as tiny and sweet, and the former aspect of the bird metaphor dominates the grotesqueries of modern women's literature. There is the "peacock of a sort of ghastly green. With one immense golden eye" who gives back the horrid *Reflections in a Golden Eye* to Carson McCullers; and *l'Opoponax,* the monstrous plant-bird who hovers over Monique Wittig's fantasy of schoolgirl interlacings. For the abnormalities of female love, no writer invented so monstrous a double bird as Virginia Woolf, in *Orlando,* her transsexual historical fantasy. "For Love," she wrote, "has two faces. . . ."

> Love began her flight towards [Orlando] with her white face turned, and her smooth and lovely body outwards. Nearer and nearer she came wafting before her airs of pure delight. All of a sudden . . . she wheeled about, turned the other way round; showed herself black, hairy, brutish; and it was Lust the vulture, not Love, the Bird of Paradise, that flopped foully and disgustingly upon his shoulders. . . .

One bird metaphor, however—that of the nesting-bird for motherhood —which so naturally occurs to male writers, seems striking by its absence from women's literature, or by the bitterness with which it is used to imply rejection of the maternal role. Edna Pontellier, the troubled, eventually suicidal heroine of *The Awakening,* is "not a mother-woman"; and Kate Chopin sets her apart from the other Creole wives with a mother-bird metaphor:

> The mother-women seemed to prevail that summer at Grand Isle. It was easy to know them, fluttering about with extended, protecting wings when any harm, real or imaginary, threatened their precious brood. They were women who idolized their children, worshipped their husbands, and esteemed it a holy privilege to efface themselves as individuals and grow wings as ministering angels.

A similar, but more violent rejection of normal married life inspires the salute to the eagle by Willa Cather's opera singer, after her lover proposes. He wonders how Thea would react if he offered her "a comfortable flat in Chicago . . . and a family to bring up"; she almost pitches him over the edge of Panther Canyon, when suddenly a great golden eagle sails overhead:

> Thea sprang to her feet . . . straining her eyes after that strong, tawny flight. O eagle of eagles! Endeavour, achievement, desire, glorious striving of human art! From a cleft in the heart of the world she saluted it. . . .

* Sylvia Plath, as is so often the case, provides an exception: *Ariel,* the title of her most important book of poems, is said to refer to a horse; while *Crow* is a title used by Ted Hughes (himself a grotesque figment of the Plath imagination).

No; the young man must admit that Thea is "not a nesting-bird."

The exception here is Anne Bradstreet, one of the few women writers to rejoice openly in the maternal role, and the only one I know to have celebrated it elaborately by means of a bird metaphor. Yet even Bradstreet's famous poem, "I had eight birds hatcht in one nest," is not quite the sentimental mother-poem that hasty readers think it. The central conceit of the poem (dated 1656) is the portrayal of the real children Bradstreet had, all eight of them, as individual birds: "Four Cocks there were, and Hens the rest." But the true subject of the poem is not the children but the poet herself—here, the "I" as hard-working mother.

> Great was my pain when I you bred.
> Great was my care, when I you fed,
> Long did I keep you soft and warm,
> And with my wings kept off all harm.

The children now are flown from the nest, and Bradstreet, after disposing of a few remaining worries about the spiritual welfare of her brood, begins upon the remarkable envoi of the poem and a transformed bird metaphor.

> Mean while my dayes in tunes Ile spend,
> Till my weak layes with me shall end. . . .

Thus the mother prepares for a solitary old age devoted to the kind of singing for which birds (without nestlings) are summoned by all poets: that is, for the poetic faculty itself. Like the bird that Yeats "set upon a golden bough to sing/To lords and ladies of Byzantium/Of what is past, or passing," Bradstreet too resolves that, in the guise of a bird,

> In shady woods I'le sit and sing,
> And things that past, to mind I'le bring.
> Once young and pleasant, as are you,
> But former toyes (no joyes) adieu.
> My age I will not once lament,
> But sing, my time so near is spent.

Then Bradstreet's bird metaphor takes on still another permutation, becoming the eternal soul bound for a heavenly afterlife:

> And from the top bough take my flight,
> Into a country beyond sight,
> Where old ones, instantly grow young,
> And there with Seraphims set song:

Such a fluent intermixing of three aspects of the bird-metaphor—the mother, the poet, and the soul—could hardly recur after the close of the seventeenth century. Among later women writers, the singing bird as paradigm for the poet evokes an uneasiness that seems distinctly female in origin. In *Jane Eyre,* for example, the only failure among Brontë's multifarious birds is the one who sings, not as a poet but as a ceaseless chatterer. " 'Oh, you are indeed there, my skylark!' " cries the blind Rochester to Jane in the reunion scene. " 'Come to me . . . I heard one of your kind an hour ago, singing high over the wood: but its song had no music for me. . . . All the melody on earth is concentrated in my Jane's tongue to my ear (I am glad it is not naturally a silent one). . . .' " Alas for the spinster's fantasy, which returns at the very end of the novel ("We talk, I believe, all day long"): Brontë's naïve belief that a spouse could take nothing but unalloyed pleasure in the fact that his mate is a chatterbox. The wife as skylark simply will not do.

The skylark makes none of this trouble for a poet like Percy Bysshe Shelley. In Shelley's Ode, the skylark is of course a blithe spirit unmarked as to sex and therefore, all would agree, appropriate for the masculine poet "hidden/In the light of thought,/Singing hymns unbidden,/Till the world is wrought/To sympathy. . . ." The only female creature in "Ode to the Skylark" is the "high-born maiden," who has nothing to do with hymns or poems or thoughts, but instead plays her birdlike role

> In a palace tower,
> Soothing her love-laden
>   Soul in secret hour
> With music sweet as love, which overflows her bower:

That particular male fantasy—the young lady locked up somewhere to warble her love for some male, presumably the poet—is the kind of association that inhibits women writers in their use of the singing bird metaphor. Willa Cather deeply regretted having given the title *The Song of the Lark* (drawn from a painting, and intended to symbolize artistic aspiration in general) to her opera singer novel. "The title is unfortunate"; Cather wrote in her 1932 preface. "Many readers take it for granted that the 'lark song' refers to the vocal accomplishments of the heroine, which is altogether a mistake. Her song was not of the skylark order." And indeed, while the skylark may do for a blithe spirit, it is a most inappropriate metaphor for a Wagnerian soprano.

Elizabeth Barrett got into all sorts of trouble avoiding the singing bird metaphor in her sonnet to George Sand, whom she has roar like a lion (instead of tweet like a bird) when under the sway of her "tumultuous senses." Miss Barrett went on in the sonnet to hope against all reason that someday Sand would emerge with a stainless reputation for sexual purity; this would have the metaphorical effect of

> Drawing two pinions, white as wings of swan,
> From thy strong shoulders, to amaze the place
> With holier light!

Like Brontë's skylark wife, the swan-winged lion is a failed metaphor.

No other family of living creatures offers the poet such a variety of size and color and habitat as the birds, such a mixture of the domestically familiar and the mysteriously exotic. But it must be the extreme nature of the *contrasts* birds offer, especially the contrast between the *esse* and the *posse* implicit in their ambivalent existence, that draws from literary women a tension in the metaphor. For birds, like the polar sea-fowl envisioned at the start of *Jane Eyre,* or like the albatross in Coleridge, can explore with unparalleled boldness and freedom the dangerous and icy regions of the earth where nothing else survives; but they are also domestic creatures, pets for the chamber and fowl for the barnyard—like Mrs. Pullet and the other chicken-ladies of *The Mill on the Floss,* through whom George Eliot discharges her acid wit on the subject of middle-class country women who never get off the ground.

Of all creatures, birds alone can fly all the way to heaven—yet they are caged. Birds alone can sing more beautifully than human voices—yet they are unheeded, or silenced. It is only when we hear the woman as well as the poet in Christina Rossetti that we sense the full force of her metaphor in "A Royal Princess":

> Me, poor dove that must not coo—
> eagle that must not soar.

It is only when we explore the agonizing splits in the meaning to a girl of the bird itself—freedom against sexual fulfillment, love that also means murder by the hunter—that we can respond fully to "A White Heron," the poignant tale by Sarah Orne Jewett.

Whenever a girl stands at a window, as Jane Eyre does, and looks toward the winding white road that vanishes over the horizon, she yearns for the wings of liberty: "for liberty I gasped; for liberty I uttered a prayer; it seemed scattered on the wind then faintly blowing." Boys too gasp for liberty, but boys do not receive, they only send such valentines to young ladies as Mary Russell Mitford describes in *Our Village* as a sample of the newest in London taste: "a raised group of roses and heartsease, executed on a kind of paper cut-work, which, on being lifted up, turned into a cage enclosing a dove—tender emblem!"

From Mary Wollstonecraft's *Maria*—to Brontë's *Jane Eyre*—to Anne Frank's *Diary of a Young Girl*—I find that the caged bird makes a metaphor that truly deserves the adjective female. And I am not at all surprised by George Eliot's and Virginia Woolf's delight in Mrs. Browning's version of the caged bird metaphor in *Aurora Leigh*. The heroine's spinster aunt, that pattern of English propriety, had lived, Aurora says,

> A sort of cage-bird life, born in a cage,
> Accounting that to leap from perch to perch
> Was act and joy enough for any bird.
> Dear heaven, how silly are the things that live
> In thickets, and eat berries!
>   I alas,
> A wild bird scarcely fledged, was brought to her cage,
> And she was there to meet me. Very kind.
> Bring the clean water, give out the fresh seed.

So in *Jane Eyre,* when Rochester proposes an illicit sexual union, Jane fights to get free of the man she loves, but will not have on the wrong terms. "'Jane, be still;'" he says, "'don't struggle so, like a wild, frantic bird. . . .'" Her reply is touched with Brontë pomposity, but there is also Brontë wit in her use of a metaphor hallowed with female associations: "'I am no bird; and no net ensnares me; I am a free human being with an independent will, which I now exert to leave you.'" In Brontë's work, both aspirations—to female freedom and moral freedom—are served by the bird metaphor, free flying.

"Do not take it to heart," Freud told his lecture audience, "if dreams of flying, so familiar and often so delightful, have to be interpreted as dreams of general sexual excitement, as erection-dreams. . . . And do not make an objection out of the fact that women can have the same flying dreams as men. Remember, rather, that our dreams aim at being the fulfillments of wishes and that the wish to be a man is found so frequently, consciously or unconsciously, in women."

At this moment, my principal objection to that passage is based not so much on sexual or spiritual grounds as on historical, for I have just finished reading the memoirs of Anne Morrow Lindbergh, the most lady-like, yet the most certifiably heroic among modern women writers. Freud may have known a good deal more about women than Mrs. Lindbergh, but she, who flew round the world several times in a biplane, certainly knew more about flying. "Flying was a very tangible freedom," she writes. "From being earth-bound and provincial, I was given limitless horizons. . . . Like the bird pushed out of the nest, I was astonished that— flapping hard—I could fly. All this was liberating." There is the bird metaphor again, and the smug voice of experience reinforces its central sense in women's literature: not flying as a way for a woman to become a man, but as a way for the imprisoned girl-child to become a free adult.

II

> I plead for my sex, not for myself. Independence I have long
> considered as the grand blessing of life, the basis of every
> virtue; and independence I will ever secure by contracting my
> wants, though I were to live on a barren heath.
>
> —Mary Wollstonecraft

Freud did know a great deal about women. More important for our purposes, he also knew a great deal about literature—the Greek and Latin,
the German of course, and he had a wonderful familiarity with the Victorians, about whom he is always worth reading. In his "Tenth Introductory
Lecture to Psycho-Analysis" (from which comes the paragraph quoted
above) he wrote most fully about all the symbols that recur in dreams.
From the fascination of the list he provides there (of what have come
loosely to be called the "Freudian symbols") modern literary criticism
has never freed itself; for Freud himself gave license to criticism to find in
the material of dreams the stuff from which literature is made. It seems
only appropriate to conclude a book of this sort, which rests on one critic's
saturated reading of women's literature, by taking out Freud's list once
again, and checking its validity.

Can one say that Freud's list is biased toward the dreams of men, that
it is useful only in reference to the literature written by men? Not at all.
"The more striking and for both sexes the more interesting component of
the genitals, the male organ," Freud writes, "finds symbolic substitutes in
the first instance in things that resemble it in shape—things, accordingly,
that are long and up-standing, such as *sticks, umbrellas, posts, trees* and so
on. . . ." Open *Jane Eyre* again, for a perfect example of this type of
"Freudian symbol" in the work of a Victorian spinster. "Who could want
me?" wonders the child Jane Eyre, when, after long isolation in the nursery, she is suddenly summoned to see a visitor. "What should I see . . .
—a man or a woman?" It is a man who waits, the Reverend Mr.
Brocklehurst come to arrange Jane's schooling, and the first adult male to
intervene decisively in her orphaned youth. His maleness more than anything else is "symbolized" by Brontë's remarkable raw metaphor:

> The handle turned, the door unclosed, and passing through and
> curtseying low, I looked up at—a black pillar!—such, at least, ap-
> peared to me, at first sight, the straight, narrow, sable-clad shape
> standing erect on the rug; the grim face at the top was like a
> carved mask, placed above the shaft by way of capital.

I run down Freud's list, further on, of those things which in dreams symbolize the female genitals: boxes, chests, pockets, ships, churches— and stop at the jewel-case, because of George Eliot. She provides two unforgettable uses of this metaphor for female sexuality, specifically for virginity on the brink of fully sexual womanhood. One is the brilliant opening scene of Book 1 ("Miss Brooke") of *Middlemarch,* where George Eliot introduces her heroine and at once raises the issue of her ambivalence toward sexual experience by means of a jewel-case. It is brought out by Celia, the younger Brooke sister, also a virgin but unlike Dorothea ripe and willing to marry in a normal fashion. The jewel-case was their mother's, and Celia is eager to divide its contents with her sister: "It is exactly six months to-day since uncle gave them to you, and you have not looked at them yet." The opening of the case—the moralistic conversation —the jewel-play—the hostile sparring between the sisters—the light and the colors and the emotions that fill the rest of the chapter bring a sharper focus than George Eliot would ever again in the novel dare to turn on Dorothea's sexuality.

The other jewel-case scene in George Eliot is Gwendolen Harleth's wedding night in *Daniel Deronda,* and it is distinguished by the greater honesty toward her sex that characterizes that novel,* and shows the power Victorian fiction derived from the then-current restraints of literary decorum. There is of course nothing that could remotely be called pornographic in George Eliot's treatment of Gwendolen's deflowering by her husband Grandcourt; the matter is not even mentioned, directly. But indirectly, by means of the jewel-case, George Eliot conveys all that need be told about Gwendolen's hysterical, virginal frigidity; about Grandcourt's sadistic tastes; and about, in addition, mercenary marriages, wedding night customs, and sexual hypocrisy in the Victorian age.

The jewel-case is sent to Gwendolen on her wedding night by Grandcourt's castoff mistress, along with a letter explaining that the diamonds in the case "were once given with ardent love" to that unfortunate woman, the mother of Grandcourt's illegitimate family. "Truly here were poisoned gems. . . ."

> . . . there was a tap at the door and Grandcourt entered, dressed for dinner. The sight of him brought a new nervous shock, and Gwendolen screamed again and again with hysterical violence. He had expected to see her dressed and smiling, ready to be led down. He saw her pallid, shrieking as it seemed with terror, the jewels scattered around her on the floor.

But that kind of female metaphor, the precious box, is not the kind that Gertrude Stein found in George Eliot, and not the kind that Freud

* Compare the unsatisfactory jewels-in-a-box scene in chapter 22 of *Adam Bede,* which points up George Eliot's deceptive treatment of Hetty Sorrel *after* the loss of her virginity.

found, in another sort of dream. "The complicated topography of the female genital parts," he said in the same lecture, "makes one understand how it is that they are often represented as *landscapes*. . . ." Most men know almost nothing of that "complicated topography," but Freud was a doctor; he would have been as capable as Gertrude Stein of perceiving the distinctly female *landscape* "In the Red Deeps":

> . . . an insignificant rise of ground crowned by trees. . . . Insignificant I call it, because in height it was hardly more than a bank: but there may come moments when Nature makes a mere bank a means towards a fateful result. . . . Just where this line of bank sloped down again to the level, a by-road turned off and led to the other side of the rise, where it was broken into very capricious hollows and mounds by the working of an exhausted stone-quarry—so long exhausted that both mounds and hollows were now clothed with brambles and trees, and here and there by a stretch of grass which a few sheep kept close-nibbled.

Nature's *means towards a fateful result* is the least of cues George Eliot provides to the sexual drama in the landscape; what most matters here, to set off the Red Deeps from other places, is its location in *The Mill on the Floss*. The most difficult moment of Maggie Tulliver's adolescence has come, the break between girlhood and growth, the choice between brother and lover. The Red Deeps are a place of seclusion that Maggie loves, and where she agrees to carry on a series of clandestine meetings with the sensitive hunchback Philip Wakem, whom her brother Tom forbids her to know, and toward whom Maggie feels affection but no physical attraction. There Maggie's sexual existence is born, abortively. "Ah, Maggie," says Philip, "you would never love me so well as you love your brother."

"In her childish days Maggie held this place, called the Red Deeps, in very great awe," George Eliot continues. The girl directs "her walk to the Red Deeps, rather than to any other spot, on the first day she was free to wander at her will—a pleasure she loved so well, that sometimes, in her ardours of renunciation, she thought she ought to deny herself the frequent indulgence in it." Guilty pleasure and renunciation are two of the themes with which women writers set off the landscape of female self-indulgence; others are ecstasy, even of a mystical nature; and freedom, and independent assertion, and fear.

The earliest of such female landscapes that I have noted, which happens also to be the closest to George Eliot's in topographical detail, occurs in Mary Wollstonecraft's first novel, *Mary, a Fiction:*

> One way home was through the cavity of a rock covered with a thin layer of earth, just sufficient to afford nourishment to a few stunted shrubs and wild plants, which grew on its sides, and nodded over the

summit. A clear stream broke out of it, and ran amongst the pieces of rocks fallen into it. Here twilight always reigned—it seemed the Temple of Solitude; yet, paradoxical as the assertion may appear, when the foot sounded on the rock, it terrified the intruder, and inspired a strange feeling, as if the rightful sovereign was dislodged.

As in *The Mill on the Floss,* the Wollstonecraft landscape has nothing to do with the plot of the novel, or the rest of its geography; it surges up, a kind of vision, when the heroine is alone. It is a time of feminine stocktaking, an atmosphere of apartness, as much as a place; to Mary Wollstonecraft, a Temple of Solitude.

The female landscape knows no nationality or century. George Sand's *Vallée-Noire,* as described for example at the beginning of *Le Meunier d'Angibault,* with its rough and dusky terrain, its *traînes* or twisting lanes leading to stagnant pools, is something more than a real place in Le Berry; it is, as Sand writes, "a continual enchantment for the imagination, with very real dangers for those who, adventurously, . . . attempt these seductive, capricious, and perfidious detours." And Isak Dinesen's Africa, which she said was "a landscape that had not its like in all the world," is remarkably like the landscapes Willa Cather saw on the mesa and on the Divide.

The very names that women writers have given to their personal landscapes—indeed, have imposed on their homeland through sheer force of language—are sexually suggestive: the Black Valley, the Divide, the Red Deeps; the first and the third of these names were entirely George Sand's and George Eliot's inventions. Before raising the serious question of the relationship of these places to external reality and to the literature they inspired, I should perhaps deal with the more trivial problem of embarrassment itself—the awkwardness of discussing female sexual imagery in women's literature.

Embarrassment was certainly my own reaction when accidentally, because of Gertrude Stein, I began to find a proliferation of this material in women's literature; and as I tried to lecture or write about it, felt concerned that even to raise the subject would tend to insult the memory and downgrade the writing of the greatest among women writers. The austere dignity of Willa Cather gave me pause, for in her work the female landscape is either a central issue or it is not there at all; Cather's greatness, finally, resides not in her womanliness as a writer but in the bardic role she played in the history of the prairie land. "The history of every country begins in the heart of a man or a woman": no line she wrote can more justly be quoted in tribute to her work.

Reflection, however, brought an end to embarrassment and produced this chapter; for why should female eroticism be less important or more demeaning to literary criticism than male eroticism? Common observation and common sense, well before the age of American sexual sociology, have long informed us that women like men have sexual desires; and sexual parts conducive through sight and touch to female sexual pleasure. Surely it would be more insulting to assume that those women writers who worked on the deepest level of the imagination toward the creation of literature should have entirely ignored their own bodies and sensations as sources for metaphor. Common sense also taught us, long ago, that Portnoy's complaint is hardly of an exclusively masculine nature; and that virgin girls are no more shut out from sexual experience than their male counterparts. In women's literature of the nineteenth century especially, the Child is here as elsewhere Mother to the Woman.

Let us therefore call a spade a spade—and there I am brought to a full stop, because the first metaphor that comes to mind is entirely inappropriate to this subject; what am I to call it? Language itself, the material which women writers have for centuries been refashioning to their needs, is at fault. For the female landscape there should be a term equivalent to "phallic symbol," to employ in civil discourse without raising a snigger of embarrassment. No one, surely, thought of Carlyle as a foul-mouthed old man when, in the *Latter-Day Pamphlets,* he fulminated against the *"new* astonishing Phallus-Worship" of the age, "with universal Balzac-Sand melodies and litanies." No one, surely, reflected at the time that "Phallus-Worship" might apply to Balzac, but would never do for George Sand.

Phallus is an *un*embarrassing word because it is Greek, meaning *penis,* which is Latin and somewhat less easy to use; the only English equivalents are unacceptable. Furthermore, in English usage *phallus* refers to an *image* of the male organ which in various lands and eras has been an object of veneration (as equivalent female images have been as well). By extension, therefore, *phallus* serves as an iconographical term, with little anatomical reference remaining, for a symbol in literature as well as art and ritual. What the criticism of women's literature requires is an equivalent female term, which does not, I believe, exist. If there is anything the recent wide availability of printed pornography has taught us, it is the meagerness in layman's English of sexual terms.

The terms of female sex that do exist were clearly fabricated by a male mind, back before the days of widespread female literacy. For example, the term for the canal leading to and from the womb is *vagina,* Latin for sheath or scabbard: thus only a single function of the canal, and biologically its less important, is evoked—that of a tight receptacle for the male organ, visualized as a sword. (As passageway to life for the newborn infant, the canal walls miraculously stretch and expand as no scabbard or sheath can do.) Even were the word *vagina* less biased toward masculine interest, the canal it refers to has almost no place, so far as I have discovered, in the female literary imagination (just as, all recent medical studies indicate, it has no nerve endings, no sensual outlet to consciousness). Instead, the female landscape is that "complicated topography" to which Freud referred: external, accessible, a prominent, uneven terrain, not a hidden passageway or chamber.

The womb, as we all know, is the most important female organ, but where it is and what it is like is information available only to the medical specialist, not to writers of either sex. (Neither of the ancient words for womb would therefore serve our present purpose: the Latin, *uterus;* or the Greek, *hystera,* with its old-fashioned psychoanalytical associations, quite unscientifically based.) *Pubes* is the Latin word and our for the pubic hair of both sexes; *vulva,* from the Latin, refers principally to an opening, not to a complex totality; and *pudenda,* which used to be genteelly translated as the private parts, derives from the Latin word for shame, which is what we are trying to dispense with.

Mons Veneris at least offers geographical suggestions, but they are the wrong ones: mountain (*mons*), as we don't need Freud to tell us, is descriptive of the male organ but not the female, which is hilly, high-lying, and hard in the female landscapes of literature, but never Alpine. And *Veneris* shows once again that a man, not a woman, invented the term: for the mountain of Venus is a place sacred to heterosexual love and masculine worship, not a Temple of Solitude consecrated to Diana, the goddess of virgins.

It would be easy enough to invent a female equivalent for "phallic symbol" by combining the Greek for place (*topos*) as in topography; and some form of the Greek for woman which gives us words like gynecology. But the air of literary debate is already so littered with Greek words used by critics who share my own ignorance of Greek and access to a dictionary that I don't have the heart for perpetrating further damage to literary ecology. I do suggest, however, that nothing be done with the female term Ivy Compton-Burnett heard as a child from her doctor father (who was of the homeopathic persuasion): "pelvic power."

. . .

Willa Cather's dissatisfaction with *The Song of the Lark,* which she severely cut and virtually repudiated in 1932 on the occasion of its republication, extended to more than its title, for it is a cluttered, disorganized work with too much detail drawn from her own and Olive Fremstad's biography, and too little evidence of the Cather fire which, especially in the short novels of the 1920s, burned away all impurities. Still, far down as *The Song of the Lark* must be placed in the Cather scale, there

are wonderful things in the novel, as well as the most thoroughly elaborated female landscape in literature. The whole Panther Cañon section of
the novel (Part IV: "The Ancient People") is concerned with female self-
assertion in terms of landscape; and the dedication to female landscape
carries with it here the fullest possible tally of spiritual, historical, national,
and artistic associations. Whether Cather's later dissatisfaction with the
novel included a realization of the unguarded sexuality of her cañon topography there is no way to know.

"Panther Cañon was like a thousand others," it begins,

> —one of those abrupt fissures with which the earth in the Southwest
> is riddled. . . . It was accessible only at its head. The cañon walls, for
> the first two hundred feet below the surface, were perpendicular cliffs,
> striped with even-running strata of rock. From there on to the bottom
> the sides were less abrupt, were shelving, and lightly fringed with
> piñons and dwarf cedars. The effect was that of a gentler cañon with-
> in a wilder one. The dead city lay at the point where the perpendicu-
> lar outer wall ceased and the V-shaped inner gorge began. There a
> stratum of rock, softer than those above, had been hollowed out by the
> action of time until it was like a deep groove. . . .

The associations come tumbling out. Thea explores "the long horizontal groove" of the cañon. She inspects the deserted, prehistoric ruins of the
Ancient People—"clean with the cleanness of sun-baked, wind-swept
places." She moves in alone, with nothing but a blanket, to take up residence in one of the ruined rooms. There she discovers the pottery made by
the Indian women, "their most direct appeal to water, the envelope and
sheath of the precious element itself." She bathes in a pool hidden at the
bottom of the cañon and, as the sun and water strike her body, ponders
the relationship between the stream, the pottery—and her own art: "what
was any art but an effort to make a sheath, a mould in which to imprison
for a moment the shining, elusive element which is life itself?" Her own artistic commitment makes her one with the Indian women, who with their
pottery began the creation of beauty "even here, in this crack in the world,
so far back in the night of the past! Down here at the beginning, that painful thing was already stirring; the seed of sorrow, and of so much delight."

Thea relishes her aloneness: it is a physical sensation—"keenly alive,
lying on that insensible shelf of stone, when her body bounded like a
rubber ball away from its hardness." She perceives that this physical
vitality—"a lightness in the body and a driving power in the blood"—is
the source of her art; of her voice as a singer. She makes then a decision
that is a major turning point: toward study in Germany, away from family
life. She will risk everything on "older and higher obligations" rather
"than meekly draw the plough under the rod of parental guidance." Then

her lover arrives; he discovers that Thea is "not a nesting-bird"; and the great golden eagle comes sailing across the sky over the cañon. "From a cleft in the heart of the world she saluted it. . . ."

The first point to be made about this section of *The Song of the Lark* is that it rests on an actual episode in the life of Willa Cather the writer, not of Olive Fremstad the opera singer. In the spring of 1912 Cather left New York and her work on *McClure's* to visit her brother in the Southwest, where she explored cañons and Indian ruins. For various reasons the experience was crucial, providing for Cather the means of self-discovery as woman and artist; from it we date her serious beginnings as a novelist.

But the second thing that must be said is that this plainly sexual landscape closely parallels other places evoked by women writers for the same purpose of solitary, feminine assertion. (All are outdoor places, with one interesting partial exception, the hard, uneven terrain of the courtyard of the German school where Miriam, the heroine of Dorothy Richardson's *Pilgrimage,* affirms her female solitude.) The height, the sky, the horizontal vistas, the aboriginal openness, the dry hard ground, the pottery colors, even the "light delicate foliage . . . in horizontal layers . . . a strange appearance as if the whole wood were faintly vibrating" are in Isak Dinesen's Africa as well as in Cather country; and exultation is sounded by both writers. Dinesen writes: "In the highlands you woke up in the morning and thought: Here I am, where I ought to be."

The whole opening chapter of *Out of Africa* is so exquisitely phrased, so deserving of its place as a classic of modern English prose (by a writer whose native language was Danish!) that Dinesen leads at once to the third point: whatever component of sexuality enters into these literary landscapes, its inspirational residue is of the highest, not the lowest order.

Cather's greatest prose as a landscapist is not in *The Song of the Lark,* but in other works where she returns, more in control, to the mesaland: "Tom Outland's Story" in *The Professor's House,* and in *Death Comes for the Archbishop.* The greatest of her landscapes are those inspired by the land she knew best, the Nebraska prairies, in *O Pioneers!* and *My Ántonia,* and some of her stories. The same sense of earthbound ecstasy fills them all, of physical dissolution on a limitless, undulating, high-lying plain under a limitless sky; of a solitary, primordial land antecedent to, perhaps hostile to human life. "There seemed to be nothing to see," she writes through the eyes of Jim Burden, the narrator of *My Ántonia,* who is transported at the age of ten from the lush mountain valleys of Virginia to the barren open land of frontier Nebraska, much as Willa Cather was herself. "There was nothing but land; not a country at all, but the material out of which countries are made. . . . Between that earth and that sky I felt erased, blotted out."

To look hard at Cather's landscapes, in fact, is to perceive not the woman in the writer so much as the mystic—an aspect of Willa Cather's temperament that requires, I believe, more examination. For the sensations I have been describing, the radiant ecstasy that comes to Alexandra Bergson from "the great, free spirit" of the Divide, or that comes to the Archbishop from the spirit of the mesa—

> Something soft and wild and free, something that whispered to the ear on the pillow, lightened the heart, softly, softly picked the lock, slid the bolts, and released the prisoned spirit of man into the wind, into the blue and gold, into the morning, into the morning!

—these are the classic experiences of mysticism.

> Earth rising to heaven and heaven descending,
> Man's spirit away from its drear dungeon sending,
> Bursting the fetters and breaking the bars.

Emily Brontë's lines—and many others of her poems—are often quoted to establish her temperament as that of the mystic. They remind us of the topographical similarity between the Brontë moors and the Cather prairies; and they suggest that a renaming is required, to take the literature of female mysticism into account, of what we call "oceanic feelings" when the central mystical experience is at issue. Women mystics are landbound. Or rather, it is from the undulating, limitless uplands that the female spirit takes flight into the limitless air that Dinesen describes as "alive over the land, like a flame burning; it scintillated, waved and shone like running water. . . ."

"Oceanic feelings" is probably the only metaphor with standing in religion, physiology, and psychoanalysis, as well as in literature. It applies to the sensation of selflessness and release from the flesh and to the comprehension of the universal Oneness that are often experienced on the open seas. From ancient times the poets have given us accounts of this experience; more recently, a monologue in *Long Day's Journey into Night* placed it in a sailor's memory, for Eugene O'Neill, Willa Cather's compatriot and younger contemporary, had been to sea. But going to sea as a sailor, at least as much as going to war as a soldier, is an experience from which women have historically been barred. Even going to the seashore has been a rare experience for literary women (until recently)—how rare, and how passionately desired, only readers of Anne Brontë and Jane Austen can know. In *Persuasion,* Jane Austen opens her delicately romantic vista toward the sea. She lets her characters find themselves on the seashore, and linger there "as all must linger and gaze on a first return to the sea, who ever deserve to look on it at all. . . ."

How much the freedom and tactile sensations of near-naked sea bathing has meant to modern women emerges at once from a glance at the imagery of the twentieth-century poets included in Ann Stanford's anthology; and among the prose writers, perhaps by coincidence, many of the moderns have lived near the sea—Katherine Mansfield, as "At the Bay" testifies; and Kate Chopin and Eudora Welty, Louisiana women with easy access to the Gulf of Mexico. But oddly enough, the one landscape that I know in Eudora Welty's work that seems to be clearly a female landscape is the upswelling land of the delta that flickers across the little girl's vision, almost subliminally, at the start of *Delta Wedding,* as she rides the train toward the family-teeming household where her individuality will be submerged in other lives.

Kate Chopin's *The Awakening* takes place almost entirely by the sea, and provides a welter of water images in the more familiar Freudian sense; an important source here, as has often been pointed out, is Walt Whitman. Indeed, learning how to swim is a central part of Edna Pontellier's story. But if there is a moment when Kate Chopin reveals herself most truly a woman writer it is when she has Edna look far back into girlhood for her first private moment of self-assertion, which took place not by the sea but in a Kentucky meadow "that seemed as big as an ocean to the very little girl walking through the grass . . . 'I felt as if I must walk on forever, without coming to the end of it.' " The land memory comes back to Edna at the end, when she swims to her death.

Am I suggesting, then, that these landscapes charged with female privacy, and with emotions ranging from the erotic to the mystical, are merely literary landscapes, merely imaginary creations of women's literature? Hardly. I have never seen Dinesen's African Highlands, or the veldt out of which both Olive Schreiner and Doris Lessing made female landscapes in their fiction; but I have visited Willa Cather's prairies and the Brontës' Yorkshire moors and can vouch, should it be necessary, for their reality. But I have also learned that the Divide is not a massive geological fact (it is not, as non-Nebraska readers sometimes assume, the Continental Divide) but is a small stretch of raised land on the outskirts of Red Cloud—a divide, without the capital letter, like many another. But one can see how a little girl could say there, as Sylvia Plath does of the Brontës' moors,

> The sky leans on me, me, the one upright
> Among all horizontals.
>> "Wuthering Heights"

I have also made my pilgrimage to the *Vallée-Noire.* People go there every spring to celebrate the *Fêtes Romantiques* which are held in and around George Sand's birthplace in tribute to the Romantic composers, artists, and writers that she drew to that otherwise ignored country place in the center of France. It is real country still, and much as Matthew Arnold found it: "a silent country of heathy and ferny landes, a region of granite boulders, holly and broom . . . of broad light, and fresh breezes, and wide horizons." It seemed to me rather ordinary farm country, neither high nor low, but perhaps a little wilder than what I think of as the normal French countryside; I was reminded of stretches of Connecticut and New York State. Chateaubriand was reminded of Brittany by Sand's landscapes; Matthew Arnold found them "strangely English"; and Stendhal paid Sand's art as a landscapist the greatest, unintentional compliment when he traveled through her countryside "quarreling, in my mind, with George Sand, who has given us such beautiful descriptions of the banks of the Indre. It's a pitiful stream. . . ."

George Sand's countryside was in fact very much her own creation, for all that Le Berry exists in the history books, and Nohant exists, a very tiny dot, on the best detailed maps of France. But *la Vallée-Noire* was the name she invented*—"a novelist's pure caprice," she wrote, "a very simple name, and the first, I confess, that came to me"—for what she calls "a natural geography," independent of administrative boundaries, which "will always exist, and which everyone has the right to reestablish in the logic of his sight and his mind." It is in this natural and highly personal geography that she located many of her stories from *Rose et Blanche* to the end of her career. Nature in *la Vallée-Noire,* wrote Sand, is "neither fierce nor welcoming . . . she is tranquil, serene, and mute under a smile of mysterious goodness . . . she has a grave amenity, a sweet majesty. . . ."

Whoever wishes to ponder the mystery of the female landscape, both literary and real, should acquire two beautiful volumes of photographs combined with literary texts, Georges Lubin's *George Sand en Berry* and *Willa Cather: A Pictorial Memoir,* by Bernice Slote and Lucia Woods. Nearby prop open Winifred Gérin's biography of Anne Brontë to the photographs she provides of the Yorkshire moors; and glance at reproductions of the art of Georgia O'Keeffe. No simple answers will emerge, but that certain lands have been good for women is clear—open lands, harsh and upswelling, high-lying and undulating, vegetated with crimped heather or wind-swept grasses, cut with ravines and declivities and twisting lanes. At the least, the brilliant landscape writing that women have devoted to open country should give pause to the next critic who wants to pronounce all literary women housebound, and the next psychologist with a theory about "inner space."

There is also matter for reflection in *Novels of Empire* by Susanne Howe Nobbe, who deals with the special effect of the African landscape

---

* Just as, according to authorities on the *berrichon* dialect, Sand invented her own use of the word *traîne* for a mysterious, twisting, hollowed-out, foliage-darkened lane.

on literature, much of it by women; and in *Virgin Land: The American West as Symbol and Myth* by Henry Nash Smith, who explores the metaphors of the West that alternately attracted or repelled Americans in their progress toward the high-lying, treeless plains beyond the Mississippi.

In spite of his title, Professor Smith takes no interest in the women who also created and responded to the myths of the West; he does not mention Willa Cather. But the two opposed metaphors he finds in the history of the opening of the West, the "Garden of the World" as against the "Great American Desert," are at the center of Willa Cather's fiction. Her testimony is that, for the woman in love with independence, the desert land—"not a country at all, but the material out of which countries are made"—exerts an attraction, and the garden of settlement a repulsion no male pioneer could feel. The gardens in Cather's work—the lush marsh at Sweet Water, in *A Lost Lady;* or the garden under the mulberry tree in *O Pioneers!*—are scenes of passion and cruel violence; they are very different from Cather's landscapes of female ecstasy out on the open prairie or the mesa.

When I reread *The Secret Garden* in the course of work for this book, to discover whether the magic it held for me as a girl would still persist, I was delighted to find that Frances Hodgson Burnett had extracted both landscapes from women's literature: the open, wind-swept, desolate moors for the little girl's arrival in England, and the walled garden for the end of the novel, when Mrs. Burnett loses interest in her heroine and concentrates on the blooming of her princely hero. But I would not want to leave the impression that female landscapes are for women only. The lush, overgrown, heavily scented *Vallée-Noire* in George Sand offers many popular attractions, as Matthew Arnold testifies, and is as different in some ways from the Brontë moors and Cather prairies as in other ways it resembles them.

Rushing water, cascading in abundance, is usually around the bend of one of Sand's twisting lanes, and cascading water is also the principal feature of Mrs. Browning's proud vision of a woman's Italy, beside which tame old England is "Not a grand nature."

> . . . Not my headlong leaps
> Of waters, that cry out for joy or fear
> In leaping through the palpitating pines,
> Like a white soul tossed out to eternity
> With thrills of time upon it. Not indeed
> My multitudinous mountains, sitting in
> The magic circle, with the mutual touch
> Electric, panting from their full deep hearts
> Beneath the influent heavens, and waiting for
> Communion and commission. Italy
> Is one thing, England one.

"Dans le Désert" is indeed the landscape of Lélia's solitary retreat, and it is indubitably a female landscape, but as far as I can calculate, George Sand does not let her heroine stick it out alone there more than a day or two. "Eh bein! Trenmor," says Lélia, "je quitte le désert."

> Ce désert est vraiment beau et Sténio le poëte eût passé là une nuit d'extase et de fièvre lyrique! Moi, hélas! je n'ai senti dans mon cerveau que l'indignation et le murmure. Car ce silence de mort pesait sur mon âme et l'offensait. . . . Oui, je détestais cette nature radieuse et magnifique, car elle se dressait là, devant moi, comme une beauté stupide qui se tient muette et fière sous le regard des hommes et croit avoir assez fait en se montrant. . . .

Which means roughly: I've had it; I'm leaving; my head aches; the silence is getting me down; true, it's all very beautiful, but I've had enough of nature with her stupid beauty, who thinks she can just stand there, show herself, keep quiet, and be looked at.

Perhaps *la Vallée-Noire* herself should have the last word. "Look at me if you wish, I don't care," Sand has that female landscape say to the traveler. "If you pass on, bon voyage; if you stay, so much the better for you."

❈ NOTES

Acknowledgments

Among all those whose kindness and generosity facilitated the work on this book, I first thank the National Endowment for the Humanities for a Senior Fellowship and a Research Grant, which gave me two unbroken years of intensive research in 1972–73 and 1973–74; and President Martha E. Peterson of Barnard College and Kenneth A. Lohf, Director of Special Collections at Columbia University, for their gracious hospitality; and Professor Allen Mandelbaum, Chairman, and my colleagues and the staff of the Graduate English Department of the City University of New York for unwavering support during the last year of writing; and Professors Maurice Kramer and Jules Gelernt, Chairmen of the Brooklyn College English Department, for their interest and understanding.

I thank Mrs. Miriam Holden, who opened the riches of her private collection of women's materials to me in 1963; and Dr. Lola Szladits of the Berg Collection, who read a late version of the whole book through for continuity. To the staff of the Columbia University Libraries, the New York Public Library, the New York Society Library, the Newberry Library of Chicago, the Boston Public Library, the Library of Congress, the British Museum Reading Room, the Bibliothèque Nationale, the Bibliothèque Sainte Geneviève, the Bibliothèque Spoelberch de Lovenjoul, the London University Library, the Graduate Library of City University, and the Houghton Library of Harvard University I am much indebted.

I thank Deborah Epstein Nord for her intelligent and dedicated work as research assistant; and Daria Lewis for heroinic assistance with the notes. Without Mrs. Rosalie Stewart this book could not have been completed.

Of all those who shared with me their scholarship, their experience as writers, doctors, clerics, editors, and teachers, and their perceptions as readers, Professor Susanne Howe Nobbe must head the list, for she trained so many of us at Columbia in the history of the novel and Victorian literature, and started many of the trains of thought in this book. There is room only to list the others by name, but my gratitude to them all is unbounded, and I apologize to those inadvertently omitted. They include Simone Balayé, Jerome H. Buckley, Rowland E. Collins, Monique Cornand, Malcolm Cowley, Maxine Cutler, John W. Donohue, S.J., Dora Edinger, Barbara Epstein, Virginia Faulkner, Roland Gelatt, William M. Gibson, Robert Halsband, Ann Harris, Iola Haverstick, Robert Hutchinson, Paul Ilie, Philip Kelley, Lewis Leary, Harry Levin, Naomi Lewis, Ruth Ann Lief, Georges Lubin, Gina Luria, Martin Mayer, Nancy Milford, Jean Baker Miller, M.D., Jo Modert, Miriam Mountford, Robert Mumford, M.D., Michele Murray of lamented memory, Tillie Olsen, Ruth Prigozy, Margherita Repetto, James Rieger, Laurence Senelick, John Shawcross, Judith Johnson Sherwin, Michael Slater, Patrick and Elizabeth Smith, Harry Stone, Marcelle Thiébaux, Patricia Thomson, Martha Vicinus, Erik Wensberg.

Guide to the Notes

The notes are arranged dictionary fashion, that is, in alphabetical order under the name of each woman writer.

Within each entry the literary works cited are arranged in order of original publication, or, where important, of composition. Thus, at the cost of some inconvenience to the reader who wishes to check sources, a rough guide to the writing career of each woman writer is provided. But a word of caution: the literary works are selectively listed, and do not always represent the complete bibliography of any one author, just as the genres given after the writer's name do not indicate all forms in which she worked, but represent an editorial judgment of those for which her literary name (the only one provided) will be remembered.

Secondary sources are also grouped within each dictionary entry— again a highly selective list mostly of those biographies and critical studies actually cited in the book. No effort has been made to mention all, or even the best critical studies of each woman writer. However, the most solid scholarly guides, especially the meticulous editors of letters and texts and the responsible biographers to whom this book is so much indebted, are generally indicated.

In the case of a comment by one literary woman on another, the reference is normally entered under the name of the writer of the comment, not of its subject. As to the literary man, when he is cited in specific reference to a literary woman, the reference appears under her name; when cited in a more general context, he is entered under the name of a woman chosen sometimes arbitrarily, often gleefully. The student of women writers, who knows how rudely they have long been handled by the makers of indexes, directories, library cards, and other such implements of research, will share my pleasure at the thought that here is one book where Thomas Carlyle is listed under his wife Jane, William Wordsworth under his sister Dorothy, and Richardson under his disciple Fanny Burney. The index to the book, which covers the notes, can be relied on to direct the reader to the placement of such entries, and also to the fullest bibliographical data for those secondary works consulted for a variety of women writers, and therefore commonly identified only by the last name of the author. For example, "Tillotson" in the index will refer the reader to the fullest entry for Kathleen Tillotson's *Novels of the Eighteen-Forties.*

Multiple references to the literary works cited throughout the book, such as *Jane Eyre* or *Aurora Leigh,* are given (under that title) roughly in the order in which they arise in this book. And chapter numbers rather than page numbers are almost invariably given, in order to facilitate, indeed encourage, the reading of a variety of editions new and old, paper- or cloth-bound. In a few cases a preferred text is indicated—for example, the Penguin editions of Charlotte and Emily Brontë, which seem likely to supplant the once "standard," always hard to find, and never wholly satisfactory Shakespeare Head Brontë edition; and the Oxford English Novels, which have brought many early women writers back into circulation. The superb Chapman edition of Jane Austen provides a special case for page numbers, as explained below; and occasionally a writer like Colette, who did not use numbered chapters, makes page-number references to a specific, indicated edition unavoidable.

As these notes took final shape and began to look like a guide to women writers as well as to a book about them, it was decided by publisher and author to contribute a few extra pages of type and a few extra days of work toward the illusion of completeness. Thus several dozen writers barely mentioned or not at all mentioned in the text are briefly included. For inadvertent omissions the author apologizes; they are inevitably most serious in the case of current writers. The aim has been accuracy within severe limitations, and the excuse for this imperfect guide is that some sort of checklist of women writers is sorely needed.

· · ·

The following symbols have been employed:

⌘means chapter (or scene of a play, or number of a poem)
§means book, section, part, or other major division of a novel or poem (or act of a play)
Capital Roman numerals mean volumes
*means additional material about a literary woman provided for the first time in the notes, and not tied to any particular page in the book
[date] means date of composition (occasionally, partial periodical publication); the date given immediately after a literary work,

without either brackets or parentheses, refers to the first edition of a book, first production of a play, or, where split years are indicated, first publication in serial form.

. . .

The following abbreviations have been employed:

AL (*American Literature*)
BM (Library of the British Museum)
BN (Bibliothèque Nationale)
CE (*College English*)
DAB (*Dictionary of American Biography*)
DNB (*Dictionary of National Biography*)
ECS (*Eighteenth-Century Studies*)
HU (Harvard University)
JRLB (*John Rylands Library Bulletin*)
KSJ (*Keats-Shelley Journal*)
MLR (*Modern Language Review*)
MWN (*Mary Wollstonecraft Newsletter*)
NCF (*Nineteenth-Century Fiction*)
NS (*New Statesman*)
NYPL (New York Public Library)
NYRB (*New York Review of Books*)
NYTBR (*New York Times Book Review*)
PFLSH (*Publications de la Faculté des Lettres et Sciences Humaines*)
PMLA (*Publications of the Modern Language Association*)
RDM (*Revue des Deux Mondes*)
RES (*Review of English Studies*)
RLC (*Revue de Littérature Comparée*)
RLMC (*Rivista di Letterature Moderne e Comparate*)
SEEJ (*Slavic and East European Journal*)
SR (*Saturday Review*)
TLS (*Times Literary Supplement*)
VP (*Victorian Poetry*)
VS (*Victorian Studies*)

Adams, Abigail   1744–1818   America   Letters
Familiar Letters of John Adams and His Wife During the Revolution 1876

> Alice S. Rossi, ed., *Feminist Papers* (1974)—AA on "a rover" and curiosity about Catherine Macaulay: pp. 9–10.

Addams, Jane   1860–1935   America   Sociology, memoirs
Twenty Years at Hull-House 1910

Akhmatova, Anna   1889–1966   Russia   Poems
Poems, trans. S. Kunitz, M. Hayward (1973)—"Epigram": p. 137.

> Sam N. Driver, *AA* (1972)—Love Lyrics: ✻3.

Alcott, Louisa May   1832–88   America   Children's books, novels
Hospital Sketches 1863

> Bessie Z. Jones, Intro., *HS* (1960)—nursing: pp. xvii–xliv.

Moods 1864
Little Women 1868–69—"Christmas": ✻1; Marmee "noble-looking": ✻1.
Little Men 1871
Work [1861] 1873—"Declaration": ✻1; hand-clasping scene: ✻20.
Eight Cousins 1875
Rose in Bloom 1876
Under the Lilacs 1878
Jo's Boys 1886

Life, Letters, and Journals, ed. Ednah D. Cheney (1889)—mother love: pp. 24, 76–77; poverty: pp. 49, 108; tomboy: p. 30; domestic service: p. 66.

> Iola Haverstick, "To See Louisa Plain" (*SR,* Oct. 19, 1968); Madeleine Stern, *LMA* (1950).

Angelou, Maya   America   Memoirs, poems
I Know Why the Caged Bird Sings 1970

Arbus, Diane   1923–71   America   Photographs
DA: An Aperture Monograph, ed. Doon Arbus 1972—"freaks aristocrats": p. 3.

Arnim, Bettina von   1785–1895   Germany   Letters, essays
Correspondence, trans. Margaret Fuller (Boston, 1842)

Ashton-Warner, Sylvia   New Zealand   Novels, pedagogy
Spinster 1958
Teacher 1963

Astell, Mary   1668–1731   England   Treatises
A Serious Proposal to the Ladies 1694; see Montagu.

Austen, Jane   1775–1817   England   Novels

> * All citations from Austen's works are from the R. W. Chapman
> Clarendon Press edition of the novels (Oxford, 1926) with the
> Juvenilia and fragments included in Vol. VI, *Minor Works*
> (1954). As the chapter numbers of this edition, derived from
> the original publication in volumes, do not accord with modern
> editions, page numbers are used below.

Juvenilia [1790–93]—*Love and Friendship* [1790]—"5th Bank-note": p. 96;
"The Female Philosopher" [c. 1793]—"My dear Neice": p. 171.

Sense and Sensibility [1795, the first version probably epistolary] 1811

Northanger Abbey [1797–1803, written and almost published; revised 1816]
1818—Tilney on Radcliffe: pp. 106–7; "noisy and wild": p. 14; "the
author she": p. 232.

Pride and Prejudice [1796–97, written and almost published; revised c.
1811–12] 1813—Bingley class, income: pp. 3, 15; Darcy income, power:
pp. 10, 250; Bingley sisters on trade: pp. 15, 139; Bennet income: p. 28;
Gardiner class: pp. 29, 36, 388; Collins reading Fordyce: p. 68.

Mansfield Park [1811–13] 1814—Mary Crawford on clergymen: p. 92.
L. Trilling, *"MP," The Opposing Self* (1959): p. 215.

Emma [1814–15] 1816—Emma's income: p. 135; upbringing: p. 5; on
Robert Martin: pp. 31–34; on yeomanry: p. 29; on baby girl, Genlis: p.
461; Knightley on Martin: p. 59; "governess-trade": p. 300.

> J. E. Austen-Leigh, *Memoir* (1870)—JA on heroine: ⚹10; L. Trilling,
> Introduction to *Emma* (Riverside edition, 1957): pp. x, xxi.

Persuasion [1815–16] 1818—Sir Walter on navy: p. 19; Wentworth on
money: p. 67; his rise in navy: pp. 26–30; his love letter: p. 237; Mary on
motherhood: pp. 56–57; Anne on Kellynch owners: p. 125; on the sea:
p. 127; on "Men have had every advantage": p. 234.

Sanditon [fragment, 1817] 1925

JA's Letters to her sister Cassandra and Others, ed. R. W. Chapman (2nd ed.,
1952)—"unlearned female": p. 443; "ordination": p. 215; on Brunton:
pp. 278, 344, 423; on Waverley: pp. 404–5; on Burney: pp. 14, 64, 180,
254, 388, 438; on Corinna: p. 242; on Genlis: pp. 82, 173, 450; on reading
women writers: see Chapman's index to JA's reading under Sévigné,
Morgan, Sykes, West, Cowley, Grant, Hamilton, More, Thrale, Porter,
Williams, S. H. Burney, Cooke, Hawkins, Edgeworth, Lennox, Radcliffe.

> R. W. Chapman, *JA, Facts and Problems* (1949)—"consummate
> aunt": pp. 6–7; Austen income: p. 22; invited to meet Mme de Staël: p.
> 132; chronology of writing, publication: pp. 175–83.
> Critical studies emphasizing JA's place in history of novel and women's
> literature—M. Lascelles, *JA and Her Art* (1939); K. L. Moler, *JA's Art
> of Allusion* (1968); M. Sadleir, *Northanger Novels* (1927); B. C.
> Southam, ed., *JA: Critical Heritage* (1968)—"man of mark and adven-
> ture" in Scott review of *Emma:* pp. 61ff.; H. Ten Harmsel, *JA Fictional*

Conventions (1964); I. Watt, *Rise of Novel* (1957); M. Wilson, *JA &
Some Contemporaries* (1938).
J. Forster, *Life of Charles Dickens* (1872–74): p. 73.

Baillie, Joanna   1762–1851   Scotland   Plays, poems
Orra: a Tragedy in *Plays on the Passions* 1812—"Tell it, I pray": §2, ⚹3.
Dramatic and Poetical Works of JB with a Life of the Author (1853). See
    Mary Shelley, *Journal*.

Barnes, Djuna   America   Novels, plays, poems
Nightwood 1937—Intro., T. S. Eliot.

Barrett, Elizabeth   See Browning

Beauvoir, Simone de   France   Novels, memoirs, essays
Le Deuxième sexe 1949
Une Mort très douce 1964—death of mother; see Leduc.

Bedford, Sybille   England   Novels, essays
A Legacy 1956—mother-daughter relationship.
The Faces of Justice 1961

Behn, Aphra   1640–89   England   Novels, plays

Benedict, Ruth   1887–1948   America   Anthropology
Patterns of Culture 1934
"The Story of My Life" [1935] in *An Anthropologist at Work: Writings of RB,*
    ed. Margaret Mead (1959)

Bengis, Ingrid   America   Fiction
Combat in the Erogenous Zone 1972

Berry, Mary   1763–1852   England   Letters, journal
*Extracts of the Journals and Correspondence of Miss Berry from the year
    1783 to 1852,* ed. Lady Theresa Lewis 1865—More and Wollstonecraft:
    I, 91–92; friendship with Mme de Staël: III, 13.

Birstein, Ann   America   Novels, stories
Summer Situations 1972—on Colette: "When the Wind Blew."

Bishop, Elizabeth   America   Poems

Blais, Marie Claire   Canada   Novels
Une Saison dans la Vie d'Emmanuel 1965—Grand-mère Antoinette: ⚹1.

Lady Blessington   1789–1849   England   Novels, memoirs
Journal of the Conversations of Lord Byron with the Countess of Blessington
    1832—Mme de Staël: pp. 22–27 in E. J. Lovell, ed., *Conv.* (1969); see
    Chopin.

Bogan, Louise   1897–1970   America   Poems, criticism
Achievement in American Poetry 1951—women poets: ⚥3.

Bowen, Elizabeth   1899–1973   Ireland, England   Novels, stories

Bowles, Caroline   1786–1854   England   Poems
        * Robert Southey, poet laureate, wrote Charlotte Brontë his
        famous discouraging letter ("Literature cannot be the business of
        a woman's life, and it ought not to be") at a time when he was
        helping Caroline Bowles, a self-supporting literary spinster, to
        publish her poetry, then the sole "business" of her life. In 1839
        he made her his second wife, and her business then was nursing
        Southey, who became senile almost immediately after their mar-
        riage.

Solitary Hours 1826
Tales of the Factories 1833

        Rubenius, *Gaskell,* pp. 281–82; J. Simmons, *Southey* (1945).

Bradstreet, Anne   1612–72   America   Poems
        * Born Anne Dudley, daughter of the steward to the Earl of
        Lincoln; married Simon Bradstreet at sixteen and at eighteen
        emigrated to the Massachusetts Bay Colony, of which her father
        and her husband were governors.

*The Tenth Muse Lately sprung up in America . . . By a Gentlewoman in those
    parts* (identified in prefatory verses as "Mistris Anne Bradstreet, . . .
    residing in the Occidentall parts of the World, in America, alias NOV-
    ANGLIA") London, 1650
Several Poems . . . By a Gentlewoman in New-England (second, expanded
    edition supervised by AB) Boston, 1678
The Works of AB, ed. John Harvard Ellis (including the Andover manuscripts:
    poems and prose meditations) 1867—* All citations from *Poems of AB,*
    ed. Robert Hutchinson (Dover Press, 1969)—"Contemplations"—Eve
    "our Grandame": ⚥12, p. 82; *"Phoebus* make haste": pp. 42–43; "In
    reference to her Children, 23. June, 1656"—"I had eight birds": pp. 47–
    49; "Prologue" to *The Tenth Muse*—"Thyme or Parsley wreath": ⚥8, p.
    120; "My thankfull heart"—"simple mite": p. 69; "To the Memory of my
    dear and ever honoured Father Thomas Dudley"—"One of thy Founders,
    him *New-England* know" (start of quatrain quoted anonymously on Har-
    vard's Dudley memorial): p. 52.

Adrienne Rich, Foreword, and Jeannine Hensley, Introduction to *The Works of AB,* ed. JH (HU, Belknap Press, 1967); Helen Campbell, *AB and Her Time* (1891); Josephine K. Piercy, *AB* (1965); Elizabeth Wade White, *AB* (1971); A. Jones, *Thomas Dudley* (1899); S. E. Morison, *Builders of the Bay Colony* (1930): pp. 320–36; K. Silverman, *Colonial Poetry* (1968)—AB's influence on Edward Taylor: pp. 41–42, 175–77; John Berryman, "One Answer to a Question" (*Shenandoah,* Autumn 1965)—on his writing *Homage to Mistress Bradstreet* (1956); R. Hutchinson, Intro., *Poems of AB* (1969).

Bremer, Fredrika   1801–65   Finland, Sweden   Novels

The Bondmaid (play, trans. from Swedish by M. L. Putnam, 1844)—"I am a slave": p. 23; autobiog. letter: pp. vi–x.
The Neighbours in *Works of FB* (trans., London, 1844)—first-person heroine: esp. pp. 14, 107; C. Brontë, *Letters,* ed. Shorter—*thought the narrator startlingly close to Jane Eyre: II, 339.

> Charlotte Bremer, ed., *Life, Letters, Works* (New York, 1868)—travels in U.S.: p. 76; George Eliot, "Belles Lettres" (*Westminster Rev.* 1855 & 1856)—on FB: LXIV, 306; LXVI, 575; Foster, *H. B. Stowe*—on women and slavery issue: p. 57; Rubenius, *Gaskell,* p. 40.

Brontë, Anne   1820–49   England   Novels, poems

Poems by C., E., and Acton Bell   1846
Agnes Grey: A Novel   1847—bird-torturing scene: ※2.
The Tenant of Wildfell Hall   1848—"taught to cling": ※3.

> W. Gérin, *AB* (1959); A. Harrison & D. Stanford, *AB* (1959); I.-S. Ewbank, *Their Proper Sphere* (1966); A.-L. Wells, *Soeurs Brontë et l'étranger* (1937)—*re* Sand: pp. 106–9, 119–22.

Brontë, Charlotte   1816–55   England   Novels, letters, poems

Juvenilia [c. 1829–39]—*Legends of Angria,* ed. Fannie E. Ratchford & C. DeVane (1933); F. E. Ratchford, *Brontës' Web of Childhood* (1941)—Zenobia: p. 87 & C. Maurat, *Brontës' Secret* (trans. M. Meldrum, 1970) pp. 76–77.
Poems by Currer, E., and A. Bell   1846.
The Professor [1846] 1857—CB on hero, work, publishers: Preface [c. 1850]; Crimsworth's appearance: ※4; on job hunting: ※7; on work for wife: ※25.

> Margaret M. Brammer, "A Critical Study of CB's *TP*" (unpublished thesis, U. of London, 1958).

Jane Eyre: An Autobiography   1847—slavery metaphors: ※1, ※2; "I was a discord": ※2; garden scene: ※23; return to Rochester: ※37; watercolors: ※13; bird metaphors—torture: ※2; china: ※3; robin: ※4; linnet, eager bird: ※27; sparrow, eagle, skylark: ※37; Bewick's: ※1; caged: ※14; "We talk all day": ※38; "For liberty I gasped": ※10; male as black pillar: ※4.

Kathleen Tillotson, *Novels of 1840s* (1954)—price: p. 22; *Quarterly Review:* see Eastlake; G. H. Lewes, "Recent Novels" (*Fraser's,* Dec. 1847)—passions and real: XXXVI, 690–93.

Shirley 1849—Monday morning real: ✻1; Eve fantasy: ✻27 & cf. ✻18 for Milton's cook; professions for women: ✻12; travel in Radcliffe: ✻23; "If men could see us": ✻20.

G. H. Lewes, "CB's *S*" (*Edinburgh Rev.*, Jan. 1850)—woman and real: XCI, 158–65.

Source of Rose Yorke: see Mary Taylor.

Villette 1853—Bretton, Mrs. Bretton: ✻1; Vashti: ✻23; Napoleon: ✻30; "morsel of affection": ✻4.

G. H. Lewes, "*Ruth* and *Villette*" (*Westminster Rev.*, 1853)—CB's genius and George Sand: LIX, 485–91; see George Eliot.

The Brontës: Their Lives, Friendships and Correspondence, ed. T. J. Wise & J. A. Symington (Shakespeare Head Brontë, 1932)—CB on Stowe, slavery: IV, 14.

Franklin Gary, "CB and George Henry Lewes" (*PMLA,* June 1936)—Lewes: *passim*; CB on Austen: p. 531.

Mrs. Gaskell, *Life of CB* (1857)—CB on woman question: ✻21; newspaper reading, research: ✻6, ✻5, ✻18; Branwell's end: ✻13; *Villette's* Paul compared to *Emma's* Knightley: ✻26.

Winifred Gérin, *CB: Evolution of Genius* (1967)—"power and will to work": p. 353; payment from publisher: p. 346; as governess: p. 170.

W. M. Thackeray, "The Last Sketch" (introduction to posthumous publication of CB's fragment "Emma," *Cornhill Maga.* April 1860)—"passionate honour": p. 279 in WMT *Works* (Smith, Elder), IV, 279; Malcolm Elwin, *Thackeray* (1932), pp. 179–83, 231–33, 265–68; Sidney Lee, "CB in London" (*Brontë Soc.*, 1909).

H. Martineau, *Autobiography,* II, 22, 323.

A. C. Swinburne, *A Note on CB* (1894), pp. 10–13.

Brontë, Emily   1818–48   England   Novel, poems
Poems by C., Ellis, and A. Bell   1846
"High waving heather" [1836]—"Earth rising to heaven": lines 4–6.

Caroline F. E. Spurgeon, *Mysticism in English Literature* (1913), pp. 80–82; I. H. Buchen, "EB and the Metaphysics of Childhood and Love" (*NCF,* June 1967); C. W. Hatfield, ed., *Complete Poems of EJB* (1941).

"Cold in the earth" [1845]

Fannie E. Ratchford, *Gondal's Queen* (1955), p. 126 and *passim* for a reconstructed "novel in verse" from the poems which are all that survive from EB's juvenile and later fantasies; Naomi Lewis, *A Peculiar Music* (1971).

Wuthering Heights 1847 (text ed. David Daiches, Penguin 1965)—Catherine's journal: ✕3; "Terror made me cruel": ✕3; "I wish I were a girl":
✕12.

R. Kiely, *Romantic Novel* (1972), p. 233; J. Blondel, *EB* (1955), p. 385;
W. Thompson, "Infanticide and Sadism in *WH*" (*PMLA*, March 1963),
p. 69; Q. D. Leavis, "A Fresh Approach to *WH*," *Lectures in America*
(1969); I.-S. Ewbank, *Their Proper Sphere* (1966), ✕4; John Hewish,
EB (1972), pp. 148–55; E. B. Gose, *Imagination Indulged: Irrational*
(1972)—* Heathcliff and Hareton as examples of "transformation" or
"Beauty and the Beast" motif in Victorian fiction: ✕3; and cf. George
Sand's *Mauprat* and Mary Shelley's "Transformation."

Winifred Gérin, *EB: A Biography* (1971)—*Athenaeum* review: p. 210;
* possible Heathcliff source in Yorkshire family saga: pp. 77–80. (EB's
disinterest in the financial aspect of the Real here strikingly distinguishes
her from Charlotte Brontë.)

Broughton, Rhoda   1840–1920   England   Novels

Browning, Elizabeth Barrett   1806–61   England   Poems, letters
* For convenience the following material is all grouped under
Browning, although Barrett is the correct name for the first forty
years of her life and about half her published work, which made
her famous before she married Robert Browning in 1846. Her
full maiden name was Elizabeth Barrett Moulton-Barrett and she
liked signing herself EBB, initials which, part of her characteristic luck, marriage preserved.

The Battle of Marathon. A Poem, by E. B. Barrett   1820
"Glimpses into My Own Life and Literary Character" [1820] ed. W. S.
Peterson, *Browning Institute Studies* II (1974), pp. 121–33 (minor punctu-
ation changes by E.M.).
An Essay on Mind, with Other Poems   1826
Prometheus Bound. Translated from the Greek of Aeschylus   1833
The Seraphim, and Other Poems, by Elizabeth B. Barrett   1838
Contributions to *The Poems of Geoffrey Chaucer, Modernized* (ed. R. H.
Horne, 1841); *A New Spirit of the Age* (ed. RHH, 1844); *The
Athenaeum* ("Some Account of the Greek Christian Poets" 1842).
Poems by Elizabeth Barrett Barrett, 2 vols.   1844
  "The Cry of the Children" [*Blackwood's,* Aug. 1843]
  "To George Sand: A Desire"—"amid the lions . . . wings of swan."
  "To George Sand: A Recognition"—"True genius, but true woman!"
  "From Catarina to Camoens"
  "A Drama of Exile"—influence on Poe: F. & W. Boos, "A Source for the
  Rimes of Poe's 'The Raven'" (*MWJ*, May 1974); Lola L. Szladits & John
  D. Gordan, *Joint Lives: EB & RB* (Berg Collection, NYPL, 1975)—
  * Poe's dedication of *The Raven* (1845) to EBB and her comment ("What

is to be said, I wonder, when a man calls you the 'noblest of your sex'? 'Sir, you are the most discerning of yours.'"): pp. 13–14.

Sonnets from the Portuguese [1845ff.] in *Poems* by Elizabeth Barrett Browning, new ed. 1850—"O liberal": ⚹8; "My letters": ⚹28; "And wilt thou have me": ⚹13; "Belovèd, dost thou love?": ⚹30; "If I leave all": ⚹35; "How do I love thee?": ⚹43; "Behold and see": ⚹5; "spread wing and fly": ⚹15; "look surprise": ⚹3; "When our two souls": ⚹22; "a mystic Shape": ⚹1.

Virginia Radley, *EBB* (1972)—writing *SftP:* p. 90; Susan Zimmerman, *"SftP:* A Negative and a Positive Context" (*MWN,* Dec. 1973).

Aurora Leigh, by Elizabeth Barrett Browning 1856/57.

> * Advertised and published late in 1856, but the first edition is dated 1857. The order of quotations below is roughly that in which they are made in this book; the text is *The Complete Poetical Works of EBB* (Cambridge Edition, Boston, 1900); § refers to the Book of *AL,* and the number following to the *first* line of the passage cited.

"Deal with us nobly": §5, 82; heavenly, Aurora imagery: §8, 310, 339, 375, 419 and §9, 500, 564, 814; "keep quiet by the fire": §1, 436; "The critics say that epics": §5, 139; "unscrupulously epic": §5, 213; "a woman and a queen": §8, 331; "Therefore come": §6, 475; "Those marriage-bells": §7, 459: Marian Erle's journey to brothel: §6, 1185; "I'm plain at speech": §8, 1127; "bounded forth": §2, 18; other walking metaphors: §2, 104, 253, 581; crowning scene: §2, 33; "The name/Is royal": §1, 934; London life: §3; "I broke the copious curls": §1, 385; "Italy/Is one thing": §1, 626; "She liked a woman to be womanly": §1, 443; "All the fields": §1, 629; "cage-bird life": §1, 304; "Not my headlong leaps": §1, 617.

A. C. Swinburne, *"AL"* [preface to 1898 edition], A.C.S., *Prose Works* (1925), VI, 5; E. Montégut, "Un Poème de la vie moderne" (*RDM,* March 15, 1857, pp. 334–37); Taine correspondence on *AL* and EBB with Sand (*RDM,* Jan. 15, 1933), pp. 336–38.

Poems before Congress 1860—"A Curse for a Nation" [Boston, *Liberty Bell,* 1856]
Last Poems 1862

Elizabeth Barrett to Miss Mitford, ed. Betty Miller (1954)—*Indiana* "brilliant": p. 156; Sand not *"second* to any genius": p. 146; book-sending project: p. 225.
The Letters of Robert Browning and EBB, ed. E. Kintner (1969)—on Sand: I, 113–14, 159; RB's first letter: I, 3–7; writing "novel-poem": I, 31.
Elizabeth Barrett to Mr. Boyd, ed. B. P. McCarthy (1955)—*Corinne:* p. 176.

Gardner B. Taplin, *Life of EBB* (1957)—chronology: pp. 456–64; laureate nomination: p. 226; on Stowe's *UTC:* p. 352; on Sand: p. 130;

Alethea Hayter, *Mrs. Browning* (1962)—bird imagery: pp. 100–1; Thackeray and "materfamilias": p. 183; Betty Miller, *Robert Browning* (1952)—early domestic life: pp. 75–85; Dorothy Hewlett, *EBB* (1953)—on women and slavery: p. 269; Frederick S. Boas, "EBB," *From Richardson to Pinero* (1936)—as novel reader: p. 154; popularity in America, England: p. 187; J. H. Buckley, *Victorian Temper* (1964)—"spasmodics": pp. 42–64; Patricia Thomson, "Elizabeth Barrett and George Sand" (*Durham U. Jnl.*, c. 1974).

Brunton, Mary   1778–1818   Scotland   Novels

Self-Control: a Novel 1811—selling paintings: I, 54–56; father's order "no more of this traffic" by which heroine "degraded into an artist": I, 198; Canadian adventure: II, 417ff.

    Gina Luria, Intro. *S-C* (Garland Pub. reprint, 1974); Brammer, "C. Brontë," p. 200.

Emmeline . . . memoir of her life . . . correspondence, ed. Alexander Brunton 1819—heroines as dolls: pp. xxxi–xxxii.

Buck, Pearl   1892–1973   America, China   Novels

The Good Earth 1931; screenplay by Tess Slesinger.

Burgos, Julia de   1916–53   Puerto Rico   Poems

    Carmen Conde, *Once Grandes Poetisas Americohispanas* (1967)—anthology and account of twentieth-century Spanish-American women poets.

Burnett, Frances Hodgson   1849–1924   America, England   Children's books, novels

That Lass o' Lowries 1877
Little Lord Fauntleroy 1886
Sara Crewe 1887
In the Closed Room 1904
The Secret Garden 1911—moor landscape: ¾3; the garden: ¾27.

    Ann Thwaite, *FHB* (1974)—begins gardening late in life: p. 182; Manchester childhood: ¾1.

Burney, Fanny   1752–1840   England   Novels, diaries, letters

Early Diary [1768–78], ed. Annie Raine Ellis 1889
Evelina, or, The History of a Young Lady's Entrance into the World 1778

    E. Montague & L. L. Martz, "FB's *E*," *Age of Johnson* (1949)

"The Witlings. A Comedy. By a Sister of the Order" [1779; ms. Berg, NYPL]
Cecilia, or Memoirs of an Heiress 1782—"Pride and Prejudice": III, ¾10.
Camilla: or, A Picture of Youth 1796

Joyce Hemlow, "FB and the Courtesy Books" (*PMLA*, 1950), pp. 732–61; E. A. & L. D. Bloom, Intro. *Camilla* (1972).

"A Busy Day" [unpublished comedy, 1800]

M. E. Adelstein, *FB* (1968), p. 112.

The Wanderer; or, Female Difficulties 1814
Diary and Letters of Madame d'Arblay, ed. Charlotte Barrett 1842–46

T. B. Macaulay review [Jan. 1843], in his *Essays Contrib. to Edinburgh Rev.* (1865), III, 389–91.

Journals and Letters, ed. Joyce Hemlow (1972ff.)—FB on de Staël: II, 10–26; on Genlis: I, 218 & IV, 483.

Joyce Hemlow, *History of FB* (1958)—Crisp letters: p. 44; Sheridan, father, Crisp and plays: ⅓5; ⅓12; earnings: pp. 87, 148, 196; subscribers: p. 250; mastectomy letter [1812]: pp. 321–24.

T. C. D. Eaves & B. D. Kimpel, *Samuel Richardson* (1971)—*Grandison* collaboration: pp. 359, 412–13; SR to M. Collier: p. 204; female circle: p. 537 & passim; Clara L. Thomson, *Samuel Richardson* (1900) —SR on "the characters of women": pp. 7–8; influence on FB: pp. 269–70.

Calisher, Hortense   **America**   **Novels, stories**

Carlyle, Jane Welsh   1801–66   Scotland, England   Letters
Letters and Memorials, ed. T. Carlyle & J. A. Froude 1883
New Letters and Memorials, ed. A. Carlyle 1903—on *Shirley:* II, 4–6.

R. A. Jones, "Mme de Staël": pp. 408–10; see Woolf, G. Jewsbury.
Thomas Carlyle, *On Heroes, Hero-Worship* (1841)—hero as king: ⅓6.

Cather, Willa   1873–1947   America   Novels, stories
Criticism and reviews 1893–1902, mostly in Nebraska and Pittsburgh periodicals, collected in *The Kingdom of Art: WC's First Principles and Critical Statements, 1893–1896,* ed. Bernice Slote (1966)—* (*KA*) and in *The World and the Parish: WC's Articles and Reviews, 1893–1902,* ed. W. M. Curtin (1970)—* (*WP*)—on Rossetti: *KA,* pp. 346–49 & *WP,* pp. 142–46; on Sand: *KA* & *WP* index.
Early stories, in *Collected Short Fiction, 1892–1912,* ed. Virginia Faulkner & Mildred R. Bennett (1970)—* (*CSF*)—"Tommy, the Unsentimental" [1896]—tomboy heroine: pp. 473ff.; "Nanette: An Aside" [1897]—opera singer on "merciless artist": p. 410; "A Death in the Desert" [1903]; "A Wagner Matinee" [1904]—opera, landscape: p. 239; "Paul's Case" [1905]; "The Enchanted Bluff" [1909]—sandbar landscape: p. 70.
April Twilights 1903 (text: *AT: Poems by WC,* ed. B. Slote, 1968)—"Dedicatory to R.C.C. and C.D.C.": pp. 3, 53–54.
The Troll Garden 1905 (WC's first collection of stories; see *CSF*)

Rossetti epigraph: see WC: *KA,* p. 346.

Alexander's Bridge   1912
O Pioneers!   1913—Alexandra's farm: §2, ⊁1; "history of every country" and "spirit of Divide": §1, ⊁5; violence in the garden: §4, ⊁7.
Uncle Valentine and Other Stories   [1915–29], ed. B. Slote (1973)
The Song of the Lark   1915, revised ed. 1937—Preface [1932]; "she is uncommon": §2, ⊁8; "her secret—passion": §6, ⊁2; Harsanyi discovers voice: §2, ⊁3; eagle metaphor: §4, ⊁5; Panther Canyon: §4, ⊁2, ⊁3, ⊁4, ⊁6.

> R. Giannone, *Music in WC's Fiction* (1968)—opera: ⊁5; B. Slote, Intro. to *KA*—metaphor: pp. 85–89.

My Ántonia   1918—"rich mine of life," "common things": §5, ⊁1; "incommunicable past": §5, ⊁3; "nothing but land": §1, ⊁1.
Youth and the Bright Medusa (stories)   1922
One of Ours   1922
A Lost Lady   1923—"life on any terms": §2, ⊁9; "Beautiful women": §1, ⊁7; blinding bird in garden: §1, ⊁2; lust in garden: §1, ⊁7 & §2, ⊁9; Niel on Ovid's *Heroides:* §1, ⊁7.

> Ovid, *The Heroides* (Loeb Classics, with G. Showerman trans.); W. S. Anderson, "The *H:* Heroine as Elegaic Figure" in *Greek & Latin Studies: Ovid*, ed. J. W. Binns (1973), pp. 64–67 & passim; Heinrich Dörrie, "L'Épître Héroïque dans les littératures modernes" (*RLC*, 1966)—on death of tradition in 19th century, and "proper" trans. of Ovid's full title, *Epistulae Heroidum* (or, "Heroines' Letters") as "Heroical Epistles" or "Heldenbriefe": pp. 48–64; H. Jacobson, *O's Heroides* (1974)—"ille novavit opus," O's boast in the *Amores* of his originality in the *Heroides:* p. 4; Simone Weil: pp. 40–41; Camille A. Paglia, "Lord Hervey & Pope" (*ECS*, Spring 1973), pp. 357–58; R. A. Day, *Told in Letters* (1966)—18th c. vogue: pp. 11–13.

The Professor's House   1925—dressmaker dummies: §1, ⊁1; mesa landscape: §2, ⊁1, ⊁2; return to earth: §3, ⊁2.

> Leon Edel, *Literary Biography* (1957), pp. 61–80.

My Mortal Enemy   1926—Myra Henshawe: §1, ⊁1.
Death Comes for the Archbishop   1927—"something soft and wild": §9, ⊁3.
Shadows on the Rock   1931
Obscure Destinies   1932—"Old Mrs. Harris"—"what are families for": ⊁13.
Lucy Gayheart   1935
Not Under Forty   1935—"Miss Jewett" (1925 preface to S. O. Jewett's stories).
Sapphira and the Slave Girl   1940—"seat of privilege": §1, ⊁2.
The Old Beauty and Others (stories)   1948

> James Woodress, *WC: Her Life and Art* (1970)—Jewett: p. 254; Isabelle McClung: pp. 173, 178, 189; 1912 journey west: pp. 149–54; Fremstad on *SotL:* p. 170; Sand portrait: p. 243; Maxwell Geismar, *Last of the Provincials* (1947)—complexity of WC: pp. 155–83; B. Slote &

Lucia Woods, *WC: A Pictorial Memoir* (1973); Henry Nash Smith, *Virgin Land: The American West as Symbol and Myth* (1950)—garden and desert: ⍟16; Eugene O'Neill, *Long Day's Journey* [1941], §4.

Catherwood, Mary   1847–1902   America   Novels

Chapone, Hester Mulso   1727–1801   England   Poems, tales, essays
Letters on the Improvement of the Mind   1774

Child, Lydia Maria   1802–80   America   Journalism, novels
An Appeal in Behalf of That Class of Americans called Africans   1833
Biography of Mme de Staël   1836—"Homage": p. 68.
Letters from New York   (Boston *Courier*) 1843, 1845
Flowers for Children   1844–46—including national Thanksgiving poem, "Over the river, and through the wood . . ."

M. Meltzer, *LMC* (1965)—*worst punishment inflicted on an outspoken literary woman: LMC barred (for her abolitionist *Appeal* of 1833) from the Boston Atheneum library: p. 35.

Chopin, Kate   1851–1904   America   Novels, stories
At Fault   1890
Bayou Folk (stories)   1894
A Night in Acadie (stories)   1897
The Awakening   1899—mother-women: ⍟4; meadow landscape: ⍟7, ⍟39; Mlle Reisz on artist's gifts, courage: ⍟21.

Per Seyersted, *KC* (1969)—*Corinne:* ⍟6; reads Lady Blessington on Byron & Staël: pp. 25–26; salon: p. 62; names daughter Lélia after Sand heroine: p. 65; Per Seyersted, ed. *Complete Works of KC* (1969); L. Leary, ed., KC, *Awakening* (1970)—sea, Whitman, bird imagery: Intro.; W. Gibson, "KC" (*TLS*, Oct. 9, 1970).

Chukovskaya, Lydia   Russia   Novels
The Deserted House   [1939–40] 1965; trans. A. B. Werth (1967)
Going Under, trans. P. M. Weston   (1972)

Colet, Louise   1808–76   France   Poems

Colette   1873–1954   France   Novels, memoirs

* All citations are to pages (for Colette rarely used chapter numbers) in the *Oeuvres Complètes*—* (*OC*) (Flammarion, 1948ff.). Virtually all her work has been or is being put into English by a variety of translators, whose work can be sampled in Robert Phelps's anthology *Earthly Paradise: C's Autobiography drawn from the writings of her lifetime* (1966).

Claudine à l'école 1900   *à Paris* 1901   *en ménage* 1902   *s'en va* 1903

    Claude Abastado, ed. *Les Claudine* (Willy et Colette)   (1969)

La Vagabonde   1910–11—farewell to men, *chichis: OC* IV, 212.

Mitsou, ou comment l'esprit vient auz filles   1919—name explained: *OC* V, 151.

Chéri   1920—adoption: *OC* VI, 17.

La Maison de Claudine   1922—Zola and birth: *OC* VII, 41–43; mother as "personnage": *OC* VII, 7–8 (Préface).

L'Enfant et les sortilèges   1925—libretto for Ravel.

La Fin de Chéri   1926

Sido   1929

Ces Plaisirs . . .   1932—later called *Le Pur et l'Impur.*

La Chatte   1933

Le Toutonnier   1939

Gigi   1944—"convenances": *OC* XIII, 8; "bas du corps": p. 26.

L'Étoile Vesper   1946 —George Sand at Work: *OC* XIII, 329 (David Le Vay trans., *Evening Star,* 1973, pp. 140–41); late pregnancy: *OC* XIII, 319–26; feminization of Baudelaire's "hypocrite lecteur": p. 301; photographs of freaks: pp. 230–33 (cf. Arbus).

Le Fanal bleu   1949

    Monique Cornand et al., *Colette* (BN, 1973)—chronologie; Margaret Crosland, *C* (1972)—Proust on *Mitsou:* pp. 125–26; Gide on *Chéri:* pp. 175–77; Elaine Marks, *C* (1960); Anne A. Ketchum, *C* (1968)— situation of French women in 1900: ⚹1; E. Moers, "Cather and C" (*World,* March 27, 1973).

Collyer, Mary   **17??–1763**   **England**   **Novels, translations**
    * Not to be confused with Fielding's and Richardson's friend, Margaret Collier.

Felicia to Charlotte   1744–50.

    E. Moers, "Richardson" (*NYRB,* Feb. 10, 1970); P. Van Tieghem, "Roman Sentimental" (*RLC,* 1940), pp. 134–35.

Colonna, Vittoria   **1492–1547**   **Italy**   **Poems**

Compton-Burnett, Ivy   **1892–1969**   **England**   **Novels**
Dolores   1911

    C. Burkhart, ed. *D* (1971)—literary background: Intro.

Pastors and Masters   1925

Brothers and Sisters   1929

A House and Its Head   1935

Manservant and Maidservant   (*Bullivant and the Lambs,* U.S.)   1947

A Heritage and Its History 1959
A God and His Gifts 1963

> Elizabeth Sprigge, *I C-B* (1973)—life with father: ⚡1; Sarraute: p. 148;
> "neuters": p. 83; F. Baldanza, *I C-B* (1964); Hilary Spurling, *Ivy When
> Young* (1973)—"pelvic power": p. 67; see Mary McCarthy.

Corelli, Marie   1855–1924   England   Novels

Corinna   ?6th to 3rd century? B.C.   Greece   Poems

> Mme de Staël, note 11 to *Corinne*—C teacher of Pindar; D. L. Page,
> *Corinna* (1953); S. Richardson, *Sir Charles Grandison,* ed. Jocelyn
> Harris (1972)—"title of *Wit* and *Poetess* disgraced by Sappho's and
> Corinna's": I, 431; 18th c. references: ed. note, I, 481; writing to
> moment defined: III, 24, n. 475.

Craik, Dinah Maria Mulock   1826–87   England   Novels

Davis, Rebecca Harding   1831–1910   America   Novels, stories
Life in the Iron Mills 1861
Margret Howth 1861–62

> Tillie Olsen, "RHD: A Biographical Interpretation," RHD, *Iron Mills*
> (Feminist Press, 1972).

Delany, Mary   1700–88   England   Letters

Desbordes-Valmore, Marceline   1786–1859   France   Poems

> George-Day, "Romantisme et poésie féminine" (*Europe,* Nov. 1964).

Deutsch, Babette   America   Poems, translations

Deutsch, Helene   Austria, America   Psychoanalysis
Psychology of Women, A Psychoanalytic Interpretation 1944–45—Sand: I,
⚡8 ("The 'Active' Woman: The Masculinity Complex").
Confrontations with Myself 1973—early study of Sand: p. 202; motherhood
combined with medical career (* a much needed doctor in World War I
Vienna, she was given an empty room beside her office in which to install
her newborn baby and a nurse, and allowed to tether two goats in the clinic
courtyard): pp. 123–25; astonished that more women don't enter psychoanalysis, "*par excellence* a profession for women": p. 209.

Dickinson, Emily   1830–86   America   Poems
Poems [1850–86] 1890, 1891, 1896 (ed. Todd, Higginson); 1914ff. (ed.
Bianchi); 1945 (*Bolts of Melody,* ed. Todd, Bingham); 1955 (*The Com-*

plete Poems, ordered, numbered, and dated by Thomas H. Johnson)—
⊁312: "Her 'last Poems'"; ⊁875: "I stepped from Plank"; ⊁280: "I
felt a Funeral"; ⊁593: "I think I was enchanted"; ⊁704: "Rearrange a
Wife's"; ⊁712: "Because I could not"; ⊁1072: "Title Divine" (cf. ⊁296,
⊁815, ⊁491); ⊁1737: "Blush my spirit"; ⊁506: "He touched me";
⊁664: "Of all the Souls"; ⊁373: "I'm saying every day"; ⊁405: "I am
not used to Hope"; ⊁540: "I took my Power."

Letters of ED, ed. T. H. Johnson   (1958)—"women, queens": II, 376; "unmentioned mourner": II, 410; "Mrs. Hunt's Poems": II, 491.

T. W. Higginson, "ED's Letters" (*Atlantic Monthly,* Oct. 1891) in
R. N. Linscott, ed., *Selected Poems & Letters of ED* (1959)—war an
"oblique place": p. 12; "dog large as myself": p. 7.
Jay Leyda, *Years and Hours of ED* (1960)—Sand: II, 37, 148; J. E.
Walsh, *Hidden Life of ED* (1971)—pp. 98–102, 130–32, 257–60;
Rebecca Patterson, "E. Browning & ED" (Kansas State TC *Educational
Leader,* July 1956); Jack L. Capps, *ED's Reading* (1966)—"intimate
kinship": p. 77; metaphors: pp. 84–85 & passim; R. B. Sewall, ed., *ED
Critical Essays* (1963)—Blackmur: p. 87; W. M. Gibson, "ED," *Lit.
Hist. of U.S.,* ed. Spiller (4th ed.); T. W. Higginson, "Americanism,"
Studies in History and Letters (1900)—passim: p. 228.

Didion, Joan   **America**   **Novels, essays**
Play It As It Lays   1970

Dinesen, Isak   1885–1962   Denmark, England, America   Tales
* Her maiden name was Karen Blixen, her native language
Danish. In a way too complicated to schematize, she wrote in
both languages and signed her books with both her pseudonym,
ID, and her maiden name (but never with her title by marriage
or her married name, which resembled her own, as she married
a cousin). Only dates and titles of first English-language editions,
some of which appeared in New York, some in London, are
given.

Seven Gothic Tales   1934

E. O. Johanneson, *World of ID* (1961)—Gothic Tale: ⊁2; see
McCullers.

Out of Africa   1937—African landscape: §1, ⊁1; heroine sups on claret: §3,
⊁8; entertains heroes: §1, ⊁2; breaks fields: §3, ⊁2; "governed in
earnest": §2, ⊁5.
Winter's Tales   1942
Last Tales   1957
Anecdotes of Destiny   1958
Shadows on the Grass   1961
Ehrengard   1963

R. Langbaum, *ID* (1964); D. Hannah, *ID* (1971).

H.D. (Hilda Doolittle)   1886–1961   America   Poems

Drabble, Margaret   England   Novels, criticism
Jerusalem the Golden 1967—intelligent girl as freak: ⚭1; "tender blurred
   world": ⚭9; death of mother: ⚭9.
The Waterfall 1969—Emily Dickinson & drowning: ⚭1; breast-feeding: ⚭2.

Duras, Marguerite   France   Novels

Lady Eastlake (Elizabeth Rigby)   1809–93   England   Art criticism
Anonymous review of *Jane Eyre, Vanity Fair*, and Report of Governesses'
   Benevolent Institution (*Quarterly Rev.*, Dec. 1848)—Becky/Jane com-
   parison: pp. 154–60; radical "tone of mind": p. 174; "forfeited society":
   p. 176.
"Mme de Staël" (*Quarterly Rev.*, July 1881)

Eden, Emily   1797–1869   England   Novels
The Semi-attached Couple 1860

Edgeworth, Maria   1767–1849   Ireland, England   Novels, pedagogy
Letters for Literary Ladies 1795—Gina Luria, Intro., *LfLL* (Garland, 1974).
Castle Rackrent 1800—G. Watson, Intro., *CR* (Oxford, 1964).
Belinda; Early Lessons; Moral Tales 1801
Leonora 1806
Tales of Fashionable Life 1809, 1812
The Absentee 1812

Letters from England 1813–44, ed. Christina Colvin (1971)—on de Staël:
   pp. 49, 254; Genlis translation [1783]: p. xxxviii.

   Isabel C. Clarke, *ME* (1949)—Genlis: p. 33; influence on Scott: pp.
   57–58; Vineta Colby, *Yesterday's Woman* (1974), ⚭3.

George Eliot   1819–80   England   Novels
          * Born Mary Ann Evans, which she preferred to spell Marian;
          published, translated, edited anonymously, mostly for John
          Chapman's *Westminster Review*—* (*WR*), also for the *Leader*
          edited by George Henry Lewes, whom she met in 1851 and lived
          with from 1854; published as George Eliot from 1857.
"Woman in France" (*WR*, Oct. 1854)—on de Staël, Sand, "Gallic race,"
   adultery: pp. 450–51; "Margaret Fuller and Mary Wollstonecraft" (*Leader*,
   Oct. 13, 1855), pp. 988–89; "Belles Lettres" (*WR*, Jan. 1856)—on
   Villette, "which we, at least, would rather read for the third time than most
   new novels for the first": p. 301; "Art and Belles Lettres" (*WR*, April
   1856)—witty response to Stendhal on the *femme-auteur* in *De L'Amour*,
   II, ⚭55: p. 649; "Silly Novels by Lady Novelists" (*WR*, Oct. 1856)—on

Stowe: p. 457; "Belles Lettres" (*WR*, Oct. 1856)—on *Dred:* pp. 571–73; "Belles Lettres" (*WR*, Jan. 1857)—on *Aurora Leigh:* pp. 306–10.

Thomas Pinney, ed., *Essays of GE* (1963)—partial reprints, bibliography.

Scenes of Clerical Life 1858 ["Amos Barton" 1857; "Mr. Gilfil's Love-Story" 1857; "Janet's Repentance" 1857]

G. H. Lewes, "Novels of Jane Austen" (*Blackwood's,* July 1859), p. 104.

Adam Bede 1859—night school: ✗21; "people . . . you should tolerate": ✗17; invitation to enter farmhouse: ✗6; Dinah's sermon: ✗2; Hetty's jewels: ✗22.

The Mill on the Floss 1860—"Red Deeps": §5, ✗1; *Corinne:* §5; ✗4; Maggie's arm: §6, ✗10; "Shakespeare and everything": §6, ✗3; "dark-eyed nymph": §6, ✗2; bazaar: §6, ✗9; chicken aunts: §1, ✗9.

Swinburne, *Charlotte Brontë* (1894), pp. 32–34.

Silas Marner 1861
Romola 1862–63
Felix Holt the Radical 1866
The Spanish Gypsy 1868
Armgart [*Macmillan's,* July 1871] in *Poems* (New York, n.d.)—"Am I a sage": ✗1; "seek the woman": ✗2.
Middlemarch, a Study of Provincial Life 1871–72—Dorothea on costs: ✗83; on male ignorance: ✗2; "Prelude": see under St. Teresa; medicine as ideal profession: ✗15; Mary Garth on man's work, also *Corinne:* ✗14 (* and note that when she writes a book after marrying Fred, it is attributed to her husband, who "might have been a clergyman if he had chosen": ✗Finale); Dorothea's voice: ✗9, ✗56; in Rome: ✗19; her entrance: ✗43; her jewel-case: ✗1.
Daniel Deronda 1876—"slavery of being a girl": ✗51; Gwendolen's gold star: ✗10; gambling: ✗1; planning to be artist: ✗23; Klesmer: ✗23.
Impressions of Theophrastus Such 1879—Shaw's reference and account of Lewes: GBS, *Our Theatres in the Nineties* (1932), II, 162.

The GE Letters, ed. Gordon S. Haight (1954)—to Stowe on *Deronda:* V, 301–2; reading her letter: II, 92; writing her: V, 322ff.; on Casaubon: V, 322; "How I Came to Write Fiction": II, 406–7; reading *Emma:* II, 327–28; quoting Margaret Fuller: II, 15; reads *Corinne:* I, 71 & II, 31; on Rousseau: I, 277; on Sand: I, 277–78; on *Villette:* II, 87, 91–93.

Gordon S. Haight, *GE: A Biography* (1968)—Robert Evans: ✗1; reading Sand: pp. 59–60; compared to Sand (*Consuelo*): p. 335; by Turgenev: p. 513; by Norton: p. 410; by Myers: pp. 450–51.
G. S. Haight, *GE and John Chapman* (1940); Anna T. Kitchel, *George Lewes and GE* (1933); K. A. McKenzie, *Edith Simcox and GE* (1961) —"uncanny": p. 97; Patricia Thomson, "The Three Georges" (*NCF,* Sept. 1963); P. G. Blount, "Reputation of George Sand" (1961), ✗6; M. C. G. Gray, "GS, Gottfried Keller, GE" (M.A. thesis, Indiana U.,

1965)—rustic novel tradition; Alice R. Kaminsky, "GE, GH Lewes and the Novel" (*PMLA*, Dec. 1955); J. P. Couch, *GE in France* (1967)— *Romola* compared to *Corinne:* p. 33; GE compared to Sand: pp. 57, 63, 74, 110, 117.

Ferber, Edna   1887–1968   America   Novels, memoirs

Fern, Fanny   1811–72   America   Sketches, tales

Ferrier, Susan Edmonstone   1782–1854   Scotland   Novels

Fielding, Sarah   1710–68   England   Novels
Adventures of David Simple 1744–53

Flanner, Hildegarde   America   Poems
If There Is Time 1942—"Hawk Is a Woman": anthologized in Ann Stanford, *Women Poets in English* (1972).

Foster, Hannah   1759–1840   America   Novels
The Coquette 1797
    Spiller, Thorpe, *Literary History of the U.S.* (1963), p. 178.

Frame, Janet   New Zealand   Novels
Faces in the Water 1961
The Edge of the Alphabet 1962
Intensive Care 1970

Frank, Anne   1929–March 1945   Holland   Diary
Het Achterhuis [1942–44] 1947; trans. B. M. Moyaart—Doubleday, as *The Diary of a Young Girl* 1952—* "feeling like a songbird whose wings have been clipped and who is hurling himself in utter darkness against the bars of his cage": Oct. 29, 1943.
Verhalen Rondom Het Achterhuis [1942–44] 1960; trans. as *Tales From the House Behind* 1960—tales, stories; and a girl's novel.

Freeman, Mary Wilkins   1852–1930   America   Novels, stories

Fuller, Margaret   1810–50   America   Essays
"The Great Lawsuit. Man versus Men. Woman versus Women," *The Dial*, July 1843, in Alice Rossi, *Feminist Papers* (1974), pp. 144–82.
Woman in the Nineteenth Century 1845; . . . *and Kindred Papers* 1855— woman and slave: p. 37; heroism: pp. 56–58; Wollstonecraft: pp. 77– 78; Eloisa. pp. 77–78; "Female Authorship" and de Staël: pp. 93–94; Sand essays: pp. 228–48.

Memoirs of Margaret Fuller Ossoli, ed. Emerson, Channing et al. 1852; London ed. in 3 vols. (read by George Eliot) 1852—"With the intellect I always have, always shall, overcome; but . . . The life, the life! O, my God! shall the life never be sweet?" [Journal, 1844]: II, 5; *Corinne* and de Staël: I, 67–68, 286–87 & II, 172–73; Sand visited [Letters, 1847]: III, 108–17; Sand read: II, 16–24.

T. W. Higginson, *MFO* (1890)—Mrs. Browning's Italy: pp. 220, 314; R. N. Hudspeth, *Ellery Channing* (1973)—MF's industry compared to her brother-in-law's improvidence: pp. 24–25, 32–33; M. Wade, *MF* (1940); Perry Miller, ed., *MF Selection* (1963); Emerson, "The Poet" [1844], *Representative Men;* see George Eliot, B. von Arnim.

Garnett, Constance   1861–1946   England   Translations

Gaskell, Elizabeth Cleghorn   1810–65   England   Novels,

**   stories, biography**

Mary Barton: A Tale of Manchester Life 1848—John Barton a Communist: ✳15; JB on labor and capital: ✳6; as Chartist: ✳8, ✳9; "by-play" of caricature: ✳16; "feeling of alienation": ✳8; singer as professional: ✳8.

Karl Marx, "The English Middle Class" (*NY Daily Tribune,* Aug. 1, 1854), p. 4; I. M. Katarsky, Foreword (trans. for E.M. by S. Hoffman) to EG, *MB* (Moscow, 1956), pp. 15–16; K. Tillotson, *Novels of 1840s* (1954) §2, ✳2; Martha Vicinus, "Literary Voices of Manchester," *Victorian City,* ed. Dyos & Wolff (1973)—working-class poetry & EG: pp. 748–50; S. Marcus, *Engels, Manchester, and the Working Class* (1974)—EG compared to Engels: pp. 48–49, 71, 99; Louis Cazamian, *Social Novel,* trans. M. Fido (1973)—compared to Tonna: pp. 240, 340.

Cranford 1851–53
Ruth 1853
North and South 1854–55
The Life of Charlotte Brontë 1857—woman author's credo: ✳16; CB as a bird: ✳6; see under CB.
Sylvia's Lovers 1863
Wives and Daughters 1864–66

Letters of Mrs. Gaskell, ed. J. A. V. Chapple and A. Pollard (1966)—"see all Quarterlies": p. 567.

Aina Rubenius, *The Woman Question in Mrs. G's Life and Works* (Upsala/Harvard, 1950)—and Mrs. Tonna: pp. 62–63, 281–83; earning and spending: pp. 31–32; Marie Belloc Lowndes, "*I Too Have Lived in Arcadia*" (1942)—friendship with Bessie Parkes: p. 11; A. B. Hopkins, *EG: Her Life and Work* (1952); Wanda Neff, *Victorian Working Women* (1929), pp. 82–87.

Mme de Genlis   1746–1830   France   Tales, pedagogy
Le Théâtre de l'éducation 1779

> Fanny Kemble, *Girlhood*—popularity of performances in England: I, 3–4.

Adèle et Théodore; ou, Lettres sur l'éducation 1782—Genlis denying self-portrait: 4th ed., 1804, Préface, p. xxx; *Adelaide and Theodore, or Letters on Education*, trans. "by some ladies" 1784—Almane/Ostalis relationship: I, 15–17; maternal legacy: III, 282–83.

> P. Fauchery, *La Destinée féminine dans le roman européen du 18e siècle* (1972), pp. 98–99, 142–43, 405–6, 492–93.

Les Veillées du Château, ou Cours de morale à l'usage des enfans 1784, trans. Thomas Holcroft as *Tales of the Castle, or Stories of Instruction and Delight* c. 1785 (* complete editions of both being difficult to find and use, I have had to compare an 1826 Genlis edition with two editions of the Holcroft translation [London: Robinson, 3rd ed., in 5 vols., 1787, and London: Walker & Edwards, ?2 vols., 1817] from which all my English citations are drawn)—father's departure: first page of all eds.; mother's punishment, and moral on virtue: "frame" before and after "The Brazier; or Reciprocal Gratitude" ("Le Chaudronnier, ou la reconnoissance réciproque"); "benevolence true happiness": "frame" after "The Heroism of Attachment" ("L'Héroïsme de l'attachement"); spoiled girl: opening and close of "Delphine; or, the Fortunate Cure" ("Delphine ou l'heureuse guérison").

Lessons of a Governess to Her Pupils: or, Journal of the Method adopted by [Mme de Genlis] in the Education of the Children of M. d'ORLÉANS, First Prince of the Blood-Royal (anon. trans., London: Robinson, 1792).
De l'Influence des femmes sur la littérature française 1811
Les Battuécas 1816—see Sand on this radical utopia: *Hist. Vie*, §2, ⚹16.

> Sainte-Beuve, "Oeuvres de Madame de Genlis," *Causeries du lundi* III [Oct. 14, 1850]; Jules Janin on Genlis (*Athenaeum*, May 6, 1837), p. 323; Violet Wyndham, *MdG: A Biography* (1958)—honors: pp. 88, 103; L. Chabaud, *Les Précurseurs du Féminisme* (1901), pp. 208, 218–19; Anna Nikliborc, "MdG contre Mme de Staël" (*Breslau Universytet Actei*, 1968), pp. 47–49; see Hemlow, "Courtesy Books" and Eaves & Kimpel, *Richardson*, pp. 525–27 under Fanny Burney; see under Hemans, Sand, Wollstonecraft, More, Austen, Lady Morgan, Staël, Edgeworth.

Gilliatt, Penelope   English   Novels, stories
A State of Change 1967
Come Back If It Doesn't Get Better 1969
Sunday, Bloody Sunday 1971
Nobody's Business 1972

Gilman, Charlotte Perkins   1860–1935   America   Economics, fiction
The Yellow Wallpaper 1892

> Elaine R. Hedges, Afterword, Feminist Press ed. (1973); re Thackeray—
> Dr. S. Cobb, "Psychiatric Case History of Isabella Shawe Thackeray,"
> App. 7, *Letters of WMT*, ed. G. N. Ray (1945–46).

Women and Economics 1898

Ginzburg, Natalia   Italy   Novels
L'Inserzione (play), trans. H. Reed as *The Advertisement*   (1969)
Caro Michele, trans. S. Cudahy as *No Way*   (1974)

Giovanni, Nikki   America   Poems
*Gemini; An Extended Autobiographical Statement on My First Twenty-Five
    Years of Being a Black Poet* 1971—birth: ⚥5.

Glasgow, Ellen   1873–1945   America   Novels

Godden, Rumer   India, England   Novels, stories

Gordimer, Nadine   South Africa   Novels, stories

Gore, Catherine   1799–1861   England   Novels
Pin-Money 1831—Austen: Preface; money, marriage, divorce: I, 21–23.
Cecil; or the Adventures of a Coxcomb 1841
Cecil, a Peer 1841
Peers and Parvenus 1846
Men of Capital 1846

> Leigh Hunt, "Blue-Stocking Revels" [1837], *Poetical Works,* ed. Milford
> (1923)—Gore: §2; and passim for virtually every woman writer of prose
> or poetry in the early nineteenth century; E. Moers, *The Dandy* (1960),
> pp. 254–56; see Lady Morgan.

Gould, Lois   America   Wit

Green, Hannah (Joanne Greenberg)   America   Novels, stories
I Never Promised You a Rose Garden (HG)   1964
The Monday Voices (JG)   1965
Rites of Passage (JG)   1972

Green, Hannah   America   Novels
The Dead of the House 1972

Hall, Radclyffe   1886–1943   England   Novels

Hansberry, Lorraine   1930–65   America   Plays, prose
A Raisin in the Sun   1959
To Be Young, Gifted and Black, adapted by Robert Nemiroff   1969—"wish to
   live": Foreword.

Hardwick, Elizabeth   America   Criticism, novels

Hays, Mary   1759?–1843   England   Novels, treatises
Memoirs of Emma Courtney   1796
Appeal to the Men of Great Britain in Behalf of Women   1798

Haywood, Eliza   1693?–1756   England   Novels, journalism
Love in Excess   1719
*Anti-Pamela: or, Feign'd Innocence Detected: Syrena's Adventures publish'd
   as a Caution to all Young Gentlemen*   1741

> B. Kreissman, *Pamela-Shamela: Richardson Parodies* (1960), p. 24.

Ed. *The Female Spectator*   1744–46
The History of Betsy Thoughtless   1751

Hellman, Lillian   America   Plays, memoirs
The Children's Hour   1934
Days to Come   1936
The Little Foxes   1939
Watch on the Rhine   1941
The Searching Wind   1944
Another Part of the Forest   1946
Toys in the Attic   1960
An Unfinished Woman   1969
Pentimento   1973

> R. Moody, *LH* (1972); E. Moers, "Family Theater" (*Commentary,*
> Sept. 1972)—review of LH, *Collected Plays* (1972).

Héloïse   c. 1101–64   France   Letters
> Étienne Gilson, *Heloise and Abelard,* trans. L. K. Shook (1960)—on
> Latin text, dating, translations, authenticity, importance of letters; Eliza-
> beth Hamilton, *Héloïse* (1967)—education, youth: pp. 13, 29; R. A.
> Day, *Told in Letters* (1966)—eighteenth-century vogue: p. 33; G. H.
> Lewes, review of C. de Remusat, *Abelard* (*For. Qu. Rev.,* 1846)—in
> love with H.: p. 292; see Fuller, Wollstonecraft.

Hemans, Felicia   1793–1835   England   Poems
Memorials of Mrs. Hemans, ed. H. F. Chorley (1837)—*Corinne:* I, 296–97;
   premature praise for beauty, recitations: I, 12–14; "partial justice to
   powers": I, 23; Genlis: I, 30; see Maria Jane Jewsbury.

Hill, Carol   **America   Novels**
Let's Fall in Love   1974

Hippius, Zinaida   1869–1945   Russia   Poems
Poems [1893–1918] in V. Markov & M. Sparks, *Modern Russian Poetry:
An Anthology with Verse Translations* (1967)—"Flowers of Night": p.
59; "She": p. 71; "Spiders": p. 69; "What is Sin?": p. 67; "And After-
wards": p. 75.

> Helen Muchnic, ZH review (*NYRB*, March 23, 1972); Olga Matich,
> "Devil and Poetry" (*SEEJ*, Summer 1972); Temira Pachmuss, *ZH*
> (1971).

Howe, Julia Ward   1819–1910   America   Poems, treatises
"George Sand," *Atlantic Monthly*, Nov. 1861
"Battle-Hymn of the Republic," *Atlantic Monthly*, Feb. 1862.
Sex and Education   1874
Margaret Fuller   1883

Inchbald, Elizabeth   1753–1821   England   Plays, novels
A Simple Story   1791
Nature and Art   1796
Lovers' Vows   1798—EI's source in a trans. provided by the manager of
Covent Garden of Kotzebue's *Das Kind der Liebe*, 1788 (or "Child of
Love"): EI's Preface, printed with *LV* in R. W. Chapman, ed., *Mansfield
Park* (Austen's *Novels*, III).
To Marry or Not to Marry   1805

Ingelow, Jean   1820–97   England   Poems, fairy tales
Mopsa the Fairy   1869—sister-brother relation: pp. 60–61 (1964 ed.)

> Naomi Lewis, "A Lost Pre-Raphaelite" (*TLS*, Dec. 8, 1972); for fairy
> tales and women, cf. Alison Lurie, "Witches and Fairies" (*NYRB*, Dec.
> 2, 1971).

Jackson, Helen Hunt   1831–85   America   Novels, poems
Verses by H.H.   1870
Ramona   1884

Jackson, Shirley   1919–65   America   Novels, stories

James, Alice   1848–92   America   Diary
The Diary of AJ [1889–92], ed. Leon Edel (1934, 1964)—memory of
brothers: pp. 127–28; Edel on "small boys": p. 3.

Jameson, Anna   1794–1860   England, Canada   Criticism
The Diary of an Ennuyée   1826—Corinne: ⚡6.
Characteristics of Women or *Shakespeare's Heroines*   1832

Winter Studies and Summer Rambles in Canada   1838
Sacred and Legendary Art   1848
Letters of AJ to Ottilie von Goethe, ed. G. H. Needler (1939)

Clara Thomas, *AJ* (1967—Italian journey: ⚡2; *Corinne:* ⚡4; E. Moers, "AJ" (*VS,* March 1970), pp. 370–71.

Janeway, Elizabeth   **America**   **Novels, essays**

Jewett, Sarah Orne   1849–1909   America   Stories, novels
Schoolgirl annotations on her copy of *Corinne* (New York: Leavitt & Allen, 1862—in French) including the Charles Kingsley poem ("Be good sweet maid"): Houghton Library, HU
Deephaven   1877
A Country Doctor   1884
A White Heron and Other Stories   1886
The Country of the Pointed Firs   1896
Best Stories, ed. Willa Cather   1925

F. O. Matthiessen, *SOJ* (1929)—on mother's death: p. 94; P. J. Eakin, "SOJ" (*AL,* Jan. 1967).

Jewsbury, Geraldine   1812–80   England   Novels
Zoe   1845
The Half-Sisters   1848
Marian Withers   1851
Constance Herbert   1855

Selections from the Letters of GEJ to Jane Welsh Carlyle, ed. Ireland   1892
—marriage and husbands: p. 369.

Susanne Howe, *GJ* (1935)—G. H. Lewes: pp. 70, 100; Fanny Lewald: pp. 130–33; V. E. A. Bewley, "George Sand and GJ" (*RLC,* 1956), pp. 396–98; see Virginia Woolf.

Jewsbury, Maria Jane   1800–33   England   Poems, sketches
Three Histories   1829—on fame: quoted in R. A. Jones, "Mme de Staël," p. 413.
Autobiographical letter in *Memorials of Mrs. Hemans,* ed. Chorley, I, 162–71; * gifted oldest daughter of a large family, overburdened with domestic responsibilities, MJJ here provides a portrait of what Elizabeth Barrett might have been, without money or luck.

E. Gillett, *MJJ* (1932)—Wordsworth's advice on "female merit": xxiii.

Johnson, Pamela Hansford   **England   Novels**

Jong, Erica   **America   Poems**
Fruits and Vegetables   1971
Half-Lives   1973—"Evidence of life?": Prologue/The Evidence.

Fear of Flying (novel)   1974
Loveroot   1975

Julian of Norwich   c. 1342–?1416   England   Mysticism
> * Also styled Lady, Dame, Mother, sometimes Juliana, Anchoress
> of Norwich.

Revelations of Divine Love [c. 1373–93] 1670—hazel-nut metaphor: ※5
(trans. from Latin in Caroline Spurgeon, *Mysticism in English Literature*
(1913), pp. 120–24).

> C. Wolters, Intro. to his modern trans. of *RDL* (Penguin, 1966).

Kaufman, Sue   America   Novels
Diary of a Mad Housewife   1967

Kemble, Fanny   1809–93   England, America   Memoirs
Journal of a Residence on a Georgia Plantation   [1838–39] 1863
Record of a Girlhood   1878 (London: Bentley, 3 vol. ed.)—"a wild desire":
I, 202–3; dislike of theater: II, 13–14.

> C. Thomas, *Jameson,* pp. 38–40.

Krüdener, Juliana (Juliette) von   1764–1824   Russia, Germany, France
                                                    Fiction, mysticism
Valérie   1803; see Staël.

Labé, Louise   c. 1525–65   France   Poems

Mme de La Fayette   1634–93   France   Novels
La Princesse de Clèves   1678

Laforet, Carmen   Spain   Novels
Nada   1944
La Mujer nueva   1955

> Isabel Calvo de Aguilar, *Antología Biográfica de Escritoras Españolas*
> (1954)—guide to twentieth-century Spanish women writers in prose.

Lagerlöf, Selma   1858–1940   Sweden   Novels, children's books

Lamb, Caroline   1785–1828   England   Novels

Landon, Letitia Elizabeth (L.E.L.)   1802–38   England   Poems
Poetical Works, ed. W. B. Scott (1880)—"The Improvisatrice": pp. 1–4.
Mme de Staël, *Corinne; or, Italy,* trans. Isabel Hill, *with Metrical Versions of
the Odes* by L. E. Landon   1833

Leduc, Violette   1907–72   France   Novels
L'Asphyxie 1946, trans. D. Coltman as *In the Prison of her Skin* (1970)
La Bâtarde 1964, Intro. Simone de Beauvoir—on female symbolism of
  asphyxiation, imprisonment in a skin: pp. 14–15. (* Cf. the bell jar image,
  as used by both Plath and Nin as titles; and in earlier writers, especially
  Dickinson, the grave/bed.)
Le Taxi 1971

LeGuin, Ursula   America   Science fiction

Lennox, Charlotte   1720–1804   America, England   Novels
The Female Quixote 1752; see Austen.

Lessing, Doris   Rhodesia, England   Novels
The Four-Gated City (final volume of the "Children of Violence" series,
  1952ff.) 1969—return to mother.

    M. Thorpe, *DL* (1973), pp. 19–25.

Leverson, Ada   1862–1933   England   Novels
The Limit 1911
Letters to the Sphinx [by Oscar Wilde] *With Reminiscences* 1930

Lewald, Fanny   1811–89   Germany   Novels

Lindbergh, Anne Morrow   America   Memoirs
Bring Me a Unicorn: Diaries and Letters 1922–28 1972
Hour of Gold, Hour of Lead: 1929–32 1973—bird metaphor: Intro.

    S. Freud, *Works*, ed. J. Strachey (Standard Ed.)—flying, landscape, and
  other dream symbols (10th *Introd. Lect. on P-Anal.*, 1916–17); XV,
  153–56; "The 'Uncanny'": XVII, 219–52.

Linton, Eliza Lynn   1822–98   English   Novels, journalism

Lowell, Amy   1874–1925   America   Poems

Macaulay, Catharine   1731–91   England   History

Macdonald, Cynthia   America   Poems
Amputations 1972—"The Insatiable Baby"—"At six months"; cf. "Twice
  Too Long."

Mallet-Joris, Françoise   France   Novels

Manley, Mary Delarivière   1672?–1724   England   Tales, plays
The New Atalantis 1709
The Adventures of Rivella 1714—"carried the passion": qu. by L. Stevenson, *English Novel* (1960), p. 61.

Mansfield, Katherine   1888–1923   New Zealand, England   Stories, journals
The Garden Party and Other Stories 1922—"At the Bay."

Marcet, Jane   1769–1858   England   Educational texts
Conversations on Chemistry, intended for the Female Sex 1806
Conversations on Political Economy 1816; see Martineau.

Marguerite de Navarre   1492–1549   France   Poems, plays

Marie de France   late twelfth century   France, England   Poems

Martineau, Harriet   1802–76   England   Fiction, journalism, autobiography

Illustrations of Political Economy 1832–34—"A Manchester Strike" [1834].
Society in America 1837
Deerbrook 1839
Household Education 1849
"What There Is in a Button" (*Household Words*, 1852, V, 106–12)
Autobiography [1855] 1877, 3 vols.—on Wollstonecraft: I, 400–1; Brougham: I, 176; Marcet: I, 138–39; "method" of research: I, 179, 193–97; C. Brontë: II, 323–28; *Jane Eyre:* II, 21–22; *Household Words* series: II, 62–67.

   R. K. Webb, *HM: Radical Victorian* (1960)—"doing something with the pen": p. 114; Doherty and Mitford: pp. 120–22; earnings: pp. 97, 114; L. Cazamian, *Social Novel* (1973), pp. 50–60; Vera Wheatley, *Life and Work of HM* (1957); R. L. Wolff, *Strange Stories* (1971), ⚔2; Vineta Colby, *Yesterday's Woman* (1974), ⚔5.

McCarthy, Mary   America   Stories, essays, novels
The Company She Keeps 1942—"Cruel and Barbarous Treatment"—pronoun strategy.
Memories of a Catholic Girlhood 1957
The Writing on the Wall and Other Literary Essays 1970—on M. Wittig, I. Compton-Burnett, N. Sarraute.

   D. Grumbach, *MMcC* (1967); E. Moers, "Fictions" (*NYTBR*, June 11, 1967).

McCullers, Carson   1917–67   America   Novels, stories
The Heart Is a Lonely Hunter 1940

Reflections in a Golden Eye   1941—"A peacock": ⚔3.
The Member of the Wedding   1946—the Freaks: §1.
The Ballad of the Sad Café   1951
"Isak Dinesen" (2 review articles, 1943, 1963) in *The Mortgaged Heart: Uncollected Writings of CMcC.*, ed. M. G. Smith (1971)—"freakish brilliance": p. 303.

  Ihab Hassan, *Radical Innocence* (1961)—her Gothic: pp. 206–16.

Mead, Margaret   **America** **Anthropology, memoirs**
Coming of Age in Samoa   1928
Blackberry Winter: My Earlier Years   1972

Meynell, Alice **1847–1922** **England** **Poems, criticism**
Preludes   1875
"Elizabeth Barrett Browning" [c. 1895] in *Selected Literary Essays,* ed. P. M. Fraser (1965), p. 160.

Millay, Edna St. Vincent **1892–1950** **America** **Poems, plays**
"Renascence"   1912
A Few Figs from Thistles   1920—"First Fig"—"My candle burns at both ends."
Second April   1921—Sonnet ⚔4—"Only until this cigarette."
Fatal Interview   1931—Sonnet ⚔1—"Up, up, my feathers."

Millett, Kate   **America** **Criticism**
Sexual Politics   1970—*Villette:* pp. 140–47.

Mistral, Gabriela **1889–1957** **Chile** **Poems**

Mitchell, Margaret **1900–49** **America** **Fiction**
Gone with the Wind   1936

Mitford, Mary Russell **1787–1855** **England** **Sketches**
Our Village, sketches of rural life, character, and scenery   [1819ff. in *Lady's Maga.*] 5 vols., 1824–32—valentine dove: "The Black Velvet Bag" (*OV,* ed. J. C. Squire, Everyman, 1963, p. 203).
Rienzi (verse tragedy)   1828
Belford Regis, or Sketches of a Country Town   1835
Recollections of a Literary Life   1852

Correspondence with Boner and Ruskin, ed. E. Lee (1914)—Sand: pp. 42–44, 120–22, 196–97, 312–14.

  Betty Miller ed., *Barrett to Mitford,* Intro.; C. Gohdes, Foreword, *Stories of American Life* [1830 anthology, ed. MRM] (1969).

Mitford, Nancy   1904–73   England   Wit, biography

Montagu, Elizabeth   1720–1800   England   Essays

Montagu, Lady Mary Wortley   1689–1762   England   Letters
Turkish Embassy Letters 1763; in *Complete Letters,* ed. R. Halsband (1965)
—Mary Astell, Preface [1724]: App. 4.

R. Halsband, *Life* (1956)—Kit-Cat Club: p. 4.

Moore, Marianne   1887–1972   America   Poems

More, Hannah   1745–1833   England   Treatises
The Search After Happiness 1773
Percy. A Tragedy 1778
The Slave Trade. A Poem 1787
Strictures on the Modern System of Female Education 1799
Hints towards Forming the Character of a Young Princess 1805
Coelebs in Search of a Wife 1808—Milton's Eve: defended: ✄1; criticized:
✄40; "*exhibiting* wife": ✄2.

    Mme de Staël review, *Le Constitutionnel* (Jan. 18, 1817)—* "Iln'y a
point de pays où les femmes auteurs sont en plus grand nombre qu'en
Angleterre. . . .": p. 4; see under de Staël—R. A. Jones.

Memoirs of the Life and Correspondence of Mrs. HM, ed. W. Roberts (1834)
—on Wollstonecraft: I, 427.

    M. G. Jones, *HM* (1952)—on *Corinne:* p. 223; "She-Bishop": pp. 137,
175; Garrick and playwrighting: ✄2; Princess Charlotte: pp. 187–90;
Annette M. B. Meakin, *HM* (1911)—on Genlis: p. 210.

Morgan, Robin   America   Poems
Ed., *Sisterhood Is Powerful: Anthology of Women's Liberation* 1970
Monster 1972—"Arraignment"; "Monster."

Lady Morgan   178?–1859   Ireland, England   Novels, memoirs
The Wild Irish Girl (by Sydney Owenson) 1806
France 1817
France, in 1829–30 1830

Lady Morgan's Memoirs: Autobiography, Diaries and Correspondence, ed.
H. Dixon & G. Jewsbury 1863—Mrs. Gore: I, 344, 466–68, 514–16;
Genlis: II, 228, 230, 346; * the best advice ever given by a man to a
literary woman: I, 254–55 (Sir R. Phillips, her publisher, to SO, Oct.
16, 1805, viz.: "I assure you that you have a power of writing, a fancy,
an imagination, and a degree of enthusiasm which will enable you to
produce an immortal work, if you will *labour* it sufficiently. Write only
one side of your paper and retain a broad margin. Your power of
improving your first draught will thus be greatly increased; and a second

copy, made in the same way, with the same power of correcting, will
enable you to make a third copy, which will be another monument of
Irish genius.").

Mortimer, Penelope   **England   Novels**
The Pumpkin Eater   1962—sterilization: ✗17.

Mowatt, Anna Cora   1819–70   America   Plays, novels
Fashion; or, Life in New York   1845 (still stageworthy farce).

Lady Murasaki   978?–1031?   Japan   Novels
The Tale of Genji   c. 1008; trans. Arthur Waley (1925–33)—A.W. Intro.
   (Anchor, 1955)

Murdoch, Iris   **England   Novels, philosophy**

Murray, Michele   1934–74   America   Poems, criticism
A House of Good Proportion: Images of Women in Literature   1973

Duchess of Newcastle   1624–74,   England   Poems, plays, letters

Nin, Anaïs   **America   Diaries, novels**
Under a Glass Bell   1944—see under Leduc.
Diary   [1931–47] 1966–71; H. T. Moore, Preface to O. Evans, *AN* (1968).

Norton, Caroline   1808–77   Ireland, England   Poems, treatises
A Voice from the Factories   1836—Intro. letter to Lord Ashley
The Child of the Islands   1845

>   Gaskell, *Mary Barton*, ✗9; Alice Acland, *CN* (1948)—*"real* occupa-
>   tions": p. 155; Rubenius, *Gaskell*, pp. 281–83; C. Weygandt, *Time of
>   Tennyson* (1936) pp. 92–94

Oates, Joyce Carol   **America   Novels, stories**

O'Connor, Flannery   1925–64   America   Stories

Oliphant, Margaret   1828–97   Scotland, England   Novels
Miss Marjoribanks   1866

>   V. & R. Colby, *Mrs. O. and Victorian Literary Market Place* (1966)—
>   "George Eliot and George Sand make me half inclined to cry": p. 1.

Olsen, Tillie   **America   Novels, stories, criticism**
Tell Me a Riddle   1961, 1969
"Silences; When Writers Don't Write" (*Harper's*, 1962)
"Women Writers" (*CE*, Oct. 1972)
Yonnondio: From the Thirties   [1932ff.] 1974

Opie, Amelia   1769–1853   England   Novels

Ouida   1839–1908   England   Novels

Parker, Dorothy   1893–1967   America   Wit

Philips, Katherine   1631–64   England   Poems

Piozzi, Hester Lynch Thrale   1741–1821   England   Memoirs
               * As friend of Dr. Johnson and Fanny Burney, she was Mrs.
               Thrale; as published writer, she was Mrs. Piozzi.

"Three Dialogues on the Death of HLT" [1779] ed. M. Zamick (*JRLB,* 1932)
Anecdotes of the Late Samuel Johnson 1786
Observations in the Course of a Journey through Italy 1789

          J. L. Clifford, *HLTP* (1941)—original style, influence: pp. 343–47.

Plath, Sylvia   1932–63   America   Poems, fiction
The Colossus and Other Poems 1960
Crossing the Water: transitional poems [c. 1960–61] 1971—"Wuthering
     Heights" [1962]—"The sky leans on me": ⌗5.
The Bell Jar by Victoria Lucas 1963; by SP 1966—"Look what can
     happen": ⌗1.

          Lois Ames, biog. note to 1st Amer. ed. (1971).

Winter Trees [c. 1963] 1972—"Stopped Dead" [1963]—"a goddam baby":
     ⌗3; *Three Women* [B.B.C. play, 1962]—second voice, miscarried.
Ariel [1963] 1965—"Lady Lazarus"—"O my enemy": ⌗4–7; "Death & Co."
     —dead baby (cf. Arbus baby photograph, 1967).

          Charles Newman ed., *Art of SP: A Symposium* (1970)—Lois Ames
          on life: pp. 155–73; M. Kinzie et al.: chronology, bibliography; A.
          Alvarez, *Savage God* (1971–72)—SP on work habits: Prologue; Eric
          Homberger, "Uncollected Plath" (*NS,* Sept. 22, 1972)—posthumous
          SP publishing industry: pp. 404–5.

Porter, Katherine Anne   America   Stories
Flowering Judas 1930
Pale Horse, Pale Rider 1939
The Leaning Tower 1944

Radcliffe, Ann   1764–1823   England   Novels
The Castles of Athlin and Dunbayne 1789
A Sicilian Romance 1790
A Romance of the Forest 1791
The Mysteries of Udolpho 1794—Ariosto: ⌗20; aunt in garden: ⌗12;
     La Vallée: ⌗1, ⌗6; father and pastoral: ⌗1; "strength of sensibility":

⅌7; "roused latent powers": ⅌30; "day devoted to business": ⅌48; "innocence shall triumph": ⅌57; "unpacked her books": ⅌19; "without a
hat": ⅌34; "bloom somewhat faded": ⅌38; "grey autumnal evening":
⅌51.
*A Journey made in the Summer of 1794 through Holland . . . Germany
. . . the Lakes* 1795—* (Real travel at last! and the trip proved just the
failure one would expect. Mrs. R. describes troubles with passports,
tipping, missed appointments, incomplete itineraries, unscrupulous foreigners; and was very happy to get home to the Lake Country, of which
her account is an interesting early Romantic document.)
The Italian, or the Confessional of the Black Penitents 1797—Ellena a
needlewoman: I, ⅌1; Schedoni a false "father" and near rapist: II, ⅌10.

Clara F. McIntyre, *AR in Relation to her Time* (1920)—"Monk" Lewis:
p. 64; "Terrorist": p. 53; Mrs. Thrale and travel books: pp. 58–61;
E. B. Murray, *AR* (1972)—popularity: p. 19; de Sade: p. 19; Aline
Grant, *AR: A Biography* (1951)—father's business: p. 29; K. Kroeber,
Styles in Fictional Structure (1971)—"transport": p. 116; Louis
Peck, *Life of M. G. Lewis* (1961), pp. 20–22; E. B. Gose, *Irrational
in 19th Century* (1972)—"stability": p. 169; W. Ruff, "AR, or the Hand
of Taste," *Essays to C. B. Tinker* (1949), pp. 186–93; A. Welsh,
Hero of Waverley Novels (1963)—Scott on his "insipid" hero: pp.
49–50; Scott, "Mrs. A.R.", *Misc. Prose Works* (1829), III, 256; W.
Hazlitt, "On the English Novelists," *Lectures on Eng. Comic Writers* ⅌6
(in *Works*, 1903, VIII, 125–28); J. M. S. Tompkins, *Popular Novel*
(1932), ⅌7; see Austen, Sand, Rossetti, C. Brontë.

Reeve, Clara   1729–1807   England   Novels, criticism
The Champion of Virtue, a Gothic Story or *The Old English Baron* 1777–78
The Progress of Romance 1785—Richardson's language: I, 133–38; Rous-
seau & adultery: II, 16–17; Genlis: II, 99.

Rhys, Jean   Windward Islands, England   Stories, novels
The Left Bank 1927 reprint in *Tigers Are Better-Looking* 1968
Postures 1928 reprint as *Quartet* 1971
Good Morning, Midnight 1939, 1970—afterbirth: §1; title from Emily Dick-
inson: Epigraph.
Wide Sargasso Sea 1966—first Mrs. Rochester, cf. *Jane Eyre:* Intro. by
Francis Wyndham.

Rich, Adrienne   America   Poems, criticism
A Change of World 1951—Foreword by W. H. Auden.
Diving into the Wreck 1973—"The Phenomenology of Anger"—"Fantasies
of murder": ⅌6; "Statement for Voices Unheard: a challenge to the
Natl. Book Awards" with A. Lord & A. Walker, in *Ms.* (Sept. 1974), p.
21; see Bradstreet.

Richardson, Dorothy   1873–1957   England   Novels
Pilgrimage 1915–38   vol. I: *Pointed Roofs* 1915—courtyard: §3, ⌗14.

J. Rosenberg, *DR* (1973)—V. Woolf on DR's invention of "the psychological sentence of the feminine gender": p. 57.

Richardson, Henry Handel   1870–1946   Australia   Novels
The Fortunes of Richard Mahoney 1917, 1925, 1929

Ritchie, Anne Thackeray   1837–1919   England   Novels, tales, memoirs

Roiphe, Anne   America   Novels
Digging Out (by Anne Richardson) 1966—dying mother scene: ⌗4.
Up the Sandbox! 1970

Rossetti, Christina   1830–94   England   Poems
Goblin Market and other Poems 1862

B. I. Evans, "Sources of *GM*" (*MLR*, 1933); W. Weathers, "CR: Sisterhood of Self" (*VP*, 1965–66); see Cather.

Verses 1847, *Goblin Market* 1862, *The Prince's Progress* 1866, *Sing-Song* 1872, *A Pageant* 1881, *Verses . . . Christian* 1893, *New Poems* 1896—collected in *Poetical Works of CGR*, ed. Wm. M. Rossetti (1906) —"Goblin Market" [1859]: pp. 1–9; "Monna Innominata: A Sonnet of Sonnets" [before 1882]: pp. 58–64; "The lowest place" [before 1886]: p. 128, cf. pp. 16–20, 233; "A Birthday" [1857]—"My heart is like a singing bird": p. 335; "A Royal Princess" [1861]—dove, eagle, mirrors: p. 35; "Noble Sisters" [1860]: pp. 348–49; "Sister Maude" [c. 1860]— "Who told my mother": p. 348.
Speaking Likenesses 1874—prose children's tale with boys as animal monsters.

L. Senelick, letter to *NYRB* (May 30, 1974).
Lona Mosk Packer, *CR* (1963)—sister and *"GM"*: pp. 149–52; interest in Mrs. Radcliffe: pp. 354–55; Hopkins: pp. 185, 430; C. M. Bowra, *Romantic Imagination* (1957), pp. 245–56; L. Stevenson, *Pre-Raphaelite Poets* (1972), ⌗4; see Woolf.

Rowson, Susanna   c. 1762–1824   England, America   Novels, plays
Charlotte Temple 1791

Spiller, Thorp, *Literary History of the U.S.* (1963), pp. 177–78.

Rukeyser, Muriel   America   Poems

Sackville-West, Vita   1892–1962   England   Novels, memoirs
"Women Poets of the 'Seventies" in H. Granville-Barker, ed., *The Eighteen-Seventies* (1929)

The Edwardians   1930
The Eagle and the Dove   1944—sex & St. Teresa: pp. 19–21; littleness & Ste. Thérèse: pp. 134–39.

Sagan, Françoise   **France   Novels**

Sand, George   1804–76   France   Novels, essays, memoirs

> *The fullest chronology of GS's work and life is provided by Georges Lubin at the head of his edition of GS's *Oeuvres autobiographiques*—* (*OA*) (Gallimard, Pléiade, 1970), I, xxxvii–lvi, and of the individual volumes of GS's *Correspondance* (Garnier, 1964ff.; vol. IX, 1972, the last published to date, through 1850). Split dates indicating serial publication have been noted, as many Anglo-American readers followed GS's work in the *Revue des deux mondes* (*RDM*). Recent scholarly editions of Sand's works are indicated.

Rose et Blanche (by J. Sand)   1831—landscape: ⌘14.
Indiana   1832—unhappy wife: ⌘6 & passim.

> Pierre Salomon ed. (1962)—marriage ideology: p. xlix.

Valentine   1832—landscape: ⌘1; heroine's ride in lane: ⌘5; education of women: ⌘6; marriage protest: ⌘22; social ideal: ⌘14, ⌘29.
Review of Senancour's *Obermann,* ed. Sainte-Beuve (*RDM,* June 1833)
Lélia   1833—bravery in the desert: §2, ⌘28; two sisters: §2, ⌘33; mal du siècle feminized: §3, ⌘1 and passim; solitude abandoned: §2, ⌘29, ⌘30.

> P. Reboul ed. (1960)—credo for revision of 1839 *Lélia:* pp. 330–31.

Le Secrétaire intime   1834—trans. G. H. Lewes as "The State Murder: A Tale" (*Fraser's,* 1844).
Jacques   1834
Lettres d'un Voyageur   1834–37—imaginary travel in masculine guise: ⌘1; Mme de Staël & *Lélia:* ⌘4; night writing, life-style: ⌘5; ideal of friendship: ⌘6; illiterates: ⌘7.
Leone Leoni   1834–35
André   1835
Simon   1836—heroine and wild bird: ⌘6; guerilla-aspiration: ⌘6, ⌘10.
Lettres à Marcie   1837
Les Maîtres mosaïstes   1837–38
Mauprat   1837—illiterate idealized: ⌘10; transformation of savage man: ⌘10, ⌘12, ⌘29; *Émile* feminized: ⌘11.

> C. Sicard ed. (1969)—historical, esp. Amer. Revolution background: pp. 16–17.

La Dernière Aldini   1838
Spiridion   1838–39; see Thackeray below.
Les Sept Cordes de la Lyre   1839–40

Gabriel 1839–40

Le Compagnon du tour de France 1840—Préface, coll. with other prefaces to popular ed. of GS Works, 1851–54, in *Souvenirs et Impressions littéraires* (1862), pp. 132–33.

Un Hiver à Majorque 1841–42; trans. Robert Graves as *Winter in Mallorca* (1956)

Horace 1841–42

Consuelo 1842–43 *La Comtesse de Rudolstadt* (conclusion) 1843–44—indoor travel: I, ⅜39–42; Mrs. Radcliffe: I, ⅜34; opera singer apotheosis: I, ⅜10; robin scene: III (*CdeR*), ⅜19.

    L. Cellier & L. Guichard ed. (1959)—Pauline Garcia, music and secret societies in *C:* pp. xxxi–lxxviii.

Jean Ziska 1843—"Le combat ou la mort," sentence addressed to delicate female reader, quoted out of context by Marx: ⅜1.

Jeanne 1844—landscape: Prologue, ⅜1.

Le Meunier d'Angibault 1845—landscape: ⅜2, ⅜3, ⅜5.

Le Péché de M. Antoine 1845

Isidora 1845–46

Teverino 1845–46

La Mare au diable 1845–46—mission of art, life & joy: ⅜1; peasant, art, & nature: ⅜2.

    P. Salomon & J. Mallion ed. with *François le Champi* (1962)—social commitment of peasant novels & "Veillées": pp. i–xii.

"La Vallée-Noire," article in *L'Éclaireur de l'Indre* [1846] in *Oeuvres* (Michel Levy, 1869)—name her invention: pp. 283, 295; address to traveler: p. 288.

    G. Lubin, *GS en Berry* (1967), pp. 8–13.

François le Champi 1847–50—creation of style: Avant-Propos.

Lettres aux riches, au peuple, à la classe moyenne 1848

    P. Salomon, *GS* (1958)—revolutionary period: §2, ⅜3, ⅜4; J. Larnac, *GS révolutionnaire* (1947); M.-L. Pailleron, *GS et les hommes de '48* (1953); E. Dolléans, *Féminisme et le mouvement ouvrier: GS* (1951); see under Milnes below.

La Petite Fadette 1848–49—twins contrasted: ⅜3.

    M. C. G. Gray, "GS, Keller, George Eliot" (M.A. thesis, Indiana U., 1965).

Le Château des Désertes 1851—dedication to Macready.

"Harriett Beecher Stowe" (*La Presse*, Dec. 20, 1852) in GS: *Autour de la table* (1876)—slaves of ignorance: p. 319: honor to Stowe: p. 327.

    * Georges Lubin informs me that *Uncle Tom's Cabin* (published as a book in March 1852 in America) ran as a serial, in translation, in 1852 in *La Presse*, to the editor of which, Girardin,

GS wrote on Dec. 9, 1852, requesting space at the end of publication for an article in which she would express her enthusiasm. Stowe included a translation of Sand's article in her own Introduction to the new ed. of *UTC* (1889).

"Quelques réflexions sur Jean-Jacques Rousseau" in *Oeuvres illustrées* (Hetzel, 1853) IV, 44–48.

Les Maîtres sonneurs 1853—motherhood learned: ✗20.

    P. Salomon & J. Mallion ed. (1958)—GS personal definition of word "traînes": note 5, p. 14.

Histoire de ma vie 1854–55, 1876—male name and dress: §4, ✗13, ✗14; escape oblivion: §1, ✗2; solidarity: §1, ✗1 (see Woolf); convent school imprisonment: §3, ✗10; *les diables*, Mrs. Radcliffe: §3, ✗11; (trans. Maria E. MacKaye as *Convent Life of GS*, Boston, 1893); adolescent boy: §1, ✗4; Genlis reading: §2, ✗16; Corambé fantasy: §3, ✗9; tame robin: §4, ✗9.

    G. Lubin, ed. *Oeuvres Autobiographiques* (1970).

Comme il vous plaira 1856—version for theater of *As You Like It*

    Dickens, *Letters,* ed. W. Dexter (1938), II, 757–58.

La Daniella 1857
Le Diable aux champs 1857
Les Beaux Messieurs de Bois-Doré 1858
Elle et Lui 1859
Promenades autour d'un village 1859
Valvèdre 1861

    F. W. H. Myers, "GS," *Essays* (1883), pp. 70–103.

Mademoiselle la Quintinie 1863
La Confession d'une jeune fille 1865
Mademoiselle Merquem 1868
Pierre qui roule 1869–70
Malgrétout 1870
Nanon 1872

    Annarosa Poli, *GS et les années terribles* (1975), pp. 253–62.

Contes d'une grand-mère 1873–76
Ma soeur Jeanne 1874
Flamarande 1875

Correspondance, ed. G. Lubin (1964ff.)—visit from G. H. Lewes, 1846: VII, ✗3383.

    * In her letter on GHL, GS mentions him as one of her three best English friends, the others W. C. Macready, the actor, and George Grote, historian and M.P. The nine presently published volumes of the *Correspondance,* though superbly indexed, give

no idea of the crowd of English and American visitors to and
correspondents with GS, such as Arnold, Milnes, Fuller, and
Browning, whose letters may come to light as post-1850 volumes
of the *Correspondance* are issued. Going to see GS, often from the
worst motives, was a Victorian pastime which inspired the one
outburst of bad temper in GS's autobiography: "a crowd of
importunate idlers . . . traveling Englishmen, who just want
to put in their notebook that they have seen you; and since I
have too much forgotten my English to make the effort to speak
with them, those who don't know three words of French speak
to me in their language, I reply in mine. They don't understand,
they go 'Oh!' and leave satisfied. . . . You cannot imagine the
eccentricities, the inconveniences . . . the stupidities which pass
in review before the unhappy artist afflicted with a little fame."
(*Histoire de ma vie*, §5, ✕2)

Influence of George Sand—general studies, all tentative for England, U.S.:
P. G. Blount, "Reputation of GS in Victorian England 1832–1886," [Un-
published dissertation, 1961] University Microfilms, 1970; C. M. Lom-
bard, "GS's Image in America 1837–1876" (*RLC*, 1966) (correcting
Howard Mumford Jones, "Amer. Comment on GS," *AL*, Jan. 1932);
Patricia Thomson, "GS and English Reviewers: the first twenty years"
(*MLR*, July 1972); and see PT under E. Brontë, Browning.

Influence on particular writers—see index for mentions of Sand in notes on
women writers; male writers are listed below in alphabetical order.

Alain (Emile Chartier)—*Propos de littérature* (1934), pp. 115, 219–25;
cf. B. Halda, *Alain* (1965), pp. 91–92; see Simone Weil.

Arnold—"GS" 1877, *Complete Prose Works of MA*, ed. Super (1960),
VIII, 216–36—"vibration": p. 235; peasants: pp. 230–31; landscape:
p. 217; "days of *Corinne*": p. 220—* MA could not remember where
GS said this; Georges Lubin has never found the phrase in GS; she may
have said it to MA when he went to see her at Nohant in 1846, and she
roused his interest in Senancour and other French Romantics.

Iris E. Sells, *MA and France* (1935); MA, *Letters to Clough* (1932);
MA, *Notebooks*, ed. Lowry (1952); D. G. James, *MA* (1961), pp. 19ff.

Carlyle—*Latter-Day Pamphlets* ✕2, March 1, 1850; cf. *New Letters*
(1904), I, 264.

Dostoevsky—V. Karenine, *GS: sa vie et ses oeuvres* (1899), pp. 33–34;
O. Watzke, "GS et D" (*RLC*, 1940)—heroines: p. 170.

Flaubert—*Correspondance*, 3rd Series, pp. 310ff.; *GS/Gustave Flaubert
Letters*, trans. A. L. McKenzie (1921), pp. 32–39, 48–49, 115, 346–57
& passim; Enid Starkie, *F the Master* (1969).

Henry James—"GS," *French Poets and Novelists* (1878)—working: pp.
208–11; passion: pp. 218–19; other HJ writings on GS, 1868–1914, reprinted in HJ, *Lit. Revs.* (1957), *Parisian Sketches* (1957), *Notes on
Novelists* (1914); HJ, "Gabrielle de Bergerac," 1869, *Complete Tales*,
ed. Edel (1962), II—heroine.

G. H. Lewes—"collective voice": "Continental Literati" (*Monthly Maga.*, June 1843), p. 584; passion & experience: "Balzac & GS" (*Foreign Qu. Rev.* 1844), p. 284.

> * Most of GHL's numerous critical articles of the 1840s—on literature English and foreign, on philosophy, history, criticism, theater—contain extended discussions or brief mentions of GS; and the same is true of a majority of his articles in *The Leader* (1850–54). His initial passion for her work, similar to Arnold's, which is also recorded in GHL's annotated volume of *Jacques* (in the Houghton Library, HU) seems to have cooled somewhat during her radical years when she was writing on *le peuple*.

Alice Kaminsky, *GHL as Literary Critic* (1968), p. 122; AK, "George Eliot, GHL and the Novel" (*PMLA*, 1955), p. 997; R. Stang, *Theory of Novel* (1959)—GHL's importance as novel critic: pp. xii, 80–85; W. Archer, Intro. to *Dramatic Essays by Lewes* (1896); Anna T. Kitchel, *GL and George Eliot* (1933); see Gary under C. Brontë, Howe under G. Jewsbury, Shaw under George Eliot.

Marx—*La Misère de la philosophie* (1847)—last line quote from Sand; see *Jean Ziska* above; trans. *Poverty of Philosophy* (1971), p. 175; M. Rubel, *Karl Marx* (1957), pp. 92–93.

Mazzini—"GS" (*People's Jnl.*, April 1847) quoted at head of Francis G. Shaw's trans. of *Compagnon* as *Journeyman Joiner* (1847).

A. Poli, *L'Italie & GS* (1960), pp. 234–45.

Mill—M. St. J. Packe, *Life of JSM* (1954), p. 153; *Subjection of Women* 1869—Sand style: ⅍3.

Milnes—J. Pope-Hennessy, *Monckton Milnes*—Paris 1848 relationship: I, 284–86; * MM's dreadful "role word" joke, on GS as France's greatest "écrevisse" rather than "écrivain": II, 188–89.

de Musset—AdeM, *Poésies* (Pléiade), I, 512–13; GS, *Correspondance*, II, 339–41.

A. Maurois, *Lélia ou la vie de GS* (1952), §4.

Proust—*À la Recherche du Temps Perdu* (Pléiade, 1954)—childhood reading: I, 41–43; GS providing a "mémoire involontaire": III, 883–86.

Ruskin—*Works,* ed. Cook & Wedderburn (1912)—GS and justice in *Fors Clavigera:* XXIX, 266 & 588; on heroines in *Letters:* XXXVI, 244.

Stendhal—*Mémoires d'un Touriste* (1838)—banks of the Indre: in V. Dellitto, "Stendhal et GS" (*Hommage à GS, PFLSH,* U. de Grenoble, 1969), pp. 16–17.

Taine—faith of GS: Dolléans, p. 16; "Lettres de GS & HT" (*RDM,* Jan. 1, 1933).

Thackeray—"Mme Sand & the New Apocalypse," *Paris Sketchbook* 1840—language & pretense: in *Works* (Biog. Ed.), LX, 192–93; cf. WMT, *Letters,* ed. Ray (1945), I, 466–67.

Turgenev—GS our saint: V. Karenine, p. 29; see Haight life of George Eliot.

Whitman—"lest stagnate": WW 1847 *Brooklyn Eagle* review of *Journey-man Joiner* (see under Mazzini, above), in Esther Shephard, *WW's Pose* (1936), p. 20; "emotions room": WW, "A Christmas Garland" 1874, in *Uncollected Poetry & Prose*, ed. Holloway (1921), II, 53.

Sappho   Seventh–sixth century B.C.   Greece   Poems

Sarraute, Nathalie   France   Novels
Tropismes 1939

Schaeffer, Susan Fromberg   America   Novels, poems
Falling 1973

Schreiner, Olive   1855–1920   South Africa, England   Novels, treatises
The Story of an African Farm 1883

Sedgwick, Catharine   1789–1867   America   Novels
Redwood: A Tale 1824—woman & American landscape: ✳1.
Letters from Abroad to Kindred at Home 1841—de Staël pilgrimage: I, 260–61.

Mary M. Welsh, *CMS* (1937); see R. L. Wolff under Martineau.

Mme de Ségur   1799–1874   France, Russia   Children's books

Séverine   1855–1929   France   Journalism

Beatrice Braude, "S: an ambivalent feminist" (*Feminist Art Jnl.*, Fall 1973).

Mme de Sévigné   1626–96   France   Letters

Seward, Anna   1747–1809   England   Poems

Sexton, Anne   1928–74   America   Poems
To Bedlam and Part Way Back 1960—"Exorcists."
Live or Die 1966
Love Poems 1969
The Awful Rowing Toward God 1975

Shelley, Mary   1797–1851   England   Novels, tales

* Born Mary Godwin; sometimes used Wollstonecraft as middle name, after her mother; P. B. Shelley's wife 1816–22; thereafter his widow and a productive writer for more than twenty years.

Frankenstein; or, The Modern Prometheus 1818—" 'How I, a young girl' "
and "curdle the blood" and "hideous progeny" and "indulging in waking
dreams": 1831 Intro. to Standard Novels ed.; birth of monster: ✂5;
"lifeless matter," "recourse to death," "painful labour," "workshop of
filthy creation": ✂4; "I am an abortion": ✂24; Justine: ✂6, ✂8.

> M. K. Joseph, Intro., ed. 1831 *F* (1971); J. Rieger, Intro., ed. 1818
> *F* (1974); M. Praz, *Romantic Agony* (trans. Davidson, 1951), p. 114;
> R. Kiely, *Romantic Novel* (1972), pp. 160–61; A. Guerard, "Prome-
> theus" (*Yale Rev.*, 1943–44); L. Nelson, "Gothic Novel" (*Yale Rev.*,
> 1962–63); I. Asimov, *Rest of Robots* (1964), pp. ix–xi; M. A. Goldberg,
> "Moral and Myth" (*KSJ*, 1959); H. Bloom, *"F," Ringers in the Tower*
> (1971); S. Rosenberg, *"F"* (*Life*, March 15, 1958); J. Rieger, *Mutiny
> Within* (1967), pp. 81–89, 237–47; Benjamin Spock, *Baby and Child
> Care* (1957 ed.), ✂71.

Mathilda [1819] ed. Elizabeth Nitchie (1959)
Valperga 1823
The Last Man 1826
Perkin Warbeck 1830
Lodore 1835
Falkner 1837

"Transformation" in *Tales and Stories*, ed. R. Garnett (1891)—transformation motif (cf. E. Brontë): pp. 174–85.

Journal, ed. Frederick L. Jones (1947)—first pregnancy: * The opening entry,
in Shelley's hand, records their elopement on July 28, 1814, and his
comment on Mary's feeling ill and faint: "in that illness what pleasure
and security did we not share!" On Feb. 22, 1815, or not quite seven
months later, another Shelley entry records the birth of "a female
child . . . not quite seven months . . . not expected to live"; "find my
baby dead": p. 39; reads *Corinne:* p. 39: Harriet's "son and heir": p. 28;
"Dream that my little baby": p. 41; reads *Orra* and other Baillie plays:
pp. 18, 28–33.

Letters, ed. F. L. Jones (1944)—Fanny's suicide: p. 16; recurring dead baby
dream: pp. 21–22; guesses new pregnancy: pp. 14–15; Byron's baby:
p. 18.

> L. A. Marchand, *Byron* (1957)—Byron on Claire: II, 681.
> Claire Clairmont, *Journals,* ed. Stocking (1968), pp. 71–76.
> Sylvia Norman, *On Shelley* (1938)—MS's late fiction: pp. 64–70.
> Eileen Bigland, *MS* (1959); W. A. Walling, *MS* (1972).

Sheridan, Frances   1724–66   England   Novels
Memoirs of Miss Sidney Bidulph 1761

> Eaves & Kimpel, *Richardson*, pp. 454–55.

Sherwin, Judith Johnson   America   Poems, stories

Sigourney, Lydia   1791–1865   America   Poems

Sitwell, Edith   1887–1964   England   Poems

Slesinger, Tess   1905–45   America   Stories
Time: The Present 1935 (reissued as *On Being Told That Her Second Husband Has Taken His First Lover and Other Stories,* 1971); see Buck.

Smith, Charlotte   1749–1806   England   Poems, novels
Elegaic Sonnets 1784

> R. Marshall, *Italy in Eng. Lit.* (1934)—women sonneteers and Petrarch revival: pp. 339–44.

Emmeline: The Orphan of the Castle 1788
The Old Manor House 1793
The Young Philosopher 1798; Garland reprint (1974)—Intro., G. Luria.

> Anne H. Ehrenpreis, Intro. to *EOC* and *OMH* (Oxford, 1969 & 1971).

Spark, Muriel   England   Novels, criticism

Mme de Staël   1766–1817   Switzerland, France   Cultural history, novels
> * Fuller documentation in standard footnote form accompanies the partial version of chapter 9 in *Harvard English Studies,* 1975.

Lettres sur les ouvrages et le caractère de J.-J. Rousseau 1787–88 (Eng. trans., 1789)—praise of R.'s *Nouvelle Héloïse:* ✳2; criticism of R.'s pedagogy: ✳3; women's right to express passion: ✳1; Richardson's *Clarissa:* ✳2; Montesquieu: ✳4; men and wives: 1814 Préface.

> Madelyn Gutwirth, "MdeS, Rousseau, and women question" (*PMLA,* 1971).

Essai sur les fictions 1795—on English novels, Richardson to Godwin, & *"l'éloquence de la passion"* in Rousseau's *NH* & recommends other passions than love to novelist: ✳3.
De L'Influence des passions sur le bonheur des individus et des nations 1796 —"De l'amour de la gloire": §1, ✳1.

> Simone Balayé, "Le Génie et la gloire dans MdeS" (*RLMC,* Dec. 1967).

De la littérature considérée dans ses rapports avec les institutions sociales 1800—women and practice, study of literature: §2, ✳4; English women, fiction, & Richardson: §1, ✳15.

> P. Van Tieghem, ed., *De la littérature* (1959): Intro.

Delphine 1802
Corinne, ou l'Italie 1807—C's first appearance, the crowd & Oswald: §2, ✳1; C's first improvisation: §2, ✳3; Corinna: note 11 (by MdeS); taran-

tella & Récamier: §6, ✗1 & note 14; C on English men loving Italian
women: §16, ✗3; Vesuvius: §11, ✗4; father's letter on C: §16, ✗7;
Italian past, future: §1, ✗5 & §2, ✗1; English hypocrisy: §6, ✗2;
spontaneity in art, love: §6, ✗1 & §4, ✗6; love and novel: §6, ✗2;
destiny and genius: §13, ✗4; C's early life: §14, ✗1; stepmother on
women: §14, ✗1; "home": §11, ✗3; Oswald on Lucile: §16, ✗5; L
and spring: §17, ✗4; North Italy: §19, ✗6.

Sainte-Beuve, Préface, *Corinne* (1839), pp. iii–iv, vii.

De l'Allemagne 1810
Réflexions sur le suicide 1813—"une sorte de rage": ✗1.
Considérations sur les principaux événements de la Révolution française 1818
Dix années d'exil 1821; Peter Gay, Intro., *Ten Years of Exile* (trans. Beik, 1972).

J. C. Herold, *Mistress of an Age: Life of MdeS* (1958)—Italian journey: ✗15; August 1804 letter on advance plan to write novel: p. 299;
father's applause: p. 36; Helen B. Posgate, *MdeS* (1968); W. Andrews,
MdeS (1963); Morroe Berger, ed. *MdeS on Politics* (1965)—"social
scientist": p. 62; Babbitt, Watt: pp. 71–72; M. Levaillant, *Passionate
Exiles* (trans. Barnes, 1958)—Récamier, Krüdener: pp. 15–18; Las
Cases, *Mémorial de Sainte-Hélène* (1961)—Napoleon on MdeS: II,
173–75 [Aug. 13, 1816]; Susan Tenenbaum, "Montesquieu and MdeS:
The Woman as a Factor in Political Analysis" (*Political Theory*, Feb.
1973); Susanne Howe, *Wilhelm Meister and His English Kinsmen*
(1930)—Carlyle on MdeS: p. 83; R. de Luppé, *Idées littéraires de
MdeS* (1969)—Grandison: pp. 30–33; G. Solovieff, ed., *MdeS: choix
de textes* (1974)—on women: §1; C. M. Lombard, "MdeS and American Literature" (*RLC*, 1967), pp. 101–6; R. L. Hawkins, *MdeS and U.S.*
(1930); R. C. Whitford, *MdeS's Literary Reputation in England* (1918)
—during her lifetime; Robert Arthur Jones, "MdeS and England" (unpublished thesis, U. of London, 1928)—influence, imitations of *Corinne*
through 1820s: ✗11. See index for other MdeS references in notes.

Stafford, Jean   **America**   **Novels, stories**

Stead, Christina   **Australia**   **Novels**
The Man Who Loved Children   1940, 1966

Stein, Gertrude   1874–1946   America   Prose
"In the Red Deeps" [1894] in Rosalind S. Miller, *GS* (1949)—Radcliffe
Manuscripts: pp. 108–10; "out of George Eliot": p. 110.
"Normal Motor Automatism" with L. Solomons, *Psychological Rev.* 1896
Q.E.D. [1903] published as *Things as They Are* 1950
Fernhurst [1904–5?] published in *The Making of Americans* 1925

L. Katz. & D. Gallup, Intro. to GS, *Fernhurst, QED, and Other Early
Writings* (1971)—reading Sand: p. x.

Three Lives   [1905] 1909
Tender Buttons   1914
Four Saints in Three Acts   1929, 1934—"pigeons on grass": §3.
The Autobiography of Alice B. Toklas   1933
"Money," "All About Money," 1936 in P. Meyerowitz ed., GS: *Look at Me Now* 1971
Ida   1841—"earning a living": p. 44.
The Mother of Us All   [1946] 1947—"women white and cold": §2, ⅍8; "interested in Saint Therese": §2, ⅍4.

> R. Bridgman, *GS in Pieces* (1970)—reading: pp. 12, 25, 178; gender in style: pp. 57–58; J. M. Brinnin, ed. *Selected Operas and Plays of GS* (1970)—Intro., pp. 42, 58, 72; Elizabeth Sprigge, *GS* (1957).

Ms. Steinem, Gloria   **America   Journalism**

Daniel Stern (Marie d'Agoult)   1805–76   France   Novels, essays

Stowe, Harriet Beecher   1811–96   America   Novels, stories
The Mayflower (stories)   1843
Introduction, *The Works of Charlotte Elizabeth* [Mrs. Tonna] (New York, 1844) 1844
Uncle Tom's Cabin; or, Life Among the Lowly   1851–52—"an exotic race," "awaken sympathy" and other phrases important to George Eliot: Preface; "land between Mississippi": ⅍8; "mothers of America": ⅍45; breakfast in Indiana: ⅍13; Topsy on "I grow'd": ⅍20; "human property in the market": ⅍30; "highest sum" for Tom: ⅍5; Haley making "a living": ⅍12; Topsy a tomboy: ⅍20; Eva preaching: ⅍27; Aunt Ophelia: ⅍17, ⅍18, ⅍20; George Harris dedication to race: ⅍43.

> HBS, Intro. to New Edition, *UTC* (Riverside Press, 1889)—reception of *UTC* in U.S., England, Europe, inc. trans. of Sand review, letters from Shaftesbury, Bremer, Dickens, Heine, Macaulay, et al.: pp. xvi–xlii; J. S. Mill, *Subjection of Women* 1869, ⅍2; K. S. Lynn, Intro. to *UTC* (1962)—history of text; F. L. Pattee, *Feminine Fifties* (1940)—Iliad of Blacks: p. 135; Amy Cruse, *Victorians Reading*—reception, sales: ⅍12; Edmund Wilson, review Modern Library *UTC* (*New Yorker*, Nov. 27, 1948); Harry Stone, "Dickens & HBS" (*NCF*, 1957); E. Moers, *"Bleak House"* (*Dickensian*, Jan. 1973); G. H. Lewes, "Contemporary French Literature" (*Westminster Rev.*, 1853) —*UTC* in France: p. 326.

A Key to Uncle Tom's Cabin presenting the Original Facts, Documents   1853 —Frederick Douglass cited: pp. 24–28; cf. F. Douglass, *Narrative of the Life* 1845, ⅍1.
Sunny Memories of Foreign Lands   1854—Lord Ashley: I, xv–xvi, xli, 276–77, 287–90; cf. Karl Marx, *Civil War in U.S.* (ed. Enmale, 1937)—importance of HBS/Ashley relationship: ⅍1 [Sept. 18, 1961].

Dred: A Tale of the Great Dismal Swamp 1856—camp-meeting: I, ✕23; Milly's story: I, ✕16; Nina: I, ✕1 & II, ✕2; Nat Turner's Confessions: App. 1.

R. K. Webb, *H. Martineau*—"work of genius": p. 38; see Geo. Eliot; Alice Crozier, *Novels of HBS* (1969), ✕2; E. Moers, "HBS" (*NYRB*, Sept. 3, 1970).

The Minister's Wooing 1859
The Pearl of Orr's Island 1862
Oldtown Folks 1869
Lady Byron Vindicated 1870
Oldtown Fireside Stories 1872
Poganuc People 1878

Life of HBS compiled from Her Letters and Journals by her Son Charles Edward Stowe (1889)—Letter to Mrs. Geo. Beecher on sink: pp. 133–39; "Now, Hattie" letter from Mrs. Edw. Beecher: p. 146; writing *UTC*: ✕6; influence of *UTC*: ✕7, ✕8; Mme de Staël: p. 67.
Annie Fields, *Life and Letters of HBS* (1897)—family letters on girlhood: ✕1; Lincoln: p. 269; writing on slavery: p. 142.

E. C. Wagenknecht, *HBS* (1965)—her reading, formation: pp. 133–53; J. R. Adams, *HBS* (1963)—literary apprenticeship: pp. 32–43; C. H. Foster, *HBS & New England Puritanism* (1954)—F. Bremer quoted: p. 57; on HBS's New England fiction: passim.

Talbot, Catherine   c. 1720–70   England   Letters
Letters between Mrs. Elizabeth Carter [the famous bluestocking, 1717–1806] *and Miss CT* 1808, qu. in Eaves & Kimpel, *Richardson*, p. 359.

Tastu, Mme Amable   1798–1885   France   Poems, children's books

Taylor, Mary   1817–93   England, New Zealand   Feminism
MT Friend of Ch. Brontë: Letters from New Zealand & Elsewhere, ed. Joan Stevens (1972)—*Shirley:* pp. 93–94; *Consuelo:* p. 49.

Gaskell, *Life of CB*, ✕6–✕11.

The First Duty of Women [*Victoria Maga.* 1865–70] 1870

J. A. & Olive Banks, *Feminism & Family Planning* (1965), p. 44.

Miss Miles, or, A Tale of Yorkshire Life 1890

St. Teresa of Avila   1515–82   Spain   Autobiography, mysticism, poems
* Also Teresa (or Theresa) of Jesus

La Vida [1562–65] 1588—childhood reading, adventure: ✕1

* Dalton's new translation (1851 ff.) of her *Autobiography* (or *Life*) revived interest in St. Teresa among Victorians, and was

probably read by George Eliot, who also may have read J. A. Froude, "Santa Teresa; a psychological study" (*Fraser's Maga.*, Jan. 1862)—"a human being conscious of sin, and thirsting to raise herself to a nobler life": p. 74 (cf. Prologue to *Middlemarch*).

E. Allison Peers, Intro. to his trans. of *The Autobiography of StToA* (1960)—quoting Crashaw's "by all the eagle . . . all the dove": p. 50; style "vivid, disjointed, elliptical, paradoxical, gaily ungrammatical": pp. 14–23; D. de Rougemont, *Passion and Society* (trans. of *L'Amour et l'Occident* by M. Belgion, 1940), §3, ⅝4; see Gertrude Stein.

St. Thérèse of Lisieux   1873–97   France   Notebooks

L'Histoire d'une Âme 1911, trans. as *Autobiography of StToL* by Ronald Knox (1958)—on littleness of souls: pp. 241–42.

John W. Donohue, "Two Women: A Centennial" (on St.T and Cather, *America,* March 31, 1973); Ida Gorres, *Hidden Face* (1959), p. 16.

Tillich, Hannah   Germany, America   Memoir
From Time to Time 1973

Mrs. Tonna (Charlotte Elizabeth)   1790–1846   England   Novels, memoir
* Citations are from an 1850 2-volume edition of the *Works* with the 1844 Stowe introduction (New York: M. W. Dodd) which includes *The Wrongs of Women* (*sic*) although English editions are entitled *The Wrongs of Woman.*

Helen Fleetwood [1839–40] 1841—Lord Ashley: I, 608–9; "Excluded from free air": I, 554–55.

Cazamian, pp. 237–40; Tillotson, p. 118; Neff, pp. 16, 25, 86.

Personal Recollections 1841—anonymity: ⅝10; truths of Gospel: ⅝11; Harlot: ⅝7; St. Giles's: ⅝16; newspaper reading: ⅝3; H. More: ⅝10, 12.
The Wrongs of Woman 1843–44—Eve: ⅝1; factory reports: ⅝5.

"CET," *DNB;* anon., *Memoir of CE* (n.d., Bristol & London; copy in BM); Vineta Colby, *Yesterday's Woman* (1974)—Evangelical novel: ⅝4; see Rubenius, *Gaskell;* Wilson, *Austen;* H. B. Stowe.

Triolet, Elsa   1896–1970   Russia, France   Novels, stories

Tristan, Flora   1803–44   France, Peru   Treatises, memoirs
Pérégrinations d'une paria 1833–34 1838—Peruvian journey undertaken in vain hope of support from her father's wealthy Tristan y Moscozo family; woman a pariah: pp. xxiii–xv.
Méphis 1838—hero's name, "Méphis le prolétaire," from Mephistopheles: I, 96–99; opera singer heroine's theme song: I, 14; great voice: I, 9; woman of future: II, 144–45, 296–99.

Promenades dans Londres 1840 (popular edition, with dedication to working classes 1842)—four trips to England in 1830s: Preface; Owen: ¾19; Chartists: ¾5; Wollstonecraft & English women: ¾17.

C. N. Gattey, *Gauguin's Astonishing Grandmother: Biography of FT* (London, Femina Books, 1970)—paraphrases and translated excerpts of *PdL*, which has never been translated and cannot be found in any form in English or American libraries: pp. 110ff.

Union ouvrière 1843
L'Émancipation de la Femme ou le testament de la Paria, ed. A. Constant 1846

J. Baelen, *FT: socialisme et féminisme* (1972); Dominique Desanti, *FT: la femme révoltée* (1971); M. Rubel, "FT et Karl Marx" (*Le Nef,* 1946), pp. 68–76; Dolléans, pp. 1, 6.

Trollope, Frances   1780–1863   England, America   Novels
Domestic Manners of the Americans 1832
Jonathan Jefferson Whitlaw; or, Scenes on the Mississippi 1836
Michael Armstrong, the Factory Boy 1840

Cazamian, pp. 235–37; L. & R. Stebbins, *Trollopes* (1945)—Ashley, p. 97; B. A. Booth, *A. Trollope* (1958), p. 69; G. Orwell, "Dickens" (*D, Dali,* 1946), ¾4

Tsvetaeva, Marina   1892–1941   Russia   Poems

Undset, Sigrid   1882–1949   Norway   Novels
Kristin Lavransdatter 1920–22 (trans. C. Archer)—Mistress of Husaby: §2.

Varnhagen, Rahel   1771–1833   Germany   Letters
Hannah Arendt, *RV: The Life of a Jewish Woman* 1957, 1974

Queen Victoria   1819–1901   England   Letters

Ward, Mrs. Humphry   1851–1920   England   Novels
Robert Elsmere 1888

Warner, Susan   1819–85   America   Novels
The Wide, Wide World 1850

Warner, Sylvia Townsend   England   Novels
Mr. Fortune's Maggot 1927

Webb, Beatrice Potter   1858–1943   Sociology, memoirs
My Apprenticeship 1926

Webb, Mary   1883–1927   England   Novels

Weil, Simone   1903–43   France   Philosophy
La Condition ouvrière [1937ff.] 1951—humiliation, contact with life: "Jour-
nal d'usine": p. 106.
L'Enracinement 1949

> T. S. Eliot preface to A. Wills trans. (*The Need for Roots,* 1952)

Attente de Dieu, ed. J.-M. Perrin   1950
La Pesanteur et la grâce   1950

> Simone Pétrement, *SW* (1973)—pupil of Alain: I, 261, 400–1; factory
> year: I, 430–31 & II, 46–47; E. Piccard, *SW: Essai, anthologie raison-
> née* (1960).

Welty, Eudora   America   Novels, stories
Delta Wedding   1946
"The House of Willa Cather" in *Art of WC,* ed. Slote & Faulkner 1974

West, Rebecca   England   Novels, essays
The Fountain Overflows 1956—girl violinist not artist, mere "desire to
please": ⚥6.

> Anthony West, *Mortal Wounds* (1973)—Sand: pp. 250–51.

Wharton, Edith   1862–1937   America   Novels, stories
The House of Mirth   1905

> Millicent Bell, *EW & Henry James* (1965)—Sand: pp. 119–23; A.
> Kazin, *On Native Grounds* (1942), pp. 89–94.

Wheatley, Phillis   c. 1753–84   America   Poems

Wilcox, Ella Wheeler   1850–1919   America   Poems
> Naomi Lewis, *A Visit to Mrs. Wilcox* (1957).

Williams, Helen Maria   1762–1827   England   Political letters, novels
Julia, a novel   1790

> Gina Luria, Intro., Garland Pub. ed. (1974).

Letters . . . from France   1790, 1792–96

> M. R. Adams, "HMW and the French Revolution," in *Wordsworth
> Studies for G. M. Harper* (1939)—numerous female Jacobins: pp. 87ff.

Wittig, Monique   France   Novels
L'Opoponax   1964; see McCarthy
Les Guérillières   1969

Wollstonecraft, Mary   1759–97   England   Treatises, letters, fiction
Thoughts on the Education of Daughters   1787

Mary, a Fiction 1788—"In delineating the Heroine": Advertisement, pp. 1–4; disgust at husband: ✗30; afterlife without marriage: ✗31; "Temple of Solitude" landscape: ✗4.

Original Stories from Real Life 1788; 2nd ed., ill. Wm. Blake, 1791—parents without judgment: Preface; "candidates for friendship": ✗25.

E. V. Lucas, Preface, *OS* (1906).

Criticism in *Analytical Review* [1788–92, 1796–97]—"write no more": rev. anon. *Seymour Castle,* Nov. 1789, *AR* V, 361; rev. Radcliffe, *Italian:* May 1797, *AR* XXV, 516–20; rev. de Staël, *Rousseau:* July 1789, *AR* IV, 360–62; on Genlis: rev. T. Day, *Sanford,* Oct. 1789: *AR* V, 217.

R. M. Wardle, "MW: Analytical Reviewer" (*PMLA,* 1947), pp. 1000–9.

A Vindication of the Rights of Men . . . to Edmund Burke   1790
A Vindication of the Rights of Woman 1792—Rousseau quoted on women: ✗5, sec. i; women in novels: ✗5, sec. ii; girl "a romp": ✗3; "Strengthen mind": ✗2; indignation at Rousseau: ✗2; MdeS, R. and passion: ✗5, sec. iv; Heloisa: ✗7; women's sexuality: ✗7; Genlis on parents: ✗5, sec. iv; "barren heath": Dedication to Talleyrand.
Letters to Imlay [1793–95] in *Posthumous Works,* ed. Godwin 1798 (cited from Kegan Paul ed., 1879)—loves Rousseau: p. 58; "Love a want": p. 150; "respect due emotions": p. 151; "unison of affection": p. 120; "looked at sea": p. 121.
Historical and Moral View of French Revolution   1794
Letters Written in Sweden   1796
Letters to Godwin [1796–97] in *Godwin & Mary: Letters of WG & MW,* ed. R. M. Wardle (1966)—"in my veins": p. 33; pregnancy "inelegant": p. 64.
The Wrongs of Woman, or Maria [1797] in *Posthumous Works,* ed. Godwin 1798—Gothic asylum: ✗1; reading Rousseau: ✗2; women's sexuality: ✗10; caged bird: ✗9.

W. Godwin, *Memoirs of MW* (1798; ed. Durant, 1927); R. Wardle, *MW* (1951); Eleanor Flexner, *MW* (1972); Janet M. Todd & Florence Boos, "Check List for MW" (*MWN,* April 1973); Gina Luria, Intro. Garland Pub. MW reprints (1974).

Woolf, Virginia   1882–1941   England   Novels, criticism
The Voyage Out 1915—Mrs. Ambrose on girls: ✗1; reading *Persuasion:* ✗4.

Aileen Pippett, *VW* (1953)—"stone woman": pp. 110–11.

Night and Day   1919
Jacob's Room   1922
The Common Reader 1925—essays on Duchess of Newcastle, Edgeworth, Austen, C. & E. Brontë, George Eliot, M. R. Mitford.
Mrs. Dalloway   1925
To the Lighthouse 1927—"Life stand still": §3, ✗3; "She was fifty": §1, ✗1; "green sand dunes uninhabited of men" (female landscape): §1, ✗1.

Phyllis Rose, "Mrs. Ramsay," *Women's Studies* (1973).

Orlando 1928—love as bird: ⚔2.

A Room of One's Own 1929—"epic age": ⚔5; "indignation," "rage," "acidity" of *Jane Eyre:* ⚔4; no grievance, no influence: ⚔6; "respectable clergyman": ⚔4.

"Professions for Women" [1931] in *The Death of the Moth* 1942—"angel in the house": p. 150.

The Waves 1931

Common Reader: Second Series 1932—on Fanny Burney, Wollstonecraft, Dorothy Wordsworth, *Aurora Leigh,* Jane Carlyle, Geraldine Jewsbury, Christina Rossetti.

Flush: A Biography 1932—on Mrs. Browning and her dog.

The Years 1937—coin, knot, center, moment metaphors: "Present Day" (pp. 295, 342–44 in Penguin ed., 1968).

Three Guineas 1938—quotes Sand on solidarity: n. 49.

Between the Acts 1941

A Writer's Diary, ed. Leonard Woolf (1953)—"The heroic woman": pp. 4–5; Cather: p. 99

Ms. Letters to Violet Dickinson [1902–4] (Berg, NYPL)—"sparroy," animals.

Qu. Bell, *VW* (1972)—incest gossip: I, 42–45; H. Marder, *Feminism and VW* (1968)—coin imagery: pp. 98–103; Leonard Woolf, *Beginning Again* (1964)—VW and money: pp. 91–93; Harvena Richter, *VW* (1970)—falling metaphors: pp. 216ff.

Wordsworth, Dorothy   1771–1855   England   Journal
Journals [1798–1803] 1897, 1941; M. Moorman ed., 1971.

Wm. Wordsworth on poetic style, Preface (1800ff.) to *Lyrical Ballads.*

Wylie, Elinor   1885–1928   America   Poems

Yonge, Charlotte M.   1823–1901   England   Novels
The Heir of Redclyffe 1853
The Daisy Chain 1856
The Dove in the Eagle's Nest 1866

Addendum to the Notes

Austin, Mary   **1868–1934**   **America**   **Novels, tales**

Glaspell, Susan   **1882?–1948**   **America**   **Novels, plays**

Guérin, Eugénie de   **1805–48**   **France**   **Journals, poems**

Hill, Susan   **England**   **Novels**

Kelley, Edith Summers   **1884–1956**   **Canada, America**   **Novels**
Weeds   1923, ed. M. S. Bruccoli (1972)

Laurence, Margaret   **Canada, Africa**   **Novels**

Mew, Charlotte   **1870–1928**   **England**   **Poems**

Phelps, Elizabeth Stuart   **1844–1911**   **America**   **Novels**

Sachs, Nelly   **1891–1970**   **Germany, Sweden**   **Poems**

Sarton, May   **America**   **Novels, poems**

Södergran, Edith   **1892–1923**   **Finland**   **Poems**

Spofford, Harriet Prescott   **1835–1921**   **America**   **Stories**

Wright, Judith   **Australia**   **Poems**
The Moving Image   1946—"South of My Days"
Woman to Man   1949

Index